INSECTS

OF BRITAIN AND WESTERN EUROPE

Michael Chinery

with illustrations by

Stephen Falk, Anthony Hopkins, Richard Lewington,
Denys Ovenden, René Préchac, John Wilkinson, David More

B L O O M S B U R Y

LONDON • BERLIN • NEW YORK • SYDNEY

First edition published in 1986
Reprinted, 1991, 1993, 1997, 1993, 1998

Second edition published in 2007
Reprinted, 2009

Third edition published in 2012 by
Bloomsbury Publishing
50 Bedford Square
London WC1B 3DP

ISBN 978-1-4081-7948-2
A CIP catalogue record for this book is available from the British Library

Printed in China by WKT Co. Ltd.

Introduction

Over a million different kinds of insects have so far been described and named, and many more certainly remain to be discovered. This is more than all the other known animal species put together. They occupy almost every known habitat outside the polar regions and the deep sea. They are represented by immense populations – perhaps 10 million individuals in a single termite colony, and 60,000 springtails in a square metre of turf. In this respect they are certainly exceeded by the nematode worms, with 20 million or more to the square metre in some soils and more than 90,000 individuals having been extracted from a single rotting apple; but nematodes do not exhibit anything like the fantastic variety of insect life.

The European insect fauna numbers about 100,000 known species, with a great range of size and form. Candidates for the largest of them include the Giant Peacock Moth (p. 138), *Saga pedo* (p. 54), *Ephippiger provincialis* (p. 56), and various chafer beetles (pp. 265-6). This book is an introduction and general guide to their identification. With its help, the general observer ought to be able to place the majority of insects that he discovers in their correct families.

The **geographical area** covered by this book is essentially western Europe - west of a line from Finland to the northern shores of the Adriatic. Many Mediterranean species are included, but generally not those found only in Peninsular Italy or the Iberian Peninsula.

All orders are covered and all the major families as well. The selection of insects to illustrate these, from a total of about 100,000 species so far discovered in Europe, was not always easy. Within each group, we have chosen those *most likely to be noticed*, because of their size, colour, habits, frequency, or association with human habitation. Many small and dull-coloured species are omitted because, although they are often abundant, only the specialist would give them a second glance - or be able to identify them with any certainty. But some quite rare or local insects have been included, simply because they are so striking that they cannot be overlooked and always cause comment when they are seen. Examples include the Spanish Moon Moth (p. 139) and the longhorn beetle *Rosalia alpina* (p. 281).

The **illustrations** show most of the insects in their natural resting positions, just as you might find them in the wild. Many species can be identified perfectly well in this way, but others need a closer examination of the venation or perhaps of the hindwings. These are shown in the 'set' position so that the relevant features can be seen. **Sexes** are indicated (♂ = male, ♀ = female) only where they are conspicuously different. **Sizes** are shown by magnifications printed beside the illustrations: × 2½ meaning that the picture is roughly 2½ times life-size. Sizes do vary a good deal, however, and the figures are no more than rough guides. Where no magnification is given, the insect has been drawn at approximately life-size.

The **text** complements the illustrations, sometimes drawing attention to important diagnostic features or to features on the underside that are not visible in the pictures. Colour variations and sexual differences are mentioned, and information is given on behaviour, habitat, and food-plant where these are helpful in identifying an insect. Closely related species can often be distinguished only by microscopic examination of the genitalia and other minute features, descriptions of which are beyond the scope of this book. In such instances, the commonest species are normally illustrated and the text indicates that there are several similar species.

There are brief introductions to each insect order and to the larger families. These give the basic features of the groups and the individual species texts should be read in conjunction with them. Many families are represented here by single species, in which case the name of the new family follows that of the species.

Where no family name is given, the insect belongs to the same family as the preceding species.

English names are given as well as scientific names where possible, but most of the smaller and less familiar species do not have English names and then only the scientific name can be given. Scientific names are recognised internationally, but unfortunately tend to change as entomologists learn more about the relationships of the insects. Names found in one book are thus not necessarily the same as those found in older or newer books. The names used here have been brought up to date as far as possible at the time of printing and show quite a number of changes from the first edition.

Time of appearance is indicated in figures for the months during which the adults may be seen: e.g. 5-8 means that the insects can be seen from May to August. These periods apply to the whole geographical range of the species concerned, and the time of appearance may be much more restricted in northern or montane regions. Only a single annual brood may be produced in such areas, while in warmer parts there may be two or even three broods in a year, with adults in evidence for several months. Species with no months given may be found throughout the year, although they may disappear into hibernation in the cooler regions.

Distribution *European* distribution is given in a simple form:

    B = Britain and Ireland

    N = Scandinavia and Finland

    C = central Europe – north of a line from Bordeaux to Venice, to include Denmark and the British Isles

    S = southern Europe – the whole area south of that line

    SW = south-western – west of Nice

    SE = south-eastern – east of Nice

The distribution for *Britain and Ireland* is given by the following symbols:

    ▲ = fairly common in suitable habitats throughout the British Isles

    ▲ = fairly common but confined to the northern half of these islands

    ▲ = fairly common but confined to the southern half of these islands

    △ = a scattered or local distribution, although possibly common where it does occur: △s = southern; △n = northern

    △ = rare in the British Isles: △s = southern; △n = northern

Southern areas are taken to be those roughly south of the Tees, but many species listed as southern will obviously have a more restricted distribution than this. There are, however, no hard and fast dividing lines for insect distributions, many of which are imperfectly known, and specimens may often be found outside the indicated areas.

Early stages. Distinctive larvae of butterflies and moths (caterpillars) have been illustrated in the main descriptive part of the book beside the adult insects. The nymphs and larvae of other groups are often very similar to each other – hard or impossible to distinguish in the field – and their study is a specialist affair. We have, however, illustrated a range of them on pp. 294-5 (terrestrial) and 296-7 (aquatic), to provide a representative survey of the different forms, cross-referenced to and from the main part of the text.

Other creepy crawlies Insects belong to the phylum Arthropoda ('jointed feet'), which also includes centipedes, millipedes, woodlice, mites, spiders, and other quite separate classes of invertebrates. Beginners can easily confuse some of these with insects, so to make the distinction clear we have included on pp. 298-307 a brief illustrated survey of them, with examples drawn from common or conspicuous species of the region.

Insect Anatomy

Technical terms are kept to a minimum in this book, but some are unavoidable when referring to various parts of insects' bodies and a basic knowledge of insect anatomy is necessary for identifying many species.

The insect body consists of three main parts: the **head, thorax**, and **abdomen**.

THE HEAD. The **vertex** is the area on top of the head, above and between the eyes. The **cheeks** (or **genae**) are the areas below and behind the eyes, and their lower portions are sometimes differentiated as the **jowls**. The head carries a pair of **antennae** or feelers, which are mainly concerned with the senses of smell and touch. Their shape varies a great deal, but in their simplest form they are a chain of more or less identical segments, each well supplied with nerve-endings. The number of segments, ranging from one to over a hundred, is sometimes of value in identifying the insects. The first or basal segment is the **scape**, and is often longer than the others. The second, usually very short, is the **pedicel**, while the rest together form the **flagellum**. In some insects, such as the ants, the scape is particularly long and the rest of the antenna hinges upon it. Such an antenna is called **elbowed** or **geniculate**.

The head also has a pair of **compound eyes**, their surfaces clothed with a number of tiny lenses called facets. Dragonflies and other active fliers have several thousand of these lenses in each eye, enabling them to detect very small movements, but some of the ants and other soil-dwellers have very few lenses or none at all. Many insects also possess some very simple eyes called **ocelli** – usually three, forming a little triangle on the vertex or sometimes on the front of the head, and looking like tiny glass beads. It seems unlikely that ocelli can produce true images, and they may be used simply for detecting variations in light intensity.

The **mouth** is surrounded by a number of greatly modified limbs, collectively known as the **mouth-parts**. The form of these appendages varies enormously with the insect's diet, but the basic set consists of a pair of **mandibles** or **jaws**, a pair of **maxillae** (sometimes called secondary jaws), and a **labium** or lower lip, formed by the fusion of two maxilla-like appendages. The maxillae and labium help first to catch and hold the food while it is cut up by the mandibles, then to shovel it into the mouth. They also have sensory arms known as **palps**, which examine and taste the food first. Several other structures may be associated with these mouth-parts, notably the **labrum** or upper lip. This is an outgrowth from the front of the head and forms a roof over the jaw area, where the food is cut and chewed before entering the true mouth.

The head of a cockroach, seen from the front and from the side, to show the major regions

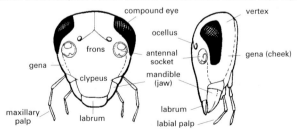

The above arrangement is designed for coping with a solid diet, and is found in a wide range of insects, including grasshoppers, mantids, dragonflies, beetles and wasps. Among the liquid-feeders we find some remarkable modifications. The mandibles are virtually absent in butterflies and moths, and the maxillae have become long and slender and linked together to form a nectar-sucking **proboscis**. Mandibles are also absent in house-flies, but among mosquitoes and horse-flies they are long and needle-like, forming part of the hypodermic syringe with which they draw blood from their victims. The true bugs also have piercing mouth-parts for sucking juices from plants or animals.

THORAX. The insect thorax consists of three segments – **prothorax, mesothorax**, and **metathorax** - each of which carries a pair of legs. Wings, when present, are borne on the second two, or if there is only one pair, on the middle one. The prothorax never carries wings and is often reduced to a narrow collar, though it is large in bugs and beetles where its dorsal surface, the **pronotum**, is a conspicuous feature. The meso- and metathorax are generally fused into a single unit and the two component sections are not easy to distinguish: the mesothorax is the larger and its dorsal covering, the **mesonotum**, commonly terminates in a prominent triangular or shield-shaped plate called the **scutellum**.

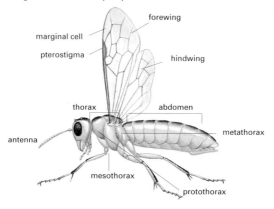

A sawfly (generalised insect)

LEGS. With the exception of a few aberrant forms – notably some female scale insects – all adult insects have three pairs of legs. One can usually recognise four main regions in each. The **coxa** is the basal segment, joining the rest of the leg to the thorax. Then comes the **femur** (plural femora), which is usually the largest segment, and beyond it is the **tibia** – often as long as or even longer than the femur, but generally much more slender. Finally the **tarsus** or foot, which consists of one to five segments and normally bears one or two claws at the tip. The **trochanter** is usually a very small segment between the femur and the coxa: it is firmly fused to the femur and normally hard to detect. The shapes and relative lengths of the different leg segments vary a great deal according to the insects' habits. Many predatory species, including the mantids, have **prehensile** or **raptorial** front legs, in which the tibia can fold back against the femur to trap and grip the prey.

A typical insect leg

WINGS are present in most insects, but not in the most primitive groups – the springtails and bristletails (p. 16). They are also missing from a number of highly specialised parasites such as lice and fleas (pp 98-101), and many high-altitude insects are wingless or virtually so. The 'typical' insect, however, has two pairs of wings. Both pairs may be membranous, as in dragonflies and butterflies, or the

6

front pair may be rather tough and function largely as protection for the more delicate hindwings at rest. Tough forewings of this kind are called **tegmina** if they are leathery but still wing-like, as in the grasshoppers and cockroaches. The forewings of beetles are known as **elytra**. They are generally very hard and horny and completely cover the flimsy hindwings at rest, making the insects look as if they have no wings at all. Hindwings are absent in all true flies (pp 190-217), where they have been converted into minute pin-like structures called **halteres**. These are also known as balancers, for they act like gyroscopes and help to stabilise the insects in flight. Hindwings are also missing from some mayfly species and from a number of flightless beetles and grasshoppers.

Membranous wings may be covered with scales, as in butterflies and moths, or with hairs as in caddis flies, but otherwise the most obvious feature is the **venation**. This varies enormously and is very important in classifying insect groups, but there is an underlying pattern based on longitudinal veins. Their full pattern, worked out from anatomical and fossil studies, is shown in the hypothetical forewing below. No living insect has the complete set and the number of branches is often greatly reduced, but the main longitudinal veins can usually be recognised in most winged species. Only two **cross-veins** are shown in the diagram. These are present in most insects, but there are often many minor cross-veins as well, especially among the dragonflies and lacewings. The areas of membrane between veins are called **cells**, and the major ones are named according to the vein in front of them: thus the costal cell is just behind the costa, the radial cell behind the radius, the 1st anal cell behind the 1st anal vein, and so on. A **discal cell** occurs in the wings of many insects and is commonly used in classification, but it does not refer to any particular cell and is merely a rather conspicuous cell near the middle of the wing. The discal cell of one insect group is not necessarily bounded by the same veins as the discal cell of another group. Cells bounded by veins on all sides are called **closed cells**, while those bounded on one side by the wing margin are called **open cells**.

Several systems have been used for naming veins, and care must be taken when referring to the older literature: a given vein then might not refer to the vein of the same name today. Dipterists and lepidopterists, whose charges often have reduced venation, commonly use a system of numbering for dealing with the longitudinal veins (p. 190).

A hypothetical insect wing, showing the full ancestral venation. Living insects all show some reduction of these major veins. R1 is the radius, while R2 to R5 are branches of a division of the radius known as the radial sector. MA and MP are the anterior and posterior divisions of the media. Cu is the cubitus, while 1A to 3A are the anal veins. a is the anterior cross vein, always linking the radius to the media, and p is the posterior cross vein which links the media to the cubitus.

ABDOMEN. The adult abdomen has up to 11 segments, although not all are visible, each with a dorsal plate called a **tergite** and a ventral one called a **sternite**. The abdomen has no real limbs but the hind end commonly carries a pair of appendages called **cerci**. These are most obvious in mayflies (p 18), where they are long and thread-like, and in the earwigs (p 68), where they form the familiar pincers. Male dragonflies and bush-crickets (p 48) use their prominent cerci to grasp the females while mating. The **genitalia** are carried on the 8th and 9th abdominal segments. They are usually concealed inside the body, although some females have a permanently exposed and often very conspicuous **ovipositor**. Blade-like or needle-like, this is used for laying eggs in the ground or in plant or animal tissues and is well seen in bush-crickets and some ichneumons (p 230). The detailed structure of cerci and genitalia is often crucial for separating closely related species, but this needs specialised microscopic techniques.

Insect life cycles

Nearly all insects begin life as eggs. protected by tough, waterproof, and often elegantly sculptured shells, these can survive a wide range of adverse conditions, from drought to severe frost. Many species pass the winter as eggs, often freely exposed on the bare twigs of their food-plants. Apart from the primitive wingless insects (see p. 16), the hatchlings rarely resemble their parents. They never have wings and often have quite different feeding habits. The considerable change that these young insects undergo as they develop is called **metamorphosis**.

Like all other arthropods (see p 4), insects have a tough outer skeleton which does not grow with the rest of the body and has to be changed periodically for a larger one. This skin change is called **ecdysis** or **moulting**. When about to moult, the insect stops feeding and becomes quiescent for several hours or even days while the inner layers of its coat or skeleton are dissolved away. A soft, new, wrinkled skin is secreted under the old layers, which by now are very thin and brittle. The insect puffs itself up by muscular action and by swallowing air or water to split the old skin and to stretch the new one, and then slowly drags itself out of the old skin. The insect is especially vulnerable until the new skin has hardened and most species try to hide themselves when about to moult.

When the new skin has become firm, the insect gets rid of the excess air or water and makes room for further growth. There is some elasticity in the skin, especially in caterpillars, but there comes a time when further stretching is impossible and another moult must take place. Some insects moult as many as 50 times, but this is unusual and most insects moult less than ten times. Most butterfly and moth caterpillars moult only four or five times. The stages between moults are called **instars**: a 2nd-instar larva being one between the first and second moults. The adult insect is the **imago**. Bristletails go on moulting throughout their lives, but other insects stop when they reach maturity. No insect grows any more once it has fully-developed wings, although mayflies do undergo one further moult in the winged state (see p. 18).

Winged insects are arranged in two divisions, according to the way in which their wings develop. Among the dragonflies, grasshoppers, bugs, and several other groups, the wings develop gradually on the outside of the body. These are the EXOPTERYGOTA (= outside wings). The young resemble the adults in general appearance, often living in the same places and having similar feeding habits. The resemblance increases as the wing buds get larger at each moult. There is thus a gradual change from young to adult form and the insects are said to show **partial** or **incomplete metamorphosis**. The young are known as **nymphs**.

Among the butterflies and moths, beetles, flies, ants, bees, wasps, and a few other groups, the young look nothing like the adults, never showing any sign or wings and often having completely different homes and habits. They are known as **larvae**. At each moult until the last, they simply emerge as larger larvae. On reaching full size, the larva splits its skin again and reveals the **pupa** or **chrysalis**, a non-feeding and generally inactive stage as far as external appearances go. Great changes take place internally, however, as the larval body is broken down and rebuilt in the adult form. Outlines of the wings and other adult features can be seen on the pupal skin, but these organs all develop inside the pupa and this group is therefore called the ENDOPTERYGOTA. Transformation takes anything from a few days to several months before the imago finally breaks out of the pupal skin. This type of development is called **complete metamorphosis**. There is now an increasing tendency to call all young insects larvae, but this disregards the fundamental differences in the development of the two groups.

Some insects can fly as soon as they leave their nymphal or pupal skins, but most of the larger species need to harden their wings before taking to the air. Most adults emerge with small and crumpled wings, and their first action is to find a perch where the wings can be unfurled without damage. Blood is gradually pumped into the wing veins, and the wings normally swell to full size within a few minutes. But they take much longer to harden, and flight is not usually possible for at least an hour.

Collecting and studying

Many of the larger and more colourful insects, notably butterflies and moths and some of the beetles, can be identified in the field quite easily without catching them. Accurate identification of most of the smaller species, however, involves catching them and taking a closer look at the venation or other details.

Nets. The traditional butterfly net is the best tool for catching free-flying insects. Good nets can be bought from entomological dealers, but satisfactory ones are not difficult to make at home. The frame should be light, but strong enough to keep its shape when the net is swept through the air. It can be circular or kite-shaped, but must be at least 30cm across – big enough to get your hands in to manipulate the catch. The bag must be strong enough to resist brambles, but the mesh not so dense that you cannot see the trapped insects. It must be at least twice as deep as the diameter of the frame, so that it can be folded around the frame to stop the insects from escaping. Dark colours are best for collecting dragonflies and butterflies, but smaller insects show up better against a light-coloured net. A short handle – up to 30cm – is good for general use. Nets with longer handles are more difficult to control, although certainly useful when trying to catch dragonflies over water or moths gyrating around street-lamps. A short permanent handle with a detachable extension is the ideal.

Trapping. Night-flying moths are nearly all attracted to light, and many can be caught simply by shining an electric light on to a white sheet in the garden and standing by with a net. A moth trap will do the same job with less effort and can be left on to sample the moth population throughout the night. Some traps can be run from car batteries out in the wilds. The heart of the trap is a mercury-vapour lamp. Lured by its ultra-violet light, the moths crash into baffles around the lamp and fall into a box below. Egg-packing material in the box provides snug resting places and the moths settle down quietly until the trap is emptied in the morning. Traps should not be positioned so that they are in full sun early in the morning: the warmth agitates the moths and they damage themselves before they can be examined. Care should also be taken when emptying the trap to ensure that the moths are not snapped up by birds – particularly when a trap is regularly used in one place, such as a garden, for birds quickly learn that the trap is a source of food. The moths should be released into dense vegetation if possible, with the birds kept away until the insects have settled down. Alternatively, cover the trap and keep it in a cool place until nightfall, when the moths can safely be released.

Crawling insects that spend their time on low vegetation can often be spotted and picked up individually, but sweeping is a more productive method and essential for any serious survey of insect life in the herbage. A very sturdy net, reinforced around the rim, is needed for sweeping to and fro through the vegetation. Huge numbers of insects can be collected in this way and the net must be examined and emptied at frequent intervals to prevent their getting damaged. White is the best colour for a sweep net, since the smaller insects in the herbage are mainly green or brown. Beetles and other ground-living insects are easily caught in simple pitfall traps, made from jam jars or plastic beakers sunk into the ground. Meat or ripe fruit can be used as bait, but baiting is not really necessary: many insects fall in without any encouragement. A piece of slate or glass should be placed over the trap to keep out rain and mice.

Insects living in **trees** and **bushes** are easily collected with a beating tray and a stout stick. The 'tray' consists of a sheet of fairly tough material stretched over a collapsible frame about a metre square, and a long handle makes it easier to hold the tray under a branch. Hitting the branch sharply with the stick usually brings an assortment of caterpillars and other insects tumbling on to the tray. The smaller ones are best picked up with the aid of a **pooter** – a simple suction device incorporating a holding chamber for the insects. This can be used for collecting insects direct from leaves and tree trunks as well as from the beating tray.

When they have been caught, most insects are best transferred to plastic tubes or boxes. Entomological dealers market these in a range of convenient sizes: 7.5 × 2.5cm is the ideal tube size, while circular boxes about 5cm across and 2cm deep are best for moths. The insects survive well in such containers as long as they are not exposed to the sun. A leaf or a piece of moss will give them something to cling to and also provide essential moisture – but watch out for condensation, which can trap and drown very small insects and also damage their diagnostic features.

A good **hand lens**, magnifying about ×10, is all that is needed to identify most of the insects in this book, but a low-power microscope (magnifying about ×30) is certainly very useful and can reveal a lot of fascinating detail, especially when used to examine living specimens.

Most insects can be released unharmed after identification, but some of the smaller species cannot be properly identified, at least by the beginner, unless they are killed and examined in detail. Ethyl acetate is one of the most useful killing agents for the amateur entomologist – although it must not be used in plastic containers – but cherry laurel leaves (*Prunus laurocerasus*) are a very good standby, especially for anyone who does not do much collecting. The crushed leaves and young shoots give off a weak cyanide vapour and, when enclosed in an air-tight jar and covered with blotting paper or tissue, make a very convenient killing bottle. But don't be in too much of a hurry to kill your insects: watch their behaviour and study their natural resting attitudes, for these will help you to identify the insects in the field on another occasion. And never kill any more insects than you really need for study.

Insect conservation

A small reference collection is necessary for the serious student of insects and will do no harm to the populations of most species, but conservation must always be kept in mind. It is unlikely that collecting alone has caused the extinction of any insect species, but when combined with the alarming rates at which many habitats are currently being destroyed it could certainly hasten the end of some of our rarer species. British conservationists, anxious to minimise the risks to our insect fauna, have issued a **Code for Insect Collecting**, of which the main points may be summarised as follows:

Take and kill no more specimens than are strictly required: a pair of each species should be enough for normal purposes.

Do not take a species year after year from the same locality. Local forms and species known to be rare should be collected with the utmost restraint, and preferably not at all. *

Leave the environment as you find it: replace logs and stones after searching beneath them, and replace bark removed from dead timber.

Breeding from a fertilised female is better than taking specimens from the wild: unwanted specimens that have been reared should be released *in the original locality*.

Never collect more larvae or other insects for breeding than can be supported by readily available supplies of food-plant.

*Many butterfly species – including the Apollo, Large Blue, Large Copper, and Purple Emperor – and various other insects are protected by law in a number of European countries, often with a complete ban on collecting.

The orders of insects

The insects are arranged in a number of **orders**, based largely on the structure of the wings and the mouth-parts. The names of the orders generally end in -*ptera*, meaning wings: Lepidoptera = scale wings, Coleoptera = sheath wings, Diptera = two wings, and so on. There is much variation in the size of the orders: some contain only a handful of species, while the world has over 300,000 different kinds of beetles (Coleoptera). The 27 orders recognised in this book are listed below, but some entomologists prefer to split some of these orders and make a total of more than 30.

Apterygotes: primitive, wingless insects which have never had wings at any stage of their evolutionary history. Many entomologists now believe that only the Thysanura are true insects.

Thysanura	Bristletails (silverfish and allies) p. 16
Diplura	Two-tailed bristletails p. 16
Protura	Minute soil-dwelling insects p. 16
Collembola	Springtails p. 16

Pterygotes: essentially winged insects, although some orders have lost their wings during their evolution. There are also wingless species or forms scattered through most of the other orders.

Exopterygotes: insects with partial metamorphosis and no pupal stage. The young are nymphs.

Ephemeroptera	Mayflies p. 18
Odonata	Dragonflies p. 22
Plecoptera	Stoneflies p. 36
Orthoptera	Grasshoppers and Crickets p. 38
Phasmida	Stick and Leaf Insects p. 64
Dermaptera	Earwigs p. 68
Embioptera	Web-spinners p. 66
Dictyoptera	Cockroaches and Mantids p. 60
Isoptera	Termites p. 66
Psocoptera	Booklice and Barklice (Psocids) p. 98
Mallophaga	Biting Lice (all wingless) p. 100
Anoplura	Sucking Lice (all wingless) p. 100
Hemiptera	True Bugs p. 70
Thysanoptera	Thrips p. 99

Endopterygotes: insects with complete metamorphosis and a pupal stage. The young are larvae.

Neuroptera	Lacewings, Alder Flies, and Snake Flies p. 102
Mecoptera	Scorpion Flies p. 108
Lepidoptera	Butterflies and Moths p. 110
Trichoptera	Caddis Flies p. 183
Diptera	True Flies p. 190
Siphonaptera	Fleas p. 100
Hymenoptera	Bees, Wasps, Ants, Sawflies, Ichneumons etc. p. 218
Coleoptera	Beetles p. 254
Strepsiptera	Stylopids (all parasites) p. 255

THE KEY

This key is designed so that adult insects of all but a few aberrant species can be assigned to their correct group. It is based on wing structure, but also makes use of feet, antennae, and a few other features, all of which are easily seen with the aid of a lens. Winged specimens will always be adults, but wingless ones can be adults or young. Nymphs of exopterygote insects, such as bugs and grasshoppers, can usually be tracked down through the key because they resemble the adults, but the larvae of beetles and other endopterygotes are not included. If you suspect that your specimen is a larva (other than a caterpillar, for which see pp 110-82), turn to the range of larvae pictured on pp 294-7. Some aquatic nymphs are also illustrated on these pages. Some insect orders occur more than once in the key, because they contain both winged and wingless species or because they cover two or more rather distinct groups: groundhoppers and grasshoppers, for example, are distinct groups within the order Orthoptera.

[1] INSECTS WITH WINGS

(This includes the beetles and other insects with hard and smooth forewings, although these might appear wingless at first sight)

[2] All wings membranous

One pair of wings

Grasshopper-like, with long back legs: pronotum extends back over the abdomen.   **Groundhoppers** p. 46

2 or 3 long 'tails' at end of abdomen; wings held vertically at rest; very small antennae.   **Mayflies** (some families) p. 18

Minute insects (<5mm long) with only one forked vein in the wing; one or more short 'tails'; antennae much longer than the head; rare.   **Scale Insects** (males) p. 96

Large fan-shaped hindwings: forewings in the form of twisted clubs (halteres).   **Stylopids** (males) p. 255

Forewings normal; hindwings in the form of tiny, pin-like structures (halteres), although these may be hidden under flaps in the stouter species; antennae often short and bristle-like.   **True Flies** pp. 190-217

Two pairs of membranous wings

Minute insects with feathery wings which are usually folded tightly over the body.   **Thrips** p 98

**Wing membrane clothed with minute scales or hairs*

Wings clothed with scales, often very colourful; usually a coiled proboscis for sipping nectar.

Butterflies and Moths pp. 110-182

Wings hairy, usually yellow, brown, or black, and held roofwise over the body at rest with antennae pointing forward; few cross-veins; hindwing normally broader than forewing; no coiled proboscis.   **Caddis Flies** pp. 183-9

Wings hairy and all alike; front tarsi swollen; (more often seen in wingless form).   **Web-spinners** p. 66

Tiny insects clothed with white powder.
Wings ± flat at rest.   **White Flies** p. 97

Wings held roofwise at rest.

Lacewings (Family Coniopterygidae) p. 107

All wings alike, very flimsy and ± veinless; usually in swarms; southern Europe. **Termites** p. 66

Head extended downwards to form a stout beak; wings usually mottled and ± alike; males mostly with upturned, scorpion-like abdomen. **Scorpion Flies** p. 109

Hindwings similar to or broader than forewings; wings held flat or rolled round body at rest; often 2 fairly stout 'tails', no longer than the body and usually much shorter. **Stoneflies** p. 36

2 or 3 'tails', as long as or longer than the body; antennae minute; wings held vertically at rest; hindwing much smaller than forewing. **Mayflies** (some families) p. 18

Antennae short and bristle-like (shorter than width of head); body at least 25mm long, often very slender; wings never held roofwise over body. **Dragonflies** pp. 28-37

Antennae relatively long, sometimes clubbed; wing veins usually fork at the margins; wings held roofwise over the body at rest; flight slow in most species except ascalaphids.
Ant-lions, Lacewings, Alder Flies etc pp. 102-9

Very small insects, often with hairy wing veins and sometimes with a few scales on the wing membrane: venation characteristic; wings held roofwise at rest; relatively long antennae with at least 12 segments.
Psocids (booklice and barklice) p. 98

Very small insects, often pear-shaped, with a slender, needle-like beak; wings normally held roofwise at rest, but sometimes flat; antennae never with more than 10 segments; often in masses on plants. **Aphids** p. 94

Stout-bodied insects with a clear, shiny, and quite stiff wing membrane; wings held roofwise at rest; a long, slender beak for sucking sap from trees and shrubs; antennae short and bristle-like. **Cicadas** p. 88

Minute to quite large insects with hindwing very much smaller than forewing and linked to it by a row of microscopic hooks; wings typically with a small number of large cells, but venation is much reduced in many of the smaller species: wings never held roofwise.

With a distinct 'waist'. **Bees, Wasps, Ichneumons, etc** pp. 226-53

Without a 'waist'. **Sawflies** pp. 222-5

[2] Forewings at least partly horny or leathery; hindwings membranous (sometimes absent)

Forewings veinless and meeting in the mid-line without overlap

Forewings short and square, leaving most of the abdomen uncovered: pincers at the rear.　　　　　　　**Earwigs** p. 68

Forewings often very hard and usually covering all of the abdomen, although some abdominal segments may be exposed (see p. 260).　　　　　　　**Beetles** pp. 254-91

Forewings with veins and normally overlapping to some extent at rest or else held distinctly roofwise

Forewings with membranous tips and laid flat over body at rest; a slender piercing beak for sucking plant and animal fluids.　　　　　　　**Heteropteran Bugs** pp. 72-87

Forewings of uniform texture throughout and usually opaque, although not always much tougher than the hindwings; held roofwise at rest; a slender beak for sucking plant juices; insects often leap when disturbed.
Homopteran Bugs: Leafhoppers (p. 92) and **Psyllids** p. 96

Body bullet-shaped, with wings wrapped tightly around it at rest; hind legs enlarged for jumping.
　　　　　　Grasshoppers and Crickets pp. 38-59

All 3 pairs of legs long and spiky; fast-running; wings laid flat over body at rest; pronotum broad and almost covering the head.　　　　　　　**Cockroaches** p. 60

Front legs enlarged and very spiny for catching prey; head very mobile on a long neck.　　　　　　　**Mantids** p. 62

[1] INSECTS WITHOUT WINGS OR WITH JUST VERY SMALL FLAPS

Free-living insects, on vegetation or in soil and leaf litter

Body long and stick-like.　　　　　　　**Stick Insects** p. 64

Body bullet-like, often with small wing flaps just behind the head; hind legs enlarged for jumping.
　　　　　　Grasshoppers and Crickets pp. 38-59

Insects with long, slender 'tails' at the rear

Small soil-dwelling creatures with 2 'tails'.
　　　　　　Diplurans (Family Campodeidae) p. 16

3 'tails'; body usually clothed with shining scales; often found indoors.　　　　　　　**Bristletails** p. 16

Insects with pincers at the rear

Slender, pale soil-dwelling insects with just one tarsal segment.　　　　**Diplurans (Family Japygidae)** p. 16

Stouter, often dark brown insects with 3 tarsal segments; often under stones.　　　　　　　**Earwigs** p. 68

14

Insects with short 'tails' or none at all

Slender, soft-bodied soil-dwellers with 2 short tails; front tarsi swollen. **Web-spinners** p. 66

Pale, slender soil-dwellers with 2 short tails: front tarsi not swollen. **Diplurans (Family Projapygidae)** p. 16

Flattened insects with spiky legs and a broad pronotum almost covering the head; 2 stumpy tails usually visible. **Cockroaches** p. 60

Elongate insects with large spiny front legs for catching prey; long neck; 2 short tails usually visible. **Mantids** pp. 62-5

Small leaping insects with vestigial wings and head extending downwards to form a stout beak. **Snow Fleas** p. 108

Small leaping creatures with no sign of wings; a forked 'spring' at the rear (usually tucked under body); mainly in soil and leaf litter. **Springtails** p. 16

Body clothed with scales or flattened hairs; wing vestiges present. **Moths** (some females) pp. 124-82

Body with a marked 'waist', often bearing small lobes or scales, at front of abdomen; antennae often elbowed. **Ants** (p. 234) and some other **Hymenoptera** p. 220

Slender, soft-bodied and pale insects, normally with 4 tarsal segments; usually in colonies in dead wood; southern Europe only. **Termites** p. 66

Small, pear-shaped insects with head much narrower than body; a needle-like beak under the head; often a pair of tubular outgrowths near the rear end; on growing plants. **Aphids** p. 94

Flattened insects with relatively broad head; antennae long and slender; hind femur often broad; commonly found indoors among dried materials. **Psocids** (booklice) p. 98

*Parasitic insects living on birds and mammals

** Insects flattened laterally

Jumping insects with long back legs; flattened from side to side; usually brown. **Fleas** p. 101

** Insects flattened dorso-ventrally

*** Head partly sunk into thorax

Antennae more or less concealed in grooves; legs relatively stout, usually with 2 strong claws to grip host; a piercing beak, although not always obvious. **True Flies** (some families) p. 214

Antennae clearly visible; legs more slender and claws less prominent; a slender, piercing beak. **Heteropteran Bugs** (some families) p. 80

***Head not sunk into thorax

Very small, oval or elongate insects; head nearly as wide as body; prothorax distinct; tarsi with 1 or 2 claws; biting mouths. **Biting Lice** p. 100

Very small, pear-shaped insects; head much narrower than body; thoracic segments fused into one unit; tarsi each with 1 large claw; sucking mouths **Sucking Lice** p. 100

15

A proturan

The insects on this page are all primitive, wingless species belonging to the sub-class Apterygota (= without wings). There is virtually no metamorphosis during the life cycle. The microscopic proturans (Order Protura) are soil-living creatures with neither eyes nor antennae. (See also p. 11).

BRISTLETAILS   Order Thysanura

Shuttle-shaped insects with 2 long cerci and a central 'tail' known as the epiproct – making 3 'tails' in all, each fringed with minute bristles. Bristletails have biting jaws and are clothed with scales.

▲ **Petrobius maritimus** Machilidae. Antennae as long as or longer than body. Eyes large, with angular outer margin. Ocelli long and slit-like. Lives as scavenger among coastal rocks in splash zone. ▲*P. brevistylis* is almost identical

△ **Dilta hibernica**. Antennae shorter than body. Eyes rectangular. Commonest of several similar species on ground in densely vegetated places.

▲ **Silverfish** *Lepisma saccharina* Lepismatidae. Body flattened. Eyes small and separated. Abundant in houses, feeding on starchy materials including spilled flour, paper, etc. Mainly nocturnal and prefers a slightly moist environment.

  Ctenolepisma lineata. Less shiny than *Lepisma* and with antennae as long as the body. 'Tails' also very long. Indoors and outside. S & C.

▲ **Firebrat** *Thermobia domestica*. Browner and more bristly than *Lepisma* and with longer appendages. Body hairs in distinct patches. Prefers warmer places: always indoors and very common in bakeries and heating ducts.

TWO-TAILED BRISTLETAILS   Order Diplura

Two cerci, of variable form, but no epiproct. Thoracic segments clearly separated, unlike Thysanura. Mostly very small, soil-dwelling scavengers and carnivores. Eyes absent.

▲ **Campodea fragilis** Campodeidae. One of several very similar species abundant in compost heaps and other decaying vegetation.

  Japyx solifugus Japygidae. Tunnels under stones and among fallen leaves, catching prey with pincer-like cerci. S &C, but rarely seen.

  Anajapyx vesiculosus Anajapygidae. Relatively stout cerci are tubular and discharge secretions from abdominal glands. A scavenger. Known only from Italy.

SPRINGTAILS   Order Collembola

The largest group of apterygotes, with about 1500 known species. Body has fewer segments than the other groups. Named for the springing organ (furcula) at rear of most species. Like a minute tuning fork, it is clipped under the abdomen at rest, but released on disturbance to shoot the animal forward through the air. All species are very small and often clothed with scales or hair. No compound eyes. Most live in leaf litter, feeding on fungi and decaying plant matter. The ventral tube on underside of abdomen is characteristic of this order.

▲ **Podura aquatica** Poduridae. Abundant on and around still water, especially where there is a good covering of duckweed. Spring reaches ventral tube when folded.

▲ **Neanura muscorum** Hypogastruridae. Grey or purplish black with very short limbs. Spring does not reach ventral tube. Insect hardly jumps. Abundant in woodland.

▲ **Isotoma viridis** Isotomidae. Spring white. Abundant in damp leaf litter and mosses.

▲ **Entomobrya nivalis** Entomobryidae. A distinctive pattern. Abundant in mosses.

▲ **Orchesella cincta**. Pale orange to deep brown or black, but 3rd abdominal segment always black. Very hairy, but no scales. Common under woodland mosses.

▲ **Tomocerus vulgaris** Tomoceridae. Body clear with silvery reflections: ciliated at hind end. One of the largest European springtails and a good jumper. Under stones and rotten wood. △ *T. longicornis* is identified by very long antennae. Pale yellow body colour shows through if scales are rubbed off. Legs very hairy.

▲ **Lucerne Flea** *Sminthurus viridis* Sminthuridae. Prefers living plants: often abundant on legumes, including garden peas. Mainly on mosses in winter.

▲ **Dicyrtoma fusca**. Brick red to deep brown: very hairy. One of the smallest springtails (1mm long). Abundant in woodland leaf litter and under loose bark.

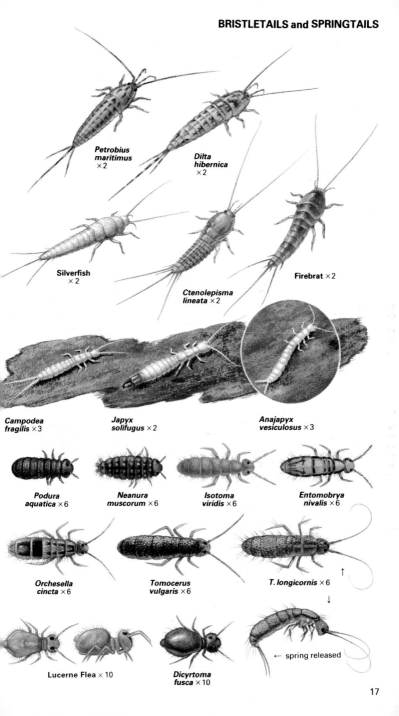

Petrobius maritimus ×2

Dilta hibernica ×2

Silverfish ×2

Ctenolepisma lineata ×2

Firebrat ×2

Campodea fragilis ×3

Japyx solifugus ×2

Anajapyx vesiculosus ×3

Podura aquatica ×6

Neanura muscorum ×6

Isotoma viridis ×6

Entomobrya nivalis ×6

Orchesella cincta ×6

Tomocerus vulgaris ×6

T. longicornis ×6

← spring released

Lucerne Flea ×10

Dicyrtoma fusca ×10

MAYFLIES   Order Ephemeroptera

Delicate, weak-flying insects with 2 or 3 long 'tails' at hind end. Front legs very long, especially in males, which can be recognised by a pair of claspers at the hind end. Usually 2 pairs of wings with complex venation: hind pair always much smaller than forewings and sometimes missing. Wings held vertically above body at rest or partly open: cannot be folded back along the body. Antennae minute. Eyes larger in male than in female, sometimes divided into two parts, with the upper parts much expanded to form turrets well above the rest of the head (see p. 20). Such eyes are known as turbinate eyes. Adults do not feed. Mainly crepuscular or nocturnal and rarely found far from the water in which they grow up.

Nymphs (p. 296) include burrowing, crawling, and free-swimming forms and feed mainly on organic debris: some are partly carnivorous. Mayflies are unique in moulting again after attaining the fully-winged state. Adults emerging from the nymphal skins are rather dull and hairy and are called duns or sub-imagines, but within hours (sometimes within minutes) they shed another very fine skin and emerge as shiny imagines, generally known as spinners. Females can sometimes be seen with egg-masses protruding from their bodies, ready to be dropped or washed into the water.

There are about 2500 known species, with some 200 in Europe. Colours fade after death and identification depends largely on the venation: a good lens is essential.

Palingenia longicauda Palingeniidae. 2 tails. Wings smoky brown throughout: hardly transparent. The largest European mayfly. Female does not shed sub-imaginal skin. Breeds in large rivers. C (mainly eastern).

Oligoneuriella rhenana Oligoneuriidae. 3 tails. Venation greatly reduced in both wings. Breeds mainly in large, clear rivers. Adults form enormous swarms over the water 7-8, usually in late afternoon or evening. S & C (mainly eastern).

Metretopus borealis Metretopodidae. 2 tails. Hindwing markedly oval. Forewing with 2 short (intercalary) veins between the last 2 long veins. 7-8. Nymph swims freely in clear, well-vegetated streams. N.

Ephoron virgo Polymitarcidae. 2 tails on male, 3 on female. Readily identified by the milky wings. Females do not shed sub-imaginal skin. 8-9, swarming in huge numbers over large, slow-moving rivers and lakes in which it breeds. Strongly attracted to light. S & C.

▲ *Ephemera danica* Ephemeridae. 3 tails. Wings always spotted. Veins in basal area of forewing run sharply backwards. Abdomen cream or greyish above with darker markings towards rear. 4-9. Nymph (p. 296) lives in lakes and rivers with muddy or sandy bottoms. There are several similar species with darker abdomens.

▲ *Siphlonurus lacustris* Siphlonuridae. 2 tails. Several wavy veinlets run back from last prominent long vein to the hind margin of forewing. Hind tarsus longer than tibia: femora unbanded. 5-9, mainly in upland areas. Breeds at edges of hill streams. There are several similar species.

△ s *Potamanthus luteus* Potamanthidae. 3 tails. Venation as in *Ephemera* but wings yellowish and never spotted with brown. 6-7. Strongly nocturnal. Breeds in large, swift rivers. S & C.

wavy veinlets

Siphlonurus wing

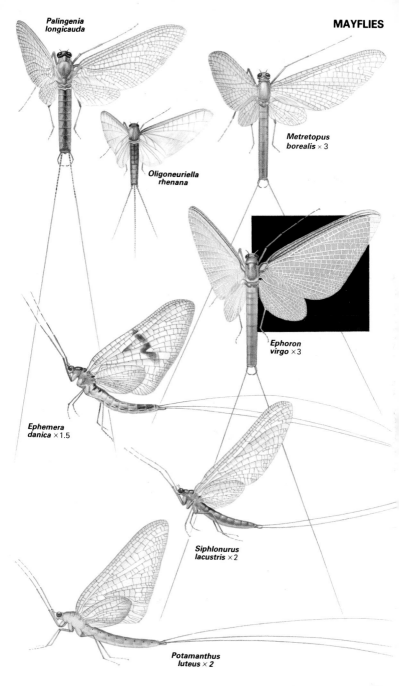

Palingenia longicauda

Oligoneuriella rhenana

Metretopus borealis × 3

Ephoron virgo × 3

Ephemera danica × 1.5

Siphlonurus lacustris × 2

Potamanthus luteus × 2

▲ **Ecdyonurus dispar** Heptageniidae. 2 tails. Forewing has 2 pairs of short (intercalary) veins between the last 2 long veins. 6-10. Nymph (p. 296) lives in stony streams and lakes. There are several similar species.

▲ **Rhithrogena semicolorata**. 2 tails. Basal half of forewing commonly bronze or golden brown: often appearing yellow in flight. Femur has brown streak in centre. 4-9. Breeds in fast, stony streams.

▲ **Caenis horaria** Caenidae. A very small mayfly with 3 tails and no hind-wings. Forewings milky and fringed with minute hairs (lens!). First 5 or 6 abdominal segments grey on top. Female has lighter thorax. 6-9. Breeds in large lakes and rivers with plenty of vegetation and debris. There are several similar species.

▲ **Ephemerella ignita** Ephemerellidae. 3 tails. Veins Cu_1 and Cu_2 are very close at the base (lens!). 4-9. Breeds in fast streams. △ **E. notata** is similar but somewhat paler and with small black marks on underside of abdomen.

Isonychia ignota Isonychidae. 2 tails. Last long vein (Cu_2) of forewing runs almost parallel to hind margin. Breeds in rivers. S & C (southern). Sometimes placed in Siphlonuridae.

▲ **Baetis rhodani** Baetidae. 2 tails. Hindwing very small. Intercalary veins in forewing always paired. Male with large turbinate eyes, as in all this family. Adult most of the year, but mainly spring and autumn. Breeds in small, fast streams. One of several very similar species, very difficult to separate.

▲ **Cloeon dipterum**. 2 tails. Hindwing absent. 3-5 cross-veins in pterostigma near wing-tip. Front margin of wing yellowish brown in female. Male eyes turbinate. 5-10. Breeds in ponds and ditches and even in water butts. ▲ **C. simile** is similar but has 9-11 cross-veins in pterostigma.

head of ♂ *Centroptilum* showing the turbinate eye (see p. 18). The facets in the enlarged upper part of the eye face upwards and detect rapid movements. The facets of the lower part of the eye face sideways and downwards and are adapted to pick out fine detail.

▲ **Centroptilum luteolum**. 2 tails. Hindwing very small and strap-like, with pointed tip. Intercalary veins around edge of forewing single (not paired as in *Baetis*). Male eyes turbinate. 4-11. Breeds in stony streams and lake margins.

▲ **Leptophlebia vespertina** Leptophlebiidae. 3 tails. Rather similar to *Ephemerella* but lens shows base of vein Cu_2 midway between Cu_1 and 1A. Front edge of hindwing without a projection. 4-8. Breeds in lakes and streams, mainly in acidic regions.
   ▲ **L. marginata** is similar but forewing is smoky brown towards tip.

▲ **Paraleptophlebia cincta**. 3 tails. Base of vein Cu_2 is nearer to 1A than to Cu_1. Hindwing without a projection on front margin. Male abdomen whitish and translucent at front. 5-8. Breeds in small, fast streams in alkaline areas.

▲ **Habrophlebia fusca**. 3 tails. Hindwing with strong projection on front margin. Forewing venation like *Paraleptophlebia* but with virtually no intercalary veins. 5-9. Breeds in slow, well-vegetated streams and ditches.

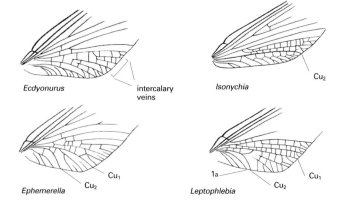

Ecdyonurus — intercalary veins

Isonychia — Cu_2

Ephemerella — Cu_1 Cu_2

Leptophlebia — 1a Cu_1 Cu_2

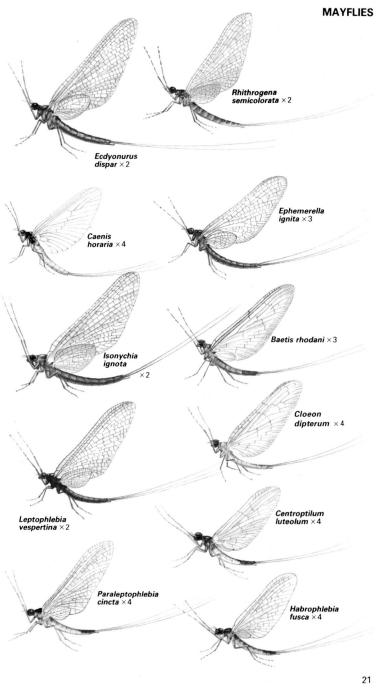

Rhithrogena semicolorata × 2

Ecdyonurus dispar × 2

Caenis horaria × 4

Ephemerella ignita × 3

Isonychia ignota × 2

Baetis rhodani × 3

Cloeon dipterum × 4

Leptophlebia vespertina × 2

Centroptilum luteolum × 4

Paraleptophlebia cincta × 4

Habrophlebia fusca × 4

DRAGONFLIES   Order Odonata

Relatively long-bodied, predatory insects with large eyes and tiny, bristle-like antennae. Wings stiff and often rustling in flight, with a dense network of veins and usually a dark spot, known as the pterostigma, on the front margin near the tip. The wings are not linked and each pair moves independently. Fight is often very fast and many of the insects are amazingly agile. They can hover and even fly backwards, which with their superb eyesight can make them very difficult to catch. Dragonflies feed on other insects, especially flies, which they normally catch in mid-air, swooping about to scoop them up in their spiky legs, which are held like a net under the head. Some prey is also plucked from the vegetation, particularly by the smaller dragonflies.

There are over 5,000 known species, mainly in the tropical regions. About 100 species occur in Europe, falling into two distinct sub-orders. The **Zygoptera** contains the damselflies, mostly delicate insects with very slender bodies and rather weak flight. Front and hind wings are roughly alike and normally held above the body at rest. The eyes are well separated on the sides of the head.

The sub-order **Anisoptera** contains larger insects, sometimes called true dragonflies to distinguish them from the damselflies. Hindwings are usually broader than forewings (Anisoptera means "unequal wings"), and the wings are always held out to the sides of the body at rest. The eyes are very large and usually meet on the top of the head. Two distinct types of feeding behaviour are found among the true dragonflies. The HAWKERS remain airborne for long periods, often hawking to and fro along a particular beat such as a stream or a hedgerow. The DARTERS, on the other hand, spend much of their time on a perch – on either ground or vegetation – and dart out from it when prey approaches. They usually return to the same perch and an individual darter may remain on its station for a whole day. European dragonflies are essentially sun-loving insects, although some may fly at dusk if food is abundant.

Life Cycle. The dragonflies have a unique system of mating, involving accessory reproductive organs at the front of the male's abdomen. These can be seen as small swellings under the 2nd abdominal segment, and are one way to distinguish the sexes. The hind end of the male abdomen bears a pair of modified cerci, technically known as superior anal appendages but more conveniently

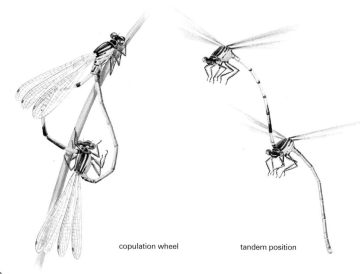

copulation wheel   tandem position

called claspers. They are usually curved, often very long and conspicuous in the anisopterans but usually less obvious in the damselflies. Male anisopterans usually have a third (inferior) anal appendage, just below the claspers and appearing between them when seen from above. Male damselflies have a pair of inferior anal appendages, just below the claspers and usually much smaller. Female anisopterans may have prominent cerci – usually straighter and more slender than those of the males – but they lack the other anal appendages. Some females have a visible ovipositor just under the tip of the abdomen.

Before courtship, the male transfers sperm from the reproductive openings at his hind end to his accessory reproductive organs. Finding an agreeable female, he then grasps her by the neck or the back of the head with his claspers – which are just the right shape for each species. The insects can fly in this tandem position, but they soon settle and the female curves the tip of her abdomen round to collect the sperm from the male's accessory organs. This position is known as the copulation wheel. The insects may separate as soon as sperm transfer is complete, but many species – particularly among the damselflies and the smaller dragonflies – remain in the tandem position until the female has laid her eggs. These may be simply dropped into the water, or washed off as the female dips her abdomen into it in flight. Some eggs are laid in silt, or placed in slits cut in plant stems. Some female damselflies go right down into the water to lay their eggs in plant stems and are often held by their partners while they do so.

The **nymphs** (p. 296) grow up in water. They eat a wide range of other aquatic creatures, which they impale on spines at the end of a remarkably extensile lower jaws known as the mask. Most damselflies complete their life cycles in one year, but the anisopterans take anything up to 5 years, especially in cooler regions. A few species in southern Europe have two generations in a year. When fully grown, the nymph crawls out of the water, usually climbing up a plant stem, and the adult soon emerges. Empty nymph skins are commonly found on the vegetation around ponds and streams in the summer.

Freshly emerged dragonflies are very pale and are called tenerals. The full colours do not develop for several days or even weeks. Many species, especially the males, develop a powdery blue coating on various parts of their bodies when mature. This is called pruinescence. Many lose their colours soon after death, however, and colour cannot always be relied on for identifying dead specimens.

Dragonfly **classification** is based largely on wing venation, and the main features used are shown in the diagrams below.

Damselfly wing

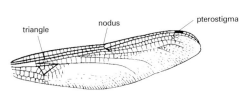

Dragonfly wing

DAMSELFLIES   Sub-order Zygoptera

Slender-bodied insects with all wings more or less the same shape and size. Eyes well separated at sides of head, which resembles a tiny hammer head. Generally weak-flying, resting with wings partly open or closed vertically above the body.

Family Platycnemididae. A fairly small family, identified by the almost rectangular quadrilateral (p. 26). The middle and hind tibiae are expanded and often feather-like in males, and also in the females of some species, but the extent of the expansion varies even within a species.

▲ **White-legged Damselfly** *Platycnemis pennipes*. Middle and hind tibiae expanded in both sexes; white with a black line down the middle. Female abdomen pale green with black markings, sometimes almost white. Frequents slow-moving rivers, canals, and large lakes without too much vegetation. 5-8. Absent from Iberia and far north. *P. latipes* is similar, but expanded tibiae without black line. Front half of abdomen often very pale in both sexes. Slow-moving water. 6-8. France and Iberia. *P. acutipennis* has orange and black body and tibiae are expanded only in male – and even then not very much. Eyes are clear blue when mature. 5-7. S & C.

Family Coenagriidae. A large family in which the quadrilateral (p. 26) is acutely pointed. Pterostigma diamond-shaped.

▲ **Large Red Damselfly** *Pyrrhosoma nymphula*. Black legs and red stripes on thorax distinguish this from the next species. Female abdomen usually more heavily marked with black; thoracic stripes sometimes yellow. Slow-moving streams and still water, including peat bogs. 4-8. Absent from extreme N & S.

△ s **Small Red Damselfly** *Ceriagrion tenellum*. Red legs and no coloured stripes on thorax. Female with largely black abdomen. Restricted to acidic bogs and marshes. 5-8. S & C.

▲ **Blue-tailed Damselfly** *Ischnura elegans*. Abdomen usually black with 8th segment bright blue in both sexes, but female sometimes lacks blue. Pterostigma bicoloured. Around still waters of all kinds, including polluted ponds: often abundant. 3-10, with 2 broods in south. Rapid development allows it to breed in rice fields of S in summer. Absent from much of Spain, where replaced by *I. graellsii*.

▲ **Red-eyed Damselfly** *Erythromma najas*. More robust than other members of the family, with prominent red eyes. No coloured spots on head. Female lacks blue tip to abdomen. Venation at tip of hindwing distinctly denser than in forewing. Shallow ponds, canals, and slow-moving waters. Flies relatively fast, keeping close to water and often settling on floating leaves. 4-9. N & C. ▲ **Small Red-eyed Damselfly** *E. viridulum* is smaller and male has sides of abdominal segments 8, 9 and 10 blue (only segments 9 and 10 in *E. najas*). S & C

▲ **Common Blue Damselfly** *Enallagma cyathigerum*. Resembles *Coenagrion* spp, but hind wing-tip is somewhat more densely veined than front, and side of thorax has a single black line instead of two. Male usually identified by mushroom or 'ace-of-spades' mark at front of abdomen. (*Coenagrion hastulatum* has similar mark, but with dark lines alongside – see below). Female green and black, with prominent spine under 8th abdominal segment. Very common over still water with plenty of floating vegetation: often settles on lily leaves. 4-8.

▲ *Coenagrion puella*. One of 11 very similar species in Europe. Male has U-shaped mark at front of abdomen. Female largely black with some green on thorax and blue at tip of abdomen. No spine under abdomen. 4-9. One of the commonest damselflies, abundant by still water almost everywhere, but rare in N.

Males of *Coenagrion* spp. can often be distinguished by the black marks on 2nd abdominal segment, although these do vary. Females are more difficult as their markings, different from those of the males, are often indistinct.

▲ *puella*   ▲ *pulchellum*   △ *mercuriale*   △ *hastulatum*

2nd abdominal segments of *Coenagrion* males

24

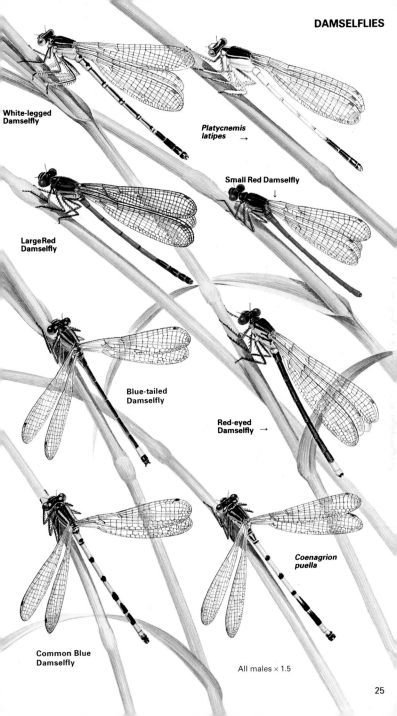

White-legged Damselfly

Platycnemis latipes →

LargeRed Damselfly

Small Red Damselfly ↓

Blue-tailed Damselfly

Red-eyed Damselfly →

Common Blue Damselfly

Coenagrion puella

All males × 1.5

Nehalennia speciosa. Europe's smallest damselfly, easily recognised by size alone. Abdomen largely black with blue or green spots. Only 1 or 2 cross-veins beyond pterostigma. Still waters with plenty of emergent vegetation. 5-7. N & C: local and usually uncommon.

Family Lestidae. A relatively small family in which pterostigma is distinctly elongated. Quadrilateral is acutely pointed at outer end. Body is generally metallic and mostly green. Males have long and strongly curved claspers.

Platycnemis (p. 24)   *Coenagrion* (p. 24)   *Lestes*

Forewings with quadrilaterals blacked in to emphasis different shapes

▲ **Common Emerald Damselfly** *Lestes sponsa.* Pale blue patches develop only on mature male. Female entirely bronzy green with reddish green eyes. Still waters, including drainage ditches and acid heathland pools as well as large lakes, but always with plenty of fringing vegetation. Insects usually keep close to the edge and rest with wings half open. 6-10. Mainly N & C: rare in S. There are several similar species. The much rarer △s **Scarce Emerald Damselfly** *L. dryas* is more robust, but safely distinguished only by examining the claspers or ovipositor. **The Southern Emerald Damselfly** *L. barbarus* is a little larger, with the outer third of the pterostigma white and the rear of the head yellow. Its body never becomes blue. A native of S & C, it has been spreading northwards in recent years and is sometimes found in B. **The Willow Emerald Damselfly** *L. viridis*, which has a pale brown pterostigma, has also been moving up from S & C and seems to be well-established in East Anglia.

Sympecma fusca. Body dull brown. Pterostigma of forewing clearly nearer to wing-tip than that of hindwing. Over still water, even where polluted. All year S & C. This and its close relative ***S. annulata*** of C are the only European dragonflies that hibernate as adults. They hide among dead leaves or in dense shrubs, but often take to the wing on sunny days, even in the middle of winter.

Family Calopterygidae. A large family, found mainly in the tropics but with four handsome species in Europe. These are our largest damselflies and are sometimes called demoiselles. Body is strongly metallic. Wings have numerous antenodal veins. There is no pterostigma, although females have a small white patch (false pterostigma). Male wings are at least partly decorated with a patch of dense colour – smoky brown at first but becoming darker with maturity and eventually assuming a deep blue or purplish sheen. The males, more agile than other damselflies, display their colours to females during fluttery courtship dances.

▲ **Banded Agrion** *Calopteryx splendens.* Male body brilliant green or blue: colour patch on wing does not start before nodus, but otherwise varies in extent and may reach wing-tip in southern races. Female body always greenish: wings colourless at first, but greenish yellow when mature. False pterostigma near wing-tip. Canals and quiet rivers with muddy bottoms, usually in open country. 4-9. Absent from far north.

▲ ***Calopteryx virgo***. Male body like *splendens*, but wing colour starts well before nodus. Female body always green: wings clear at first and then brownish – never greenish. False pterostigma well away from wing-tip. Prefers faster-flowing streams with sandy or gravelly bottoms; often among trees. 5-9.

Calopteryx haemorrhoidalis. Body shining brown, that of male distinctly pink at rear of abdomen. Male wings dark nearly all over, but with a clear base. Female wings like those of *virgo*, but tip of hindwing dark brown. 5-8. Clear running water. S.

C. haemorrhoidalis
female hindwing

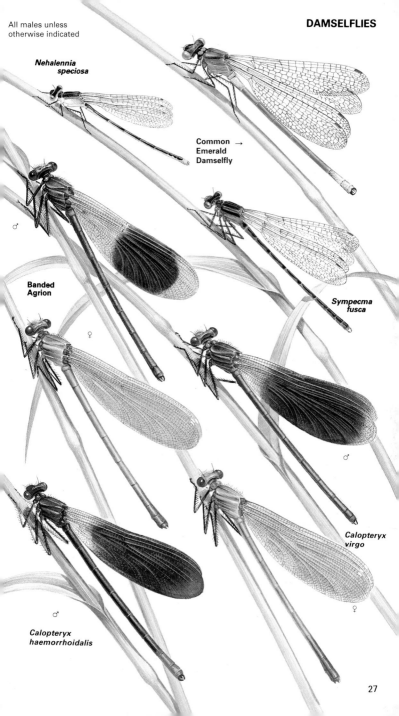

All males unless
otherwise indicated

*Nehalennia
speciosa*

Common →
Emerald
Damselfly

♂

Banded
Agrion

*Sympecma
fusca*

♀

♂

*Calopteryx
virgo*

♂

♀

*Calopteryx
haemorrhoidalis*

TRUE DRAGONFLIES   Sub-order Anisoptera

Stouter than damselflies and with hindwings broader than front. Eyes usually meet on top of head. Wings held more or less flat at rest: never brought together above the body except when first emerged from nymphal skin. Mostly strong fliers, either hawking up and down for long periods (hawkers) or perching for long periods and periodically darting out to snatch prey (darters).

Family Gomphidae. Hawker dragonflies with widely separated eyes: ocelli more or less in a straight line. Abdomen swollen at end, especially in males. Triangles similar in both wings. Base of hindwing angular in male, rounded in female.

△s **Club-tailed Dragonfly** *Gomphus vulgatissimus*. The only British species, and the only European gomphid appearing more black than yellow. Legs black. Relatively slow-flying, with a short beat along streams, although often flying far from water. Rests on rocks and bare ground as well as on vegetation. Mainly rather swift rivers, but also lakes. Eggs are laid at the water surface and nymphs burrow in silt or mud. 4-8. Absent from most of the Mediterranean region, but otherwise widely distributed.

Gomphus pulchellus. Legs almost entirely yellow. Abdomen less swollen than in other *Gomphus* spp. Much less black on sides of thorax than in *vulgatissimus*, and altogether paler. Yellow never very bright and dark markings often grey. Rests on paths and other bare ground and also on trees – a rare habit in *Gomphus*. Still waters, where nymphs burrow in mud. 5-7. Spain and south-west France.

Onychogomphus uncatus. General body colour is clear, bright yellow, but older insects may become greenish around the thorax. Eyes greyish blue. Male claspers not forked at apex, but bent sharply inwards to give the abdomen a distinctly blunt tip. Rests on ground. Very clear, fast-flowing streams. Nymphs crawl on to waterside rocks and stones ready for adult emergence. 6-9. SW Europe, north to the Rhine. *O. forcipatus* is similar, but smaller and paler yellow with forked male claspers. Much of Europe.

Family Cordulegasteridae. Large hawkers in which the eyes just meet at a point in both sexes. Triangles similar in both wings. Base of hindwing angular in male and rounded in female. Latter has long ovipositor, reaching beyond tip of abdomen, which she digs into stream bed to lay eggs.

▲ **Gold-ringed Dragonfly** *Cordulegaster boltonii*. Occipital triangle, just behind eyes, is yellow. Male claspers strongly divergent when seen from above. Male hindwing usually with 5-celled anal triangle. Flies strongly at low levels along streams, but often far from water. Rests on ground or vegetation. Clear, shallow streams with silty bottoms. Nymphs burrow in the silt. 5-8. Widely distributed, especially in upland areas.

Cordulegaster bidentatus. Occipital triangle, just behind the eye, is black. Male claspers more or less parallel when seen from above. Male hindwing has 3-celled anal triangle. Habits similar to *boltonii*, but breeds in still waters of bogs and marshes as well as in streams. 5-8. S & C: mainly montane in S.

Gold-ringed Dragonfly laying eggs in the silt of a shallow heathland stream

DRAGONFLIES

Gomphus pulchellus

Club-tailed Dragonfly

Onychogomphus uncatus

Gold-ringed Dragonfly

Cordulegaster bidentatus

29

Family Aeshnidae. A family of relatively large hawkers in which the eyes touch for an appreciable distance in the mid-line. The triangles are similar on both wings. Claspers are well developed in both sexes, although often straighter and narrower in the female. Male are usually easily distinguished by the inferior anal appendage below the claspers. Most of the European species belong to the genus *Aeshna,* in which the base of the male hindwing is very angular and possesses a well-marked anal triangle. The number of cells in this triangle is useful in identifying the species (see below).

△s **Hairy Dragonfly** *Brachytron pratense.* Extremely hairy, with a very long, slender pterostigma. Female lacks conspicuous green thoracic stripes: her abdominal spots are green or yellow and her wing bases are yellow. Still and slow-moving water: enjoys sunbathing. 3-6: one of the earliest dragonflies. S & C, but very local in S.

▲ **Emperor Dragonfly** *Anax imperator.* Male, easily identified by deep blue abdomen with black line and no inferior anal appendage, is one of Europe's largest dragonflies. Base of hindwing is rounded, instead of pointed as in *Aeshna* spp, and has no anal triangle. Female has greenish blue abdomen. Neither sex has stripes on top of thorax. A very fast-flying species, usually keeping to still water and often breeding in small ponds and ditches. 5-10. S & C. △ **The Lesser Emperor Dragonfly** *Anax parthenope,* which has a bright blue patch at the front of the abdomen, has recently been moving northwards from its base in southern Europe and colonies now exist in B and various other parts of C & N.

▲ **Brown Hawker** *Aeshna grandis.* Easily distinguished by the amber wing membrane. Female lacks blue spots at front of abdomen. Still waters of lakes, canals, gravel pits, etc: often flying close to the edge but sometimes far from water. 4-9. Most of Europe, but mainly montane in S.

▲ **Southern Hawker** *Aeshna cyanea.* One of the commonest species. Broad green thoracic stripes in both sexes. Abdominal spots all green or yellow in female. In both sexes, the last two abdominal segments carry complete bands of colour, not broken into spots. Anal triangle of male usually with three cells and sometimes more. Mainly still waters, from marshes to large lakes: often flies far from water and commonly hawks along hedgerows and woodland clearings. 6-10. Most of Europe apart from far north.

▲ **Common Hawker** *Aeshna juncea.* Narrow thoracic stripes, blue spotting throughout abdomen, and 2-celled anal triangle distinguish male from Southern Hawker. Female is like Southern Hawker, but without stripes on top of thorax, although she has bright yellow stripes on the sides. Coloured patches on last two abdominal segments are clearly divided. Well-vegetated ponds and other still waters. 6-10. All Europe, but mainly montane in S.

▲ **Migrant Hawker** *Aeshna mixta.* Very like Common Hawker, but smaller and top of thorax virtually without stripes in both sexes and there is a small yellow triangle or T-shaped mark at front of abdomen. Male has 3-celled anal triangle. Both sexes have very long claspers – at least as long as the last two abdominal segments. Mainly still waters. Often migrates in swarms. 6-10. S & C.

Common Hawker (2 cells)   Migrant Hawker (3 cells)

Hindwing bases showing the anal triangles

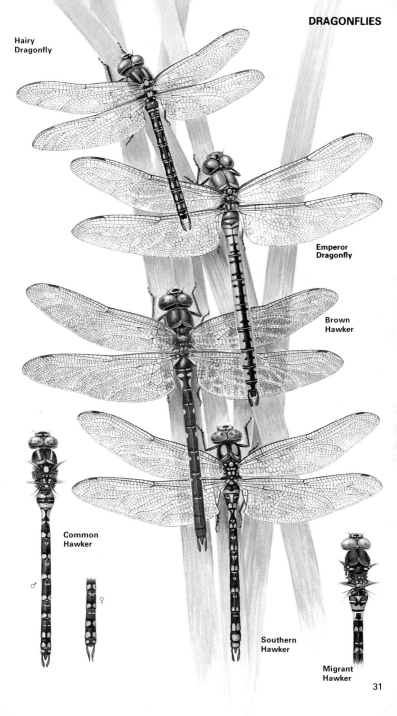

DRAGONFLIES

Hairy
Dragonfly

Emperor
Dragonfly

Brown
Hawker

Common
Hawker

♂

♀

Southern
Hawker

Migrant
Hawker

Family Corduliidae. Medium-sized hawkers with distinctly metallic bodies – usually bronze or green. Triangles of the two wings differ in shape, that of the forewing having front and basal sides about equal. Claspers usually well developed in both sexes. Male abdomen distinctly narrowed in the front half.

△ s **Downy Emerald** *Cordulia aenea.* Shiny green thorax, densely clothed with golden hair. Abdomen dark bronze with sides of 2nd segment clear yellow in male. Inferior anal appendage of male deeply forked and resembling an extra pair of claspers. Hindwing triangle undivided. Female stouter than male. Flies swiftly over lakes and ponds and rarely settles. 4-8. Most of Europe, but rare in S.

△ **Brilliant Emerald** *Somatochlora metallica.* Thorax much less hairy than *Cordulia* and abdomen much brighter green – detectable even in flight. Claspers much longer than in *Cordulia*, especially in female. Inferior anal appendage of male unforked. Triangle of hindwing 2-celled. Female stouter than male and easily identified by a sharp spine under the abdomen just before the tip. Still and slow-moving water in lowlands and mountains. Flies rapidly. 6-9. Most of Europe, but not Iberia. Two distinct populations in B: one in SE England and one in NW Scotland.

△ n **Northern Emerald** *S.arctica,* a similar but more northerly species, has strongly curved claspers in male and no abdominal spine in female.

Family Libellulidae. A large family of darters in which triangles are of different shapes in the two wings: that of the forewing has front side very much shorter than basal side. Body not metallic in European species. Mature males often have pale blue pruinescence. Claspers sometimes prominent in females. Often perch on exposed twig or reed and rest with body horizontal. In hot weather the wings may be lowered to shade the thorax (see below). Most of the European species belong to the genus *Sympetrum,* in which the last antenodal vein (see p 22) is usually incomplete.

▲ **Black-tailed Skimmer** *Orthetrum cancellatum.* Wing bases completely clear. Pterostigma black. Only mature male is blue: young male resembles female. Marshes, ponds, and lakes. 5-9. Absent from far north.

△ **Keeled Skimmer** *Orthetrum coerulescens.* Wing bases clear. Shorter and more slender than *cancellatum:* pterostigma yellowish brown. Only mature male is blue: young male resembles female. Mainly on bogs and marshes. Male commonly rests on ground. 6-9. Absent from far north. Several similar species in S.

▲ **4-spotted Chaser** *Libellula quadrimaculata.* Named for the prominent spot on each nodus. There may also be a brown patch near each wingtip. Always a triangular brown patch at base of hindwing, with amber shading at base of forewing. Sexes alike: female claspers about as long as those of male. Male never becomes blue. Bogs and marshes, often high in mountains and by the sea. 4-9. All Europe, often migrating in swarms.

▲ **Broad-bodied Chaser** *Libellula depressa.* All wings brown at base. Abdomen very broad, blue only in mature males: young males resemble females. A very fast darter, often perching on bushes. Frequents ponds and slow-moving streams and often breeds in garden ponds and similar small bodies of water. 4-8. The much rarer △ s **Scarce Chaser** *L. fulva,* also known as the **Blue Chaser,** is similar but lacks yellow spots and has much less dark shading on wing bases, especially on forewing. Abdomen is marked with black at the rear.

Broad-bodied Chaser in typical warm-weather pose, with wings lowered slightly to shade thorax. Wings are horizontal in cooler weather, when the insects often choose to rest on the ground.

DRAGONFLIES

Downy
Emerald

Brilliant
Emerald

Black-tailed
Skimmer
♀

Keeled
Skimmer

♀

Broad-bodied
Chaser
♀

4-spotted
Chaser

33

Crocothemis erythraea. Resembles *Sympetrum*, but broader: last antenodal vein may or may not be complete. Body yellow or brown at first, becoming red with age: especially vivid in male. No trace of black on upper surface apart from a very thin black line along the abdomen, and even this is not always visible. Costa and radius red: other veins black. Patch on hindwing orange or red in male, yellow in female. Likes to perch on bare twig or reed. Still water, including Mediterranean rice fields. 5-10. S & C, with two broods in southernmost areas.

▲ **Common Darter** *Sympetrum striolatum*. Commonest member of the genus. Legs dark with a yellow stripe. Black band across the head just in front of eyes does not continue down the side of each eye. Thoracic sutures well marked with black. Female is orange-brown with dark marks on end of abdomen. Still waters. 6- 10. All Europe: a great migrant. There are several similar species. △s **Vagrant Darter** *S. vulgatum* has black line on head running down side of each eye. ***S. meridionale*** has no black sutures on sides of thorax: legs almost entirely yellow. ▲ **Ruddy Darter** *S. sanguineum* has entirely black legs: male abdomen deep red. △n **Highland Darter** *S. nigrescens* has a very broad dark stripe on side of thorax.

△ **Red-veined Darter** *Sympetrum fonscolombei*. Distinguished from *striolatum* by yellowish pterostigma sharply edged with black. Many veins are red or yellow, especially near base. Female body sand coloured. Still waters, including Mediterranean rice fields. 5-11. Resident in S, with two broods per year: migrates to C each spring.

Sympetrum pedemontanum. The only European *Sympetrum* species with clouding in outer part of wing. Marshland. 7-10. S & C.

△ **Black Darter** *Sympetrum danae*. Black triangle on top of thorax clearly identifies female and teneral male. Mature male is jet black. Mainly on peat bogs. 7-9. N & C.

△ **Yellow-winged Darter** *Sympetrum flaveolum*. Extensive yellow patch at base of each wing identifies this species. Pterostigma red. Bogs and marshes. All Europe. A strong migrant.

△ **White-faced Darter** *Leucorrhinia dubia*. White face. Pterostigma short and broad: reddish brown in male and black in female. Female has yellow markings instead of red, and dark wing bases are surrounded by a yellow cloud. Teneral males also have yellow body markings. Rarely far from peat bogs or wet heaths. 5-8. Most of Europe: mainly montane in S.

Leucorrhinia caudalis. Pterostigma short and broad: pale in male and brown in female. Abdominal segments 6-9 enlarged. Female and immature male lack blue in middle of abdomen. Bogs and marshes. 5-7. C.

White-faced
Darter

Leucorrhinia
caudalis

Crocothemis erythraea

All males unless
otherwise indicated

DRAGONFLIES

Common
Darter

*Sympetrum
pedemontanum*

...veined
...r

Yellow-winged
Darter ♀

Black
Darter ♀

35

STONEFLIES   Order Plecoptera

Weak-flying or flightless insects with rather soft and flattened bodies: often with two long cerci. Never brightly coloured. Wings folded flat over body or wrapped around it at rest. Forewings often with two prominent rows of cross-veins forming a 'double ladder'. Hindwings usually much broader than forewings. Venation very variable, even within a species. Males commonly smaller than females and often with very short wings. Nymphs (p. 296) are aquatic and usually prefer cool, running water. They crawl on to waterside stones ready for adult emergence. Adults rarely move far from water, usually crawling on stones and tree trunks close to the streams. Some scrape algae or nibble pollen, but many do not feed at all. There are about 3000 known species, but less than 150 occur in Europe.

▲   **Leuctra fusca** Leuctridae. One of many similar species known as needle flies because wings are wrapped tightly round body at rest. Cerci very short. Stony streams and lake shores, including chalk streams. Lowlands and uplands. 4-11, but most commonly 7-9; probably all year in S.
    Members of the family Nemouridae are similar but they have an oblique vein in apical cell of forewing, and the wings are less tightly rolled around the body. Members of the Taeniopterygidae are also similar, but their tarsal segments are about equal in length: Leuctridae and Nemouridae have 2nd tarsal segment very short.

LEUCTRIDAE

TAENIOPTERYGIDAE

hind tarsi

▲   **Isoperla grammatica** Perlodidae. Anal region of hindwing much enlarged, with 2 prominently forked veins. One of several very similar species, but the only large yellow species in B (commonly called yellow sally by anglers). Stony and gravelly streams: very common in limestone regions. 4-9.

▲   **Perlodes microcephala**. Distinguished from most other large species by the irregular network of veins near the wing-tips. Male normally has very short wings. Stony streams and rivers: the only large stonefly commonly found in chalk streams. 3-7. Several similar species in Alps and Pyrenees.

▲   **Capnia bifrons** Capniidae. Forewing has no 'double ladder' of cross veins. A single cross-vein in apical space. Hindwing distinctly shorter than forewing and more rounded. Male has very short wings – no more than 2.5mm long and often just minute stumps. Basal tarsal segment about as long as third segment – distinguishing the Capniidae from other families with long cerci, in which basal tarsal segment is always shorter. Common by stony rivers and lake shores. 2-5. Mainly S & C. A few similar species occur mainly in N and on mountains.

▲   **Chloroperla torrentium** Chloroperlidae. Anal area of hindwing small, with no forked veins. Lake shores and sandy or gravelly streams, mainly in upland areas. 4-8. Called small yellow sally by anglers. One of several similar species.

▲   **Dinocras cephalotes** Perlidae. One of the largest stoneflies. No network of veins near wing-tip. Three long cells are prominent near middle of hindwing, and hindmost of these has 1-3 cross-veins (often very faint and occasionally absent). Pronotum black. Male no more than half size of female. Common on stony rivers with firm beds and fixed, moss-covered stones: especially in upland regions, where it may reach 2000m. 5-8.

▲   **Perla bipunctata**. Resembles *D. cephalotes* but has a paler body. Pronotum yellowish with dark central stripe and dark borders. Hindwing lacks cross-veins in hindmost long cell. Cerci extend well beyond wings at rest. Male 1/2 to 3/4 size of female. A very common species, preferring rivers with beds of loose stones. Mainly uplands, but not as high as *Dinocras*. 5-7.

cross-vein

Forewing of NEMOURIDAE
showing cross-vein in
apical space

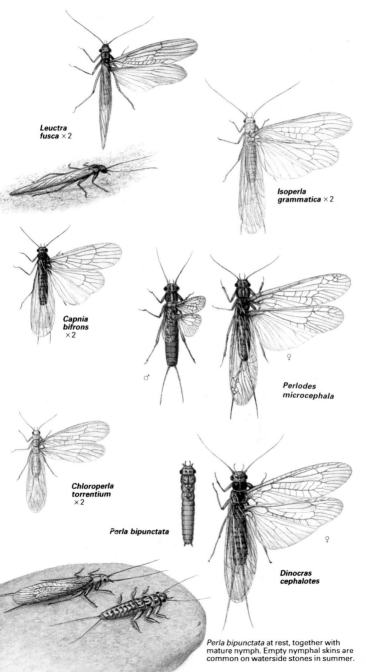

Leuctra fusca × 2

Isoperla grammatica × 2

Capnia bifrons × 2

♂

♀

Perlodes microcephala

Chloroperla torrentium × 2

Perla bipunctata

♀

Dinocras cephalotes

Perla bipunctata at rest, together with mature nymph. Empty nymphal skins are common on waterside stones in summer.

GRASSHOPPERS and CRICKETS   Order Orthoptera

There are some 17,000 known members of the order, of which more than half are grasshoppers. Over 600 species occur in Europe, but the great majority of these are confined to the south – notably in Iberia and Greece – and only about 250 species extend into central Europe. Only 30 occur in the British Isles. The main groups of European Orthoptera may be distinguished with the key opposite.

Orthopterans are mostly rather stout insects, with hind legs enlarged for jumping. There is a prominent, saddle-shaped pronotum, the top (known as the disc) often with a central keel. There may also be side keels where the disc joins the side flaps of the pronotum. A transverse groove, known as the sulcus, normally runs across the centre of the disc, and there may be other grooves in front of it. The forewings (tegmina) are thicker and tougher than the hindwings and usually quite narrow. They may completely cover the abdomen at rest, but many species have very short forewings and some have none at all. The hindwings are similarly variable, but when fully developed they are broad and membranous. Flight is normally weak, although some species fly very well. The jaws are of the biting type.

The males of most species 'sing' by rubbing one part of the body against another. This is known as stridulation and serves to bring the sexes together. Allowing for differences in pitch and volume, the sounds may be likened to sewing machines and other pieces of machinery. In the presence of females, many males produce special courtship songs.

The orthopterans all begin life as eggs, and the great majority of European species pass the winter in the egg stage. There is no pupal stage and the youngsters pass through several nymphal stages before reaching maturity. Older nymphs are easily distinguished from adults of short-winged species because their wing buds are twisted and the front edges are uppermost: in adults the front edge of the forewing lies along the side of the body.

Grasshoppers (Family Acrididae) are almost entirely vegetarian and the majority are active only in sunshine. The males usually stridulate by rubbing the hind legs against the forewings. One of these surfaces bears a row of tiny pegs and the other a hard ridge. Moving one over the other produces a buzzing sound, just like that produced by running a finger nail over the teeth of a comb. The pitch varies with the number of pegs and also with the rate at which the legs are moved. Each species has its own characteristic song, but some species do not stridulate at all. Some female grasshoppers can stridulate, but their pegs are small and their songs are usually very soft. Hearing organs are on the sides of the body.

In one major group of grasshoppers the stridulatory pegs are carried on the inner face of each hind femur, with the ridge running along the centre of the forewing. In the other major group the pegs are borne on the forewing and the ridge is on the femur. The songs of this last group are usually rather weak. Their heads tend to be blunter than those of the first group, although there are some exceptions.

Colours are very variable and cannot always be relied on for identification. The shape of the pronotum and the arrangement of the keels are often of greater use.

male   female

Grasshopper sexes are easily distinguished
because the hind end of the male turns up
like the prow of a boat.

Locusts are large grasshoppers which assume gregarious habits from time to time and build up huge populations, although this rarely happens in Europe. Insects of the gregarious phase differ from the solitary insects in several anatomical features.

Bush-Crickets (Family Tettigoniidae) are mostly omnivorous, eating other insects as well as plant material. A few are entirely carnivorous. Long antennae readily distinguish them from the grasshoppers, and females are further distinguished by the blade-like ovipositor. Species with short, curved ovipositors normally lay their eggs in plants, after cutting slits with the saw-like teeth at the tip of the ovipositor. Other species lay eggs in the ground. During mating the male produces a large, jelly-like spermatophore, which is then attached to the hind end of the female. Sperms enter her body from it, but she eats most of the jelly. Many bush-crickets are crepuscular or nocturnal. They sing by raising the forewings and rubbing their bases together. The songs are often much higher-pitched than those of grasshoppers and often more prolonged. Both sexes sing in some species. The hearing organs are on both sides of the front tibiae.

True Crickets (Family Gryllidae) resemble bush-crickets in many ways but the forewings are usually broader across the top and the female ovipositor is needle-like. The songs are produced in the same way except that the right forewing overlaps the left one – the reverse of the bush-cricket condition. True crickets are either vegetarians or omnivores.

Key

Front legs greatly enlarged for digging

Mole Crickets, p. 58

Front legs normal
  Antennae shorter than body
    Pronotum extends back over abdomen

Groundhoppers, p. 46

    Pronotum does not extend back over abdomen

Grasshoppers, pp 38-47

  Antennae longer than body
    Palps very long; always wingless

Cave-crickets, p. 56

    Palps not particularly long; usually with at least traces of wings

      Tarsi 4-segmented   **Bush-crickets**, pp 48-57

      Tarsi 3-segmented   **True Crickets**, p. 58

GRASSHOPPERS Family Acrididae. Essentially diurnal, sun-loving insects with short antennae. Shape of pronotum and arrangement of keels often help to identify species. Female usually larger than male: sometimes much larger. Songs described are those of isolated males (p. 38). Unless otherwise stated, the stridulatory pegs are on the hind femur.

Arcyptera fusca. Female heavy and flightless. Song up to 8 short, croaky notes followed by harsh rustle which becomes very loud for 2-3 secs and then dies away with 2 or 3 more short notes. 7-9. Montane grassland, mainly in Alps & Pyrenees.

Pyrgomorpha conica. Head conical with rather stout antennae. Male grey or brown, often tinged with green: female green. Hindwings slightly pink at base. No stridulation. Dry grassy places. 3-9. S.

△s **Large Marsh Grasshopper** *Stethophyma grossum.* Stridulatory pegs on forewing, but male's normal call is a soft ticking made by tapping tip of forewing with hind tibia. Marshy areas, especially peat bogs with extensive sphagnum cover. 7-10. N & C: very local.

  ▲ **Mottled Grasshopper** *Myrmeleotettix maculatus.* Brown, green, or black: always mottled. Tip of antenna less swollen in female. Song a series of 10-30 short chirps, increasing in volume over 10-15 secs and rather like the sound of winding a clock: repeated at irregular intervals. 6-10. Heathland and other dry places.

 ▲ **Rufous Grasshopper** *Gomphocerippus rufus.* Normally brown: female sometimes purple. Antenna tipped with white. A small bulge on front edge of forewing. Song a soft chirp, fluctuating in volume like a sewing machine and lasting about 5 secs. 7-11. Mainly on limestone.

 ▲ **Field Grasshopper** *Chorthippus brunneus.* One of many similar species. Grey, green, brown, purple, or black. A small bulge on front edge of forewing. Very hairy below thorax. Song 6-10 short chirps, like time-signal pips at a lower pitch: sequence repeated irregularly. Female sings before mating. Mostly dry and often sparse grassland. 6-10. *C. biguttulus* is very similar, but front edge of forewing is strongly curved, especially in male. Song loud and metallic, like an old-fashioned dentist's drill, in chirps of 1-1.5 secs: chirps often in threes. Most of Europe, but not B.

 ▲ **Meadow Grasshopper** *C. parallelus.* Green, brown, or purple. A small bulge on front edge of forewing. Hindwings absent (the only flightless grasshopper in B.) Song like a sewing machine in bursts of up to 3 secs, getting louder: repeated every 5-15 secs. All kinds of grassland, but especially where moist. 6-10.

 ▲ **Lesser Marsh Grasshopper** *C. albomarginatus.* Green and/or brown. Female has a small bulge on front edge of forewing, and usually a white stripe near the front edge. Side keels of pronotum virtually straight. Song like *brunneus* but softer and slower: 2-6 chirps, each under 1 sec and separated by about 2 secs: series repeated at irregular intervals. Dense grassland, both dry and moist: mainly low-lying. 7-10.

▲ **Common Green Grasshopper** *Omocestus viridulus.* Green or brown in any combination, but female always green on top and sometimes with purple sides. Forewing often dark towards tip. Abdomen yellowish green below. Song a fluctuating hiss lasting 10-20 secs and getting louder – rather like an approaching moped – before ending abruptly. Full volume is reached about halfway through song. 7-10. Mainly on the lusher grasslands. Absent from far south.

▲ **Woodland Grasshopper** *O. rufipes.* Usually brown: female may be green above. Palps very white at tip. Abdomen red at hind end. Song like *viridulus* but only 5-10 secs and stops as soon as full volume is reached. Heaths and woodland clearings and margins. 6-10.

 brunneus forewing

 biguttulus forewing

GRASSHOPPERS

Pyrgomorpha conica ×1.5

Arcyptera fusca

♂

♀

Mottled Grasshopper ×1.5

Large Marsh Grasshopper

Field Grasshopper ×1.5

Rufous Grasshopper ×1.5

♂

Meadow Grasshopper ×1.5

♀

Common Green Grasshopper ×1.5 ▶

Lesser Marsh Grasshopper ♀ ×1.5

Woodland Grasshopper ×1.5

Euchorthippus declivus × 1.5

Euchorthippus declivus. Forewings short in both sexes, usually with a clear white stripe. Flightless. Side keels of pronotum almost straight. Song a prolonged succession of short croaks, each consisting of a few distinct pulses. Abundant in both dry and damp grassland, including woodland clearings and montane pastures. 6-10. S & C.

Gomphocerus sibiricus. Male immediately identified by swollen front tibia. Female has no swelling and less strongly clubbed antennae. Pronotum usually clearly humped in front half and often with a clear X-shaped mark on top. Song begins with well-separated chirps, getting quicker, rather like the rapid winding of a watch, and then becomes a constant loud call reminiscent of a small cicada: this lasts for up to a minute and then dies away with a few more short chirps. 7-9. Montane pastures, mainly in Alps and Pyrenees.

Chorthippus scalaris. Usually dark brown: sometimes green. Male has greatly enlarged front region of forewing. Median area of forewing enlarged in both sexes, with prominent parallel cross-veins in male and irregular cross-veins in female. Hindwings dark. Song starts with slow build-up of short croaks, getting quicker and louder until it becomes a constant rattle like a free-wheeling bicycle. This lasts about 10 secs and is punctuated by short, higher-pitched notes. Both sexes rustle loudly in flight. 7-9. Montane pastures from southern Sweden southwards.

Dociostaurus maroccanus. Pale to dark brown. Side keels of pronotum form a cross with pale outer edges. Central keel clearly cut by transverse sulcus. Female up to 37mm long. Song a soft staccato croak, not unlike a clock ticking. 4-10 in a wide range of habitats. Becomes gregarious and develops into a serious pest in some years, especially in Corsica and Italy and other parts of the far south. The gregarious form has less strongly marked forewings and a less clear white cross on the thorax. S & C.

Small Gold Grasshopper *Chrysochraon brachypterus*. Flightless, with short pink or golden green forewings in both sexes – mere lateral flaps in the female. Body with a bright, silky lustre. Song of repeated short buzzing sounds, rather like striking matches. 6-9. Short turf and stony places, wet or dry, in the mountains. S & C.

Large Gold Grasshopper *C. dispar*. Sharply angled forehead. Male forewing distinctly oval. Flightless, with greatly reduced hindwings. Female is often pale brown. Song a very harsh, ratchet-like chirp, lasting about 1 sec and repeated at short intervals. Heathland, woodland clearings, hedgerows, and damp grassland. 6-9.

Stripe-winged Grasshopper *Stenobothrus lineatus*. Mainly green, sometimes with brown forewings and legs. Median area of forewing enlarged, with prominent parallel cross-veins. Female usually with white stripe near front edge of forewing. End of abdomen orange-red when mature. Song a rather high-pitched whine, lasting 10-20 secs and with a marked rhythmic rise and fall in volume. The male's hind legs move remarkably slowly during stridulation, but he has up to 450 pegs on each femur and the pitch thus remains high. Warm, dry grassland, especially on limestone. 6-10. S & C.

Paracinema tricolor. Stridulatory pegs on forewing. Pronotum with a straight, dark stripe on each 'shoulder'. Forewings become clear towards the tip. Hind tibiae red with black-tipped white spines. Female 30-40mm, male only 25mm. Rustles in flight. Moist grassland. Quite rare in most places, but not uncommon in the rice fields of the Camargue, where it causes some damage. 7-10. S.

Gomphocerus sibiricus
♂ × 1.5

Chorthippus scalaris
♂ × 1.5

Dociostaurus maroccanus
♂ × 1.5

Small Gold Grasshopper × 1.5

♂

♀

Paracinema tricolor

♀

Large Gold Grasshopper × 1.5

♂

♀

Stripe-winged Grasshopper × 1.5

♂

♀

FLASH COLOURS. Several grasshoppers have brightly coloured hindwings. When disturbed, they fly on an erratic course and flash their colours. A bird chasing one of these insects latches on to the colourful 'hunting image', but then the grasshopper drops to the ground, covers its hindwings, and 'disappears', leaving the bird searching in vain for a colourful object. Human observers are often deceived by this flash coloration and even mistake the grasshoppers for butterflies. Most of the colourful species, including all those on this page, have stridulatory pegs on the forewings, but stridulation is at best very weak.

Psophus stridulus. Central keel of pronotum quite pronounced and not crossed by the sulcus. Hind femur smoothly curved on upper edge. Greyish brown to black. Female forewings only just reach tip of abdomen. Both sexes produce a grating sound. They also produce a rustling noise in flight, especially loud in the male, and the species has been called the rattle grasshopper. Rough grassy places, mainly in upland areas. 7-10. Southern Scandinavia southwards.

Acrotylus insubricus. Hairy. Large head stands above pronotum, especially in male. Pronotum knobbly in front half: hind margin ± rounded, not sharply pointed. Brown to black. Dry places, especially on sandy soils: common on sand dunes. All year in warmest regions: hibernates elsewhere and active mainly 3-11. S.

Oedipoda germanica. Superficially like *Psophus*, but central keel clearly interrupted by sulcus. Upper edge of hind femur has a distinct notch just beyond the middle. Light or dark brown. Rough ground in dry, sunny places, including roadsides and cultivated land. 7-11. Locally common in S & C.

O. caerulescens is similar but has blue hindwings. Forewings and body grey or brown. Commoner and more widely distributed than *germanica* in warm, dry places: often on sand dunes. 7-11. S & C.

Oedaleus decorus. Head large and rounded. Strong central keel on pronotum, hardly or not at all interrupted by sulcus. Usually a distinct white cross on top of pronotum. Body and forewings green or brown. Hot, dry places. 6-10. S & C.

Sphingonotus caerulans. Central keel of pronotum very weak and present only in hind region. Forewings clear and distinctly membranous towards tip. Hindwing with no trace of black band. Hind femur with just one complete pale band on inner surface. Warm, sandy places. 6-10. S & C.

Aiolopus thalassinus. Pronotum with weak central keel and no side keels. Proportion of green and brown very variable. Hindwings colourless. Stridulatory pegs on forewing. Grassland and woodland clearings, especially where damp: also on cultivated land. 3-10, but may be all year in far south. S & C.

Bryodema tuberculata. Side keels virtually absent: central keel prominent only at front. Disc very flat: hind end ± right-angled or obtuse. Surface markedly rough. Rustles in flight. Mainly sandy places. 7-10. N & C.

GRASSHOPPERS

**Psophus
stridulus**
×2

**Acrotylus
insubricus**
×1.5

Hind
wing of
O. caerulescens

**Oedipoda
germanica** ×2

**Oedaleus
decorus** ×2

**Sphingonotus
caerulans** ×2

**Aiolopus
thalassinus** ×2

△ **Migratory Locust** *Locusta migratoria*. Solitary phase has swollen pronotum with arched central keel. Male, often brown, averages only 35mm long. Female usually green. Flies rapidly. Stridulatory pegs on forewing. Male screeches loudly in presence of female. Dense vegetation, including cultivated land, but not a serious pest in Europe. 7-11: sometimes through winter in far south. S & C: rare visitor to B. Gregarious phase, more rarely seen in Europe, is greyish brown or yellowish: sexes ± alike.

nymph of Egyptian grasshopper

showing reversal of wing buds

Underside of
Podisma thorax
showing peg

△ **Egyptian Grasshopper** *Anacridium aegyptium*. Like gregarious phase of *Locusta*, but clearly distinguished by indented pronotal keel, striped eyes, and a blunt peg under the thorax between the front legs. Male about 35mm long: female 50-65mm. Flies well. On trees and shrubs in warm, dry areas. Causes little damage. Silent. All year. S: sometimes carried north in produce. Nymphs are bright green or orange-brown.

Brown Mountain Grasshopper *Podisma pedestris*. Pronotum with straight or smoothly curved rear edge. A peg between front legs. No stridulation, but insects make crackly sounds by rubbing jaws together. Flightless. Male is quite sprightly, but heavier female drags herself over the ground. Stony, sparsely vegetated places in mountains, usually above 1000m, but lower in north: often near snow line. 7-10.

Pezotettix giornai. Hairy. Peg between front legs is tongue-like and bent backwards. Central keel runs length of pronotum: side keels only in front half. Forewings very short in both sexes. Grey to reddish brown or almost black. Dry, scrubby places and cultivated land. Silent. All year in S: 6-10 in southern C.

Calliptamus italicus. Peg between front legs. Very blunt forehead. Central and side keels well developed: pale stripes on side keels and forewings not always present. Hind femur reddish pink internally, with three dark spots: middle and posterior spots of equal size. Male 14-25mm long, with long curved cerci: female 22-40mm. No stridulation, but male 'sings' by rubbing jaws together. Common and often abundant on grassland and cultivated areas: sometimes a pest. 7-11. S & C. *C. barbarus* is very similar, but middle spot on hind femur is much larger than others.

Acrida ungarica. Unmistakable shape, with blade-like antennae. Green or brown. Female 50-70mm long, much stouter than male and often mottled. Damp, grassy places, including coastal marshes. Silent. 7-10. S.

GROUNDHOPPERS Family Tetrigidae Superficially like grasshoppers, but pronotum extends back to tip of abdomen. Forewings reduced to small scales, but hindwings usually well developed. Active all year in sunshine, preferring bare and sparsely-vegetated ground. Eat mosses and other small plants. Silent. Several species in Europe: 3 in Britain.

▲ **Common Groundhopper** *Tetrix undulata* is pale brown to black. Hindwings do not reach tip of pronotum. Heaths, open woods, and other dry places. ▲ **Slender Groundhopper** *T. subulata* has a relatively longer pronotum and hindwings reach its tip. Pale brown to black. Flies and also swims well. Damp places.

T. depressa has central keel only in front half of pronotum, and two dark depressions near centre. Damp places, including seashores. S & C.

hind end of male,
showing large *cercus*

Calliptamus italicus

solitary phase
♀

gregarious
phase ♀

Migratory Locust

Brown Mountain Grasshopper
♂
♀

Egyptian Grasshopper

Pezotettix giornai ×1.5
♀
♂

Calliptamus italicus ×1.5
♀

Slender Groundhopper ×1.5

Common Groundhopper ×1.5

Tetrix depressa ×1.5

Acrida ungarica
♂

BUSH-CRICKETS Family Tettigoniidae Orthoptera with long, slender antennae and 4-segmented tarsi. Female has a blade-like ovipositor, either short and strongly-curved like a sickle or long and sabre-like. Mated female often seen with a gelatinous spermatophore attached to base of ovipositor (p. 39). Wings often short and sometimes absent, but male usually retains enough of his forewings to produce his song. An ear on each face of the front tibia. Many are crepuscular or nocturnal insects.

'ear'

front leg of
Phaneroptera

'ear'

front leg of
Tylopsis

ovipositor of
I. pyrenea

Phaneroptera nana. Ear on front tibia is oval. Hindwings extend well beyond forewings at rest. Side lobe of pronotum well-rounded, especially on hind margin. Insect covered with tiny dark, often rust-coloured dots. Ovipositor short and strongly curved. Song a high-pitched staccato ticking, mostly at night. On a wide range of bushes. 8-10. S. The almost identical *P. falcata* of C. Europe is now established in a few places in southern England.

Tylopsis liliifolia. Like *Phaneroptera* but side lobes of pronotum are rectangular and 'ears' are slit-like. Green or brown. Antennae up to 5 times body length. Ovipositor short and curved. Song of 2-4 weak chirps, like striking a match, repeated irregularly: mainly at night. Scrubby places (brown form) and grassy areas (green form). 7-10. S & C.

Isophya pyrenea. Stout, with many tiny red dots on back. Forewings very small in both sexes, those of female half covered by pronotum. Song is a very weak squeak, like turning a cork in a bottle. Grassy places in mountains: mainly ground-living. 5-8. S & C. Many similar species in SE.

Barbitistes fischeri. Bright green when young, becoming heavily speckled and then almost black as it matures: always shiny. Forewings very short in both sexes, those of male inflated as in *Leptophyes.* Song a series of 20-40 feeble grinding sounds, produced over a period of 10-20 secs and repeated at irregular intervals: mainly at night, although insect often active by day and enjoys sunbathing. On trees and shrubs: often abundant and sometimes damaging vines. 5-8. SW.

Polysarcus denticauda. Heavy-bodied. Forewings very short in both sexes and almost entirely hidden in female. Ovipositor 15-25mm long, curved towards apex and toothed at tip. Male cerci very large. Song a prolonged series of soft but monotonous metallic chirps, produced in sunshine. Montane pastures. 6-9. S & C.

▲ **Speckled Bush-cricket** *Leptophyes punctatissima.* Densely speckled, with very short forewings in both sexes, those of the male inflated and perched saddle-like on the back. A narrow brown line along the top of the abdomen. Song a very short and feeble scratching sound repeated every few seconds: interval gets shorter as temperature rises: day and night. Superbly camouflaged on nettles, brambles, and other vegetation, including many garden plants. 7-11. S & C.

▲ **Oak Bush-cricket** *Meconema thalassinum.* Fully winged in both sexes, often flying to lights at night, although flight is rather weak. Male has long curved claspers. Ovipositor about 9mm long and gently curved. No stridulation, but male drums gently on leaf surface with hind foot. Forewings are raised while doing this and sound can be heard several metres away. Inhabits a wide range of deciduous trees, including garden apples. Rarely seen by day. 7-11. *M. meridionale,* a Mediterranean species recently established in southern Britain, is flightless and has wings less than half the body length.

Cyrtaspis scutata. Readily identified by the enlarged pronotum, completely covering forewings in both sexes. Hind end of pronotum raised in male. Pale green to pinkish grey. Song very feeble, rather like the ticking of a watch. On trees and shrubs. 8-12: sometimes surviving until spring in mild years. S: mainly western.

Speckled Bush-cricket ♀ × 1.5

Tylopsis liliifolia ×1.5

Phaneroptera nana ×1.5

Speckled Bush-cricket ×1.5

Isophya pyrenea ×1.5

Oak Bush-cricket ×1.5

Barbitistes fischeri ×1.5

♀

Cyrtaspis scutata ×2

Polysarcus denticaudata

Short-winged Conehead

Long-winged Conehead

△s **Short-winged Conehead** *Conocephalus dorsalis*. Forewings short in both sexes; hindwings vestigial. Ovipositor 8-11mm long. Song long bursts of faint high-pitched sound consisting of alternating periods of hissing and ticking – like a knife-grinding machine when the blade is alternately pressed firmly and lightly against the wheel. Marshes, river-banks, and other moist grassland, including coastal saltmarshes. More active by day than by night, but hard to see when stretched along reed stems and leaves. 7-10. Mainly coastal in Britain.

△s **Long-winged Conehead** *C. discolor*. Resembles *dorsalis* but is fully winged and ovipositor is longer and nearly straight. Both species occasionally all brown. Song long bursts of high-pitched, quiet sound of constant tone – like a distant knife-grinder. Mainly diurnal in areas of tall grass and other rough vegetation, both dry and moist. 7-10. S & C. Restricted to a few southern, mainly coastal localities in Britain until recently but now extending its range inland.

Ruspolia nitidula. Green or brown. Fully winged. Head acutely pointed. Ovipositor longer than abdomen and almost straight. Song a prolonged and strident sound: very loud, like a knife grinder or even an alarm clock ringing at a low pitch: strictly nocturnal. Mainly in damp places, such as river-banks, with tall grass or other dense vegetation. Sits more or less vertically on leaves and stems. 7-10. S & C.

△ **Great Green Bush-cricket** *Tettigonia viridissima*. The largest British bush-cricket. Fully winged, but not a great flier. Stridulatory area of male forewings always brown and about 1/6th of total wing length. Ovipositor about 20mm long and slightly down-curved: just reaching tip of forewings. Song loud and harsh, like a sewing machine, continuing for long periods with short breaks every few seconds. Becomes active in afternoon and carries on for much of the night, with peak of activity in the evening. In trees, shrubs, and rough vegetation in general. Can bite hard if handled, in common with most large species. 7-10. *T. cantans* is similar, but forewings shorter and more rounded, with stridulatory area covering about 1/4 of total length. Ovipositor straight and reaching well beyond tip of forewings. Song more rasping than *viridissima*, starting slowly and then increasing in speed and volume: continuous for long periods. 7-10, mainly in upland areas.

△s **Wart-Biter** *Decticus verrucivorus*. Green or brown, often heavily mottled. Pronotum flat, with central keel running its whole length. Fully winged. Ovipositor about 20mm long, with very gentle upward curve. Named because once used in Sweden to bite warts from the skin. Song long bursts of clicking sounds, starting slowly and then speeding up to resemble the sound of a free-wheeling bicycle: continues for several minutes. Mainly diurnal, usually singing only in sunshine. Open grassy places, including marshy habitats, heaths, and montane pastures. 7-10. Very rare in Britain and confined to just a few localities in southern England (green form only).

D. albifrons. Similar to *verrucivorus*, but larger and never green: face very pale. Song very high-pitched, beginning with isolated chirps more like a bird than an insect but then speeding up and becoming louder and finishing with a strident ratchet-like sound. Diurnal in dry, scrubby habitats: sometimes a pest of cereals and fruit crops. 7-11. S.

This Great Green Bush-cricket nymph shows the characteristic bright green colour and brown dorsal stripe. The reversed wing-buds, typical of the later nymphal stages of orthopterans, are clearly visible.

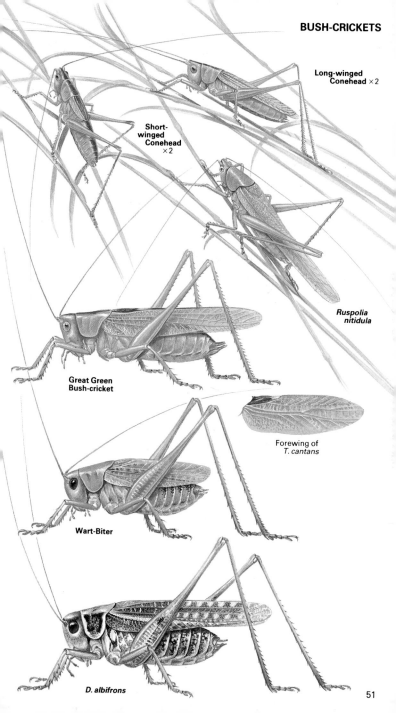

Long-winged Conehead ×2

Short-winged Conehead ×2

Ruspolia nitidula

Great Green Bush-cricket

Forewing of *T. cantans*

Wart-Biter

D. albifrons

51

Grey Bush-cricket

P. tessellata

P. affinis

△ s **Grey Bush-cricket** *Platycleis albopunctata*. Fully winged and flies readily. Sometimes green on top. Central keel on posterior half of pronotum: side keels converge towards the front. Ovipositor (left) 8-11mm long. Song a prolonged series of short (½ sec) buzzing sounds like winding a watch. Active mainly afternoon and evening. Dry, scrubby places. 7-10. S & C: mainly coastal in B. One of several very similar species, often difficult to separate.

P. tessellata is smaller and distinguished by heavy markings in centre of forewing: female easily recognised by 4-6mm ovipositor (left). Song a few well-spaced chirps, followed by several rapid ones and then a few more well-spaced ones: harsh and scratchy like drawing a comb over a finger nail. 7-10. Dry places. S and most of France.

P. affinis is like a large *albopunctata* (20-25mm long), but vein running along sharp fold of forewing just behind the pronotum is distinctly yellow. Ovipositor (left) 13-16mm. 6-10. Rough and cultivated land. S.

Sepiana sepium differs from the above in being short-winged and in lacking side keels on the pronotum. Pinkish brown, sometimes reddish, with very long hind feet. Ovipositor 11-15mm. Song a prolonged strident hiss at night: shorter bursts by day. Rough vegetation, especially in damp places. 7-9. S.

△ **Bog Bush-cricket** *Metrioptera brachyptera*. Forewings normally short in both sexes, hindwings vestigial. A short central keel on posterior half of pronotum. Pale band normally only on hind margin of pronotal flaps. Green may be missing from upper parts, but always green underneath. Ovipositor 8-10mm: moderately curved. Song a prolonged series of short, shrill chirps – 2-6 per sec and resembling the rapid ticking of a clock. Mainly diurnal. Peat bogs and damp heaths. 7-11. N & C. One of several similar species.

△ s **Roesel's Bush-cricket** *M. roeselii*. Pale yellow or green stripe all round pronotal flaps. Head and body brown or green, but the short forewings are always brown. Ovipositor 5-6mm: strongly curved. Song long bursts of high-pitched sound, like a high-speed drill. Active day and night. Although most common in moist areas, especially coastal marshes, the insect has now invaded many other areas, including chalk grassland and other relatively dry grasslands in southern England and has become very common in some places. 6-11.

Zeuneriana abbreviata differs from the above in its slightly longer forewings (c. 10mm) and in the much shorter male cerci, which are very stout at the base and largely covered by the last abdominal segment. Ovipositor 6-7mm. Moist mountain slopes with lush grass. 6-9. SW (mainly Pyrenees).

△ **Dark Bush-cricket** *Pholidoptera griseoaptera*. No central keel on pronotum. Light brown, through chestnut, to almost black: but top of head and pronotum always brown and underside of body always greenish yellow. Female usually paler than male. Forewings vestigial in female. Song a single, very short high-pitched chirp repeated irregularly. Will sing in daytime, especially in afternoon, and likes sunbathing, but becomes most active in evening and sings well into the night. 7-11. Rough vegetation of hedgerows, woodland clearings, and roadsides. Also in garden shrubberies. Absent from heathland and other open habitats. Several similar species in southern Europe, especially SE.

Sepiana sepium

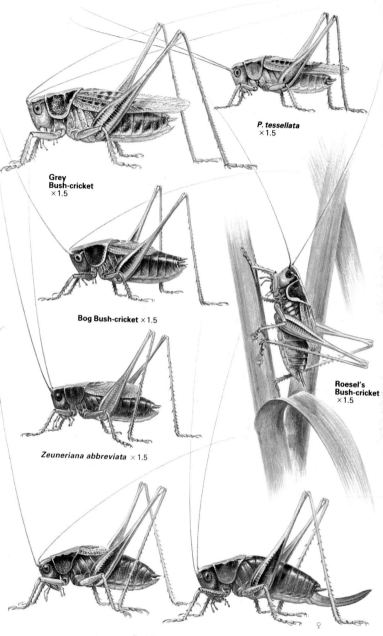

P. tessellata
×1.5

**Grey
Bush-cricket**
×1.5

Bog Bush-cricket ×1.5

Zeuneriana abbreviata ×1.5

**Roesel's
Bush-cricket**
×1.5

Dark Bush-cricket ×1.5

Eupholidoptera chabrieri. One of the most beautiful bush-crickets, easily identified by bright green top of pronotum, which is strongly rounded at the rear. Rest of body generally green or yellowish green above and often orange below: abdomen sometimes largely brown. Face lime-green with black spots. Female forewings almost completely hidden under pronotum. Ovipositor 18-24mm: very slightly curved. Song a series of shrill, staccato chirps, about 2 per sec., rather like striking matches but higher pitched: mainly after dusk. On bushes and low vegetation, mostly in upland areas. 7-10. S & C (southern).

Anonconotus alpinus. Upper surface generally dark brown or black, often heavily mottled with olive green: sometimes chestnut-coloured. Cream or pale grey below. Female forewings only 1mm and carried at sides. Front tibia with 3 spines on outer edge. Ovipositor 11-16mm: slightly curved. Song short bursts of rather soft warbling sound, like a sewing machine: produced only in sunshine. Insect enjoys sunbathing. Often infested with red mites. Stony ground and low-growing vegetation in mountains, usually above 600m. 7-10. S & C. ***A. apenninigenus***, a rare species from the mountains of S. France and Italy, is similar but has only one or two spines on front tibia.

Rhacocleis germanica. Basically brown with darker markings: sometimes marbled with grey or yellow. Pronotum elongate and lightly rounded behind, with a pale stripe in mid-line: stripe often extends along abdomen. Female forewings are minute flaps. Ovipositor 14-19mm: very slightly curved. Long flaps under hind tarsi. Dry habitats, especially woodland margins and olive groves. Mainly crepuscular. 7-10. S & C (southern). Several similar species in SE.

Antaxius pedestris. Grey or light brown above, generally with darker markings: sometimes entirely greyish, relieved only by pale border of pronotum and dark spot above it. Often pinkish below. Male forewings black at base and pale at apex: female forewings hardly visible beyond pronotum. Ovipositor 13-19mm: almost straight. Song a low-pitched scratching sound, ratchet-like with fluctuating volume: in bursts of 1-2 secs. Active largely by day. Shrubby habitats, mainly in uplands. Usually falls to ground when disturbed. 8-9. S & C (southern). Several similar species.

Gampsocleis glabra. Mainly light green as a rule, but sometimes brown: top of pronotum always brownish. Fully winged in both sexes. Forewings heavily spotted with brown. Ovipositor 15-23mm, curving gently downwards towards tip. Song a rather weak, but continuous warble lasting for as much as a minute: produced mainly by day. Lush vegetation in moist habitats. 7-9. S & C.

Yersinella raymondi. Like a small *Rhacocleis*, but no large flaps under tarsi. Shiny, with a smoothly rounded pronotum. Sometimes chestnut but more often light brown with dense speckling. A dark stripe along each side of the body. Forewings minute in both sexes. Ovipositor 10mm; quite strongly curved. Rough areas and shrubby habitats, especially near water. Attracted to lights at night. 7-9. S & C (southern).

Saga pedo. One of Europe's largest insects. Occasionally grey with a pale yellow stripe on the side, but stripe may be absent from both green and grey forms. Wings completely absent. Male unknown, female reproducing by laying parthenogenetic eggs. Grassy and shrubby habitats, especially on limestone: lives on ground or vegetation and feeds almost entirely on other bush-crickets and grasshoppers, which are held down by the spiky front legs. Quite rare. 7-9. S (rarely far from Mediterranean coasts). Several similar species, with males as well as females, occur in SE. The males have flap-like forewings, just enough for stridulation.

Yersinella raymondi × 1.5

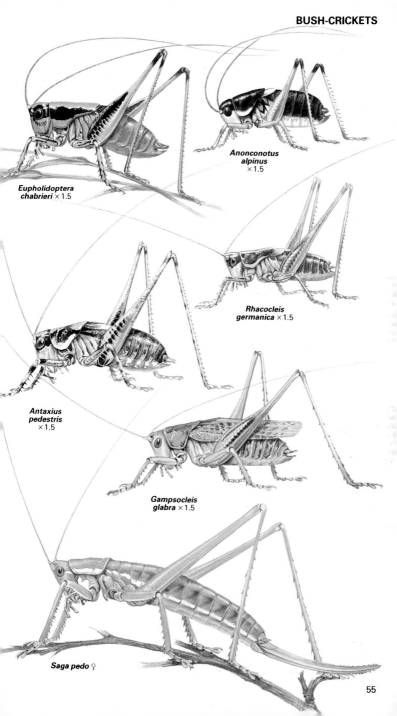

Eupholidoptera chabrieri × 1.5

Anonconotus alpinus × 1.5

Rhacocleis germanica × 1.5

Antaxius pedestris × 1.5

Gampsocleis glabra × 1.5

Saga pedo ♀

Ephippiger provincialis. Pronotum strongly raised in posterior half, producing a very distinctive saddle-shape: top of pronotum joining side in a smooth curve. Forewings very short and with stridulatory apparatus in both sexes. Antennae attached below eyes. These features are shared by all *Ephippiger* species, but *provincialis* is easily distinguished by its size. Ovipositor about 30mm; gently curved. 6-9. On a wide range of shrubs, including vines. Populations fluctuate markedly from year to year, sometimes becoming very high and causing severe damage in vineyards. Confined to southern France.

Ephippiger ephippiger. One of several very similar species. Green or brown, often with a clearly banded abdomen. Ovipositor up to 25mm: gently curved. Known as 'le tizi' in France for its characteristic song – a short, high-pitched rasping, double chirp, sounding like *tizi* and repeated irregularly, sometimes in quick succession. Female also chirps, as in all *Ephippiger* species, but less readily than male. Rough ground and scrubby habitats, often damaging vines when abundant. 7-11. S & C.
E. cruciger resembles *E. ephippiger* but is generally a little larger and usually has a dark cross on top of the pronotum, which is shinier and less wrinkled than that of *ephippiger*. The species appears to be confined to southern France.

Uromenus rugosicollis. Resembles *Ephippiger* but pronotum has side keels in rear half, forming a distinct angle between top and sides. Ovipositor 10-12mm: quite strongly curved towards tip. Occasionally greyish green. Song rather like a slowed-down tizi song (see above), each chirp lasting about 2/3 sec and repeated about 20 times a minute: not unlike winding a watch or running a comb over a finger nail. Female chirp is shorter, more like typical tizi song. Scrubby places. 7-10. SW. Several similar species, mainly in Iberia.

Pycnogaster inermis. Greenish or reddish brown. Pronotum virtually flat on top with a shallow V-shaped notch at the rear: side keels run all along it, interrupted by two transverse grooves. Forewings almost covered by pronotum, especially in female. Antennae attached near base of eyes (attached between the eyes in most other bush-crickets). Ovipositor 30-35mm. Scrubby places. 5-8. Spain.

CAVE CRICKETS Rhaphidophoridae

Completely wingless insects with very long antennae: legs, palps, and cerci are also unusually long and slender. Tarsi 4-segmented. Ovipositor blade-like, as in bush-crickets. Most species inhabit caves and scavenge on dead animal matter. They are also called wingless camel-crickets. About 30 species live in Europe, mostly in SE.

Dolichopoda azami. One of several very similar species. Plain or mottled brown. Ovipositor about 14mm, almost straight and lightly toothed near tip. Cave-dwelling but often seen on vegetation outside in summer. Strictly nocturnal. Adult all year, but most common in late autumn, when mating occurs. Confined to SE France and N Italy, often high in hills.

⚠ **Greenhouse Camel-cricket** *Tachycines asynamorus*. Very similar to *Dolichopoda* but with much spinier hind tibia (50-80 closely-packed spines, compared with less than 30 in *Dolichopoda*). Usually mottled. Ovipositor 11-12mm: very gently curved. A native of eastern Asia, but now established in heated greenhouses throughout Europe. May nibble plants, but probably compensates by eating insect pests, although it feeds mainly on dead animal matter. Strictly nocturnal.

Ephippiger eggs are laid in the ground. Raising herself up on her long legs, the female drives her ovipositor into the soil for its full length.

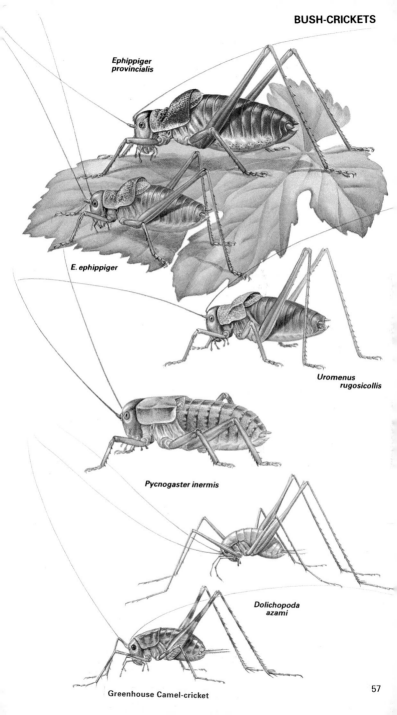

*Ephippiger
provincialis*

E. ephippiger

*Uromenus
rugosicollis*

Pycnogaster inermis

*Dolichopoda
azami*

Greenhouse Camel-cricket

57

TRUE CRICKETS Gryllidae Orthoptera with long, slender antennae, globular head, 3-segmented tarsi, and long cerci. More flattened than bush-crickets, with forewings, when present, fitted over body like a lid. Hindwings, when present, rolled up and protruding beyond abdomen like tails. Ovipositor straight and needle-like. Front tibia usually with an ear on inner and outer faces, although inner one often very small.

▲ **House Cricket** *Acheta domesticus*. Fully winged. Song a bird-like warble: 2-3 chirps per sec and continued for long periods. Mainly nocturnal. Native of SW Asia and N Africa, but well established in houses, bakeries, etc in Europe. Often on rubbish dumps and sometimes in gardens in summer.

△s **Field Cricket** *Gryllus campestris*. Pale yellow at base of forewing often obscure, especially in female. Her forewings less shiny and with denser venation. Hindwings vestigial in both sexes. Hind femur orange below. Song like that of House Cricket, but usually 3-4 chirps per sec: very musical. Lives in burrow and male sings at entrance. Active day and night. Grassland. 4-9. Absent from far north. **G. bimaculatus** of S Europe is very similar, but has a narrower head and is fully winged, with hindwings projecting behind body.

Eugryllodes pipiens. Front tibia has ear only on outside. Female forewings hardly longer than pronotum: obliquely truncated. Song a shrill, musical chirp, like a cheeping chick, with occasional trills. Dry, stony places, including old walls and buildings. Mainly nocturnal. 7-10. SW.

Gryllomorpha dalmatina. Wingless. A pale cross on pronotum. No 'ears'. Damp, rocky places, often in and around buildings. Mostly nocturnal. Mainly 9-12. S.

Melanogryllus desertus. Forewings may reach end of abdomen. Hindwings short or fully developed. All legs entirely black. Song short, shrill chirps: 30-40 per minute. Among stones and turf, often on cultivated land. 5-8. S & C.

Modicogryllus frontalis. Wings vary from very short to fully developed. Front tibia has ear on outer face only. Pale band between eyes. Hind tibia with short spines. Sunny woodland edges and scrub: also vineyards. 5-8. S & C.

△s **Wood Cricket** *Nemobius sylvestris*. Front tibia has ear on outer face only. Forewings shorter in female, not or only just meeting in centre. No hindwings. Hind tibia with long spines (distinctly longer than width of tibia). Song a soft prolonged warble with brief pauses every second or two. On ground in woodland and scrub. Active day and night. 6-11. S & C.

Pteronemobius heydeni. Like Wood Cricket but smaller. Forewings cover at least half of abdomen. Hindwings rudimentary or fully developed. Song shrill, but soft, in bursts of about 3 secs: repeated every 2-3 secs. Damp grassland. 5-8. S & C.

Arachnocephalus vestitus. Wingless: clothed with fine scales. No ears. Male drums by tapping end of abdomen on leaves. On shrubs in dry places. 7-10. S.

Italian Cricket *Oecanthus pellucens*. Very delicate. Female forewings much narrower than male. Song a soft warbling *griii-griii-griii*, produced mainly at night and continued for long periods. On trees, shrubs, and tall herbage. Sometimes called Tree Cricket. 7-10. S & C.

Italian Cricket

♂

△s **Mole Cricket** *Gryllotalpa gryllotalpa* Gryllotalpidae. A burrowing insect with much enlarged front legs. Body furry. No visible ovipositor. Forewings short, but hindwings fully developed. Flies on warm evenings. Song long periods of quiet churring, usually produced at mouth of burrow in the evening. Moist meadows, especially near rivers, sometimes causing damage to the roots of vines and other crops. Adult all year, but dormant in winter. Absent from far north.

Mole Cricket

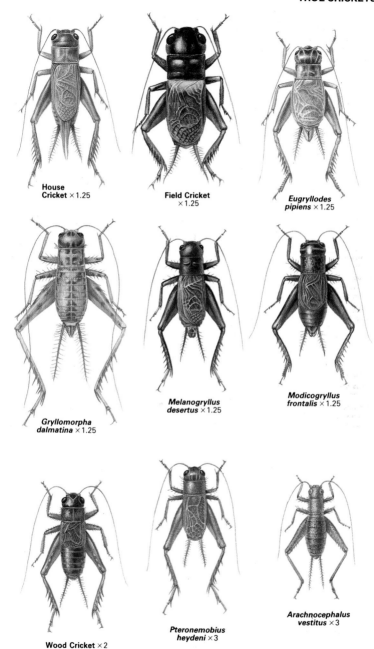

House Cricket ×1.25

Field Cricket ×1.25

Eugryllodes pipiens ×1.25

Gryllomorpha dalmatina ×1.25

Melanogryllus desertus ×1.25

Modicogryllus frontalis ×1.25

Wood Cricket ×2

Pteronemobius heydeni ×3

Arachnocephalus vestitus ×3

COCKROACHES   Order Dictyoptera:
Sub-order Blattodea

♀

♂

Common Cockroach

Rather flat insects with long antennae and long, spiky legs. Mostly fast-running, ground-living scavengers, feeding largely on dead plant matter. Broad pronotum almost completely covers head. Central area of pronotum is called the disc. Forewings (tegmina) leathery: often shorter in female than in male, but sexes otherwise alike. Hindwings membranous, but often absent. Eggs laid in horny cases (oothecae), which female may carry protruding from her rear end. Nymphs very like adults without wings. There are about 3500 known species, mostly in the warmer parts of the world. Several tropical species have become cosmopolitan pests in houses and other buildings. Native European species are all rather small.

▲ **Common Cockroach** *Blatta orientalis* Blattidae. Commonly called the black beetle. Wings vestigial in female: both sexes flightless. Introduced from Africa or Asia. Usually found indoors in Europe – in houses, bakeries, etc. Sometimes on rubbish dumps in summer, and may survive there in winter in warmer regions.

▲ **American Cockroach** *Periplaneta americana*. Introduced from Africa, despite its name. Rarely out of doors in Europe, and usually near ports. Inhabits bakeries, warehouses, greenhouses, sewers, etc., but rare in dwelling houses. Common on ships. Flies well in warm conditions.

▲ **Australian Cockroach** *P. australasiae* is also probably African. Slightly smaller than *americana*, with distinct yellow margin to pronotum. Habits and distribution like *americana*.

▲ **German Cockroach** *Blattella germanica* Blattellidae. Introduced from N. Africa. Mostly in bakeries and other buildings in Europe, but also on rubbish dumps in summer. Pronotal stripes vary. Both sexes can fly, but reluctant to do so.

▲ **Brown-banded Cockroach** *Supella longipalpa*. An African species only recently established in European houses. Ground colour yellowish to deep brown. Female darker and with shorter wings, leaving part of broad abdomen exposed. Male can fly.

Loboptera decipiens. Wings form minute flaps on sides of thorax. Pale margin of pronotum may extend round abdomen. Under stones and debris: often by sea. 4-8. S.

△s **Tawny Cockroach** *Ectobius pallidus* Ectobiidae. Fully winged in both sexes and flies in warm weather. Like other *Ectobius* species, it inhabits woods, heaths, and rough grassland: mostly in turf and leaf litter but sometimes in the trees. 4-10. S & C.

E. sylvestris. Pronotal disc entirely black, sharply angled behind. Female forewings cover only about half of black abdomen. Male can fly. 5-9. *E. vittiventris* Body and forewings unspotted. Pronotal disc rounded. Fully winged in both sexes. 7-10. SE & C.

△s **Dusky Cockroach** *E. lapponicus*. Like *sylvestris* but unspotted and pronotal disc rounded. Male often very pale. Female shorter, broader, and browner, with forewings not usually reaching tip of abdomen. 4-10.

△s **Lesser Cockroach** *E. panzeri*. Always under 9mm long. Pale to dark brown, sometimes greyish: heavily speckled. Male forewings narrow and pointed: female short and truncated. Mainly coastal areas and sandy ground. 6-10. S & C.

Phyllodromica subaptera. Forewings minute, not wider than pale margin of pronotum. Male cerci black: female cerci yellowish brown. Under leaves and stones: rare. 5-9. S.

P. maculata. Female forewings roundly truncated, but more or less meeting in centre. In debris. 5-9. C. The forewings in *Phyllodromica* spp are stiffer than in *Ectobius* and less distinctly veined.

P. marginata has unmistakable pattern. In leaves and debris. 4-7. SE.

German Cockroach × 2
with ootheca

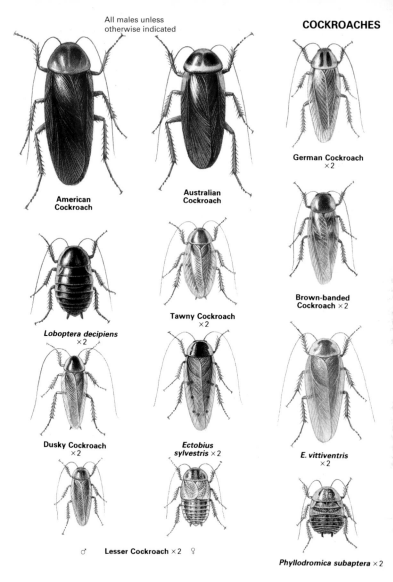

All males unless otherwise indicated

COCKROACHES

American Cockroach

Australian Cockroach

German Cockroach ×2

Loboptera decipiens ×2

Tawny Cockroach ×2

Brown-banded Cockroach ×2

Dusky Cockroach ×2

Ectobius sylvestris ×2

E. vittiventris ×2

♂ **Lesser Cockroach** ×2 ♀

Phyllodromica subaptera ×2

P. maculata ×2

P. marginata ×2

female *Mantis*
laying her eggs

MANTIDS   Order Dictyoptera:
Sub-order Mantodea

Predatory insects related to cockroaches, with thickened, leathery forewings (tegmina) and a long neck. They usually lie in wait for their prey with the front legs folded in front of the face. The highly mobile head turns to face any movement, and when prey comes within range the spiky front legs shoot out to impale it. Females of the larger species often eat the males during copulation, starting with the head – quite an efficient arrangement, for the male then helps to nourish the eggs as well as fertilising them. Eggs are laid in frothy 'souflées' which harden into horny cases. There may be several hundred eggs in each case. Most European species pass the winter in the egg stage. There are some 2000 known species. Most are tropical, but about 18 reach S & C Europe. They feed on a variety of other insects, including grasshoppers. None lives in B.

hindwing of *R. baetica*

Praying Mantis *Mantis religiosa* Mantidae. The commonest European species: green or brown. Male much more slender than female. Both sexes fly well in warm weather. When disturbed, it puts on a threat display, raising front legs to reveal dark eye-spots on their insides and making a hissing sound by rubbing abdomen against the partly raised wings. Rough grassland, scrub, and gardens. 7-11. S & C.

Rivetina baetica. Truncated forewings immediately identify female: male forewings reach end of abdomen. Pronotum has strongly toothed edges, especially in female, and usually has a dark stripe down the centre. Hindwing with large apical eye-spot. Hot, dry places. 6-9. Far south.

head of *A. spallanzania*

Ameles spallanzania. A small mantid that scuttles over low vegetation in warm, dry places. Male flies when disturbed, but female is almost wingless. Eyes moderately pointed, especially in male. Not a cannibalistic genus. 6-10. S.

head of *A. decolor*

A. decolor inhabits the same dry, scrubby habitats as *spallanzania* and is more common. Generally a little larger, but female lacks the swollen abdomen. Eyes rounded. 7-10. S. Several similar species occur in far south.

Geomantis larvoides. Because of its small size and lack of wings, this species may be taken for a young *Ameles*. The prothorax, however, is widest near the front and finely toothed along the margins, whereas the *Ameles* prothorax is smooth-edged and widest in the middle. Runs rapidly on the ground in dry, sunny places. 7-9. S.

Iris oratoria. May be green or brown, sometimes with a rosy tinge. Forewings of male completely cover abdomen. Smaller size and coloured hindwings distinguish it from *M. religiosa*. Male often comes to light at night. Common on bushes in warm places. 6-10. S.

A male *Mantis* has already lost his head, but continues to pump sperm into the female as she devours him

Praying Mantis ♀

threat
display
→

*Rivetina
baetica* ♀

♀   ♂

Geomantis larvoides

Ameles spallanzania

♀   ♂

Ameles decolor

*Iris
oratoria* ♀

Empusa pennata Empusidae. Identified by the tall crest on the head, this species is green or brown. Male antennae rather feathery. Flies well in warm weather, especially the male, which regularly comes to lights at night. Eats relatively small prey – mainly small flies. Female never eats male. Rough, grassy places. 5-9. SW. Unlike most other European mantids, nymphs appear in summer, feeding through autumn and sporadically in winter. Growth is completed in late spring. Nymph always rests with abdomen curled upwards. *E. fasciata* of SE is very similar but has broader flaps on its legs.

Perlamantis alliberti Amorphoscelididae. Wings well developed in both sexes: forewings almost transparent with a clear network of veins. Pronotum very short and not dilated in middle, thus separating this small mantid from *Ameles* species. Front tibia has no spines apart from terminal spur. Rough vegetation, the males readily flying to lights at night. 6-9. SW.

STICK INSECTS   Order Phasmida

Leaf-eating insects with stick-like bodies. Extremely well camouflaged on shrubs and grasses, but can be found by careful searching, especially at night when they do most of their feeding. Males of *Bacillus* and *Clonopsis* are extremely rare, the females reproducing parthenogenetically by laying unfertilised but viable eggs for generation after generation. The seed-like eggs are simply dropped to the ground, where they remain throughout the winter and hatch in the spring. Some may remain dormant for two or three years. The sausage-shaped eggs of *Leptynia* are readily identified. Those of *Bacillus* and *Clonopsis* are best distinguished by using a lens to examine the micropylar plate – the elongate area on one side of the egg enclosing microscopic pores. Young stick insects resemble the adults in all but size. The half dozen species living in southern Europe are completely wingless, but many tropical species are winged and able to fly. There are about 2500 known species, including the very flat and amazingly leaf-like leaf insects. The majority live in SE Asia.

Bacillus rossius Phylliidae. Green or brown, the surface of green specimens being smooth while that of brown ones is rather granular. Female 65-100mm long: antennae with 20-25 segments. Eggs oval and very dark, with micropylar plate running the full length of one side. Common on many kinds of shrubs in warm, dry places. 6-12. S.

Clonopsis gallica. Very similar to *B. rossius*, but female rarely over 75mm long and antennae with only 12-13 segments. Green or brown, the green specimens being rather smoother. Eggs are mottled brown and usually a little larger than those of *rossius*, with micropylar plate much shorter than the egg. More common than *rossius* on shrubs in warm, dry places. 5-10. S, but extending well up into central France.

Leptynia hispanica Phasmatidae. Green or yellowish brown. Male up to 46mm: female to 58mm. Male cerci extend beyond tip of abdomen. Male antennae usually 16-segmented: female antennae usually 11-segmented. Although still heavily outnumbered by females, males are more common than among the last two species. Egg is sausage-shaped. Local in rough grassy places. 5-9. SW.

Carausius morosus. Known as the laboratory stick insect because it is widely bred in schools and laboratories, this oriental species sometimes escapes and becomes temporarily established in gardens. Completely wingless: female green or brown and up to 80mm long. Base of front leg pink. Male very rare.

Bacillus rossius

Clonopsis gallica

Stick insect heads showing different lengths of antennae

MANTIDS and STICK INSECTS

Empusa pennata

♀

nymph

Perlamantis alliberti ×2

Bacillus rossius ♀

Leptynia hispanica ♀

Carausius morosus ♀

B. rossius egg

C. gallica egg

L. hispanica egg

TERMITES   Order Isoptera

Soft-bodied, social insects, forming long-living colonies headed by a king and a queen. Most individuals are juvenile workers: large-jawed soldiers, which defend the colony, form about 5% of population. Only the reproductive forms have wings. These are very flimsy, with forewings and hindwings almost identical (Isoptera means 'equal wings'). There are over 2000 known species, with just two native to southern Europe. Both live in tree stumps and other dead wood, chewing out their living quarters and digesting the timber with the aid of hordes of protozoans in their digestive canals. Swarms of reproductive forms periodically emerge, but they lose their wings after a short flight and, after mating, some become kings and queens of new colonies.

Kalotermes flavicollis Kalotermitidae. Small colonies of a few hundred individuals in dry wood. Workers all youngsters, many of which later grow into soldiers or reproductives. Pronotum rectangular in all castes. Soldiers with toothed jaws. Winged insects emerge mainly in early spring. Widespread in S, mainly near coast.

Reticulitermes lucifugus Rhinotermitidae. Colonies of several thousand insects, usually in damper wood, including building timbers at or below ground level. Workers are juveniles and remain so all their lives, never turning into other forms. Pronotum of all castes is more rounded and often heart-shaped. Soldiers' jaws not toothed. Swarms appear mainly 4-6, usually in the morning. Throughout S: slightly hardier than *Kalotermes* and extends further from coast. Colonies sometimes become established in S. England.

WEB-SPINNERS   Order Embioptera

Slender insects with first tarsal segment of front leg conspicuously swollen. Male may be winged in some species: female always wingless and somewhat larger than male. Female cerci slender and symmetrical: male cerci strongly asymmetrical. Live among leaf litter and turf, usually under stones or logs, where they make silken tunnels with silk from glands in the swollen front legs. They wriggle rapidly along the tunnels, moving backwards and forwards with equal ease. Feed mainly on dead leaves, with some animal matter. Adult females can be found all year, but they go deeper into ground to avoid desiccation in summer. Adult males occur in spring, but are rarely found. Many females can reproduce parthenogenetically. Nymphs resemble adult females and remain in mother's tunnel for some time. They may build their own tunnels under the same stone, but they do not co-operate like social insects. Most of the 300 or so known species are tropical, but a few live in S. Europe. Males can usually be identified by the shape of their cerci: females are much harder to separate.

Haploembia solieri Oligotomidae. Very like *Embia ramburi* but often paler. Best distinguished by 1st segment of hind tarsus, which has two tubercles on lower surface compared with just one in *Embia* (but a microscope is needed to see this feature!). Fairly common throughout S, often living with *E. ramburi*.

Embia amadorae Embiidae. One of the few European species with winged male. Female paler. Iberia only. **E. ramburi** is wingless in both sexes. Male jet black: female brownish, often with purplish tinge, and with pale intersegmental membranes. Head more rounded than in *amadorae*. SW. One of the commonest European species.

part of a *Reticulitermes* colony with developing winged forms

a web-spinner emerging from its tunnel

Kalotermes flavicollis
queen ×8

K. flavicollis
king ×8

king

K. flavicollis
worker ×8

worker

K. flavicollis
soldier ×8

soldier

Reticulitermes lucifugus
heads and pronota
×8

Kalotermes
forewing

Reticulitermes
forewing

**Haploembia
solieri** ×5

**Embia
amadorae**
×5

EARWIGS Order Dermaptera

Elongate insects with pincer-like cerci – usually strongly curved in male, slimmer and straighter in female and often just meeting or crossing at tip. Forewings (elytra), when present, short and horny. Hindwings, when present, very thin: elaborately folded under elytra and often projecting beyond them at rest. Many species lack hindwings and some lack elytra as well. Even fully-winged species generally reluctant to fly. Essentially ground-living, nocturnal scavengers of both plant and animal matter. Hide under stones and in crevices by day. Many species can be found as adults all year, although they hibernate in the coldest months. Females of most species guard their eggs, and some prolong this parental care until the young are well grown. Nymphs resemble adults, but have very slender cerci. Newly-moulted individuals are white or cream. About 34 of the 1300 known species occur in Europe: only 4 are British.

Anisolabis maritima Anisolabididae. Elytra and hindwings absent. Body reddish brown below. Male cerci asymmetrical. Among debris on seashores and stream banks: also in damp woodlands. 3-9. S: occasionally carried elsewhere by ships.

Euborellia moesta. Elytra reduced to minute flaps at sides of thorax. Male cerci asymmetrical: female cerci stout and usually held together. Antennae usually 18-segmented. Leaf litter. S. **E. annulipes** is paler than *moesta*, with no trace of elytra. Antennae usually 16-segmented. Under stones in damp places. 6-10. S: sometimes carried north in produce.

▲ **Labia minor** Labiidae. Smallest European earwig. Flies readily. Common near human habitation, especially on compost heaps and rubbish dumps.

Marava arachides. Hindwings usually very small or absent. Tropical but sometimes temporarily established in bakeries and other buildings in Europe, mainly S.

Giant Earwig *Labidura riparia* Labiduridae. Largest European earwig: generally reddish brown, but sandy grey in some areas, notably on the Atlantic coast of France. Sandy places, especially seashores and river banks: makes long tunnels in sand or hides under debris. Also on rubbish dumps. Partly predatory. Mainly S but local in C: not recorded in B for many years.

Nala lividipes. Slightly downy and rather flat. Elytra with markedly parallel margins and abdomen usually parallel-sided. Pronotum rounded at back. In debris of various kinds. 6-9. SW.

Family Forficulidae The largest family. 2nd tarsal segment expanded and heart-shaped (see below). Mostly fully-winged, although hindwings often completely concealed under elytra at rest. *Forficula* spp are primarily vegetarians and often found quite high in trees and shrubs in summer.

Chelidura aptera. Elytra form collar-like flaps: no hindwings. Male cerci very long, with no teeth. Female generally much lighter. Under stones on north-facing slopes of Alps. 7-10. **C. pyrenaica** is similar but male cerci short and strongly curved: female usually dark. 6-10. Pyrenees.

Chelidurella acanthopygia. Elytra collar-like: no hindwings. Cerci very thin in both sexes. On woodland shrubs and in leaf litter. Absent from far N.

Anechura bipunctata. Elytra distinctly longer than pronotum. Male cerci not flat at base, where they almost form a circle: curving downwards at tip. Female cerci distinctly crossed at tip. Under stones in uplands. 6-10. S & C.

Pseudochelidura sinuata. Elytra equal to or shorter than pronotum: hind margin of elytra very oblique. In turf and under stones in mountains of SW.

△s **Short-winged Earwig** *Apterygida media*. Hindwings vestigial. Regularly climbs vegetation and, like *Forficula* spp, commonly rests in flowers and chews petals.

▲ **Common Earwig** *Forficula auricularia*. Commonest European earwig and the only one commonly seen in B. Hindwings project beyond elytra. Male cerci broad and flat at base, with a tooth at the end of the flat part: a form with much longer cerci is not uncommon.

F. decipiens is similar but hindwings concealed. Flat part of male cerci about one third of their length. S & C.

F. pubescens is downy: flat part of male cerci over ½ length. Damp places. S.

△ **F. lesnei** is smoother and slightly larger: flat part of male cerci about ½ length. S & C.

swollen 2nd tarsal segment.

Female *Forficula auricularia* tending her eggs. Constant licking keeps them free of mould and bacteria.

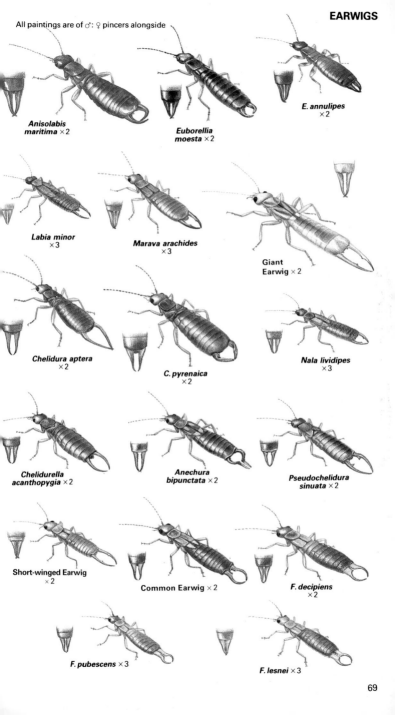

EARWIGS

All paintings are of ♂: ♀ pincers alongside

Anisolabis maritima ×2

Euborellia moesta ×2

E. annulipes ×2

Labia minor ×3

Marava arachides ×3

Giant Earwig ×2

Chelidura aptera ×2

C. pyrenaica ×2

Nala lividipes ×3

Chelidurella acanthopygia ×2

Anechura bipunctata ×2

Pseudochelidura sinuata ×2

Short-winged Earwig ×2

Common Earwig ×2

F. decipiens ×2

F. pubescens ×3

F. lesnei ×3

69

BUGS   Order Hemiptera

An order of some 80,000 known species of hemimetabolous insects, of which some 8000 occur in Europe and about 1700 in Britain. The range of form within the order is very great, but all species possess a piercing beak (the rostrum) like a minute hypodermic needle, with which they suck juices from plants or other animals. The aphids and many others are serious crop pests, reducing yields through mechanical damage to the plants and also by transmitting an assortment of disease-causing viruses. Two pairs of wings are normally present, the front ones usually hardened to some extent, but there are many wingless species. There is also great variation within many species, with fully-winged (macropterous), short-winged (brachypterous), and wingless (apterous) forms often present in the same population. Males and females often differ in wing length and other features.

There are two very distinct sub-orders – the Heteroptera (p. 72) and the Homoptera (p. 88) – with no obvious connection apart from the beak or rostrum: the two are often treated as entirely separate orders.

A heteropteran bug, showing the membranous tips of the forewings

In the **Heteroptera** the forewing, when fully developed, is clearly divided into two regions – a horny or leathery basal area and a membranous tip. The hindwings are always membranous and all wings are folded flat over the body at rest. The head is more or less horizontal and clearly visible from above. The antennae never have more than five segments and the beak clearly arises from the front of the head. The pronotum is very large and the scutellum is generally very conspicuous as well, sometimes extending back to cover the whole body and making the insect appear wingless.

Forewing of an anthocorid bug, showing the major divisions

Family classification of the Heteroptera depends on various features, including the number of segments in the antennae, tarsi, and rostrum, and the structure of the forewing (when present), whose main regions are shown above. All winged species have a claval suture, dividing the toughened area of the forewing into the clavus – which is next to the scutellum when the wings are folded – and the corium. The corium may be further divided by sutures marking off the embolium along the front edge and the cuneus at the tip. The membrane commonly contains visible veins, whose number and shape are useful in identification.

The heteropterans include both plant and animal feeders, and all the water bugs, both surface-dwelling and submerged. The latter generally breathe in the same way as the water beetles (p. 255), but the water scorpion and its relatives (p. 86) have solved the problem with a long breathing tube that conducts air down from the surface.

In the **Homoptera** the forewings, when present, are generally of uniform texture throughout, although they may be either horny or membranous. They are usually held roofwise over the body at rest. The head is commonly deflected backwards and the rostrum appears to spring from its rear – almost between the front legs in some species.

A homopteran bug, showing the roof-like resting position of the wings

The homopterans are entirely vegetarian and generally far less active than the heteropteran bugs. Many spend virtually their whole lives sucking sap from a single host plant. The sap has a relatively low protein content but is very rich in sugars. In order to get enough protein, the bugs have to take in a large excess of sugar, but most of this passes straight through the gut and is exuded through the anus as honeydew. The aphids and psyllids are the most prolific producers of this sticky material and infested trees and other plants become covered with it in the summer. Bees, ants, and many other insects feed on it, but much remains on the leaves and is later colonised by a black fungus.

The bristle-like antenna of the cicada

peripheral vein

Hindwing of a froghopper, showing the peripheral vein

Two distinct groups can be recognised within the Homoptera. Members of the **Auchenorrhyncha** generally have short antennae with a terminal bristle, and 3-segmented tarsi. Their forewings are often opaque and brightly coloured, and usually quite stiff. Many jump well, and the group as a whole are often called hoppers. There are many families and they are not always easy to separate, but the presence of a peripheral vein just inside the margin of the hindwing – at least in the hind part of it – distinguishes the froghoppers (p. 90) and the leafhoppers (p. 92) from other superficially similar groups of plant hoppers.

The other main group within the Homoptera is the **Sternorrhyncha**, in which the antennae are relatively long and thread-like and the tarsi 1- or 2-segmented. This is a very diverse group containing the aphids, psyllids, whiteflies, and scale insects (p. 96).

Young. Being hemimetabolous, the bugs do not go through a pupal stage. The young nymphs may or may not resemble the adults, but the beak readily identifies them as bugs. There are usually five instars, during which the young gradually get more like the adults, although the wing-buds are not usually clear until the 4th instar. It is sometimes difficult to decide whether a specimen is a fully-grown nymph or a brachypterous adult, but if the wings meet the scutellum with a well-defined junction the insect is almost certainly an adult. There are often considerable colour changes during development, especially between the last nymphal stage and the adult. *Nezara viridula*, for example, has a multicoloured nymph (p. 74) and an almost plain green adult.

HETEROPTERAN BUGS

Sub-order Heteroptera

Bugs in which the forewings, when fully developed, are horny at the base and membranous at the tip.

▲ **Pine Flat-bug** *Aradus cinnamomeus* Aradidae. Very flat, with head narrowing strongly behind eyes. Antennae 4-segmented. Forewings very narrow and lacking membrane: even smaller in female. Feeds on pine sap. Most members of the family are fully winged and feed on fungi under loose bark.

▲ **Aneurus laevis** Aneuridae. One of the bark bugs. Very flat: forewings almost entirely membranous. Antennae 4-segmented. Feeds on fungi under bark.

typical shield bug showing beak

The following bugs are known as shield bugs, from their general shape. All have 5-segmented antennae. They are also known as stink bugs because many species emit pungent fluids when alarmed. Many hibernate as adults and are seen mainly in autumn and spring. The group contains both herbivorous and carnivorous species. Their colours often fade after death.

▲ **Hawthorn Shield Bug** *Acanthosoma haemorrhoidale* Acanthosomatidae. Tarsi 2-segmented, as in whole family. Feeds on leaves and fruit of hawthorn and other trees.

▲ **Parent Bug** *Elasmucha grisea*. Named for female's habit of standing guard over eggs and young nymphs, probably protecting them from attack by parasites. Mainly grey or yellow, usually tinged with purplish red. Mainly on birch.

▲ **Pied Shield Bug** *Sehirus bicolor* Cydnidae. Tarsi 3-segmented and tibiae very spiny, as in whole family. On deadnettles and other labiates. ▲ *S. dubius* is metallic green or violet, sometimes black. It lives on various labiates.

Cydnus aterrimus. Legs very spiny, with flattened front tibiae. Pronotum with a marked transverse depression. Feeds on various plants in sandy places, including coastal dunes. S & C.

▲ **Negro Bug** *Thyreocoris scarabaeoides*. Large rounded scutellum covers most of abdomen. In leaf litter and dry turf, especially on sandy and chalky soils.

△s **Odontoscelis dorsalis** Scutelleridae. As in all members of the family, tarsi are 3-segmented and scutellum covers whole abdomen. Forewings (covered by scutellum) largely membranous. Very hairy. Light bands may be reduced. Mainly on coastal dunes, feeding on stork's-bill. S & C.

▲ **Eurygaster testudinaria**. Damp grassy places, feeding mainly on rushes and sedges. 2nd antennal segment hardly longer than 3rd. ▲ **European Tortoise Bug** *E. maura* varies from yellowish to black, with or without brown stripes. Scutellum parallel-sided and 2nd antennal segment much longer than 3rd. Polyphagous. Often damages cereal grains.

Family Pentatomidae. The largest shield bug family, with a total of about 3000 species. Scutellum usually triangular and reaching at least to middle of abdomen. Tarsi 3-segmented. Nymphs usually rounded, often brightly coloured. Abundant on continent, but relatively few in B owing to short, cool summers.

▲ **Eysarcoris fabricii**. Greenish bronze, golden, or brownish violet: always heavily punctured. On hedge woundwort and other labiates.

△s **Eurydema dominulus**. Orange or red. A common pest of brassicas on the continent. △s **Brassica Bug** *E. oleracea* Metallic green, blue, or violet, often with red, yellow, or cream spots. Mainly on crucifers and often a pest of cultivated brassicas.

▲ **Zicrona caerulea**. Dark green, blue, or violet. A carnivorous species, sucking juices from eggs and young larvae of various beetles, butterflies, and moths – including such pests as the Colorado Beetle and cabbage white butterflies.

▲ **European Turtle Bug** *Podops inuncta*. Resembles Scutelleridae in its large scutellum covering most of abdomen, but readily distinguished by two small anvil-shaped projections at front of pronotum. Grassy places.

▲ **Bishop's Mitre** *Aelia acuminata*. Rough grassland and cereal fields, occasionally attacking ripening grain. *A. glebana* is similar but larger. S & C (southern).

Graphosoma italicum. Abundant on umbellifers 5-10. Bold colour warns of foul taste. Legs often much blacker than shown here. S & C. *G. semipunctatum* has pronotal stripes broken into dots and tibiae almost entirely red. S.

Ancyrosoma albolineatum. Ground colour yellowish to violet brown. Shape unmistakable. On various plants in dry habitats. S.

Pine Flat-bug ×3

Aneurus laevis ×3

Pied Shield Bug ×3

Sehirus dubius ×3

← **Hawthorn Shield Bug** ×2

Cydnus aterrimus ×2

← **Parent Bug** ×2

Negro Bug ×3

Odontoscelis dorsalis ×3 →

Eurygaster testudinaria ×2

European Tortoise Bug ×2

Eysarcoris fabricii ×2

Eurydema dominulus ×2

Brassica Bug ×2

Zicrona caerulea ×2

European Turtle Bug ×3

Bishop's Mitre ×2

Graphosoma italicum ×2

Ancyrosoma albolineatum ×2

73

▲ **Forest Bug** *Pentatoma rufipes*. Distinguished from most shield bugs by its rather square 'shoulders' and almost rectanglar pronotum. 6-10 on a wide range of trees and shrubs, sometimes attacking other insects as well as feeding on sap. Often common in orchards, especially on cherries. Nymphs are yellow with dark spots.

▲ *Picromerus bidens*. Pronotum slopes sharply back from head and then expands to form a sharp 'thorn' on each side. Common on bushes and other vegetation, especially in damp habitats. 7-10. Predatory on larvae of butterflies, moths, and beetles.

▲ **Green Shield Bug** *Palomena prasina*. Sides of pronotum slightly concave. Abundant on trees and shrubs, and in rank herbage in autumn. Becomes bronze coloured in late autumn before going into hibernation, but bright green again when it re-emerges 4-5. There are several similar species. *P. viridissima* has slightly convex sides to the pronotum.

Green Vegetable Bug *Nezara viridula*. Slightly narrower than *Palomena*, with paler membrane at wing-tip and 3-5 pale spots on front edge of scutellum. Head and front of pronotum may be pale brown. The nymph (left) is brightly coloured. Abundant on a wide range of herbaceous plants, often causing damage to peas and potatoes. Widely distributed in S & C, the bug has recently established itself in southern England after arriving with imported produce. It cannot survive hard frosts, but may spread further north if the climate continues to warm up.

▲ **Gorse Shield Bug** *Piezodorus lituratus*. The red colour is present only in young adults 7-10: after hibernation the insects are yellowish green, often with a bronze tinge. Always heavily punctured. Mainly on gorse, but sometimes on broom and other leguminous plants, often in very large numbers. S & C.

Green Vegetable Bug
nymph × 1.5

Carpocoris fuscispinus. Ground colour ranges from yellow to reddish brown. Pronotal angles slightly raised and extending as dark points well beyond the wing margins. Double-brooded in south, where only mid-summer insects have the sharp pronotal angles: the autumn-spring brood have smaller and blunter angles. Polyphagous, but especially common on composites and umbellifers.

▲ **Sloe Bug** *Dolycoris baccarum*. Very hairy when seen under a lens: often tinged purple or red. On a wide range of herbaceous plants as well as blackthorn and other rosaceous shrubs, usually feeding on flowers and fruit. Very common on dunes.

▲ *Coreus marginatus* Coreidae. Two tiny horns on head between antennae. Latter are 4-segmented in this and all remaining families of land-living heteropterans. Often much darker brown than shown here. On docks and related plants, feeding mainly on the seeds, but also feeds on blackberries and other fruits in the autumn. Like most members of the family, it hibernates as an adult and is most often seen in autumn and spring. There are many rather similar species. Most members of the family are dull brown and they are commonly known as squash bugs because several species are pests of squashes in North America: nearly all are fruit-feeders.

Philomorpha laciniata. On silvery paronychia in dry, sunny places. Eggs are usually laid on other bugs of the same species and thus carried to fresh food plants. S & C.

△s *Syromastes rhombeus*. Abdomen diamond-shaped and extending sideways well beyond the wings. In dry habitats, usually on sandy soils, including heaths, grassland, and open woods. On sandworts and related plants. Mainly coastal in B.

▲ *Coriomeris denticulatus*. A rather spiky bug found on trefoils and other leguminous plants. Generally only on light, well-drained soils.

△s *Chorosoma schillingi* Rhopalidae. Straw-coloured to green. Forewings sometimes even shorter than shown. In long grass, mainly on coastal dunes: rarely on inland dunes and heaths. 7-9.

▲ *Rhopalus subrufus*. Resembles some coreids but head is broader (almost as wide as pronotum) and pronotum not expanded sideways. Woodland clearings and other lush, flowery places, on St John's-wort and many other plants. Flies readily.

▲ *Myrmus miriformis*. Males green or brown: females always green. Usually brachypterous. Forewings always with prominent pink veins. 6-10 in all kinds of grassland from dry heaths to water meadows. Feeds mainly on ripening grass seeds.

△s *Corizus hyoscyami*. Superficially like some of the ground bugs (p. 76) but distinguished by its hairiness and numerous veins in the apical membrane (ground bugs never have more than 5). Sandy areas, feeding on a wide range of plants. Mainly on coastal dunes in B.

Coptosoma scutellata Plataspidae. 2 tarsal segments. Scutellum covers almost whole of abdomen. Hind edge of scutellum strongly indented in male, weakly so in female. On legumes in damp grassland in summer. S & southern C.

Coptosoma scutellata
× 3

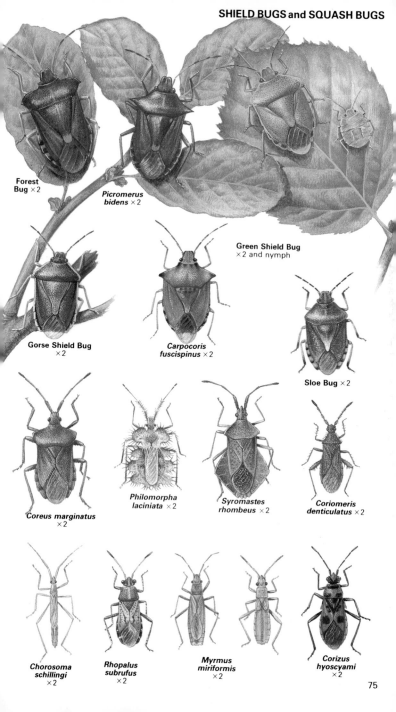

Forest
Bug ×2

*Picromerus
bidens* ×2

Green Shield Bug
×2 and nymph

Gorse Shield Bug
×2

*Carpocoris
fuscispinus* ×2

Sloe Bug ×2

Coreus marginatus
×2

*Philomorpha
laciniata* ×2

*Syromastes
rhombeus* ×2

*Coriomeris
denticulatus* ×2

*Chorosoma
schillingi*
×2

*Rhopalus
subrufus*
×2

*Myrmus
miriformis*
×2

*Corizus
hyoscyami*
×2

75

Alydus calcaratus Alydidae. 4th antennal segment much longer than 3rd and distinctly curved. Fast-flying in sunshine, with red abdomen exposed in flight. Heathland and other dry habitats, associated with a variety of plants and also partly carnivorous: sometimes feeds at carrion. Nymphs are ant-like and often found in ants' nests.

Camptopus lateralis. Like *Alydus* but pronotum much squarer. 4th antennal segments only slightly curved. Larger than *Alydus* and with yellowish brown underside marked with brown (underside bronzy black in *Alydus*). Dry habitats in S & C.

△s **Fire Bug** *Pyrrhocoris apterus* Pyrrhocoridae. Generally brachypterous: rarely macropterous. On many kinds of vegetation: often swarms on ground to feed on fallen seeds, especially in early spring after hibernation. Also attacks other insects. S & C.

Fire Bug ×2

GROUND BUGS Lygaeidae.
A large family of essentially sombre-coloured bugs, although some display bright warning colours. Membrane of forewing, when present, has no more than 5 veins (see p. 70). Antennae basically 4-segmented, although some individuals may have only 3 segments. Many species resemble mirid bugs (p. 80) but the forewings are much tougher and lack the distinct cuneus of the mirids. Ground bugs also have ocelli, which are lacking in mirids. Mainly seed-eating, although some are partly predatory, and mostly ground-living – often in sandy areas. Most species hibernate as adults.

△s **Aphanus rolandri**. Pale spot varies from yellow to red. In dry places with plenty of stones or leaf litter: occasionally under loose bark. Mostly nocturnal, feeding on fallen seeds. Mainly coastal counties in B.

▲ **Megalonotus chiragra**. Antennae often all black. Forewing membrane may extend beyond abdomen. In moss and leaf litter in sandy places, feeding on various plants. Mainly coastal in B.

▲ **Scolopostethus decoratus**. One of several rather similar species. Abundant on heathland, often swarming over heather shoots. Active all winter, feeding on shoots and seeds and partly on other insects.

▲ **European Chinch-bug** *Ischnodemus sabuleti*. Long and short-winged forms equally common. Swarms on reeds and other tall grasses, including cereals, in damp and dry habitats. Adults and young hibernate in masses in leaf sheaths. Abdomen of nymph is largely red.

Lygaeus saxatilis. Underside of abdomen red with a black band at base of each segment. Common on a wide range of plants in sunny habitats. S & C. **L. equestris** is similar but forewing membrane is marked with white. Underside of abdomen has 2 black spots on each side of each segment.

▲ **Spruce Cone Bug** *Gastrodes abietum*. Very flat. Usually high up in Norway spruces, hiding in old cones by day and feeding on needles and young seeds at night. Overwinters in cones or bark crevices. ▲ **Pine Cone Bug** *G. grossipes* is readily distinguished by its rich chestnut colour. It lives mainly on pines but is less confined to the cones than *abietum* and commonly found on the lower branches.

Trapezonotus ullrichi. Largest of several species with bicoloured pronotum and black scutellum. Among grasses in dry habitats, mainly on coast. S & C (southern). ▲ **T. arenarius**, with 2nd and 3rd antennal segments black instead of brown, is common in dry grassland everywhere.

▲ **Rhyparochromus pini**. An active runner on dry heathland. Found mainly around the bases of heathers and other plants, but higher up in the vegetation in warm weather. Feeds mainly on seeds.

▲ **Nysius thymi**. Pronotum without a keel. On dry sandy or gravelly areas, especially waste land, with short turf or scattered vegetation. 6-11 (occasionally living through winter). On numerous plants, especially composites such as Canadian fleabane, but also partly carnivorous.

Geocoris grylloides. Short forewings distinguish it from some related species. Mainly on coastal sand dunes. N & C.

Phymata monstrosa Phymatidae. A predatory bug with enlarged raptorial front legs. Abdomen angular and toothed. Yellowish brown to black. S. **P. crassipes** is similar but a little larger and without teeth on sides of abdomen. Usually reddish brown. S & C (southern).

Phymata monstrosa ×3

GROUND BUGS

Alydus calcaratus ×2

Camptopus lateralis ×2

Aphanus rolandri ×2

Megalonotus chiragra ×4

Scoloposthetus decoratus ×4

long-winged   short-winged
European Chinch-bug ×4

Lygaeus saxatilis ×2

L. equestris ×2

Spruce Cone Bug ×3

Pine Cone Bug ×3

Trapezonotus ullrichi ×3

Rhyparochromus pini ×3

Nysius thymi ×4

Geocoris grylloides ×3

Gampsocoris punctipes Berytidae. One of the stilt bugs, named for the very long legs and antennae of most members of the family. A spine on the scutellum distinguishes this species. On restharrow, usually in sandy areas: often plentiful on coastal dunes. Nymphs are bright green in this family. S & C.

Neides tipularius. Superficially like *Empicoris* and other assassins, but with no distinct neck or enlarged front legs. Rostrum straight. Short-winged form has narrower forewings just reaching tip of abdomen. In dense vegetation in dry places, such as heaths, dunes, and weedy arable fields. Feeds on a wide range of plants and 'freezes' when disturbed.

Gampsocoris punctipes × 3

▲ **Berytinus minor**. Commonly short-winged. In dry grassy places, feeding on grasses and various leguminous plants. Absent from far south.

▲ **Cymus melanocephalus**. Resembles ground bugs (p. 76), but distinguished by scutellum being much shorter than commisure and by inflated edges of forewings. In rank vegetation in damp places. Feeds on various rushes. Several related species have a pale keel on scutellum. S & C.

ASSASSIN BUGS Reduviidae.
Predatory bugs with distinct neck and stout, curved, 3-segmented rostrum hardly longer than the head (left). Some have enlarged, raptorial front legs. All European species feed on other insects, but some of the larger ones can pierce human skin. Some tropical species feed on vertebrate blood.

△s **Fly Bug** *Reduvius personatus*. Chocolate brown to black. Among rocks and in tree holes, but most common in and around buildings. Nocturnal and often attracted to light. Feeds on a wide range of insects, including bed bugs. Stridulates by rubbing tip of rostrum in a ridged groove on underside of thorax. 5-9.

▲ **Heath Assassin Bug** *Coranus subapterus*. Sometimes fully winged, especially in north. 6-10 on heaths and sand dunes, usually on bare patches of ground. Stridulates loudly if touched, like previous species.

R. iracundus showing beak or rostrum

Rhinocoris iracundus. Variable red and black pattern: pronotum may be all-black. 1st segment of rostrum red (black in *R. erythropus*). On flowers. 5-9. S & C (southern).

Pirates hybridus. Anterior part of pronotum much longer than posterior part. Waves antennae is it walks over the ground. 4-10. S & C.

▲ **Empicoris vagabundus**. Readily distinguished from stilt bugs by raptorial front legs and strongly curved rostrum. Lives mainly in trees and looks like a gnat at rest. Feeds on aphids and other small insects. Pale sides of abdomen separate it from several similar species.

Ploiaria domestica. Always wingless. Nocturnal, usually in and around buildings. Feeds on mosquitoes and other small flies. S.

DAMSEL BUGS Nabidae.
Predatory bugs resembling assassins but with a longer, 4-segmented rostrum. 2nd antennal segment longer than first and antennae never clearly elbowed. Larger species will pierce human skin if handled.

Prostemma guttula. Usually short-winged. At the bases of various plants in dry, sandy places. S & C. Common in Channel Islands.

▲ **Kalmanius flavomarginatus**. Upper surface and sides of abdomen with golden hair. Forewings occasionally reach beyond tip of abdomen. 6-10 in rough, damp grassland.

▲ **Common Damsel Bug** *Nabis rugosus*. Pale to dark brown: one of several very similar species. Forewings long or short. Grassy places everywhere.

♂

▲ **Marsh Damsel Bug** *Dolichonabis limbatus*. Very rarely with longer wings. 7-11 in damp, grassy places, feeding on a wide range of insects.

▲ **Tree Damsel Bug** *Himacerus apterus*. Forewings occasionally reach tip of abdomen. One of very few tree-dwelling damsel bugs. 6-10. S & C.
　▲ **Ant Damsel Bug** *Aptus mirmicoides* lives on the ground and has much shorter antennae. Its nymphs are extremely ant-like.

▲ **Loricula elegantula** Microphysidae. A very tiny bug with fully winged male and short-winged or virtually wingless female. 6-9 among lichens on trees and old walls. Males uncommon: rarely seen after July. Feeds on mites, springtails, etc.

♀

Loricula elegantula × 6

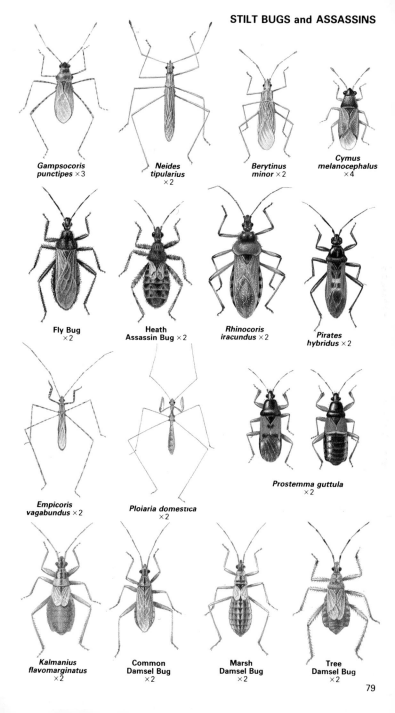

Gampsocoris punctipes ×3

Neides tipularius ×2

Berytinus minor ×2

Cymus melanocephalus ×4

Fly Bug ×2

Heath Assassin Bug ×2

Rhinocoris iracundus ×2

Pirates hybridus ×2

Empicoris vagabundus ×2

Ploiaria domestica ×2

Prostemma guttula ×2

Kalmanius flavomarginatus ×2

Common Damsel Bug ×2

Marsh Damsel Bug ×2

Tree Damsel Bug ×2

Common Flower Bug feeding on aphid

■ *Piesma maculatum* Piesmidae. Superficially like lacebugs, with strongly punctured forewings and pronotum, but latter does not cover scutellum. Pronotum has 2 keels at front. On sea purslane, orache, goosefoot, and other chenopods on coastal salt marshes and waste ground. Occasionally on beet. △ *P. quadratum* has 3 keels on pronotum and may be green or brown. Male stridulates by rubbing wings on abdomen. Most of European coastline: inland in parts of C, where it carries virus disease of sugar beet. Both species are known as beet bugs.

▲ **Spear Thistle Lacebug** *Tingis cardui* Tingidae. One of the lacebugs, named for the densely punctured and reticulate pronotum and forewings. Pronotum extends back to cover scutellum. Clothed with powdery wax. On spear thistle, where nymphs live in dense clusters on underside of flowerheads. There are many similar species. ▲ **Pear Lacebug** *Stephanitis pyri*, which sports a delicate glassy dome on its thorax, is common under the leaves of pears and apples in S & C, although only recently arriving in southern B.

▲ **Bedbug** *Cimex lectularius* Cimicidae. Orange to deep brown and completely wingless. In and around houses, hiding in crevices by day and emerging to suck blood from man and other animals at night. Common in zoos.

▲ *Oeciacus hirundinis*. Smaller and hairier than bedbug. Feeds on house martins and swallows (occasionally on other birds) and over-winters in and around their nests. May enter houses when birds leave in autumn.

▲ **Common Flower Bug** *Anthocoris nemorum* Anthocoridae. Forewings shiny throughout – distinguishing this from several similar species. Abundant everywhere on a wide range of trees, shrubs, and herbaceous plants – on leaves as well as flowers. A useful predator of aphids and spider mites, it will pierce human skin and suck blood if handled. This and other members of the family are distinguished from mirids by the clear embolium in the anterior part of the forewing (see p. 70).

▲ *Orius niger*. One of several similar, very small species. Colour varies, but can be identified by black hind tibiae. Male has swollen antennae. On a wide range of plants, especially gorse, heather, and mugwort.

▲ **Hot-bed Bug** *Xylocoris galactinus*. Antennae distinctly hairy (lens!). Named for its liking for compost heaps and similar places. Also in stables, birds' nests, etc, feeding on other insects and also sucking birds' blood.

MIRID or CAPSID BUGS Miridae.
The largest family in the Heteroptera, with some 6,000 known species. Body and forewings are relatively soft. Forewings, when present, have a well-developed cuneus (see p. 70), which distinguishes this family from most other bugs. The embolium is not distinct and the membrane generally contains one or two distinct cells at the base. Most species are herbivorous, feeding largely on developing fruits and seeds. Most pass the winter as eggs.

△s *Deraeocoris olivaceus*. 6-8 on hawthorn, feeding on young fruits as well as on various small insects. S & C. ▲ *D. ruber* is smaller and shinier: generally brick coloured but ranging from yellow to black: cuneus always red. Tibiae not ringed. On a wide range of plants. 6-9. S & C.

▲ *Systellonotus triguttatus*. 5-9, mainly on heathland, feeding on shoots and fruits of many plants and also on aphids. Often associated with ants, which nymphs and females resemble closely, although not in movements.

▲ *Phylus melanocephalus*. Yellow or brick coloured and distinguished from related species by black head. On oak and hazel, feeding partly on the plants and partly on aphids and other small insects. 5-8.

▲ *Psallus varians*. Reddish, yellow, or greyish brown. 5-9 on various deciduous trees, especially oaks. Partly predatory. There are many similar, closely related species.

▲ *Amblytylus nasutus*. One of many rather similar mirids. Green at first, often becoming brown with age. 5-8 in dry, grassy places. S & C.

▲ *Dicyphus errans*. 5-10 in rough herbage, including stinging nettles. Partly predatory. Most members of the genus are entirely herbivorous, with just one food-plant.

▲ *Macrotylus paykulli*. Tibiae clothed with minute black spines. 6-9 on restharrow in dry grassland and waysides. Usually gregarious.

▲ **Fern Bug** *Bryocoris pteridis*. Forewing membrane commonly absent, the shortened wings leaving tip of abdomen exposed: in this form the forewings get wider towards the tip, giving a pear-shaped outline. 6-9, on bracken and other ferns in damp woods. N & C.

Fern Bug
(short-winged) × 5

Piesma maculatum ×4

Bedbug ×3

Piesma quadratum ×4

Spear Thistle Lacebug ×5

Pear Lacebug ×6

Common Flower Bug ×3

Orius niger ×6

Oeciacus hirdundinis ×3

Hot-bed Bug ×6

Deraeocoris olivaceus ×2

D. ruber ×2

♂   ♀

Systellonotus triguttatus ×3

Phylus melanocephalus ×3

Psallus varians ×3

Amblytylus nasutus ×3

Dicyphus errans ×3

Macrotylus paykulli ×4

Fern Bug ×5

81

▲ **_Orthocephalus saltator_**. Rather hairy. Head not noticeably wider than front of pronotum. Antennae black. Tibiae red or brick-coloured (black in _O. coriaceus_). Hind femora enlarged for jumping, especially in female. Male always fully winged: female usually brachypterous as illustrated. 6-9 in rough grassland, mainly on composites.

▲ **_Orthotylus virescens_**. 6-9 on broom. Partly predatory. One of many rather similar green bugs in this genus, although rather darker than most. Specific identification is difficult in this genus, although host plant is a good guide. The genus may be confused with some species of _Lygus_ and _Lygocoris_, but these genera are generally more robust and they have a distinct collar at the front of the pronotum.

▲ **Black-kneed Capsid** _Blepharidopterus angulatus_. Named for the black patches at the tips of the tibiae – especially prominent in the nymphs. Antennae much shorter in some males. 6-10 on a wide range of trees, especially apple and lime. Partly predatory, destroying large numbers of red spider mites in orchards.

▲ **_Pilophorus perplexus_**. Pale bands are due to silvery hairs. 6-10 on oaks and other deciduous trees, feeding mainly on aphids and sometimes on leaves and young fruits. Rather active and sometimes mistaken for ants. ▲ **_P. cinnamopterus_** is similar but lives on pines.

▲ **_Campyloneura virgula_**. Bright yellow cuneus with red apex distinguishes this from several otherwise similar bugs. 6-10 on a wide range of trees, feeding on aphids and other small insects and on red spider mites. Nymphs are bright yellow and orange.

▲ **_Mecomma ambulans_**. Sexes markedly different, but fully-winged females occasionally occur in north and on mountains. 6-9 among rushes and other vegetation, especially in and around damp woods. Partly predatory.

▲ **_Halticus apterus_**. Head noticeably wider than front of pronotum. Wings occasionally fully developed and covering abdomen. Femora black: tibiae and antennae yellowish brown. Leaps with aid of enlarged hind femora. 6-9 on legumes and bedstraws in grassy places: sometimes a pest of clovers and related crops. Related species have pale head and sometimes pale thorax as well.

▲ **_Myrmecoris gracilis_**. Almost always micropterous and extremely ant-like, running rapidly on ground. 6-9 on heathland and other dry habitats. Largely predatory: sometimes in ant nests, feeding on brood but not on adults. N & C.

▲ **_Pithanus maerkeli_**. Usually micropterous and ant-like, the pale wing pads giving the illusion of a narrow waist. Female occasionally fully-winged. 5-9 in grassy places, especially where damp. Partly predatory.

▲ **_Lygus pratensis_**. In northern half of Europe and on mountains both sexes are light brown, usually with no marks on pronotum. Elsewhere males are darker red with a yellowish scutellum and females are greenish brown, both usually with dark marks on the pronotum. Both forms occur in B. Feeds on a wide range of plants and hibernates as adult.

▲ **Tarnished Plant Bug** _L. rugulipennis_ varies from yellow to brick red or brown. Dense coat of short, fine hair distinguishes it from _pratensis_. Abundant on a wide range of plants, including stinging nettle, causing white spotting on leaves. Also attacks flowers and frequently causes malformation of peas and beans. Although sometimes a serious agricultural pest on the continent, it is more of a garden pest in B. Hibernates as adult.

▲ **_Liocoris tripustulatus_**. Young adults (late summer) are light brown with yellow spots. After hibernation they are deep reddish brown with bright orange scutellum and cuneus. Mainly on nettles. ▲ **_Capsodes gothicus_** is superficially similar but is parallel-sided and has a dark head.

▲ **Common Green Capsid** _Lygocoris pabulinus_. Abundant 5-10 on a very wide range of woody and herbaceous plants: woody plants, on which over-wintering eggs are laid, are infested mainly in spring. Often a pest of soft fruit, potatoes, and several other crops. Pale brown tibial spines distinguish this from several closely related species: narrow pronotal collar distinguishes it from _Orthotylus_ spp.

▲ **_Polymerus unifasciatus_**. Fine golden pubescence on forewing (strong lens!). Tibiae with strong black spines. 5-9 in rough, grassy places, feeding on various bedstraws.

▲ **_Phytocoris tiliae_**. White or pale green with black markings. 6-10 on a wide range of deciduous trees. Largely predatory, taking small caterpillars, aphids, red spider mites, etc. There are several similar species but they lack the pale patch at junction of corium and cuneus.

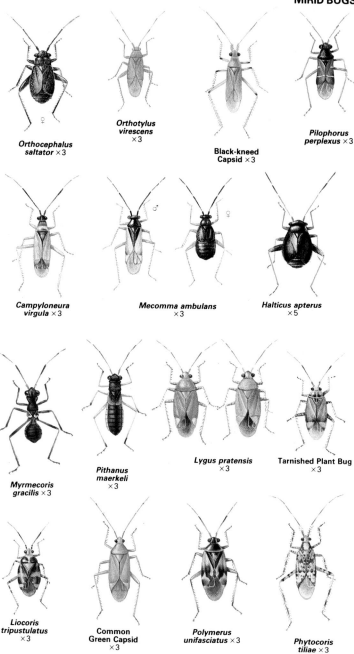

*Orthocephalus
saltator* ×3

*Orthotylus
virescens*
×3

Black-kneed
Capsid ×3

*Pilophorus
perplexus* ×3

*Campyloneura
virgula* ×3

Mecomma ambulans
×3

Halticus apterus
×5

*Myrmecoris
gracilis* ×3

*Pithanus
maerkeli*
×3

Lygus pratensis
×3

Tarnished Plant Bug
×3

*Liocoris
tripustulatus*
×3

Common
Green Capsid
×3

*Polymerus
unifasciatus* ×3

*Phytocoris
tiliae* ×3

△ **Miris striatus**. A very striking bug, found mainly on oak and hawthorn in B but on alder, birch, sallow, and many other trees on the continent. 5-8. Partly predatory.
▲ **Calocoris quadripunctatus** has similar colours but is smaller and much more oval in outline and the orange cuneus has a black tip.

▲ **Calocoris stysi**. Light areas are yellow or pale green: cuneus always orange. 5-8, mainly in wooded areas. Feeds on the flowers and young fruits of stinging nettle, and also on aphids. Adults visit umbellifer flowers.

▲ **Lucerne Bug** *Adelphocoris lineolatus*. Tibial spines at least as long as tibial width distinguish this genus from *Calocoris*, which has very short spines. 6-10 in damp grassland, almost always on legumes although adults may attack composite flowers. A pest of lucerne in parts of C and in the USA.

△ **Stenotus binotatus**. Both sexes yellow and black at first: with age male becomes orange and black and female becomes greyish and black. 2 black pronotal spots always present. 5-10 in rough grassland, feeding largely on flowerheads of grasses.

▲ **Capsus ater**. Head and pronotum often black. 2nd antennal segment greatly swollen, as in all members of the genus. 6-9 in long grass everywhere, including gardens and woodland clearings. Feeds mainly on lower parts of stems.

▲ **Heterotoma merioptera**. Inhabits dense vegetation, especially nettles and other hedgerow plants, and various trees and shrubs. Partly predatory. 6-10.

▲ **Pantilius tunicatus**. Dull yellowish green at first, becoming reddish later. Mature insects have red patch at tip of abdomen. Clothed with short black hairs. Last 2 antennal segments very short. 9-10 on hazel, alder, and birch.

△ **Miridius quadrivirgatus**. Cuneus not always red. Waste places and rough grassland, on wall barley and other grasses, especially where fairly damp. S & C: coastal in B.

▲ **Stenodema laevigatum**. 1st antennal segment stout and hairy. Pronotum strongly punctate. Young adults (7-8) are pale yellow with reddish brown stripes, but stripes soon fade and bugs become browner. Hibernate as adults and become green in spring to match fresh grass, although male darker than female. Abundant in long grass of all kinds.

△ **Notostira elongata**. Tibiae and 1st antennal segment very hairy. Pronotum smooth. 2 broods per year. Males of both broods largely black, margined with greyish or yellowish green. Summer females mainly green: autumn females pinkish brown, developing a green abdomen after hibernation. Males do not survive winter. Abundant in rough grassland.

▲ **Teratocoris antennatus**. Varies from pale green (mainly females) to deep orange, with varying amounts of black: males generally blacker than females. Wing length variable, usually leaving part of abdomen exposed. 1st antennal segment always reddish brown. 6-10 in marshes and damp grassland. N & C.

▲ **Leptopterna dolabrata**. Black and yellow or black and orange. Legs and antennae very hairy. Males generally fully-winged: females mostly brachypterous. Emits a very pungent odour. Abundant 5-9 in grassy places, as long as not too dry. Feeds on cocksfoot and other tall grasses: sometimes a cereal pest in north. The very similar ▲ **L. ferrugata** inhabits the drier grasslands.

———————————

▲ **Common Shore Bug** *Saldula saltatoria* Saldidae. Rather flat, with prominent ocelli and eyes. Rostrum 3-segmented. Predatory and, like most members of the family, living on mud at edges of ponds and ditches: very active in sunshine. Rather variable and not easily separated from its numerous relatives.

△ **Marine Bug** *Aepophilus bonnairei*. No ocelli. Always short-winged. Lives in rock crevices and among seaweeds on lower part of the shore, usually in family groups. Predatory. Atlantic, Irish Sea, and Channel coasts.

Leptopus marmoratus Leptopodidae. Resembles shore bugs but has ocelli on stalked platform. Under stones at edges of ponds and streams. S & C.

Isometopus mirificus Isometopidae. On old, lichen-covered trees, feeding on aphids and psocids. Sometimes placed in Miridae, but differs from mirids in having ocelli. S & C (southern).

Ochterus marginatus Ochteridae. A semi-aquatic bug living at the edges of rivers. Differs from true water bugs (p. 86) in having ocelli and visible antennae. Flies rapidly. Predatory, feeding mainly on fly larvae. S & C (southern).

Ochterus marginatus × 3

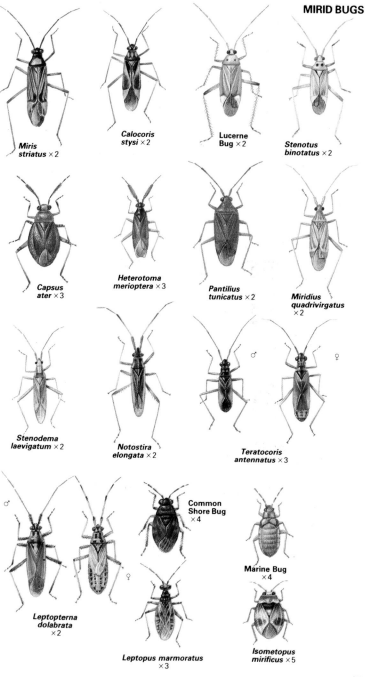

Miris striatus ×2

Calocoris stysi ×2

Lucerne Bug ×2

Stenotus binotatus ×2

Capsus ater ×3

Heterotoma merioptera ×3

Pantilius tunicatus ×2

Miridius quadrivirgatus ×2

Stenodema laevigatum ×2

Notostira elongata ×2

♂ ♀

Teratocoris antennatus ×3

♂ ♀

Leptopterna dolabrata ×2

Common Shore Bug ×4

Leptopus marmoratus ×3

Marine Bug ×4

Isometopus mirificus ×5

SURFACE DWELLERS Antennae clearly visible. All are predatory and are clothed, at least on the lower surface, with water-repellent hairs that prevent them from becoming wet. Most hibernate as adults.

▲ **Water Measurer** *Hydrometra stagnorum* Hydrometridae. Head very long and thin. Virtually wingless as a rule but sometimes with partly or fully developed wings. Walks slowly over surface, usually among vegetation, at margins of ponds and streams. Spears small prey with beak. △ *H. gracilenta* is slightly smaller and much rarer.

▲ **Common Pond Skater** *Gerris lacustris* Gerridae. Wings range from minute to fully developed. Skates rapidly over surface of still and slow-moving water, using front legs to grab other insects that fall on to the surface. Winged individuals often fly far from water to hibernate. There are several similar species.

▲ *Aquarius najas*. Like a large *Gerris* but prefers flowing water. Usually wingless. Sides of 7th abdominal segment produced into long points, but these do not reach tip of abdomen. ▲ *A. paludum* is similar but usually fully-winged.

▲ **Water Cricket** *Velia caprai* Veliidae. Winged or wingless. Underside orange. On still and slow-moving waters with little vegetation, especially in wooded areas and uplands. It feeds like *Gerris*.

▲ *Mesovelia furcata* Mesoveliidae. Usually wingless. Runs rapidly on floating leaves of pondweeds and other aquatic plants, on which it is well-camouflaged. 7-9, feeding on small insects on or just below the surface. S & C.

SUBMERGED BUGS Antennae concealed in pits or grooves on head. Mainly carnivorous. Most hibernate as adults, or at least become quiescent for the winter, usually in mud.

▲ **Water Scorpion** *Nepa cinerea* Nepidae. Very flat. Creeps slowly over mud and vegetation in shallow water, drawing air from surface through hollow 'tail'. Catches prey, including small fishes, with raptorial front legs. Fully-winged, but few individuals ever fly. Active all year.

△ s **Water Stick Insect** *Ranatra linearis*. In deep ponds with plenty of vegetation, on which it lies in wait for small prey to pass. Breathes like *Nepa*. Flies by day in warm weather. S & C.

▲ **Saucer Bug** *Ilyocoris cimicoides* Naucoridae. Fully-winged, but flightless. In weedy and muddy ponds, carrying a large air-bubble under forewings and on underside of body. Fiercely carnivorous and may pierce skin if handled.

▲ *Aphelocheirus aestivalis* Aphelocheiridae. Varies from micropterous to fully-winged, but usually micropterous in B. Mainly in swift streams with gravelly beds and scattered vegetation. Feeds on various young insects and may stab fingers if handled. Breathes with a plastron (p. 255) and never needs to surface.

▲ **Common Backswimmer** *Notonecta glauca* Notonectidae. Swims on its back with a large air-bubble attached to ventral surface. Dorsal surface strongly keeled. Active all year in still waters, flying readily in warm weather. Fiercely carnivorous, commonly attacking tadpoles and small fishes – and fingers! Also called water boatman. ▲ *N. maculata* has mottled brick-coloured forewings.

▲ *Plea atomaria* Pleidae. A small, back-swimming predator living in still and slow-moving water with plenty of weed. Often present in vast numbers.

▲ *Corixa punctata* Corixidae. One of several similar species, often known as lesser water boatmen. Swims right-way-up: dorsal surface not keeled. Middle and hind legs more or less same length. Feeds largely on unicellular algae and plant debris in weedy ponds and slow-moving water. Active all year and flies well. Males stridulate loudly during courtship, as do most species in the family.

△ s *Sigara striata*. In still water. Males stridulate very loudly and can be heard yards away if placed in a shallow dish of water. There are many similar species, some very common in B. They are usually much slenderer than *Corixa* spp.

▲ *Cymatia coleoptrata*. Distinguished from *Corixa* and *Sigara* by smaller size, unbanded pronotum, and long front tarsi. Usually micropterous. In weedy ponds and ditches, darting out to catch small prey.

Plea atomaria ×5

Mesovelia furcata ×5

Cymatia coleoptrata ×5

86

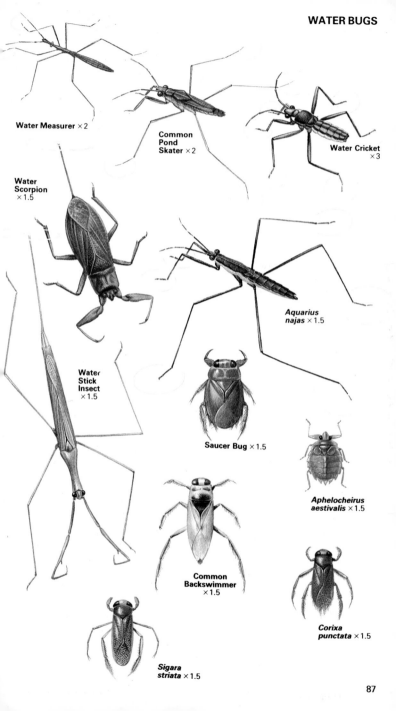

Water Measurer ×2

Common Pond Skater ×2

Water Cricket ×3

Water Scorpion ×1.5

Aquarius najas ×1.5

Water Stick Insect ×1.5

Saucer Bug ×1.5

Aphelocheirus aestivalis ×1.5

Common Backswimmer ×1.5

Corixa punctata ×1.5

Sigara striata ×1.5

Cicada orni freshly emerged from nymphal skin

HOMOPTERAN BUGS

Sub-order Homoptera

Bugs in which the forewings, when present, are of uniform texture – either horny or membranous – and usually held rooflike over the body at rest. Antennae are short and bristle-like in the cicadas and hoppers but much longer in the aphids and psyllids (pp. 94-96).

CICADAS Cicadidae. Large homopterans with transparent and usually shiny wings. They live mainly on trees and shrubs. Males produce very shrill sounds by vibrating small membranes (tymbals) on each side of the body. Flaps called opercula protect the tymbals on the underside and may act as sounding boards. Female has a long ovipositor with which she lays eggs in bark, but nymphs fall to ground on hatching and burrow down to feed on roots for several years. They have massive front legs for tunnelling. The group is largely tropical, but several species live in southern Europe and one reaches B.

Tibicen plebejus. The largest European cicada, with an extremely loud song. Tymbals completely concealed. Opercula very large and overlapping. 6-9, mainly on pines. S.

Cicada orni. Forewing with 11 small dark spots. Body often covered with dense grey bloom. Rostrum longer than in any other species, reaching back to base of abdomen. Tymbals partly exposed, especially at the sides. Opercula oval and well-separated. Abundant on trees, mainly pines, 6-9. Can sometimes be seen in hundreds on fences and telegraph poles when freshly emerged and drying their wings. S & C (southern).

Tibicina haematodes. Tymbals completely exposed from above. Opercula very small and widely separated. 2 spines on front femur. Extensive reddish colour on pronotum. Costa and basal parts of other veins very red. 6-9 on various trees. S & C (southern).

△ s *Cicadetta montana*. Tymbals completely exposed from above. Opercula rather small. Pronotal colour and pattern vary, but usually dark. Front femur with 3 spines, the posterior one sloping sharply forward. 5-8 in woodland clearings and scrubby places, on a wide range of shrubs and herbaceous plants, but possibly now extinct in B. Song is soft and warbling and easily missed. *C. argentata* is very similar but has larger opercula and much more red on the pronotum. Wing veins are distinctly paler than in *montana*. Scrubby areas 6-9. S. *C. pygmea*, the smallest species, lives on a wide range of trees and shrubs, especially oaks, pines, and junipers. 6-9. SW. *C. tibialis* is similar to *pygmea* but with very bright red bands on the abdomen. SE.

Cicadatra atra. Tymbals partly exposed from above and from the sides, as in *C. orni*. 2 dark spots near tip of forewing. Pronotum with extensive yellow mottling. Front femur with three or four spines, the basal one being the longest. 6-9 on a wide range of trees and shrubs. S.

TREEHOPPERS Membracidae. A large family of jumping bugs in which the pronotum extends back over the body. Mainly tropical, with only 4 species in western Europe. Pronotum often ornate, frequently resembling prickles or thorns in tropical species and thereby affording protection. Nymphs are rather spiky and pointed at the rear.

△ s *Gargara genistae*. Rear extension of pronotum straight, reaching about half way back along the abdomen. 6-10 on broom and other leguminous plants.

▲ *Centrotus cornutus*. Pronotum horned on each side, horns being larger in south than in north. Rear extension of pronotum sinuate on lower edge and reaching back to about tip of abdomen. 4-8, on a variety of herbs and shrubs in wooded habitats. *Acanthophyes chloroticus* resembles *Centrotus* but is much shorter and pronotum is usually brown or yellowish. 5-8 on various herbs and shrubs. S.

Buffalo Treehopper *Stictocephalus bisonia*. Green fades to dirty yellow after death. Rear extension of pronotum wider than in the other species and usually completely covering scutellum. 7-9 on a wide range of woody and herbaceous plants: often causes damage to apples and other fruit trees by laying eggs in bark of twigs. An American species now widely distributed in S & C (western).

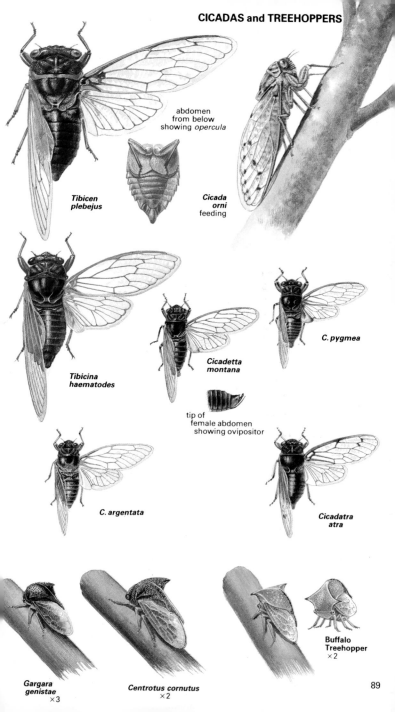

CICADAS and TREEHOPPERS

Tibicen plebejus

abdomen from below showing *opercula*

Cicada orni feeding

Tibicina haematodes

Cicadetta montana

C. pygmea

tip of female abdomen showing ovipositor

C. argentata

Cicadatra atra

Gargara genistae ×3

Centrotus cornutus ×2

Buffalo Treehopper ×2

89

FROGHOPPERS Cercopidae. Jumping homopterans, mostly brown, in which the hind tibiae are rounded and bear just a few spines. This distinguishes them from the cicadellids (p. 92), which have many spines. Antennae arise from between the eyes. Forewings horny and pitted. Hindwings have a peripheral vein, at least in hind region. Nymphs of most species live in masses of froth, giving rise to their other common names of spittle bugs and cuckoo-spit insects.

▲ **Neophilaenus lineatus.** Forewings light or dark brown, generally with a pale stripe along the costa. Basal half of costa more or less straight. 6-9 on grasses: dark form generally in cooler and damper areas. There are several similar species.
Lepyromia coleoptrata. Yellow to dark brown. Costal margin of forewing very convex. 5-9 on grasses in marshes and damp grassland. N & C.

▲ **Aphrophora alni.** Pronotum has central keel. Forewing may lack one or both pale patches on costal margin: whole wing may be darker. 5-10 on many kinds of trees and shrubs. There are several similar species.

▲ **Common Froghopper** *Philaenus spumarius*. Ground colour basically buff, with a very variable dark pattern: occasionally dark all over. Abundant 6-9 on a wide range of woody and herbaceous plants.

▲ **Cercopis vulnerata.** Anterior margin of pronotum straight, not arching forward between eyes as in other cercopids. Nymphs live communally on roots, surrounded by solidified froth. 4-8 on various plants, mainly in wooded areas. S & C. There are several similar species on the continent.

▲ **Cixius nervosus** Cixiidae. Forewings membranous with well-defined veins. Hindwings without peripheral vein. Pronotum yellowish brown with prominent lateral keels. Scutellum dark brown or black with 3 keels. 5-10 on various trees. There are several similar species.

▲ **Issus coleoptratus** Issidae. Forewings rather horny with a network of cross-veins. Hindwings smoky brown with no peripheral vein. Pronotum bulges strongly forward between eyes: hind margin almost straight. 5-10 on various trees and in moss. Several similar species live on the continent, mainly in S.

△ s **Tettigometra impressopunctata** Tettigometridae. Forewings horny and distinctly pitted: veins weak. Hindwings with no peripheral vein. Hind tibia with an apical circlet of spines. On dry grassland, hibernating as adult. S & C: mainly on sand dunes and chalk in B. Many similar species live on the continent, mainly in S.

Dictyophara europaea Dictyopharidae. Becomes yellowish after death, but easily identified by conical head and network of veins towards tip of forewing. 6-10 on a wide range of herbaceous plants, especially umbellifers. Leaps strongly. S & C.

Bursinia genei. 6-9 on a wide range of shrubby and herbaceous plants. S.

Family Delphacidae. A family of small hoppers, distinguished from similar groups by a large movable spur at apex of hind tibia. Forewings rather tough: hindwings with no peripheral vein. Antenna springs from a notch in lower margin of eye. Sexes are often very different. Most species have brachypterous and fully-winged individuals.

▲ **Delphax pulchellus.** Female usually brachypterous, with few dark marks on forewing. Latter reaches about half way along abdomen. 6-9 on reeds in marshy places and on river banks.

▲ **Megamelus notula.** Forewings may be almost entirely brown: sometimes fully-winged. 4-10 in marshy habitats. Absent from most of S.

▲ **Delphacodes pellucida.** Forewings always reach at least to tip of abdomen in male: long or short in female. Pronotum and scutellum may be black. 5-9 in grassland nearly everywhere. There are many similar species.

▲ **Asiraca clavicornis.** Front and middle legs broad and flat. 1st antennal segment long and broad. Scutellum with 4 keels. 4-10 in damp, grassy places. S & C.

▲ **Stenocranus minutus.** Always fully-winged. Forewings transparent and iridescent, with prominent veins. Dark patch often indistinct, but may cover inner half of wing. On grasses in many habitats.

△ **Delphacinus mesomelas.** Lateral keels of pronotum arched round eyes. Long-winged form equally common. 6-8 in wooded and scrubby areas, especially on broom.
Tropidocephala elegans 1st two antennal segments very short. Head, pronotum, and scutellum green or yellow. Scutellum with 3 keels. 5-10 in well-vegetated habitats. S.

hind leg of CERCOPIDAE

hind leg of CICADELLIDAE

hind leg of DELPHACIDAE

spur ↗

*Neophilaenus
lineatus* ×3

Lepyromia coleoptrata
×3

Cercopis vulnerata
×2

*Aphrophora
alni* ×2

Common Froghopper ×3

Cuckoo-spit and nymph

*Cixius
nervosus* ×3

*Issus
coleoptratus* ×3

*Tettigometra
impressopunctata*
×3

*Dictyophara
europaea* ×2

*Delphax
pulchellus* ×3

*Megamelus
notula* ×3
♀

*Delphacodes
pellucida* ×3
♂

*Bursinia
genei* ×3

*Asiraca
clavicornis* ×3

*Stenocranus
minutus* ×3

*Delphacinus
mesomelas* ×5

*Tropidocephala
elegans*
×5

Ledra
aurita
× 2

LEAFHOPPERS Cicadellidae A large
family of jumping homopteran bugs with
relatively soft forewings and a peripheral
vein in hindwing (see p. 71). Distinguished from
froghoppers by numerous spines on hind tibiae
(see p. 90). Identification of many species depends
on detailed facial features and measurements. Winter is
spent as adult or egg.

▲ *Ledra aurita*. Ear-like flaps immediately identify this bug. 5-10 in woodlands, especially on oaks. Well-camouflaged on lichen-covered branches. S & C.

▲ *Aphrodes bifasciatus*. Very variable: anterior white band on forewing often broken or absent. 6-9 in damp or dry grassland, mainly in lowlands. Males of several related species all have light and dark bands on forewings – a generic characteristic.

▲ *Eupteryx aurata*. Pale areas often tinged with orange. Abundant 5-11 on a wide range of plants, especially nettles and labiates. Often a pest of tomatoes. As in all leafhoppers, its saliva is toxic to plants and destroys chlorophyll: feeding punctures are surrounded by pale spots, and if infestation is severe the spots join up and destroy large areas of leaf.

▲ *Iassus lanio*. Head and thorax yellowish or green, always heavily mottled with brown. Forewings green or reddish brown. 7-10 in woodland, especially on oak.

Penthimia nigra. Brown or black, with or without red spots on pronotum. Forewings overlap slightly at tip. 5-8 on various trees, especially oaks. S & C.

▲ *Elymana sulphurella*. Greenish face with broad black spot around base of each antenna. Sides of thorax with black spots: sometimes a dark patch on top of head. 7-10 among grasses, often in quite dry places.

▲ *Idiocerus vitreus*. Head broadly rounded in front. Forewings overlap slightly at apex and are often redder, especially after hibernation. 3-10 on poplars. N & C. There are several similar species, not easily separated.

▲ *Thamnotettix confinis*. Forewings with prominent greenish veins. Pronotum may have darker markings. 5-9 on a wide range of trees, shrubs, and herbage. N & C.

▲ *Eupelix cuspidata*. Dark markings vary in density. Head has sharp keel on top. Pronotum has 3 keels. Forewings with prominent veins. 3-9 in dry, grassy places.

▲ *Macropsis scutellata*. Top of head largely covered by pronotum. Veins dark brown, with some clear cells in middle of forewing. 6-10 on nettles.

▲ *Macrosteles variatus*. Head and thorax yellow or greenish. Dark areas of forewing less distinct in male. 5-9 on nettles and other herbage. Several very similar bugs.

▲ *Psammotettix sabulicola*. Pronotum and scutellum yellowish brown, often with dark markings. 6-10 among grasses on coastal dunes, often resting on bare sand. N & C.

▲ *Cicadella viridis*. Top of head (vertex) smoothly rounded in front, clearly bi-coloured. Pronotum yellow at front, dark green behind. Forewings generally green in female, purplish brown or black in male. 7-10 in marshy places, generally on grasses.

▲ *Agallia laevis*. Pronotum with fine transverse ridges. Black marks on scutellum meet side margins. 7-9 on sand dunes. S & C.

▲ *Arboridia ribauti*. Top of head (vertex) with 2 black spots. Scutellum pale with 2 black triangles at front. All year on various trees. S & C.

▲ *Eupterycyba jucunda*. Vertex with 2 black spots. Pronotum with 3 large black spots. Scutellum has 2 black triangles at front. Forewing apex greyish. 7-10 on alder. S & C.

▲ *Evacanthus interruptus*. Pronotum black, with or without pale central stripe. Wings shorter than abdomen in female. 6-10 on a wide range of herbage, especially in damp places.

▲ *Edwardsiana geometrica*. Apex of forewing greyish. Dark streak on forewing and dark scutellum distinguish this from many related species. 7-10 on alder.

▲ *Balclutha punctata*. Head and thorax green or dirty yellow, often marked with brown. Forewings pale green or yellow to reddish brown, often spotted. All year, mainly on grasses but often passing the winter on conifers.

▲ *Ulopa reticulata*. Vertex very flat in front. Forewings horny, distinctly pitted and strongly convex. No hindwings. All year on heathers.

▲ *Graphocephala fennahi*. Red stripes on forewing readily identify this North American bug now established on rhododendrons in southern B. 6-10.

Aphrodes bifasciatus ×4

Eupteryx aurata ×4

Iassus lanio ×3

Penthimia nigra ×3

Elymana sulphurella ×4

Idiocerus vitreus ×4

Thamnotettix confinis ×3

Eupelix cuspidata ×3

Macropsis scutellata ×4

Macrosteles variatus ×4

Psammotettix sabulicola ×4

Cicadella viridis ♀ ×3

Agallia laevis ×4

Arboridia ribauti ×4

Eupterycyba jucunda ×4

Evacanthus interruptus ×3

Edwardsiana geometrica ×4

Balclutha punctata ×4

Ulopa reticulata ×4

Graphocephala fennahi ×3

APHIDS Very small, pear-shaped, sap-sucking homopteran bugs. Both wings, when present, are membranous: generally held rooflike at rest. Hind end of abdomen generally has a pair of 'horns', known as cornicles, that exude waxy secretions. Honeydew is produced in abundance (see p. 71). Life cycles are generally complex, with winged and wingless forms in most species. Winter is usually passed in the egg stage, although many species can remain active in mild winters. Spring aphids are generally wingless and all female, building up dense colonies through parthenogenetic reproduction. Most give birth to active young - sometimes several in a day - instead of laying eggs. Winged aphids gradually increase in late spring and summer and spread to new plants. Most species have more than one host plant during the year. The Aphididae is the largest of several families. The forewings in this family have at least 4 oblique cross-veins. The Pemphigidae is similar but cornicles are very short or absent.

△ **Grape Phylloxera** *Daktulosphaira vitifoliae* Phylloxeridae. Wings, when present, held flat at rest. No cornicles. An American vine pest, causing extensive damage when introduced to Europe in the 19th century, but not now a serious problem. It feeds on leaves and roots, often inducing abundant galls on the leaves. Winged forms are rare in Europe.

▲ **Phylloxera glabra.** No cornicles. Wingless females abundant under oak leaves in spring, surrounded by eggs (this family of aphids does not give birth to active young). Yellow spots develop around feeding sites on leaves. Winged forms appear in summer.

▲ **Adelges viridis** Adelgidae. Only 3 oblique cross-veins. No cornicles. One of several very similar species causing cone-like pineapple galls on spruce. Galls are green at first and open 6-7 to allow aphids to escape; they then become brown and woody. New aphids fly to larch and other conifers, where they produce several generations without galls, although this is not true of all the species.

▲ **Woolly Aphid** *Eriosoma lanigerum* Pemphigidae. Purplish brown body densely clothed with waxy fluff. In dense clusters on bark of apple and other rosaceous trees and shrubs in summer, especially where trees have been damaged. Winter is passed in bark crevices and, occasionally, on the roots.

▲ **Tetraneura ulmi.** Causes smooth, stalked bladder-like galls on elm leaves in spring. Summer generations feed on grass roots and are orange or brown. Galls of **T. nigriabdominalis** are similar but hairy. Larger, irregular pouch galls are caused by ▲ **Eriosoma lanuginosum.**

▲ **Pemphigus bursarius.** Causes pouch galls on poplar leaf stalks in spring. Summer aphids are cream-coloured and very waxy and live on roots of lettuce and other composites, often causing the plants to wilt. ▲ **P. spyrothecae** causes spiral galls on poplar leaf stalks in spring and then moves to the trunks and branches. It has no herbaceous host plant.

Baizongia pistaciae. Causes huge red, candle-like galls on leaves of pistachio trees. Greyish aphids live in the galls all summer, escape in autumn and fly to grass roots where they spend the winter. S.

▲ **Cabbage Aphid** *Brevicoryne brassicae* Aphididae. Cornicles short. Wingless forms green with mealy white coating. Abundant on brassicas in spring and early summer, causing severe damage. May remain active all year if mild.

▲ **Black Bean Aphid** *Aphis fabae* The familiar garden 'blackfly', with black or olive-green body. Passes winter as egg on spindle and a few other shrubs and spends summer on beans, sugar beet, docks, and many other herbaceous plants. There are several very similar species.

▲ **Peach-Potato Aphid** *Myzus persicae* Yellow or pale green: sometimes pink, especially the nymphs. Winged form has black patch on abdomen. Cornicles swollen in middle (lens!). Curls peach leaves in spring and then moves to a wide range of herbaceous plants, including potatoes, but does not form dense colonies. A major vector of virus diseases.

▲ **Rose-Grain Aphid** *Metopolophium dirhodum* Shiny green with a darker dorsal stripe. Overwinters as egg on roses. Aphids migrate to cereals and other grasses 5-6. Often swarm off the cereals in summer.

gall of
Baizongia
pistaciae

▲ **Rose Aphid** *Macrosiphum rosae* The gardener's 'greenfly'. Relatively large: green or pink. Long black cornicles distinguish it from other rose-inhabiting species. On roses in spring: scabious or teasel in summer.

▲ **Bird Cherry Aphid** *Rhopalosiphum padi* Wingless forms darker, with large rust-coloured patch at rear. Rolls bird cherry leaves in spring, when insects are clothed with white wax. On cereals and other grasses in summer: may remain there through winter if mild.

half natural size

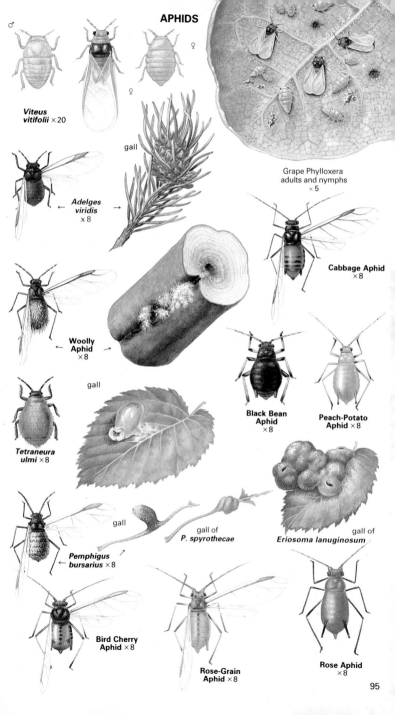

APHIDS

♂

♀

♀

Viteus vitifolii ×20

gall

Adelges viridis ×8 →

Grape Phylloxera adults and nymphs ×5

Cabbage Aphid ×8

← Woolly Aphid →
×8

Black Bean Aphid ×8

Peach-Potato Aphid ×8

gall

Tetraneura ulmi ×8

gall

Pemphigus bursarius ×8 →

gall of *P. spyrothecae*

gall of *Eriosoma lanuginosum*

Bird Cherry Aphid ×8

Rose-Grain Aphid ×8

Rose Aphid ×8

JUMPING PLANT LICE Also known as psyllids, these small homopterans resemble miniature cicadas. They leap well with the aid of their enlarged hind legs. Antennae are much longer than in the superficially similar leafhoppers (p. 92). Forewings relatively tough, with prominent veins: hindwings very flimsy. Nymphs are very flat and usually gregarious, secreting large amounts of honeydew and wax.

△ **Livia juncorum** Liviidae. The head is elongated in this family. Lives on rushes (*Juncus* spp) in damp meadows. Nymphs live in flowerheads and induce growth of red tassel-like galls in summer.

▲ **Homatoma ficus** Carsidaridae. Very flat, bristly antennae darken distinctly towards the tip. Veins hairy. On figs 6-8. S & C: introduced to B.

▲ **Apple Psyllid** *Psylla mali* Psyllidae. Abundant on apple trees 4-10. Green at first, becoming red and brown in late summer. Nymphs damage blossom and stunt young shoots by gregarious feeding. △ **P. buxi** has distinctly yellowish forewings and bright green or yellowish body. 4-9. Nymphs live in young shoot tips of box, causing leaves to cluster tightly together. The presence of this insect is usually marked by abundant white wax.

▲ **Psyllopsis fraxini**. One of several similar species living on ash. Nymphs cause leaves to curl and swell up to form red-veined galls. 5-10.

▲ **Trioza urticae** Triozidae. Wing membrane pale yellow. Body green to cream with dark markings. On stinging nettles in summer and evergreen trees in winter. There are several similar species.

WHITEFLIES Aleyrodidae. Tiny homopterans with waxy white wings spanning about 3mm. They resemble minute moths. There are numerous species, not easily separated although many are host-specific. They usually feed on the undersides of leaves.

Best known is the ▲ **Cabbage Whitefly** *Aleyrodes proletella*, common on brassicas in spring and summer. △ **Greenhouse Whitefly** *Trialeurodes vaporariorum* infests many greenhouse plants and is especially injurious to tomatoes and cucumbers.

SCALE INSECTS A large group of homopterans, belonging to several families, named for the waxy or horny scales under which most of the females live. Most females are wingless and legless and only the sap-sucking beak reveals their relationship to other bugs. In fact, these female scale insects don't really look like insects at all. A few, such as the mealy bugs, retain their legs and some mobility. Male scale insects have one pair of wings and resemble small midges, but they are rarely seen. Most species reproduce by parthenogenesis, and lifting a female scale may reveal hundreds of eggs. 1st instar nymphs wander freely, but then lose their legs and settle down to feed in one place. Because they exist in vast numbers, scale insects cause serious damage to crops, although they are less of a problem in Europe than in tropical areas.

Icerya purchasi and *Planococcus citri* are both citrus pests. ▲ **Mussel Scale** *Lepidosaphes ulmi* is abundant on the bark of apple and many other fruit trees. ▲ **Rose Scale** *Aulacaspis rosae* should be looked for on wild and cultivated roses, especially on the older parts. △ **Parthenolecanium corni** infests many cultivated trees and shrubs, including vines and currants, while △ **Pseudococcus longispinus** is a mealy bug found on a wide range of greenhouse plants.

Icerya purchasi
♀ × 2

Planococcus citri
♀ × 2

Mussel Scale
♂ × 20

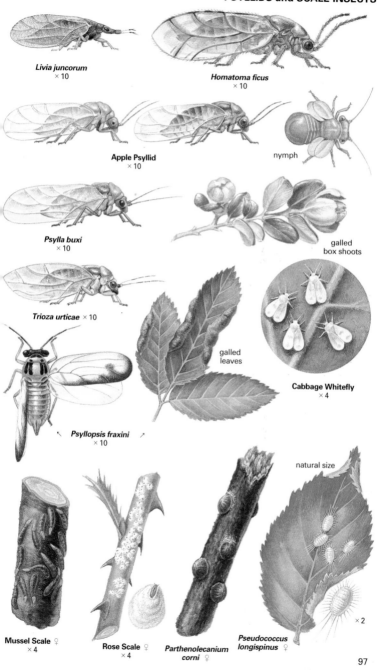

Livia juncorum
× 10

Homatoma ficus
× 10

Apple Psyllid
× 10

nymph

Psylla buxi
× 10

galled
box shoots

Trioza urticae × 10

galled
leaves

Cabbage Whitefly
× 4

Psyllopsis fraxini
× 10

natural size

Mussel Scale ♀
× 4

Rose Scale ♀
× 4

*Parthenolecanium
corni* ♀

*Pseudococcus
longispinus* ♀

× 2

97

PSOCIDS   Order Psocoptera

Very small, winged or wingless insects also known as booklice, barklice, and dustlice. There are about 2000 known species, but many thousands more undoubtedly await discovery. All have biting jaws and a rather wide head. Wings, when present, have a rather characteristic venation, although this is occasionally much reduced.

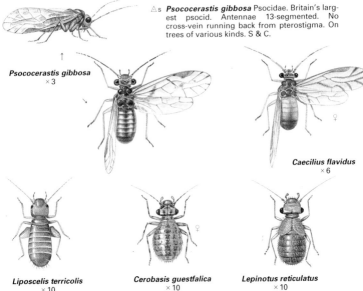

△s *Psococerastis gibbosa* Psocidae. Britain's largest psocid. Antennae 13-segmented. No cross-vein running back from pterostigma. On trees of various kinds. S & C.

Psococerastis gibbosa
× 3

Caecilius flavidus
× 6

Liposcelis terricolis
× 10

Cerobasis guestfalica
× 10

Lepinotus reticulatus
× 10

Two cells are of particular importance in classification: the pterostigma on the front edge of the forewing is generally semi-circular or lens-shaped, and the areola postica is a similar cell on the hind margin of the forewing. The areola postica is absent in some families. Wings are held roofwise over the body at rest, the insects then resembling the psyllids (p. 96) although the venation is quite different. Psyllids also have sucking beaks. Psocids are found mainly on shrubs and other vegetation, where they chew pollen, fungal spores, and bark-living algae. Many occur indoors, where they feed on a variety of starchy materials and cause some damage. Parthenogenesis is common, with males very rare or even absent in some species. Nymphal stages are similar to adults. Because of their small size, the psocids are not easy to identify, but those shown here are fairly distinctive and should be recognised without much trouble.

▲ *Caecilius flavidus* Caeciliidae. One of the commonest outdoor species, easily recognised by its yellow body and bristly wings. Antennae 13-segmented. No cross-vein running back from pterostigma. Males unknown. On broad-leaved trees, mainly on foliage.

▲ *Liposcelis terricolis* Liposcelidae. Widespread in buildings, often damaging books and paper, stored food, and also insect collections. Occasionally found out of doors. Antennae 15-segmented. One of several similar species with a flat body and broad hind femur with a distinct 'hump' near the base. A cosmopolitan pest. Males unknown.
    ▲ *L. bostrychophilus* is the commonest domestic species.

▲ *Cerobasis guestfalica* Trogiidae. A wingless species easily recognised by its densely speckled body. Antennae with more than 20 segments. Abundant on tree bark and fences: also in buildings. Males almost unknown.

▲ *Lepinotus reticulatus*. Forewings reduced to small flaps with dense reticulate pattern: hindwings absent. Antennae with more than 20 segments. A widespread domestic species, feeding on debris of all kinds. Will destroy insects collections.
    ▲ *L. patruelis* is similar but forewings not reticulate.

THRIPS   Order Thysanoptera

Minute, usually dark insects with very narrow body and usually two pairs of tiny, feather-like wings. Some are wingless. Very common in flowers, where many species pierce and scrape cells to get sap. Thousands take to the air in still, thundery weather – hence a common name of thunderflies. Most females have a curved, saw-like ovipositor for laying eggs in plants. Male abdomen usually smoothly rounded. Thrips are exopterygote insects, but nymphal development is complex, with one or more resting stages. Over 3000 species are known.

tip of abdomen of
Phlaeothripidae

down-curved ovipositor
of *Thripidae*

▲ **Phlaeothrips annulipes** Phlaeothripidae. Somewhat stouter than most thrips. As in whole family, abdomen is tubular at tip in both sexes and wings overlap strongly at rest. On dead birch twigs and branches (look at fire brooms in forests!), feeding on fungal spores and threads. 5-9.

Phlaeothrips annulipes × 10

Aeolothrips intermedius × 10

Aeolothrips albicinctus × 10

Aeolothrips intermedius Aeolothripidae. One of many species with banded wings. 5-9, mainly on yellow crucifer and composite flowers. In this family, wings are more or less parallel at rest, forewings rounded at tip, body not flattened, and ovipositor curved upwards. ▲ **A. albicinctus**, virtually wingless and antlike, is very common at bases of grasses 5-9. Possibly predatory.

▲ **Pea Thrips** *Kakothrips pisivorus* Thripidae. Relatively large, with yellow tarsi. Breeds in flowers of peas and related plants and damages young pods. 5-9.

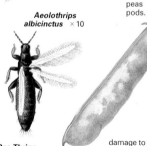

Pea Thrips × 10

damage to pea pod

Limothrips cerealium × 10

damage to wheat ear

▲ **Limothrips cerealium**. Breeds in cereal ears and emerges in swarms as grain ripens. Male 6-9: female all year, but hibernates – often in houses. Wings in this family are rather pointed at tip: body flattened: ovipositor curved downwards.

LICE

Columbicola claviformis × 10

Shaft Louse × 10

Philopterus passerinus × 10

Damalinia bovis × 10

Human Louse × 10   *Linognathus vituli* × 10   Hog Louse × 6

LICE Wingless parasites of birds and mammals, all strongly flattened and with strong claws to grip feathers and hair. Sometimes placed in a single order – the Phthiraptera – but mouth-parts are of two very different kinds and the insects are here regarded as belonging to two separate orders. Nymphs are very like adults, with virtually no metamorphosis.

BITING LICE Order Mallophaga Head quite large, with biting jaws: eyes and antennae generally very small. Prothorax distinct. Mainly on birds, feeding on flakes of skin and feather and also on blood from wounds. Longer-bodied species generally among longer plumage: short species generally on head and neck. Examine freshly-dead birds to find lice. There are many species, but most have strong host preferences.

▲ *Columbicola claviformis* Philopteridae. A common parasite of pigeons.

▲ *Philopterus passerinus*. One of several similar species infesting sparrows and other passerine birds.

▲ **Shaft Louse** *Menopon gallinae* Menoponidae. Less flattened than *Philopterus* and with less obvious antennae – more or less concealed in grooves. A very common cosmopolitan pest of poultry and other game birds.

▲ *Damalinia bovis* Trichodectidae. Antennae prominent and clearly 3-segmented. Tarsi 1-clawed. Widely distributed on cattle: closely related species on other hoofed mammals.

SUCKING LICE Order Anoplura Blood-sucking lice confined to mammalian hosts. Head very narrow and body pear-shaped. Prothorax indistinct.

▲ **Human Louse** *Pediculus humanus* Pediculidae. Eyes distinctly pigmented. Exists in 2 forms – head and body lice, of which latter is the larger (about 4mm long). Carries typhus fever, but unlikely to be a problem in hygienic conditions.

▲ *Linognathus vituli* Linognathidae. Eyes absent. Front legs smaller than others. A parasite of cattle. Related species on other hoofed mammals and also on dogs.

▲ **Hog Louse** *Haematopinus suis* Haematopinidae. All 3 pairs of legs equally developed. Eyes virtually absent. On pigs.

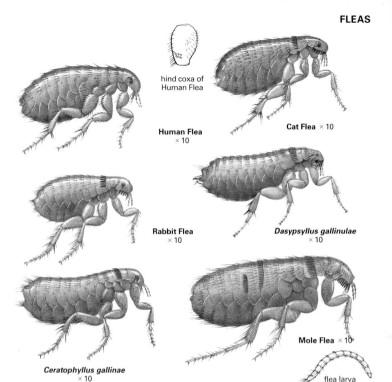

hind coxa of
Human Flea

Human Flea
× 10

Cat Flea × 10

Rabbit Flea
× 10

Dasypsyllus gallinulae
× 10

Ceratophyllus gallinae
× 10

Mole Flea × 10

flea larva

FLEAS   Order Siphonaptera

Wingless insects, strongly flattened from side to side and with enlarged hind legs for jumping. Generally dark brown or black. Adults all blood-suckers living on birds and mammals. Pearly white eggs are scattered in host nest, including sleeping quarters of domestic cats and dogs, and worm-like larvae feed there on debris, including droppings of adult fleas. Identification of fleas generally requires a microscope, and specimens should first be soaked in 10-20% caustic potash for a day or two: this makes them more transparent and easier to examine. The combs of strong bristles on head and thorax are important features. The illustrations are paler than living fleas to show up the bristles.

▲ **Human Flea** *Pulex irritans* Pulicidae. Small spines on inner side of hind coxa characterise this family. Front of head smoothly rounded. Cosmopolitan in dwellings: also on fox and badger, which may have been original host.

▲ **Cat Flea** *Ctenocephalides felis*. Distinguished from human flea by elongate head and strong genal and pronotal combs. The commonest household flea, often biting man.
△ **Dog Flea** *C. canis* has a more rounded head, with 1st spine of genal comb much shorter than 2nd. Much less common than cat flea in B.

▲ **Rabbit Flea** *Spilopsyllus cuniculi*. Antennal club symmetrical. Genal comb of 4-6 blunt spines. On rabbits, usually attached to ears: carrier of myxomatosis. S & C.

▲ *Dasypsyllus gallinulae* Ceratophyllidae. Distinguished from *Ceratophyllus* spp by many more bristles (3 rows) in front of antenna. Male readily identified by prominent spurs at rear. Abundant on small birds.

▲ *Ceratophyllus gallinae*. Pronotal comb with at least 24 spines: no genal comb. On a very wide range of birds, especially those with rather dry nests. Commonest bird flea in B: abundant in tit nest-boxes and a real pest in poultry houses.

▲ **Mole Flea** *Hystrichopsylla talpae* Hystrichopsyllidae. One of our largest species – up to 6mm long. On moles, shrews, and some small rodents.

ANT-LIONS, LACEWINGS, and ALLIES   Order Neuroptera

Soft-bodied holometabolous insects with wingspans ranging from about 3mm to more than 100mm. Wings are membranous, usually with a dense network of cross-veins that gives the order its name: Neuroptera means nerve-winged. Except in the alder flies (p. 108), the veins usually fork prominently at the wing margins. Flight is weak in most species and the wings are generally held roofwise over the body at rest. Antennae usually thread-like: sometimes moniliform (composed of bead-like segments) and occasionally toothed or clubbed. Compound eyes large, sometimes accompanied by 3 ocelli. Tarsi 5-segmented. Largely carnivorous, feeding mainly on other small insects, although some eat pollen and some hardly feed at all. Larvae are carnivorous or parasitic, with several species living in water. More than 6000 species are known, of which about 300 occur in Europe. The snake flies and alder flies are sometimes placed in a separate order – the Megaloptera.

ANT-LIONS Myrmeleonidae. Dragonfly-like insects with long narrow body and narrow wings spanning up to about 100mm in European species. Antennae short and stout, and always clubbed in European species. Males have prominent claspers at the rear. Flight slow and fluttery: mostly nocturnal or crepuscular and often coming to artificial light. Nocturnal species often take flight when disturbed by day. Difficult to see when resting among vegetation with wings pulled tightly back along the body. Mostly carnivorous, plucking small insects from plants, but some also nibble pollen. All like warm, dry areas.

The larvae prey on a wide range of spiders and small insects, which are captured with large jaws. Some larvae roam in soil and leaf litter: others construct pitfall traps in sandy soil. The pit is conical and the larva buries itself at the bottom. Insects blundering into the pit slither to the bottom, often helped by sand grains hurled by the ant-lion, and are grabbed by the large jaws. Ants are among the commonest victims – hence the name. There are 41 European species, mainly in the Mediterranean region. Only one occurs in B.

> **Dendroleon pantherinus.** Characteristic eye-spot on hind edge of forewing may be rather indistinct. Dry, open oakwoods with many old trees. 7-8. Larva lives in old leaf litter and makes no pit. S & C.
>
> **Myrmeleon formicarius.** Top of head black or brown. Wings clear. Dry, open places. 5-8. Larva makes pit in soil, rarely in leaf litter. One of the commonest European ant-lions, from southern Scandinavia southwards. **M. inconspicuus** has top of head yellow with brown spots. Wings clear, spanning 50-70mm. Veins dark with just a few clear spots (several similar species have pale veins with a few dark spots). Abdomen chequered. Open habitats, especially near the sea. 5-8. Larva makes pit in fine sand, especially on dunes and in stream banks. S & C.
>
> **Palpares libelluloides.** An unmistakable insect, flying mainly by day and often forming dense colonies on dunes, rough grassland, and rocky maquis (not too dense). Avoids the driest places. 5-9. Larva (p. 294) lives in soil and debris around vegetation but makes no pit: head protrudes from ground and larva rushes out to grab passing prey in its huge jaws. Mediterranean.
>
> △s **Euroleon nostras.** Both wings spotted, but hindwing has just a few small spots in front half. Several cross-veins between radius and media in basal part of hindwing (see below). Open woodland, but avoids driest places: sometimes flies with *M. formicarius.* 6-9. Baltic islands southwards, but very local. Larva makes small pit in bare ground. The only ant-lion in B, found on sand-dunes of East Anglia.

The hind wing helps to identify the smaller ant-lions. *Myrmeleon* and *Euroleon* (left) have several cross-veins between radius and media in basal region: *Creolon, Distoleon,* and *Macronemurus* (right) have just one such cross-vein.

ANT-LIONS

Myrmeleon inconspicuus

Dendroleon pantherinus

Myrmeleon formicarius

Palpares libelluloides ♂

Euroleon nostras ♀

larva and pit of *M. formicarius*

103

Creoleon lugdunensis
♂

**Distoleon
tetragrammicus**

Creoleon lugdunensis. Yellowish thorax with dark brown central stripe. Female abdomen does not extend beyond wings. Two branches of cubital vein in forewing run parallel to hind margin. Hindwing with just one cross-vein between radius and media in basal region (see p. 102). Common in rough grassland and rocky places 5-8. Larva lives in soil and debris, but makes no pit. SW, as far north as Loire Valley. *C. plumbeus* of SE is very similar.

Distoleon tetragrammicus. Conspicuously spotted, similar to *Eurolean nostras* but with only 1 cross-vein between radius and media in basal part of hindwing (see p. 102). 6-8 in dry oak and pine woods: local but sometimes abundant. Larvae lies in dry leaf litter and makes no pit. S & C.

Acanthaclisis baetica. One of our largest ant-lions. Wings virtually unspotted and with two rows of cells along front edge of forewing. 6-9, mostly on coastal dunes. Larva lives in sand but makes no pit. SW, as far north as Normandy.

Macronemurus appendiculatus. Thorax yellow with 3 brown stripes on top. Abdomen yellow and brown, extending beyond wings in male, who has very long claspers. Often swarms over roadsides and waste land and also among cereals and other crops. Larva lives in soil but makes no pit. S.

ASCALAPHIDS Ascalaphidae.
Fast-flying relatives of the ant-lions, generally shorter and stouter but with very long, clubbed antennae. Males have prominent claspers. Mostly diurnal, with fast undulating flight, commonly 2-3 metres above the ground. Capture flies and other small insects in flight. May bask on plants with wings open, as illustrated, in dull weather, but normally rest with wings folded roofwise over body. Larvae are like those of ant-lions, but make no pits. They live on the ground, among debris and under stones, often camouflaging their bodies with debris. Ascalaphids prefer warm, dry places and the 15 European species occur mainly in the south. None lives in B.

Libelloides longicornis. Black area at base of hindwing stops well short of anal angle. Yellow veins run through dark area of forewing. General venation pale yellow to deep gold. 6-8 in sunny meadows. SW (including southern Switzerland).
L. macaronius of eastern Europe is similar but base of forewing is yellow and there is a dark bar in the centre of the wing. **L. coccajus** has black area at base of hindwing extending almost or quite to anal angle, and no yellow veins in dark areas of forewing. Pale patches white or yellow, often deep yellow in Iberia. Dry, open woods and grassy areas (rarely far from trees). 4-7. S & C.

Puer maculatus. Forewing clear: hindwing densely spotted and sometimes almost black in distal part. Garrigue and rough grassland in summer. Almost confined to southern France: uncommon.

Deleproctophylla dusmeti. Forewing clear: hindwing with brown patch near tip. 6-8 in dry, grassy places. SW. (Insects found from Corsica eastwards have brown patch on all four wings and have recently been treated as a separate species – **D. australis**.)

Bubopsis agrioides. Wings very narrow: first 2 long veins very dark and forming a prominent streak near front edge of all wings. Active at dusk and most often seen at artificial light. 5-8, mainly in and around open woodland, especially pinewoods. SW.

ANT-LIONS and ASCALAPHIDS

Acanthaclisis baetica

Macronemurus appendiculatus

♂

Libelloides longicornis

L. coccajus

Puer maculatus

Deleproctophylla dusmeti

Bubopsis agrioides

Mantis Fly *Mantispa styriaca* Mantispidae. Resembles mantis but wings flimsy and insect more timid, feeding mainly on small flies. Active day and night in warm, dry places, especially light woodland with plenty of ground cover. 5-8. Larva enters egg cocoons of spiders, especially wolf spiders, and feeds on eggs. S & C. 4 other similar species in S.

Mantis Fly × 2

Nemoptera bipennis Nemopteridae. Easily recognised by ribbon-like hindwings and lazy, up-and-down flight. Dry, stony and grassy hillsides and coastal pinewoods. 4-8. Larva has long neck and lives on ground. Iberia only. There are 2 similar species in SE, *N. sinuata* being powder-blue with black markings.

▲ *Conwentzia psociformis* Coniopterygidae. One of many very similar small insects clothed with mealy white powder. Resembles a whitefly (p. 96) but rests with wings steeply roofwise. Common in many habitats 4-11 and often comes to lights at night. Larva eats aphids on trees.

▲ *Osmylus fulvicephalus* Osmylidae. Identified by large size and spotted wings. Streamside vegetation, especially in woods. 4-8. Larva hunts in wet moss and debris. Most of Europe but absent from much of N.

GREEN LACEWINGS Chrysopidae.
Long veins reduced, with one – the pseudomedia – almost straight and very prominent in centre of wing. Two zig-zag veins – the gradates – rise stair-like in outer part of wing. Generally green, but there are some brown species. Mainly nocturnal. Eggs on slender stalks (p. 294). Larvae (p. 294) mostly aphid-eating, some species camouflaging themselves with empty skins of victims.

▲ *Chrysopa perla* is bluish green, heavily marked with black. Deciduous woodland. 5-8.
▲ *C. pallens* is large and bright green with 7 tiny black spots on head. Woods, hedges, and gardens. 5-8. Larvae of both species naked.

▲ *Chrysoperla carnea* is pale green, becoming pinkish in autumn when it seeks hibernation sites in buildings. All kinds of well-vegetated habitats. Larva naked. There are several other pale green lacewings and accurate identification necessitates a detailed examination of the veins and the genitalia.

Chrysoperla carnea × 2

Chrysopa perla × 2

△ *Nothochrysa fulviceps* is large and brown, with central yellow band on thorax. Pseudomedia runs into inner gradate vein. Oakwoods. 6-9. S & C, but very rare in B, where *N. capitata*, with no pale thoracic stripe, is more common.

Italochrysa italica resembles *Nothochrysa* but, as in most other chrysopids, pseudomedia runs into outer gradate. Yellow-brown thorax with red-brown side stripes. Dry, well-vegetated areas. 6-9. Larva feeds on grubs in nests of the ant *Crematogaster scutellaris* (p. 234). S.

▲ *Sisyra fuscata* Sisyridae. The non-forking veins along front of wing distinguish this family from Hemerobiidae (p. 108). All-dark antennae separate *S. fuscata* from similar species. Streamside vegetation. 4-10. Larva feeds on sponges.

Dilar meridionalis Dilaridae. Recognised by pectinate antennae of male or long, slender ovipositor of female. Flies weakly at dusk. Lush vegetation, especially in woodland clearings. 6-9. Larvae live under bark. SW.

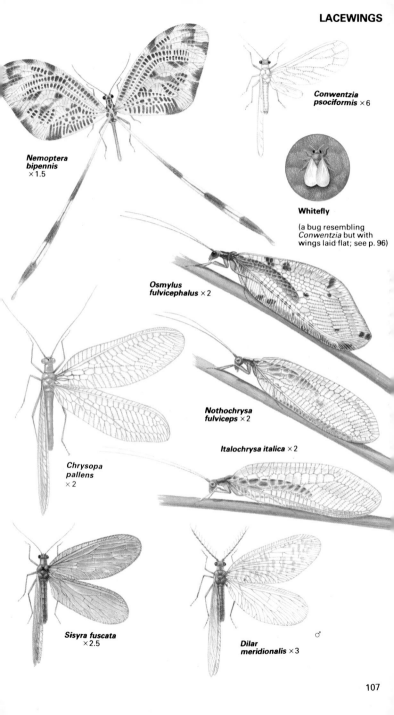

LACEWINGS

Conwentzia psociformis ×6

Nemoptera bipennis ×1.5

Whitefly

(a bug resembling *Conwentzia* but with wings laid flat; see p. 96)

Osmylus fulvicephalus ×2

Nothochrysa fulviceps ×2

Italochrysa italica ×2

Chrysopa pallens ×2

Sisyra fuscata ×2.5

Dilar meridionalis ×3

♂

BROWN LACEWINGS Hemerobiidae. A large family of mainly small greyish or brown insects. Distinguished from Chrysopidae by numerous long veins and from Sisyridae by the forked veins along front edge of wing. Larvae (p. 294) less bristly than chrysopids: mainly aphid-eating.

▲ **Wesmaelius quadrifasciatus** flies in dry, warm habitats, especially among conifers. 5-9. ▲ **Micromus variegatus** prefers low-growing vegetation and is common in gardens and hedgerows. 4-9. △ **Drepanepteryx phalaenoides** is immediately identified by its pointed and hooked wing-tips, but easily passed over as a dead leaf. It flies in light woodland with well-vegetated clearings. 4-10. N & C.

   ▲ **Hemerobius humulinus** is one of several very similar species. Forewing pattern varies. Abundant in hedgerows and deciduous woods 3-11.

▲ **Alder Fly** *Sialis lutaria* Sialidae. One of 6 very similar species in N & C. Veins not forked at margins. Flies near water, but spends much time resting on vegetation. 4-8. Eggs laid in batches on reeds and other waterside objects. Larva (p. 296) aquatic.

SNAKE FLIES Raphididae. Named for the long 'neck', on which the head can be raised way above the body. Mainly woodland insects and largely aphid-eating. Female with long ovipositor. Larvae (p. 294) eat various insects under bark and in dead wood. Several very similar species in Europe, differing in detailed wing venation and also in shape of head.

▲ **Phaeostigma notata** is associated mainly with oaks. Usually 2 cross-veins in pterostigma. 4-8. Larva in stumps of various trees, but mainly oak. N & C.
   △ **Subilla confinis** is smaller (c. 20mm wingspan), with only 1 cross-vein in pterostigma. Associated with pines. 5-7. S & C. ▲ **Atlantoraphidia maculicollis**, one of the commonest species, is confined to conifers. About the same size as *S. confinis*, but with narrower head. 1 cross-vein in pterostigma. 5-7. S & C: mainly western.

Inocellia crassicornis resembles the above but has no ocelli and no veins crossing pterostigma. Associated with conifers. 5-7. N & C.

Phaeostigma wing

Inocellia wing

SCORPION FLIES   Order Mecoptera

Named because male abdomen is often up-turned, but main diagnostic feature is downward extension of the head to form a stout beak. There are some 400 known species and about 30 – mostly *Panorpa* species – live in Europe. These fly weakly in shady places, eating mainly dead animal matter and fruit. They fly mainly 5-8, but there are two or more broods in S and may fly all year in Mediterranean area. Larvae (p. 294) are caterpillar-like. The species are often difficult to separate, especially the females.

▲ **Panorpa communis** is a typical species with fairly heavy spotting on wings.
   △ **P. germanica** is similar but spotting may be lighter, and absent altogether in N. Distinguished from *communis* by the parallel appendages on male abdomen (caliper-shaped in *communis*). △ **P. cognata** is slightly smaller and usually paler: 6th abdominal segment in male is square and appendages divergent. **P. alpina** of S & C has almost spotless wings but is best identified by the short subcostal vein.
P. rufostigma of SE has a red pterostigma. **P. meridionalis** is a heavily spotted species from Iberia and southern France.

Bittacus italicus Bittacidae. clings to vegetation with front legs and grabs small insects with its long back legs. Male has no up-turned tail. All four wings long and narrow. Shady places in spring and summer. S.

▲ **Snow Flea** *Boreus hyemalis* is flightless, with much reduced wings and no up-turned tail. Lives among mosses. 10-4: often seen hopping over snow.

P. alpina

P. rufostigma

P. meridionalis

Snow Flea

Wesmaelius quadrifasciatus
×2.5

Micromus variegatus
×2.5

Drepanepteryx phalaenoides
×2.5

Hemerobius humulinus
×3

Alder Fly
×2

P. notata

A. maculicollis

S. confinis

Phaeostigma notata
×2

Panorpa communis ×2
♂

Bittacus italicus
×1.5

view from above

P. communis

P. germanica

P. cognata

P. cognata
×2.5
♀

BUTTERFLIES and MOTHS   Order Lepidoptera

A very large order, with some 150,000 known species. About 5000 species occur in Europe and about half of these live in Britain. A few moths have wingless females, but the insects generally have two pairs of membranous wings clothed with minute scales. The scales provide the wing colour and pattern, but they are easily detached: touch the wings and you will find scales on your fingers. Insects that have been flying around for several weeks often look dull and worn as a result of losing many of their scales. Lepidopterans show little variation in general structure and are easily recognised as such, but they do exhibit a remarkable range of sizes. European species have wingspans ranging from 3mm to 150mm, and some tropical species exceed 300mm.

Adult **mouth-parts** are almost always in the form of a slender tube called the proboscis. They use this to drink nectar from flowers, and sometimes to suck up other fluids. When not in use, the proboscis is coiled neatly under the head. Many moths lack a functional proboscis and take no food in the adult state. Some of the more primitive moths, including the *Micropterix* species (p. 124) have retained biting jaws and feed on pollen.

The simple division of the order into **butterflies** and **moths** is an artificial split, based on simple observations and having no real scientific basis. There are about 25,000 known butterfly species and over 120,000 moths. No one feature separates all the butterflies from all the moths, and moth groups differ from each other just as much as they do from butterflies. Nevertheless, the butterfly/moth distinction is well established in the English language and unlikely to be abandoned.

Butterflies are day-flying insects, usually brightly coloured, generally resting with their wings brought together vertically above the body, and with clubbed antennae. Moths are generally nocturnal, rather dull in colour, hold their wings either flat or roofwise over the body at rest, and seldom have clubbed antennae. But there are exceptions: in Europe, the burnet moths (p. 134) are colourful and diurnal and have clubbed antennae – while some butterflies are quite drab. Most moth antennae are either hair-like or feathery, those of the male being more feathery than those of the female because the greater surface area helps him to pick up the female's scent more easily during courtship.

Many moths, including the burnets, also have a **frenulum** on the underside of the hindwing. This is a bristle springing from the 'shoulder' of the wing and running forward to be held in a small catch on the underside of the forewing. Its function is to link the wings together in flight. Only one butterfly – an Australian skipper – is known to have a frenulum. Butterflies generally link their wings together simply by means of a large overlap, and the same is true of those moths without frenula.

retaining hook on forewing

frenulum

front edge of hindwing

Underside of a moth's wings, showing how the frenulum connects them

The Lepidoptera are arranged in numerous **families**, based largely on wing-venation. This can sometimes be seen through the covering of scales, and one can usually make out a prominent cell (called the discal cell, or simply the cell) near the centre of the wing. But venation is of little use with living insects and one must rely on general appearance to assign them to their families. With a little practice, this is not difficult. Colour alone may be enough with the butterflies: predominantly white or yellow species belong to the **Pieridae** (p. 114), blue ones to the **Lycaenidae** (p. 122), and brown ones with eye-spots to the **Satyridae** (p. 120). Moths are a little more difficult, but many families have characteristic shapes. The **Noctuidae** (p. 156) are generally rather stout-bodied with drab brown or grey wings laid flat or held roof-like over the body at rest. The **Notodontidae** (p. 148) are similar but have a slightly different forewing venation. The **Geometridae** (p. 170) are rather flimsy and generally rest with their wings flat. Some members of the **Pyralidae** (p. 128) look like them but are distinguished by the hindwing venation. The presence or absence of tympanal 'ears' may also help to distinguish certain families. These membranes, when present, occur either at the rear of the thorax or at the front of the abdomen. At least some moths are known to be able to pick up bats' echolocation signals and to take avoiding action.

Venation of hindwing of pyralid (*left*) and (*right*) geometrid moths

Life Histories Among the butterflies the sexes are usually brought together initially by visual signals emanating during flight, although scent signals come into play during the later stages of courtship. Most moths rely entirely on scent, and this is why it is much easier to breed moths in captivity than butterflies, which need plenty of flying space. **Eggs** are usually laid on the appropriate food-plant, and a lens will reveal that many are exquisitely sculptured. Some species pass the winter in the egg stage, but most eggs hatch within a couple of weeks or so and the **larvae** or **caterpillars** start to feed. Almost all lepidopteran larvae are vegetarian, feeding on or in almost every kind of terrestrial plant and attacking every part from the root to the flower and seed, although most species feed on the leaves. Many are serious agricultural pests. A few, such as the wool-eating clothes moth larvae, feed on animal matter. Their natural habitats are the nests of birds and mammals, where they find plenty of fur or hair to eat.

The typical caterpillar has three pairs of true legs at the front and five pairs of stumpy or fleshy prolegs at the back. The last pair are known as claspers. All the prolegs are furnished with numerous minute hooks, with which the caterpillar keeps a firm hold on its food-plant. Some species have fewer than five pairs of prolegs. Geometrid larvae have only two pairs, including the claspers. They move by stretching out along a twig and taking a grip with the front legs, and then bringing the claspers right up behind them. In doing so, the body is arched up (see p. 176), and these caterpillars are commonly known as loopers.

After three or four moults the caterpillar is ready to turn into a **pupa** or **chrysalis**. Many moth larvae spin silken cocoons in which to pupate – usually among the leaves of the food-plants. Others burrow into the soil and make silk-lined chambers. Most butterfly larvae pupate naked on the food-plants, either hanging from the tail-end or held upright against a stem by a silken girdle. Many butterfly and moth species pass the winter in the chrysalis stage. Others overwinter as larvae, either completely quiescent (hibernating) or remaining active and feeding when conditions allow. A few species hibernate as adults.

A typical moth pupa

Butterfly pupae: suspended (*left*)
and (*right*) upright or succinct

Apollo

SWALLOWTAIL and APOLLO BUTTERFLIES Papilionidae.

Mostly large and brightly coloured butterflies, often with tails on the hindwings. Hind margin of hindwing generally concave. Antennal club generally rather slender. When disturbed, larvae stick out a colourful tuft – the osmeterium – just behind the head: a strong odour from this deters enemies. Pupae usually attached to food-plant in an upright position and secured by a silken belt.

Apollo *Parnassius apollo.* Colours vary slightly from place to place. A mountain butterfly, rarely below 700m except in north. 6-8. Flies lazily in sunshine: basks on flowers and stones. Larva on stonecrops and houseleeks: pupates in loose cocoon. Most European mountains. **Small Apollo** *P. phoebus* is similar but a little smaller and has a small red spot near front edge of forewing. It lives in the Alps, usually between 1500 and 2500m, where its larvae feed on saxifrages and houseleeks.

Clouded Apollo *P. mnemosyne* is like a Black-veined White (p. 114) but black spots and concave margin of hindwing distinguish it. Wings become almost transparent with age. Dark form only in female. As in all members of the genus, mated females have a large, horny pouch (the sphragis) below abdomen – secreted by male to prevent further mating by the female. 5-7. The larvae feed on *Corydalis*. Damp meadows in N: mountain pastures elsewhere.

△ **Common Swallowtail** *Papilio machaon.* 4-9 in open habitats with plenty of flowers. Single-brooded in N: 2 or 3 broods further south. First brood has less yellow dusting on black areas and a completely black abdomen: later broods have yellow abdomen with a black dorsal stripe. Larvae on wild carrot, fennel, and other umbellifers. All Europe, but only in Norfolk Broads in B. The British race can survive only in moist habitats, for the male genitalia are very sensitive to humidity and become hard and unable to function in drier climates.

Corsican Swallowtail *P. hospiton* is quite similar but the dark band on the underside of the forewing has distinctly wavy margins. Confined to Corsica and Sardinia and in some danger of extinction, it flies 5-7, mainly in upland areas.

Southern Swallowtail *P. alexanor* has no black patch at base of forewing but a prominent black stripe runs right across the basal part of both wings. It has a scattered distribution in southern Europe from Provence eastwards. 5-7.

Scarce Swallowtail *Iphiclides podalirius.* 3-9 in scrubby habitats, including orchards and gardens. 1 or 2 broods: spring insects pale yellow and summer ones almost white. Larva on blackthorn and various cultivated fruit trees. Common in S & C, despite its English name: absent from B other than as a vagrant.

Spanish Festoon *Zerynthia rumina.* Red spots in forewing cell: translucent 'window' near tip. 2-5 on rocky hillsides. Larva on birthworts (*Aristolochia* spp.). Iberia and southern France only. **Southern Festoon** *Z. polyxena* has no red spots in cell and no 'window'. 4-5. SE, overlapping with *rumina* in Provence.

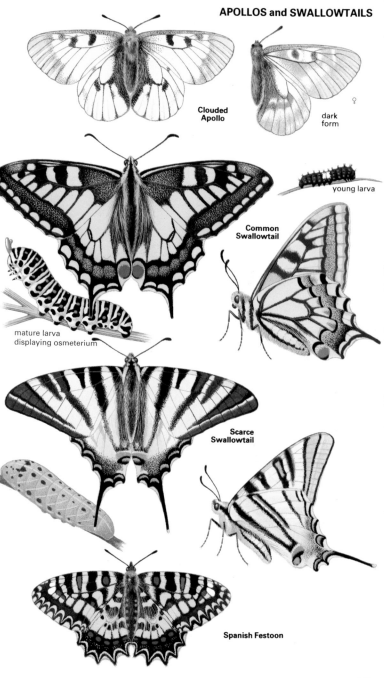

Clouded Apollo

dark form ♀

young larva

Common Swallowtail

mature larva displaying osmeterium

Scarce Swallowtail

Spanish Festoon

WHITE and YELLOW BUTTERFLIES Pieridae. A large family whose European members are basically white or yellow, often with black markings. Often marked differences between the sexes. Pupae are attached in an upright position on food-plant or other vertical surface and supported by a silken belt. The single point on the head distinguishes them from the pupae of all other butterfly families.

Small White

▲ **Small White** *Pieris rapae.* Male may lack spot on upper side of forewing: female has two spots. 3-10 in 2 or more broods. Dark markings much greyer in 1st brood. Open country and cultivated land everywhere. Larva on wild and cultivated brassicas: a serious pest. This and the next species have often been placed in the genus *Artogeia.*

▲ **Green-veined White** *P. napi* is easily identified by greenish black or grey lines along veins of underside of hindwing. Female has 2 spots on upperside of forewing: male has only 1. 3-10 in 2 or 3 broods. Open country and light woodland, often in damp areas. Larva resembles that of *rapae:* on various crucifers but rarely on cultivated forms.

Large White

Large White pupa

▲ **Large White** *P. brassicae.* Only female has black spots on upperside of forewing. 4-9 in 2 or 3 broods. Spring insects have greyer wing-tips. Hindwings range from white to deep yellow on underside, often dusted with greenish black scales. Larvae gregarious and serious pests of cultivated brassicas: also on nasturtiums and wild crucifers. Vast numbers of larvae destroyed by *Cotesia glomerata* (p. 230). Adults strongly migratory, with large numbers arriving in B from the continent each summer.

Black-veined White

Black-veined White *Aporia crataegi.* Veins black or dark brown. Wings thinly scaled, especially in female where brown membrane is clearly visible. 5-7 in open habitats, often at altitude. Larva on hawthorn and other rosaceous trees and shrubs: gregarious and hibernating in web when young. S & C.

Orange-tip

▲ **Orange-tip** *Anthocaris cardamines.* Only male has orange wing-tips. Female is distinguished from several similar species by rounded wing-tips with solid grey or black patch. 4-6 in flowery meadows, especially where damp: not uncommon in country gardens. Larva on cuckooflower and other crucifers, including garden honesty and sweet rocket.

Clouded Yellow

△ **Clouded Yellow** *Colias croceus.* Female generally like male but black borders contain yellow spots. About 10% of females are very pale (form *helice*). 4-10 with up to 3 broods. Flowery fields and hillsides. Larva on clovers and other legumes. Resident in S, spreading northwards each spring and reaching as far as southern Sweden. There are several similar species, some of them a good deal paler.

▲ **Brimstone** *Gonepteryx rhamni.* Male sulphur yellow: female greenish white. Both sexes very leaf-like at rest, showing pale yellow or green underside. 6-9 and again in spring after hibernation: one of the first butterflies to appear in spring in cooler regions. Light woodland, gardens, and open country. Larva on buckthorn and alder buckthorn, and possibly on other *Rhamnus* species. **G. cleopatra** is similar but male has large orange flush on upperside of forewing. S.

Brimstone ♀

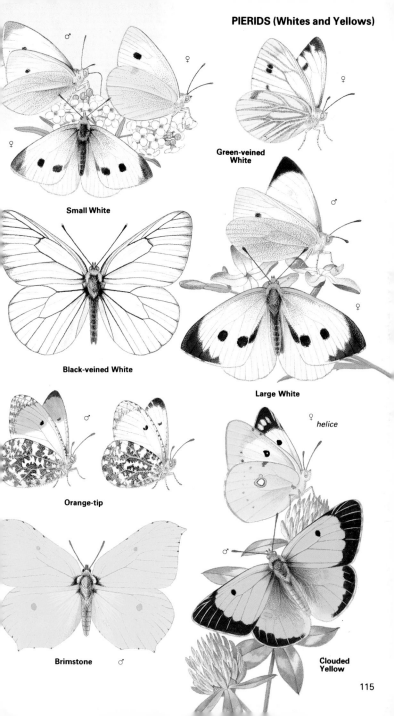

PIERIDS (Whites and Yellows)

Green-veined White

Small White

Black-veined White

Large White

Orange-tip

♀ *helice*

Brimstone ♂

Clouded Yellow

115

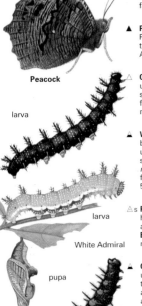

Nettle Tree Butterfly *Libythea celtis* Libytheidae. The only European member of its family, this butterfly is easily recognised by its wing pattern, its strongly toothed forewing, and its very long palps. Female has all three pairs of legs fully developed. Open and lightly-wooded country: 6-9 and again in early spring after hibernation. Larva is green with pink and white stripes and feeds on nettle tree (*Celtis australis*). S & C (southern and eastern).

Nettle Tree Butterfly

ADMIRALS, TORTOISESHELLS and kin Nymphalidae. A family of about 5,000 species, which also includes the fritillaries (p. 118). Upperside generally very colourful: underside commonly drab and cryptically coloured, especially in those species that hibernate as adults. Front legs much reduced and not used for walking. Larvae are generally spiny. Pupae often bear bright metallic spots and are suspended freely from food-plant or other support.

Two-tailed Pasha *Charaxes jasius*. 5-6 and 8-9. Fast-flying: commonly attracted to ripe fruit. Larva is green with yellow stripes, two eye-spots on the back, and reddish horns on the head. It feeds on strawberry tree (*Arbutus unedo*). S: rarely far from coast other than in Spain.

▲ **Peacock** *Inachis io* 6-9 and again in spring after hibernation. Flowery places, including gardens. Hibernates in hollow trees and buildings. Larva (left) feeds on stinging nettle. Absent from far north.

Peacock

△ **Camberwell Beauty** *Nymphalis antiopa* Underside similar to upperside, but duller and with less blue. 6-9 and again in spring after hibernation. Light woodland. Larva (bottom left) feeds on sallows and other trees. Most of Europe, sometimes migrating as far as North Cape, but a rare visitor to B.

larva

▲ **White Admiral** *Limenitis camilla* Velvety black when fresh, becoming browner with age. Two rows of black dots on underside of hindwing. 6-7 in woodland. Larva on honeysuckle. S (northern) and C. **Southern White Admiral** *L. reducta* has a conspicuous white spot near middle of forewing and only one row of black dots under hindwing. 5-10. S & C.

larva

△ s **Purple Emperor** *Apatura iris*. Female lacks purple sheen and has larger white markings. 7-8 in woodland, especially around oaks. Larva feeds on sallows. S & C. **Lesser Purple Emperor** *A. ilia* is smaller, with an orange-ringed dark spot near outer edge of forewing. 5-9. S & C.

White Admiral

▲ **Comma** *Polygonia c-album* Named for comma-like mark on underside of hindwing. Summer brood, flying 6-7, is paler than autumn brood shown here. Autumn brood flies 8-9 and again in spring after hibernation. Larva is black and white and resembles a bird-dropping. It feeds on nettle, elm, and hop. **Southern Comma** *P. egea* is less heavily marked, with 'comma' replaced by an indistinct 'v'. SE.

pupa

Camberwell Beauty larva

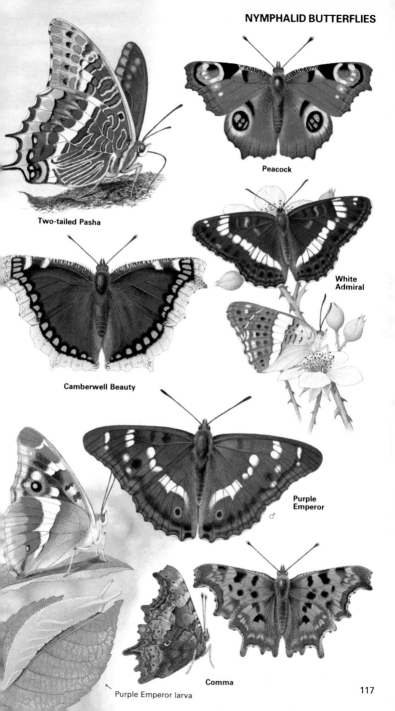

NYMPHALID BUTTERFLIES

Two-tailed Pasha

Peacock

White Admiral

Camberwell Beauty

Purple Emperor ♂

Comma

Purple Emperor larva

117

Painted Lady

Red Admiral

Map Butterfly

▲ **Painted Lady** *Vanessa cardui*. 3-10 in open, flowery places: very fond of thistles and various garden flowers. Larva mainly on thistles and burdock. Resident, if at all, only in extreme S, migrating northward each spring and producing a summer brood all over Europe. Some insects move south again in autumn.

▲ **Red Admiral** *Vanessa atalanta*. 3-10 in flowery places, especially gardens and woodland margins. Very fond of over-ripe fruit. Larva on nettles. Resident in S & C, including southern B in recent years, hibernating as adult and moving north in spring like Painted Lady.

Map Butterfly *Araschnia levana*. 4-9 in open woodland. 2 or 3 broods, with spring and summer insects markedly different. Larvae, black with brownish spines, feed gregariously on nettles. SW & C.

▲ **Small Tortoiseshell** *Aglais urticae*. 3-10 in gardens and other flowery places. Hibernates as adult: underside very dark for concealment. Larva on nettles: gregarious at first.
△ **Large Tortoiseshell** *Nymphalis polychloros* is larger and lacks deep black patch on hindwing. A rare visitor to B.

▲ **Dark Green Fritillary** *Argynnis aglaja*. All spots on underside of hindwing are silver. 6-8 in rough, flowery places – open grassland, woodland clearings, and moorland. Very fond of knapweed and scabious flowers. Larva is black and spiny with white stripe on back and red spots on sides. It feeds on violets.

Lesser Marbled Fritillary *Brenthis ino*. One of several rather similar species, but distinguished from most by the continuous heavy brown margins on upperside together with purplish brown band across underside of hindwing. 6-8 in damp meadows and open woodland. Larva on meadowsweet.

△ **Silver-washed Fritillary** *Argynnis paphia*. Male much brighter than female, with smaller black markings on upperside and black streaks (scent scales) on some forewing veins. 6-8 in woodland: very fond of bramble flowers. Larva, black and brown with yellow stripe and long brown spines, feeds on violets.

△ **Queen of Spain Fritillary** *Issoria lathonia* is instantly identified by the large and very shiny silver spots on the underside. 2-9 in rough, flowery places, with up to three broods: adults hibernate in S. Larva on violets. Most of Europe, with much northward migration in spring: rare visitor to B.

△ **Pearl-bordered Fritillary** *Clossiana euphrosyne*. Distinguished from several superficially similar species by silver marginal spots on underside of hindwing together with large silver spot in middle of the yellow band. 4-8 in open woodland. Larva, black and grey with yellow spines, feeds on violets.

△ **Marsh Fritillary** *Eurodryas aurinia*. Very variable, but always with a row of black dots in outer part of underside of hindwing. Female larger than male. 5-7 in rough, grassy places – not necessarily damp – with plenty of flowers: often on moorland. Larvae are black and spiny and feed in a communal web on plantains and scabious.

Queen of Spain Fritillary

larva

pupa

△s **Duke of Burgundy** *Hamearis lucina* Riodinidae. The only European member of its family. Often called Duke of Burgundy Fritillary because of its colour. Male front legs much reduced. 5-8 in light woodland and scrubby places. Larva on primrose and cowslip. S & C.

Duke of Burgundy

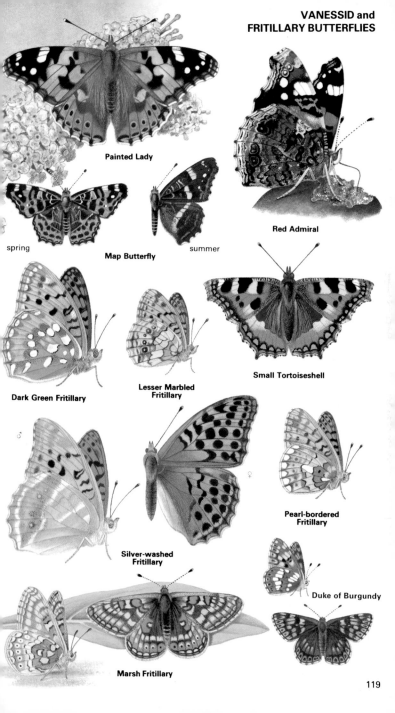

Painted Lady

Red Admiral

spring

Map Butterfly

summer

Dark Green Fritillary

Lesser Marbled Fritillary

Small Tortoiseshell

♂

♀

Pearl-bordered Fritillary

Silver-washed Fritillary

Duke of Burgundy

Marsh Fritillary

BROWN BUTTERFLIES Satyridae. A large family of predominantly brown butterflies characterised by prominent eye-spots (ocelli) near wing margins. The spots lure birds away from the head to the less-vulnerable wing-tips. Several veins are distinctly swollen near base. Sexes similar, but females often larger and somewhat paler: males often have dark patch of scent scales in middle of forewing, the scent being important in courtship. Front legs much reduced and brush-like in both sexes. Larvae all feed on grasses and are generally green or brown, with two prongs at the rear. Pupae either hang upside-down like nymphalids or lie in a flimsy cocoon in the turf.

Marbled
White

Grayling
↓

Speckled
Wood

Meadow
Brown

Scotch Argus

Wall Brown

▲ **Marbled White** *Melanargia galathea*. Pattern variable, often much darker in mountains. 6-8 in rough, grassy places: very fond of knapweed flowers. Larva has brown and green forms. S & C. **Western Marbled White** *M. occitanica* has a black line across cell in forewing and veins under hindwing are brown. 5-7. SW. There are several similar species in S.

▲ **Grayling** *Hipparchia semele*. Rather variable pattern: female has more extensive pale patches on upperside. 5-8 on heaths and dry grassland, usually resting on ground with wings closed and tilting over to reduce shadow. Absent from far north.

▲ **Ringlet** *Aphantopus hyperantus*. Upperside very dark brown in both sexes. Ocelli of upperside indistinct or absent in male, but always present in female. 6-8 in woodland margins and clearings, hedgerows, and scrubby places, especially where slightly damp. Larva like that of Grayling, but hairier.

▲ **Gatekeeper or Hedge Brown** *Pyronia tithonus*. 6-8 in hedgerows and open woodland, especially on bramble blossom. Larva like that of Grayling, but yellower and more hairy. S & C.

▲ **Small Heath** *Coenonympha pamphilus*. Upperside almost plain orange. 4-10 in grassy places and heathland everywhere. Normally rests on grass or ground, rarely on flowers, and never opens its wings. Larva like green form of Marbled White, but smaller.

Dryad *Minois dryas*. Eye-spots with blue pupils. Female paler, with larger eye-spots. Hindwings distinctly scalloped. 7-9 in open woods and scrub. Larva dirty yellow with darker lines and brown head. S (northern) & C.

▲ **Speckled Wood** *Pararge aegeria*. 3-10 in woodland clearings. Orange-spotted form (*P.a. aegeria*) occurs in SW and Italy and cream-spotted form (*P.a. tircis*) elsewhere, although the two grade into each other where they meet. Not in far north.

▲ **Meadow Brown** *Maniola jurtina*. Upperside of male with little, if any orange, but with dark patch of scent scales in middle of forewing. 6-9 in grassy places everywhere.

△n **Scotch Argus** *Erebia aethiops*. Size rather variable. Female paler and often with an extra eye-spot on forewing. Underside like upperside but hindwing has a greyish band containing 3 tiny white dots. 6-9 in damp grassland, mainly in uplands: often associated with conifers. C.

▲ **Wall Brown** *Lasiommata megera*. Female often paler and less heavily marked, without broad brown band of scent scales in middle of forewing. 3-9 in rough, grassy places, including roadsides. Basks on rocks and walls. Larva is pale green with white spots and lines. Absent from far north.

Great Banded Grayling *Brintesia circe*. Upperside very dark brown, with cream band crossing both wings and reaching hind edge of hindwing. Forewing with just one eye-spot (always blind on upperside). No eye-spots on upperside of hindwing. 6-8 in open woodland and on scrubby hillsides. Larva is brown with paler stripes on sides. S & C.

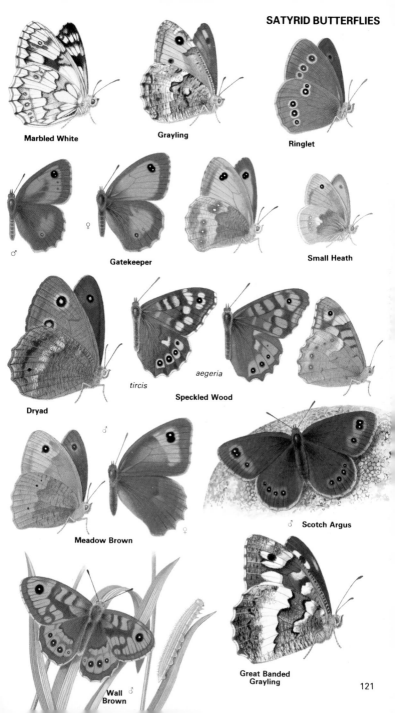

SATYRID BUTTERFLIES

Marbled White

Grayling

Ringlet

♂

♀

Gatekeeper

Small Heath

Dryad

tircis

aegeria

Speckled Wood

♂

♀

Meadow Brown

♂ **Scotch Argus**

Wall Brown ♂

Great Banded Grayling

121

HAIRSTREAKS, COPPERS and BLUES Lycaenidae. Relatively small butterflies, often brilliantly coloured in male: sexes often markedly different. Hairstreaks, named for the fine streaks on underside, have small 'tails' on hindwings. Larvae are short and squat, with legs concealed from above to give a slug-like or woodlouse-like appearance. Pupae attached upright to the food-plant or fixed to debris on the ground by a few strands of silk. There are about 100 species in Europe.

△ **Purple Hairstreak** *Quercusia quercus*. Male has purple sheen all over upper surface. 7-8 in oakwoods, often high in trees and feeding on honeydew. Larvae on oak. Absent from the far north.

△s **White-letter Hairstreak** *Satyrium w-album*. One of several similar species, but distinguished by plain upperside and conspicuous white W-shaped line on underside of hindwing. Female is paler, with no sex brand near front of forewing. 7-8, in and around woods: very fond of bramble blossom. Larva is yellowish green with a dark head and diagonal green stripes on sides: mainly on elm.

▲ **Green Hairstreak** *Callophrys rubi*. 3-7 in scrubby habitats, including woodland clearings, hedgerows, and damp heathland. Larva is bright green with oblique yellow stripes and feeds on gorse, broom, heathers, and many other shrubs.

Scarce Copper *Lycaena virgaureae*. Distinguished from several similar species by yellowish green underside. Male upperside may bear small black spots in mountainous areas. 7-8 in flowery places. Larva on docks.

▲ **Small Copper** *Lycaena phlaeas*. 3-11 in grassy and flowery places, including gardens. Larva on docks and sorrel. All Europe below 2000m.

▲ **Common Blue** *Polyommatus icarus*. Male distinguished from several rather similar species by distinctly violet tinge. Amount of blue on female very variable and often absent. 4-9 in flowery grasslands, including roadsides. Larva on legumes.

△s **Chalkhill Blue** *Lysandra coridon*. Silvery blue upperside distinguishes male from most other blues. Female is dull brown, with or without some blue scales near base. 7-8 on flowery chalk and limestone hillsides. Larva, green with yellow stripes and a black head, feeds on legumes – mainly horseshoe vetch. S & C. *L. hispana* of southern Europe is similar, but flies 4-5 and again 9.

▲ **Holly Blue** *Celastrina argiolus*. 4-5 and 7-9: females of summer brood with much more black than spring insect shown here. Open woods, gardens, parks, and hedgerows. Larva is yellowish green to brownish green with yellow and red markings. Summer larvae on holly and several other shrubs: autumn larvae on ivy: mainly in flowerheads.

Large Blue larvae are pink at first and feed on wild thyme flowers. They are taken into ant nests, where they receive ant grubs to eat in return for a sugary secretion eagerly lapped up by the adult ants.

△s **Large Blue** *Maculinea arion*. Greyish underside with blue flush at base distinguishes this from several similar species. Spots vary in size: generally larger in female. 6-7 on rough hillsides. Most of Europe but not far north.

SKIPPERS Hesperiidae. Small butterflies with rapid, darting flight. Antennae widely separated at base: club gradually thickens and often ends in hooked point. Larvae feed and pupate in silken shelters on food-plant. Only the Dingy Skipper occurs in Ireland.

▲ **Small Skipper** *Thymelicus sylvestris*. Male has dark stripe (sex brand) in centre of forewing. Wings held vertically above body when truly at rest but, like most skippers, when feeding or basking the wings are usually held as illustrated, with forewings partly raised and hindwings flat. 6-9 in grassy places. Larva, yellowish green with darker head, feeds on grasses. S & C. △s **Essex Skipper** *T. lineola* is similar but has black under tip of antennae instead of orange.

▲ **Dingy Skipper** *Erynnis tages*. 5-9 in rough, flowery places. Rests moth-like, with wings roof-like over body. Larva on various legumes. Absent from far north.

▲ **Large Skipper** *Ochlodes venatus*. Underside mottled orange. 6-9 in rough, grassy places, including roadsides and woodland clearings. Perches like Small Skipper. Larva on various grasses. Not in far north. △s **Silver-spotted Skipper** *Hesperia comma* has silvery spots on underside.

▲ **Grizzled Skipper** *Pyrgus malvae*. Distinguished from several similar species by clear row of small white spots in outer part of hindwing: underside never very green. 4-9 in flowery places: basks with wings almost flat. Larva, purplish brown above and green below, feeds on many low-growing herbs.

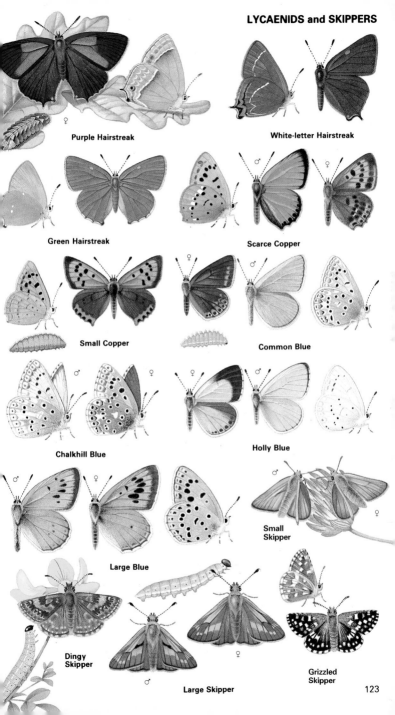

LYCAENIDS and SKIPPERS

Purple Hairstreak

♀

White-letter Hairstreak

Green Hairstreak

Scarce Copper

♂ ♀

Small Copper

♀ ♂

Common Blue

♂ ♀

Chalkhill Blue

♀ ♂

Holly Blue

♂ ♀

Large Blue

♂ ♀

Small Skipper

Dingy Skipper

♂ ♀

Large Skipper

Grizzled Skipper

123

△ **Micropterix mansuetella** Micropterigidae. One of several similar pollen-feeding moths with functional jaws. Hindwings purplish brown. Diurnal in damp places on flowers of sedges and marsh marigold. 5-6. Larvae live in leaf litter. N & C.
   ▲ *M. calthella*, common on buttercups, has golden head and unbanded wings.

▲ **Eriocrania semipurpurella** Eriocraniidae. One of several very similar day-flying moths with scattered bright blue scales on forewings. Swarms on birches 3-4. Larvae make blotch mines in young birch leaves, but pupate in soil. N & C.

▲ **Stigmella aurella** Nepticulidae. One of many very similar tiny moths with leaf-mining larvae. 1st antennal segment expanded to form pale orange cap over eye. 5-9, in 2 broods. Larvae make serpentine mines in bramble leaves, but escape before pupation. Most of Europe, but not in coldest regions because larvae overwinter in mines.

▲ **Tischeria marginea** Tischeriidae. Distinguished from several similar species by dark-edged forewings. All rest with front end raised and wing-tips pressed against surface. 4-8. Larvae make blotch mines in bramble leaves. Absent from far north.

△ **Nemophora degeerella** Incurvariidae. Male has longest antennae of all British moths: female antennae much shorter. Hindwings purplish brown. 4-6, fluttering slowly up and down at dusk. Usually in woodland. Larva feeds in leaf litter, living in a case made from small fragments.

▲ **Adela reaumurella**. Female antennae much shorter. Hindwings purplish brown. 4-6. Males swarm round trees and shrubs in sunshine, drifting slowly with antennae more or less vertical. Larva lives in leaf litter like *Nemophora*.

▲ **Incurvaria masculella**. Female antennae filamentous. 4-6: diurnal. Young larva mines leaves of hawthorn and other trees and shrubs, then makes itself a small leafy case and falls to ground to feed on dead leaves. S & C. ▲ *I. pectinea* is similar, but pale and with greyish head.

▲ **Lampronia rubiella**. Spots pale yellow or cream in varying patterns. 5-6. Larvae feed in central stalk of raspberry fruit in summer, overwinter in soil, and complete growth in buds in spring. ▲ *L. praeletella* flies 4-6. Larva mines near leaf-tip of strawberry in summer and then makes a small case for itself and continues to feed externally on the leaf. N & C.

▲ **Tapestry Moth** *Trichophaga tapetzella* Tineidae. Largest of the 'clothes moths', whose larvae feed on wool and other animal fibres, although this species does not do much damage to normal fabrics indoors. Its larva prefers coarser materials, such as horse hair, and is more often found in stables and other buildings with high humidity. Common in owl pellets, which may be its natural food. Adult 6-7.

▲ **Case-bearing Clothes Moth** *Tinea pellionella*. Hindwings quite dark. Larva lives and pupates in portable case made of silk and collected fibres. It eats a wide range of animal fibres and damages clothes, carpets, etc. Adult all year indoors: 6-10 out of doors, where it commonly breeds in birds' nests. It needs a relatively high humidity and is less common in houses with central heating.

▲ **Common Clothes Moth** *Tineola bisselliella*. Hindwings rather pale. All year in houses: rarely seen out of doors. Reluctant to fly, preferring to scuttle into crevices. Larva, white with a pale brown head, makes no portable case, although it builds a shelter of fibres. The commonest and most destructive clothes moth, attacking a wide range of woollen fabrics and furs.

▲ **Yponomeuta padella** Yponomeutidae. Forewings with light grey fringes: hindwings grey. Larvae feed communally in silken tents on hawthorn and blackthorn and also pupate in the tents. There are several similar species, some of which have pure white fringes. They are all known as small ermines.

▲ **Diamond-back Moth** *Plutella xylostella*. Named for row of pale diamonds appearing along back of male when wings are folded. Female forewing ± uniformly grey. 5-9. Larva, green with brown or black head, feeds on various crucifers and is often a serious pest of cultivated brassicas.

▲ **Ypsolopha dentella**. 7-8 in woods and hedgerows. Rests in characteristic pose resembling bud or twig. Larva feeds on honeysuckle.

Diamond-back Moth ♂ × 2

Yponomeuta padella × 2
with larval tent

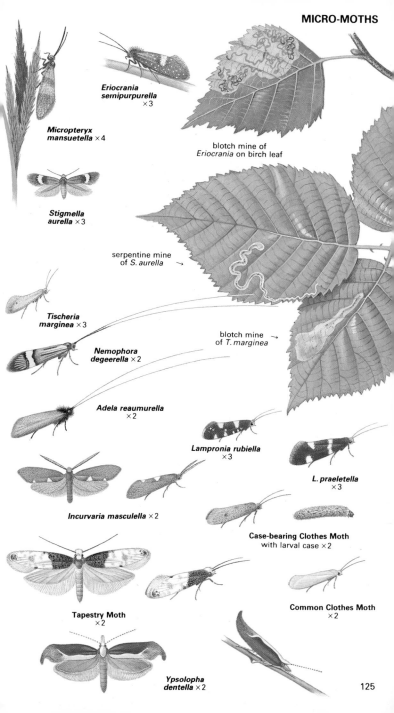

*Eriocrania
semipurpurella*
×3

*Micropteryx
mansuetella* ×4

blotch mine of
Eriocrania on birch leaf

*Stigmella
aurella* ×3

serpentine mine
of *S. aurella* →

*Tischeria
marginea* ×3

*Nemophora
degeerella* ×2

blotch mine →
of *T. marginea*

Adela reaumurella
×2

Lampronia rubiella
×3

L. praeletella
×3

Incurvaria masculella ×2

Case-bearing Clothes Moth
with larval case ×2

Tapestry Moth
×2

Common Clothes Moth
×2

*Ypsolopha
dentella* ×2

125

larva
cases

*Coleophora
caespititiella*
× 2

▲ *Coleophora caespititiella* Coleophoridae. Larval cases are abundant on seed heads of rushes. Each larva spins a silken case and remains in it until maturity. There are many similar species on other plants. Adults are all small and brown or cream, with pointed wings.

▲ *Depressaria pastinacella* Oecophoridae. One of many rather similar flattened moths. As in most members of the family, antennae have a tiny comb of hairs near base. 9-4, hibernating as adult. Grey with black spots, feed communally in silken webs on umbellifers.

▲ *Esperia sulphurella*. Day-flying in open woodland 5-7. Rests with antennae held forward. Pale grey larva feeds in dead wood. S & C.

▲ **Brown House Moth** *Hofmannophila pseudospretella*. 5-9 in and around buildings: one of the commonest household pests. Larva, white with a brown head, feeds on a wide range of stored foods, fabrics, and debris. Also breeds in old birds' nests.

▲ **White-shouldered House Moth** *Endrosis sarcitrella*. All year in buildings. Larva resembles that of previous species: also eats dried animal droppings in nests.

▲ *Carcina quercana*. Hindwings pale yellow with rosy apex. 7-8 in woods and hedges. Pale green larva feeds in silken envelope under leaves in spring. S & C.

▲ *Alabonia geoffrella*. Palps very long. Hindwings dingy brown. Day-flying, 5-6 in wooded areas. Larva, white with black dots, feeds in rotting wood. S & C.

Family Tortricidae. A large family of rather small moths with more or less rectangular forewings. Most hold wings roofwise over body at rest, many resembling bird droppings and leaf fragments. Hindwings usually greyish brown. Larvae generally live in folded or rolled leaves, but some tunnel in plants.

▲ **Pine Shoot Moth** *Rhyacionia buoliana*. Silvery markings often reduced. 6-9 in pinewoods. Reddish brown larva feeds on buds and shoots, causing much damage in plantations. ▲ *R. pinicolana* is similar but less orange.

▲ **Codlin Moth** *Cydia pomonella*. 5-10, wherever apples grow. Larva, cream at first and then pink or red, tunnels in apples and some other fruits, eating flesh and seeds: leaves fruit to pupate in bark crevices.

▲ *Pammene regiana*. 5-7 in wooded areas, including town parks. Usually high in trees. Larva, greyish white with a brown head, feeds on maple and sycamore. N & C.

▲ *Epiblema cynosbatella*. One of several very similar 'bird-dropping' species, distinguished by its yellow palps. 5-6 in gardens and hedgerows. Reddish brown larva lives in rose buds and shoots.

▲ *Acleris emargana*. Colours vary, but deep notch in forewing readily identifies this species. Falls to ground like a piece of leaf if disturbed. 6-9 in wooded areas. Green larva feeds in folded leaves of sallow and other trees. ▲ *A. literana* is easily identified by colour, although pattern varies. Woodland, 8-10 and again in spring after hibernation. Greyish green larva feeds on oak. ▲ *A. variegana* is very variable: black spots often absent from white patch. 7-9 in hedges and other rough places. Greenish larva feeds on roses and related shrubs.

▲ *Ancylis badiana*. 4-8 in rough grassy places. Greyish larva feeds on clovers and vetches, first as a leaf-miner and then in a pouch of folded leaves.

▲ *Hedya nubiferana*. Often much browner. 5-7 in hedges and other scrubby places. Larva, greenish with a black head, feeds on flowers and shoots of trees and shrubs.

△n *Philedonides lunana*. Male has slightly feathery antennae and greyer wings, with less obvious brown areas. 3-6 on heaths and moors. Greenish larva feeds on flowers and leaves of various plants. N & C.

▲ *Cacoecimorpha pronubana*. Day-flying 5-9 in gardens, hedgerows, and other scrubby habitats. Polyphagous larva is greyish green to brown.

▲ *Archips podana*. One of several similar species with prolonged wing-tips. Rests with wings fairly flat, like a dead leaf. 6-8, especially in gardens and orchards. Larva is greenish and feeds on leaves, buds, and fruits of apple.

▲ *Pandemis corylana*. Like *Archips* but without prolonged wing-tips. Hindwings never orange. 6-9 in woodland. Green larva feeds on many trees and shrubs. N & C.

▲ *Exapate congelatella*. Female has vestigial wings. 10-12 in woods and other scrubby places and moorlands. Light green larva feeds on various shrubs. N & C.

▲ **Green Oak Tortrix** *Tortrix viridana*. 5-8 on oaks. Larva feeds in buds and rolled leaves, often defoliating small trees in summer.

▲ *Croesia bergmanniana*. Amount of brown banding and spotting varies. 6-7 in hedgerows and gardens. Larva, greenish grey or yellowish, feeds on roses. N & C.

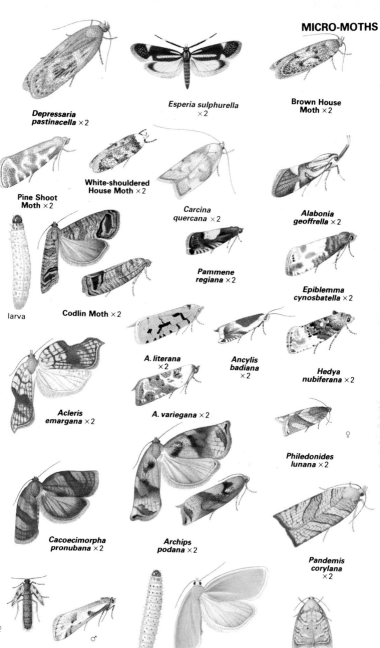

Depressaria pastinacella ×2

Esperia sulphurella ×2

Brown House Moth ×2

Pine Shoot Moth ×2

White-shouldered House Moth ×2

Carcina quercana ×2

Alabonia geoffrella ×2

Pammene regiana ×2

Epiblemma cynosbatella ×2

larva

Codlin Moth ×2

A. literana ×2

Ancylis badiana ×2

Hedya nubiferana ×2

Acleris emargana ×2

A. variegana ×2

♀

Philedonides lunana ×2

Cacoecimorpha pronubana ×2

Archips podana ×2

Pandemis corylana ×2

♀

Exapate congelatella ×2

♂

larva

Green Oak Tortrix ×2

Croesia bergmanniana ×2

127

Family Cochylidae. A family closely related to the Tortricidae (p. 126) but differing in details of wing venation.

▲ *Agapeta hamana*. Ground colour pale to deep yellow: markings pale to dark brown. 5-9 in rough grassy places in lowlands. Larva is greyish and feeds in roots of thistle.

▲ *A. zoegana* occasionally has orange ground colour. 4-9 in rough grassy places. Larva is pale yellow and feeds in roots of scabious and knapweeds.

▲ *Aethes cnicana*. One of several very similar species. Ground colour pale yellow to light brick. 5-8 in rough vegetation, especially where damp. Larva is pale yellow and feeds in stems and seed-heads of thistles.

▲ *Cochylis roseana*. 5-9 on rough ground and waste land. Larva is pale green with a brown head and feeds in seed-heads of teasel. N & C.

Family Pyralidae. A very large family whose members generally have rather narrow forewings. The two front veins in hindwing are fused for a short distance (see below). Tympanal organs present on abdomen. Legs are relatively long and spiky. Many of the larvae live in silken tubes or webs. Several are serious pests of crops and stored food.

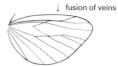

↓ fusion of veins

Venation of *Pyralid* hindwing

▲ *Crambus pratella*. Forewings generally paler in female. 5-9 in grassy places. One of many rather similar slender species, known as grass moths, that rest vertically on grasses, usually head-down with wings wrapped tightly around body. Larvae of all species live in silk tubes at base of grasses and chew the stems at or below ground level.

▲ *Catoptria pinella*. 6-9 in damp habitats, especially in or near woods. Larva feeds on cotton grass (a sedge) as well as on various true grasses.

▲ *Chrysoteuchia culmella*. Wings relatively short. 5-9. Abundant in grass everywhere.

▲ *Agriphila tristella*. Ground colour ranges from straw to deep brown, and central stripe from white to pale orange. 6-9 in grassy places everywhere.

Ancylolomia tentaculella. Female larger and brighter, with nearly white hindwings. 7-9 in grassy places. Larva lives in silken tunnel at base of grass. S & C.

▲ **Garden Pebble** *Evergestis forficalis*. 5-9 in hedges and cultivated land. Larva is greyish green with black and white spots and feeds on wild and cultivated brassicas, often drawing leaves together with silk to form a retreat.

▲ *Nymphula stagnata*. One of a group of moths known as 'china-mark', because their wing patterns are thought to resemble the markings under plates and other china articles. The markings vary in intensity and are sometimes absent. 6-8, usually near water. Larva, yellow or pale brown, feeds underwater on bur-reed and other aquatic plants, usually inside the stems at first.

▲ **Brown China-mark Moth** *Elophila nymphaeata*. 5-8, usually near still or slow-moving water. Larva is brown and hairy and lives underwater. It cuts pieces from leaves of pondweeds and other plants and sticks them together with silk to form a little case, in which it lives attached to the undersides of leaves.

▲ *Pyrausta purpuralis*. 5-8 in open grassy habitats. Larva, dull green with black spots, feeds on wild thyme and related labiates. ▲ **Mint Moth** *P. aurata* is similar but forewings have just one or two small golden spots: often on wild and cultivated mint.

Scoparia pyralella. One of many similar moths with a tuft of scales in centre of forewing. Markings vary from black to brown: occasionally much reduced. 5-7 in dry grassland, including dunes. Larva feeds on various roots at ground level.

△ **European Corn Borer** *Ostrinia nubilalis*. Male is pink to dark brown: female cream to brick-coloured, often bright yellow. 5-9 on cultivated land. Whitish larva tunnels in stems of many plants and causes much damage to stems and cobs of maize. Much of Europe, but a sporadic visitor to B.

▲ **Small Magpie** *Eurrhypara hortulata*. 6-8 in hedges and waste land. Larva, greenish white at first and then pinkish yellow, feeds in rolled leaf of stinging nettle and various labiates.

▲ *Phlyctaenia coronata*. 5-7 in hedgerows and woodland margins. Pale green larvae feed in silken web on elder. S & C.

▲ **Mother of Pearl** *Pleuroptya ruralis*. 6-8 in hedges and waste land, with slow, ghost-like flight. Pale green larva feeds in a rolled stinging nettle leaf.

▲ **Rush Veneer** *Nomophila noctuella*. Pale to dark brownish grey. 5-9 in grassy places. A strong migrant. Dirty green larva feeds on grasses, clovers, and other herbs.

MICRO-MOTHS: GRASS MOTHS and other PYRALIDS

Agapeta hamana ×2

A. zoegana ×2

Aethes cnicana ×2

Cochylis roseana ×2

Crambus pratella ×1.25

Catoptria pinella ×1.25

Chryso-teuchia culmella

Agriphila tristella

Ancylolomia tentaculella ×1.25

Garden Pebble

Nymphula stagnata ×1.25

Pyrausta purpuralis ×1.25

Scoparia pyralella ×2

larva in case

Brown China-mark Moth ×1.25

♂

♀

European Corn-borer ×1.25

larva

Small Magpie ×1.25

Mother of Pearl ×1.25

Phlyctaenia coronata ×1.25

Rush Veneer ×1.25

- ▲ **Gold Fringe** *Hypsopygia costalis*. 7-10 in and around hedges and grassy places. Rests with wings outstretched and pressed flat against surface, usually with abdomen pointing upwards. Larva is dirty white with a brown head and feeds on dead grasses, including stored hay and even roof thatch. S & C.

- ▲ **Orthopygia glaucinalis**. Often with a coppery sheen when fresh. 6-9. Larva lives in a silken web among dead grass and other plant material: often in old birds' nests. S & C.

- ▲ **Dioryctria abietella**. 6-8 in pinewoods, where it is very well camouflaged at rest on the pine trunks. Greyish larva feeds in pine cones and shoots.

- ▲ **Wax Moth** *Galleria mellonella*. Marked sex differences. 6-10 around apiaries and wild honey bee colonies. Larvae are pale grey and feed on honeycomb, rapidly chewing through the wax and destroying it. Once a serious pest in beehives, but now much less common.

- ▲ **Meal Moth** *Pyralis farinalis*. Forewings often tinged with purple. 5-9, usually in and around buildings. Rests with wings flat and abdomen often raised, rarely moving far when disturbed, even if touched. Larva lives in a silken tube and feeds on stored cereal products.

- ▲ **Myelois cribrella**. Easily confused with *Yponomeuta* species (p. 124), especially at rest, but distinguished by clear white fringe on hindwing. 6-8 in rough habitats where thistles grow, but easily overlooked at rest on shiny leaves. Larva is pale grey and feeds in seed-heads and stems of thistles.

- ▲ **Oncocera semirubella**. White streak often missing from front margin of forewing. 6-8 in grassy places. Larva is greenish black and feeds on white clovers and other legumes. S & C. Mainly on chalk in B.

- ▲ **Pempelia palumbella** flies 6-8 on heathland. Larva is greenish grey and feeds on heather, *Erica* species, and wild thyme.

PLUME MOTHS Pterophoridae. A small family, closely related to Pyralidae, in which the forewings are generally split into two feathery plumes and hindwings into three similar plumes. Wings are usually rolled around each other at rest and held at right angles to the body, forming a slender T. Legs are long and spiky and flight is rather weak.

- ▲ **Agdistis bennetii**. Wings not divided, although other features are just like those of typical plume moths. 5-9 in coastal areas, especially on salt marshes. Larva is green with a yellow line on each side and feeds on sea lavender. S & C.

- ▲ **Capperia britanniodactyla**. 6-8 on heathland, open woods, and scrubby grassland. Larva, yellowish green with brown dots, feeds on wood sage. S & C.

- ▲ **White Plume Moth** *Pterophorus pentadactylus*. The most familiar and unmistakable plume moth, flying 5-8 in hedgerows and on waste land. Attracted to light at night and often found on window panes. Larva is green and yellow, with tufts of hair, and feeds in a rolled leaf of hedge bindweed.

- ▲ **Platyptilia gonodactyla**. Ground colour and intensity of markings rather variable. 5-9 in rough habitats, including roadsides and railways. Larva, dirty white with black dots, feeds in leaves, flowers, and seed-heads of coltsfoot.

- ▲ **Many-plumed Moth** *Alucita hexadactyla* Alucitidae. Each wing is divided into 6 slender plumes. 7-10 and again 5-6 after hibernation as adult (occasionally seen on mild winter days). Hedgerows and woodland margins. Larva is pink and feeds in buds and leaves of honeysuckle.

   Thyris fenestrella Thyrididae. Clear membranous areas of wing (characteristic of this small genus) are larger in north of range. Abruptly narrowed abdomen is another generic characteristic. 5-8 in hedgerows and other scrubby habitats. Swift, darting flight in sunshine: often drinking from wet ground. Slightly hairy green larva feeds on *Clematis* species. S & C.

- ▲ **Horse Chestnut Leaf Miner** *Cameraria ohridella* Gracillariidae. This tiny moth, first discovered in SE Europe in the 1970s, has now spread to most parts of the continent. The forewing, about 4mm long, is light brown with 2 or 3 silvery cross-lines. 4-9, wherever there are white-flowered horse chestnut trees. The larvae tunnel through the leaves, causing irregular, pale blotches and there may be dozens of these on a single leaf. It is rare to find a horse chestnut tree that has not been affected and the foliage may be completely brown by the end of the summer. The red horse chestnut does not seem to be affected by this insect.

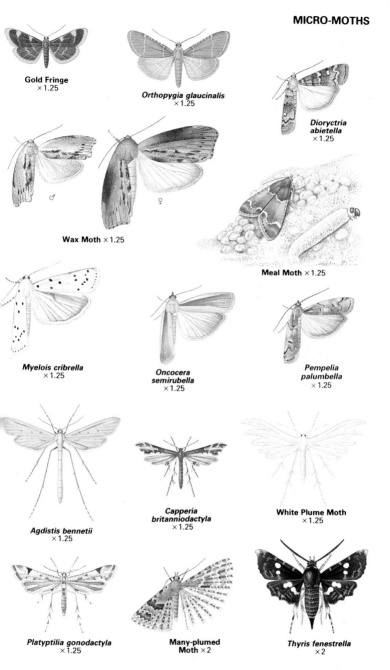

Gold Fringe
×1.25

Orthopygia glaucinalis
×1.25

Dioryctria abietella
×1.25

♂

♀

Wax Moth ×1.25

Meal Moth ×1.25

Myelois cribrella
×1.25

Oncocera semirubella
×1.25

Pempelia palumbella
×1.25

Agdistis bennetii
×1.25

Capperia britanniodactyla
×1.25

White Plume Moth
×1.25

Platyptilia gonodactyla
×1.25

Many-plumed Moth ×2

Thyris fenestrella
×2

SWIFT MOTHS Hepialidae. Moths with no proboscis and with very short antennae. Forewings and hindwings of similar shape, with no frenulum. At rest, wings are held tightly along sides of body. Flight is usually fast and darting, with rapid beating of wings. Females generally larger than males and less boldly marked. Eggs are scattered in flight and larvae feed underground on the roots of a wide variety of plants.

▲ **Ghost Swift** *Hepialus humuli*. Named for the ghost-like, hovering flight of male, which rises and falls slowly over the vegetation at dusk. The flashing of its pure white upperside attracts the yellowish female. Both sexes are dull brown below. 6-8 in grassland and arable land, especially where damp. Larvae (below) damage crop roots and are also harmful in forest nurseries. N & C.

▲ **Orange Swift** *H. sylvina*. Male forewing sometimes tinged with red: hindwing reddish brown. Female much larger and duller: hindwing greyish. 6-8 in open country. Absent from Ireland and SW.

▲ **Map-winged Swift** *H. fusconebulosa*. Forewing pattern very variable, but distinguished from other swift moths by chequered fringes on all wings. The form *gallicus*, found mainly in north, has no more than a white spot near middle of forewing. 5-8, mainly on heathland and woodland margins. Larva feeds mainly on bracken roots and rhizomes.

▲ **Common Swift** *H. lupulinus*. Variable forewings: markings often absent in female. Hindwings greyish brown. 5-8. Abundant in open habitats, including gardens and other cultivated land, where larva is often a pest. Adults commonly come to lighted windows. Absent from SW.

▲ **Gold Swift** *H. hecta*. Light spots often reduced. Hindwings dingy brown. Male with hovering flight. 6-8 on heathland and other bracken-covered habitats. Larva feeds on bracken roots and rhizomes. N & C.

▲ **Goat Moth** *Cossus cossus* Cossidae. A stout moth with conspicuously ringed abdomen. Hindwings same colour as forewings. 6-8. Larva is purplish and lives inside trunks of various broad-leaved trees. It takes two or more years to mature and then pupates in soil, leaving a strong smell of goat on the tree.

▲ **Leopard Moth** *Zeuzera pyrina*. Wings thinly scaled in outer part and almost transparent: pulled tightly to sides of body at rest, with abdomen protruding beyond them. Female much larger. Male antennae feathery in basal half. 6-8, often coming to lights. Common in orchards and town parks. Larva in broad-leaved trees and shrubs and can weaken trunks and branches of young trees. S & C.

Dyspessa ulula. Pattern variable: grey areas often very pale. 5-7 in well-drained places, usually on sandy soil. Larva in bulbs of wild and cultivated onions. S & C.

CLEARWING MOTHS Sesiidae. Day-flying, sun-loving moths whose wings lose most of their scales during first flight. Many mimic bees and wasps, often buzzing in flight. Usually rest with wings partly open. Larvae live inside roots and stems, usually for two years: pupa works its way partly out of stem before adult emerges.

▲ **Lunar Hornet Clearwing** *Sphecia bembeciformis*. Wasp-like, with black head and clear yellow collar. 6-7, usually in wooded areas, where larva feeds in willows and poplars. C.

△ **Hornet Clearwing** *Sesia apiformis*. Yellow head and two yellow patches on thorax, but no complete collar. Hornet-like in flight. 5-6. Larvae in roots and lower trunks of poplars, usually just under the bark.

△ **Welsh Clearwing** *Conopia scoliaeformis*. Brick-red tuft at tip of abdomen distinguishes this from most other clearwings. Named because first British specimen was found in Wales. 6-8. Larvae in birch trunks. N & C. ▲ **Red-belted Clearwing** *C. myopaeformis* sometimes has orange or yellow belt. 5-8, mainly in gardens and orchards. Larvae in apple and pear trees, especially old and weak ones. S & C. △ **Large Red-belted Clearwing** *Synanthedon culiciformis*, living in birch and alder trees, is very similar but has a red patch at the base of each forewing.

▲ **Currant Clearwing** *Synanthedon tipuliformis*. Tip of forewing tinged orange. Male usually has 4 yellow abdominal belts. Basks on leaves of currant bushes 5-8. Larva in stems of red and black currant, causing them to wilt and die.

△s **Fiery Clearwing** *Bembecia chrysidiformis*. Extensive red colour on forewing identifies this species. Usually 2 yellow belts: sometimes 3 in male. 5-7. Larvae in roots of docks. S & C.

larva of Ghost Swift

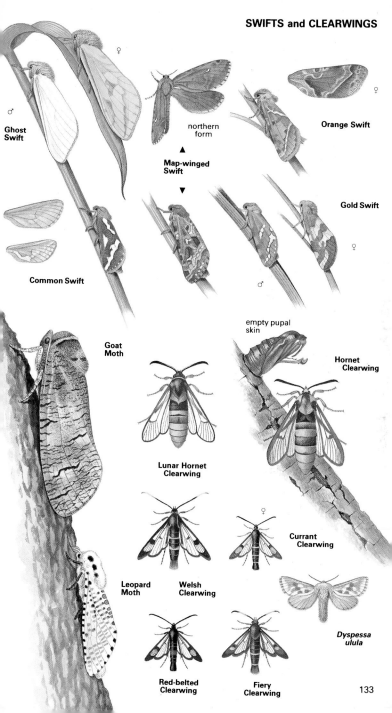

Ghost
Swift

♂
♀

northern
form

▲

Map-winged
Swift

▼

Orange Swift
♀

Common Swift

Gold Swift
♀

♂

Goat
Moth

empty pupal
skin

Hornet
Clearwing

Lunar Hornet
Clearwing

Currant
Clearwing
♀

Leopard
Moth

Welsh
Clearwing

*Dyspessa
ulula*

Red-belted
Clearwing

Fiery
Clearwing

133

Nine-spotted Moth *Syntomis phegea* Ctenuchidae. Day-flying, with weak, drifting flight. 6-7 in flowery habitats, including town gardens: often abundant in sunny valleys in southern Alps. Larva (left) feeds on various low-growing plants. S & C. One of several similar species. Although burnet-like, the family is unrelated to the burnets and is quite close to the tiger moths (p. 152-4).

Syntomis larva

Dysauxes ancilla. Spot pattern varies. Day-flying in scrubby places, especially south-facing slopes with scattered trees. Larvae feed on tree-trunk lichens. S & C.

Zygaena larva

BURNETS and FORESTERS Zygaenidae. Brightly coloured diurnal moths with slow, drifting flight, although wings beat quite rapidly. Generally lethargic and easily picked from flowers. Antennae slightly clubbed in burnets and toothed in foresters, especially in the males. Larvae are rather plump and usually pale with black spots (left), and the species are not easy to separate. Burnets pupate in papery cocoons, commonly attached to grass stems: foresters usually pupate low down in the vegetation. Pupa partly emerges from cocoon before adult escapes.

▲ **6-spot Burnet** *Zygaena filipendulae.* 6 red spots on each forewing, but outer 2 may fuse. Red occasionally replaced by yellow. Common in flowery grassland 5-8: strongly attracted to knapweed and scabious flowers. Larvae feeds on trefoils and other legumes.

▲ **5-spot Burnet** *Z. trifolii* has only one spot near wing-tip: central spots usually touching. Hindwing has thicker border than 6-spot Burnet. S & C.

△ **Transparent Burnet** *Z. purpuralis* exists in several forms, all with thinly-scaled wings and red stripes reaching nearly to tip of forewing. 6-8 in grassy areas. Larvae feed on various plants.

Z. osterodensis is similar but is more thickly scaled and hindwing has a broader margin. 6-7 in upland meadows. Less sluggish than most burnets. Larva is golden yellow and feeds on various low-growing plants.

Z. fausta often lacks the red belt. Abundant in rough grassy areas 5-9. Larva feeds on various low-growing plants. S & C.

Variable Burnet *Z. ephialtes* is extremely variable: red is replaced by yellow in *Z. e. coronillae* from Austria and northern Italy. Hindwings and all spots may also be red or yellow. 6-9 on scrubby hillsides, mainly in upland areas. Larva feeds on crown vetch and other legumes. S & C.

Z. lavanduli is easily recognised by its bluish-black hindwings and white collar. 4-6, usually resting head-down. Less fond of flowers than most burnets. Larva has red underside and feeds on *Dorycnium.* S.

Z. carniolica has white collar and white-ringed spots, and may have a red belt. 6-8 in scrubby habitats in upland areas. Larva is bluish green with black and yellow dots and feeds on various legumes. S & C.

Rhagades pruni. Forewings range from green to blue or brown. Male antennae are toothed right to the tip. 6-8 in scrubby places. Larva feeds on heathers and *Prunus* species. N, SE, & eastern parts of C, although the brown-winged, heather-feeding northern race *R.p. callunae* is sometimes treated as a separate species.

Aglaope infausta. Rather transparent. 6-8 in scrubby places but, unlike its relatives, it has no tongue and rarely visits flowers. Larva feeds on hawthorn, blackthorn, and other rosaceous shrubs. SW & SE.

△ **Common Forester** *Adscita statices.* One of several similar species, with male antennae toothed only in basal region. 5-7 in grassland: usually on flowers. Larva is pale green or yellow with a brown stripe on each side and hairy spots on back. It feeds on sorrel.

BAGWORMS Psychidae. A small family named for the larval habit of constructing cases of vegetable fragments held together with silk. The larva carries the case about as it feeds, and then fixes it to a leaf or other object before pupating inside it. Males often fly by day, but females are wingless and remain in their larval cases, where they mate and lay eggs. Neither sex feeds in adult state.

△ *Sterropterix fusca.* Male flies 6-8 in wooded areas, using feathery antennae to detect females in their cases. Nocturnal. Larva feeds on various trees. C.

▲ *Psyche casta.* 6-8 in rough grassy places. Males fly soon after daybreak, drifting lazily in search of females, whose cases are usually quite conspicuous on grass stems. Larvae feed on grasses and lichens.

BURNETS and BAGWORMS

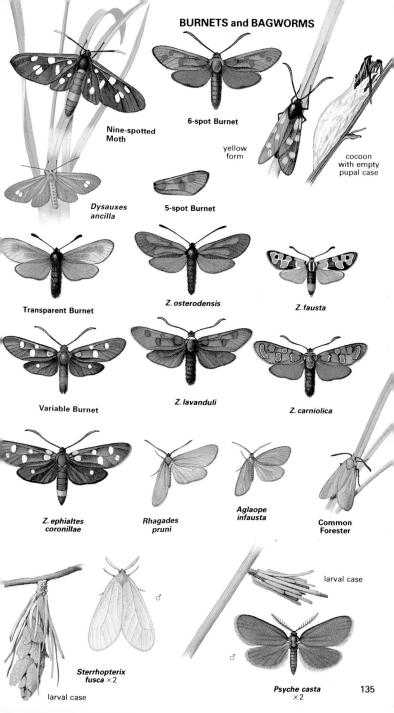

Nine-spotted Moth

6-spot Burnet

yellow form

Dysauxes ancilla

5-spot Burnet

cocoon with empty pupal case

Transparent Burnet

Z. osterodensis

Z. fausta

Variable Burnet

Z. lavanduli

Z. carniolica

Z. ephialtes coronillae

Rhagades pruni

Aglaope infausta

Common Forester

larval case

Sterrhopterix fusca ×2

larval case

Psyche casta ×2

135

EGGAR MOTHS Lasiocampidae. Mostly heavy-bodied moths with sombre colours – usually brown. Females considerably larger than males. No proboscis and no frenulum, the wings being linked merely by a large overlap. The larvae are stout and hairy and usually spin strong silken cocoons on the vegetation. The hairs commonly have irritating properties and the larvae should be handled with care. Several of the species pass the winter as hibernating larvae: most of the others overwinter in the egg stage.

▲   **Oak Eggar** *Lasiocampa quercus.* Hindwing resembles forewing. Male flies rapidly by day, but female flies and lays eggs at night. 4-9, mainly on heathland and other open country: sometimes in light woodland. The velvety larva feeds mainly on heather, bramble, and hawthorn.

△s **Grass Eggar** *L. trifolii* has uniformly brown hindwing, with white line often absent: cross-band may also be missing from forewing. Female usually paler, with less prominent white spot. 7-9 on heathland and rough grassland, including coastal dunes: largely nocturnal. Larva like that of Oak Eggar but blacker. It feeds on grasses and many other low-growing herbs and shrubs. Coastal in B.

▲   **Lappet** *Gastropacha quercifolia.* Varies from deep purple to pale brown, the latter most common in the south, where it can be confused with *G. populifolia*, although the latter has no obvious cross-lines. Female often twice as big as male. Rests with wings in unusual position, resembling a bunch of dead leaves. 5-8 in hedgerows and wooded areas, including orchards. The dark brownish grey larva has 2 bluish bands near the front and feeds on blackthorn and other rosaceous trees. It hibernates openly on the stems when still very small, but is very well camouflaged on the dark bark.

▲   **Drinker** *Euthrix potatoria.* 6-8 in grassy places, including roadsides, usually where damp. Named for larval habit of drinking from water droplets on leaves. Larva feeds on various tall grasses and pupates in a tough, yellowish, sausage-shaped cocoon.

▲   **Fox Moth** *Macrothylacia rubi.* Female much paler and usually greyer. 5-7. Males fly day and night: females only at night. Heaths, moors, open woodland, and hedgerows. Larva is velvety black or deep brown, with orange inter-segmental bands. Feeds on bramble, heather, and other low-growing shrubs, hibernating when fully grown and pupating in spring.

Pine Lappet *Dendrolimus pini.* Very variable: female forewing may be almost uniformly grey with just the central white spot. 5-9. Coniferous forests and plantations. Larva is greyish brown with 2 blue patches behind head. Feeds on pine and spruce.

▲   **Lackey** *Malacosoma neustria.* Ranges from pale buff to brick-red. 6-8 in woods and hedgerows: often common in gardens and orchards, and even town streets. Larva has 2 black spots on face and is remarkably large compared with adult. It lives communally for most of its life on hawthorn and many other trees. Less hairy than many of its relatives, it relies on its warning colours for protection. The species overwinters in neat batches of eggs on the twigs of the food-plant.

▲   **December Moth** *Poecilocampa populi.* Thinly-scaled wings. Flies 9-12, usually at dusk, in woods and hedgerows. In northern regions it may be on the wing as early as August. Larva is pale brown, heavily speckled with black.It feeds on a wide variety of deciduous trees. N & C.

▲   **Small Eggar** *Eriogaster lanestris.* Wings thinly scaled. Female, with much longer wings, has prominent tuft of grey hair at tip of abdomen. 2-4 in lightly wooded areas and especially in hedgerows. Larvae feed communally on blackthorn and hawthorn, forming dense silken tents. The species often spends 2 or 3 years in the pupal stage and has been known to take 7 years to emerge. Becoming scarce in B as a result of mechanical hedge-trimming in summer.

E. catax. Female much larger and mostly brown, with narrow yellow band across forewing and a large grey anal tuft. White spot prominent in forewing of both sexes. 9-11 in wooded and scrubby places. Larva is hairy, yellowish brown with velvety black and blue spots. It feeds communally in a silken web on hawthorn and many other trees and shrubs.

Lemonia dumi. Female lighter. 9-10 in open woodland, especially northern and montane coniferous forests. Males fly fast and erratically, like most of the family, and are largely diurnal: females fly at night. Larva, dark brown with yellowish brown hairs, feeds on dandelions and other low-growing herbs. N & C.

▲   **Pale Eggar** *Trichiura crataegi.* Sexes about same size, but female often more uniformly grey. 7-9 in wooded areas. Larva is dark grey or black, decorated with red and white. It feeds mainly on hawthorn and blackthorn. In southern and central Europe it overwinters in the egg stage, but further north, including parts of Scotland, it may have a 2-year life cycle, spending the first winter as an egg and the second as a larva.

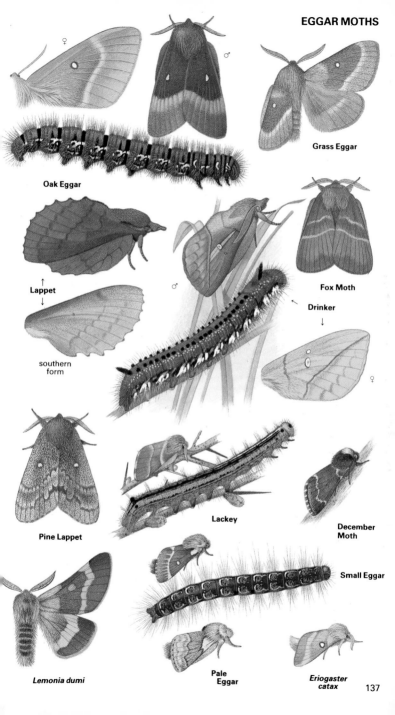

EGGAR MOTHS

Grass Eggar

Oak Eggar

Lappet

southern form

Fox Moth

Drinker

Pine Lappet

Lackey

December Moth

Small Eggar

Lemonia dumi

Pale Eggar

Eriogaster catax

137

Emperor Moth

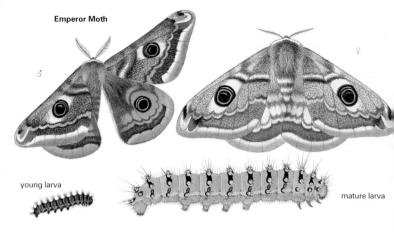

young larva

mature larva

Giant Peacock Moth *Saturnia pyri* Saturniidae. Europe's largest moth, with a wing-span up to 15cm. 4-6, both sexes flying at night and often mistaken for bats. Lacks proboscis, as do all members of the family. Larva starts off black with red or orange rings, becoming yellowish green with long clubbed spines and bands of blue warts. Feeds on ash, blackthorn, and various other trees. Spins a very fibrous cocoon. S, extending here and there into southern parts of C.

▲ **Emperor Moth** *Saturnia pavonia*. Male flies rapidly by day and can detect female up to 2km away. She flies and lays her eggs at night, but flight is weak. 4-6 on heathland and other open country. Larva, black and orange to start with, feeds on heather, bramble, blackthorn, and various other plants 5-7.

Tau Emperor *Aglia tau* Ranges from yellow to very dark brown. Female larger. Eye-spots vary in size: underside with eye-spots only on forewing. 3-6, male flying by day and female at night. Mainly in woodlands. Larva is pale green, with fine red spines in early stages, and feeds on various trees, especially birch, oak, and beech.

Kentish Glory

△n **Kentish Glory** *Endromis versicolora* Endromidae. Flies 3-5, associated with birches of moorland and open woodland. Does not feed. Bright green larva has a prominent hump at the rear. It feeds on various trees, but especially birch and alder. Widespread, but in B now confined to northern Scotland.

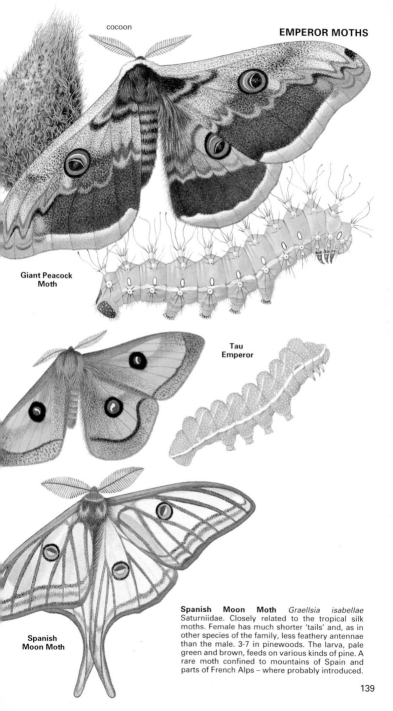

cocoon

Giant Peacock
Moth

Tau
Emperor

Spanish
Moon Moth

Spanish Moon Moth *Graellsia isabellae*
Saturniidae. Closely related to the tropical silk
moths. Female has much shorter 'tails' and, as in
other species of the family, less feathery antennae
than the male. 3-7 in pinewoods. The larva, pale
green and brown, feeds on various kinds of pine. A
rare moth confined to mountains of Spain and
parts of French Alps – where probably introduced.

HAWKMOTHS Sphingidae. Stout-bodied and generally fast-flying moths, mostly with narrow, pointed forewings. A few have broader, scalloped wings and fly more slowly. Most have a very long proboscis and feed while hovering at flowers, but some have no proboscis and do not feed at all as adults. The wings are commonly held flat and swept back like arrowheads at rest. Many species are strong migrants. The larvae often sport oblique stripes, which camouflage them remarkably well, but species feeding on low-growing plants are often protected by warning colours. There is often a marked colour change before pupation. Most caterpillars have a curved horn at the rear end.

Lime Hawkmoth *Mimas tiliae*. Ground colour of forewings ranges from greenish, through orange-brown, to buff. Pattern also varies. One of the slower fliers, it does not feed. The wings are spread rather widely at rest. 5-7. Larva feeds mainly on lime but also on other trees.

Poplar Hawkmoth *Laothoe populi*. Wings range from ash grey to pinkish brown. The moth flies relatively slowly and does not feed. There is no frenulum and the hindwing projects in front of forewing at rest. Orange spot on hindwing is concealed at rest, but exposed when disturbed, as in the Eyed Hawkmoth. 5-9 in 2 broods. Larva, sometimes blue-green, feeds on poplars, willows, and sallows.

△s **Pine Hawkmoth** *Hyloicus pinastri*. Hindwings dark grey. Especially fond of honeysuckle. Very well camouflaged at rest on tree trunks by day. 6-8. Larva feeds on pine and spruce needles. It is green with white stripes at first, when it rests among the needles. It becomes browner and rests on the twigs later. Pine and spruce forests throughout Europe, although absent from the native pine forests of Scotland.

Eyed Hawkmoth *Smerinthus ocellata*. Flies faster than Poplar Hawkmoth, but rests in the same way with hindwings projecting forward. The eye-spot on hindwing is exposed when the moth is disturbed, the body heaving up and down at the same time and scaring away inquisitive birds. Does not feed. 5-9 in 2 broods. Larva feeds on sallows and apple, almost always in an upside-down position.

Privet Hawkmoth *Sphinx ligustri*. Superficially similar to Convolvulus Hawkmoth (p. 142), but pink banding on hindwing easily distinguishes it: thorax also blacker and forewings much browner than Convolvulus Hawkmoth. At rest, wings are pulled back and held roofwise or tent-like over the body. 6-7. Larva feeds on privet, lilac, and ash, commonly in an upside-down position.

HAWKMOTHS

Lime Hawkmoth

Poplar Hawkmoth

Pine Hawkmoth

Eyed Hawkmoth

Privet Hawkmoth

△ **Convolvulus Hawkmoth** *Agrius convolvuli*. Grey thorax and speckled grey wings, with no pink on hindwings, distinguish this from Privet Hawkmoth (p. 140). It feeds on the wing, with a proboscis much longer than the body (the proboscis has a special sheath in the pupa, sticking out from the body like a jug handle). 6-11. Larva feeds on convolvulus leaves. Its ground colour may be apple green or purplish brown. A summer visitor to Europe from Africa, spreading to all parts but rare in N.

△ **Death's Head Hawkmoth** *Acherontia atropos*. The largest European hawkmoth, named for the skull-like pattern on the thorax. The proboscis is short and the moth, which is less streamlined than most other hawk-moths, settles to feed. It sometimes enters beehives to take honey. In the normal resting position, the wings are pulled back and held roofwise over the body. It squeaks when handled. 5-11. Larva feeds on potato and nightshades. It may be brown, green, or yellow. A summer visitor to Europe from Africa: sporadic in N, but more common in S, where it may survive the win-ter in the pupal state.

△ **Oleander Hawkmoth** *Daphnis nerii*. This unmistak-able moth flies 6-10. Larva feeds on oleander and peri-winkle, but is rarely found north of the Alps. Essentially a tropical and sub-tropical species, visiting Europe each year from Africa but not surviving the winter. Not uncommon in S, but only an occasional vagrant else-where.

△ **Spurge Hawkmoth** *Hyles euphorbiae*. Forewings are essentially greenish brown and buff, often with a clear pink tinge when freshly emerged. Resembles Bedstraw Hawkmoth, but hindwings are usually much pinker and there is no continuous brown band along the front edge of the forewing. 5-9 in 2 broods. The striking larva feeds on various spurges, especially the larger species. Common in S & C (southern): a rare summer visitor to N & B.

△ **Bedstraw Hawkmoth** *Hyles galii*. Resembles Spurge Hawkmoth in looks and habits, but can be distin-guished by the continuous broad brown band along the front edge of the forewing. The hindwing also has a less extensive pink flush. 5-9 in 2 broods. Larva is greenish, brown, or black, with large cream spots, and feeds on bedstraws and willowherbs. Resident in most of S & C: summer visitor to N and B (rare).

Spurge Hawkmoth hindwing

Bedstraw Hawkmoth hindwing

HAWKMOTHS

Convolvulus Hawkmoth

Spurge Hawkmoth

Death's Head Hawkmoth

Bedstraw Hawkmoth

Oleander Hawkmoth

143

△ **Silver-striped Hawkmoth** *Hippotion celerio* A very slim hawkmoth with prominent black veins on hindwing. The wings are swept strongly backwards at rest. 4-10 in 2 broods. Larva feeds on vines and bedstraws. When alarmed, the head and thorax can be pulled back into the abdomen, which swells up as in the Elephant Hawkmoth larva (p. 146) so that the eye-spots present a threatening appearance to any would-be predator. The larva becomes much darker just before pupation. A great migrant, it is a summer visitor to Europe from Africa. It occurs regularly, often in large numbers, in S, but appears sporadically further north – usually only in autumn.

△ **Striped Hawkmoth** *Hyles lineata*. This is the European race (ssp *livornica*) of a species that occurs almost throughout the sub-tropical and temperate regions of the world. The white veins on the forewing clearly distinguish it from the Bedstraw Hawkmoth and Spurge Hawkmoth (p. 142). 4-9 in 2 broods, often flying by day as well as by night. Larva varies from green to black, with yellow spots and lines. It feeds on a wide range of plants, but especially bedstraws and vines. Resident in Mediterranean region, this is a great migrant, reaching far into the north each summer, often in great numbers, although it is a scarce and irregular visitor to B.

Hyles vespertilio. Flies mainly in hilly regions. Mainly 6-7, but may be earlier in warm valleys and there may then be a second brood 8-9. Larva is green at first, but becomes greyish brown as it grows. Spots may be red or yellowish. There is no horn. It feeds on willowherbs, especially the slender-leaved *Epilobium rosmarinifolium*. Local in S & C, from France eastwards.

Hyles hippophaes. Resembles Bedstraw Hawkmoth (p. 142) but forewing is much darker. In addition, hindwing has a much broader pink patch and this is sometimes quite red. 6-7. Larva feeds on sea buckthorn, often basking on upper twigs. Local, from Spain and southern France through the Alps to Switzerland and southern Germany.

Hyles nicaea. Resembles Spurge Hawkmoth (p. 142), but larger and with no prominent white spot on the hindwing. 6-7. The unmistakable larva feeds mainly on spurges. Confined to the Mediterranean area and, unlike many other *Hyles* species, it does not make extensive migrations.

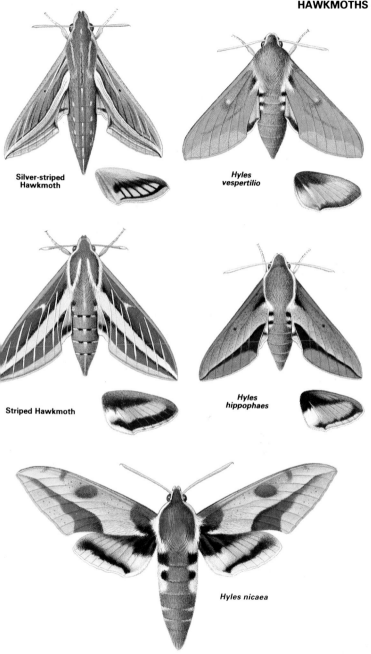

Silver-striped Hawkmoth

Hyles vespertilio

Striped Hawkmoth

Hyles hippophaes

Hyles nicaea

▲ **Elephant Hawkmoth** *Deilephila elpenor.* Bronzy green of forewing may become yellowish with age. Hindwing is pink and black. Often seen at honeysuckle at dusk. 5-7. The trunk-like snout of the caterpillar gives the insect its name. When disturbed, the snout is retracted into the eye-spot region, which swells up while the whole front end sways menacingly from side to side. The caterpillar is sometimes green. It feeds on willowherbs and bedstraws and occasionally on garden fuchsias.

▲ **Small Elephant Hawkmoth** *D. porcellus.* Smaller and much yellower than its larger relative: hindwing yellow with a pink margin. It feeds at dusk, especially at honeysuckle and rhododendrons. 5-7. Larva is green or brown, with no horn. It feeds mainly on bedstraws and behaves like the previous species.

△ s **Broad-bordered Bee Hawkmoth** *Hemaris fuciformis.* Day-flying. Resembles bumble bee at rest, but flight is much faster and more darting than bumble bee. Wings are lightly covered with scales at first, but most of the scales fall during first flight, leaving just the brown margins. Feeds in flight, especially at bugle flowers. 4-7, sometimes with a partial 2nd brood in late summer. Woodland clearings and margins. Larva feeds on bedstraws and honeysuckle.

△ **Narrow-bordered Bee Hawkmoth** *H. tityus.* Resembles the previous species but has narrower brown wing margins and a blacker abdominal belt. Day-flying, 5-6, in woodland clearings and margins, moors, and damp heaths and meadows. Larva feeds on devil's-bit scabious and field scabious.

Oak Hawkmoth *Marumba quercus* Less streamlined than most other hawkmoths and relatively slow-flying. Hindwings largely orange-brown. 5-7. Larva feeds on various oaks, especially cork oak. Confined largely to the cork oak forests of the Mediterranean region.

Proserpinus proserpina. Ground colour of forewings usually green, but may be brown or grey, always with a darker central band. Hindwings yellow with a brown margin. Size also varies: often much smaller than illustrated here. 6-8, often flying by day. Larva feeds on willowherbs and purple loosestrife. It is dull green at first and has a small horn at this stage. Mature larva has a prominent eye-spot on the rear in place of the horn. S & C (southern).

▲ **Hummingbird Hawkmoth** *Macroglossum stellatarum.* Day-flying and most often seen hovering in front of flowers to feed. Also 'sunbathes' by hovering in front of sunny walls. It makes an audible hum while hovering. Common in gardens. All year, especially in S, in 2 or more broods. Larva is green or brown and feeds on bedstraws. Resident in S, it is a strong migrant and reaches all parts of Europe in spring and summer. Hibernates as adult, but rarely survives the winter north of the Alps.

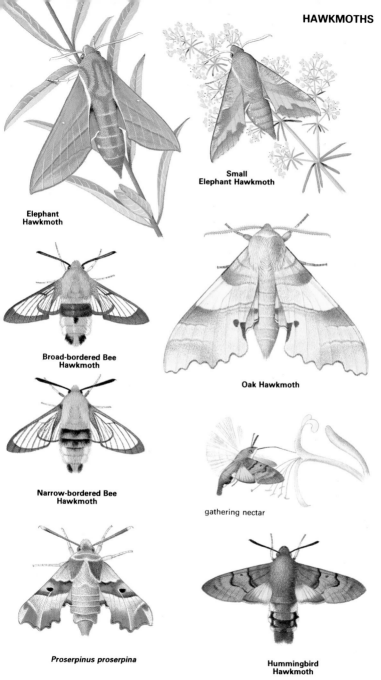

Elephant
Hawkmoth

Small
Elephant Hawkmoth

Broad-bordered Bee
Hawkmoth

Oak Hawkmoth

Narrow-bordered Bee
Hawkmoth

gathering nectar

Proserpinus proserpina

Hummingbird
Hawkmoth

Family Notodontidae. Rather stout and often hairy moths with sombre colouring. Resemble noctuids (p. 156-8) in many ways, but vein M_2 is not close to M_3 at base. Many are called prominents because the rear edge of the forewing has a tuft of hair that sticks up in the mid-line at rest. Larvae usually with little or no hair but often with fleshy growths on the back: often rest with front and hind ends raised.

forewing venation of Notodontidae

▲ **Puss Moth** *Cerura vinula*. Female slightly darker and more strongly marked. 4-7 in lightly wooded areas, including parks and gardens. Larva, green with a brownish saddle, is well camouflaged among leaves. It rears head if disturbed and waves highly modified, whip-like hind legs. Feeds on willows and poplars.

▲ **Poplar Kitten** *Furcula bifida*. Inner margin of dark band straight and edged with black: outer margin well defined and smoothly curved. Hindwing pale grey. 5-7 in lightly wooded areas, including town parks and gardens. Larvae like small Puss Moth larva. On poplars.

▲ **Sallow Kitten** *F. furcula* resembles *bifida* but has yellow inner edge to forewing band, with outer margin distinctly toothed. 5-8. Larva like that of *bifida* but with paler saddle. On sallows.

▲ **Alder Kitten** *F. bicuspis* has darker central band than the last two species, with both edges concave. 5-7. Larva like that of *furcula*: on alder and birch. N & C.

▲ **Lobster Moth** *Stauropus fagi*. Wings may be much darker or much greyer than shown here. 4-7 in woodland, especially beechwoods. Pinkish brown larva gives the species its name: it has long, slender front legs and an up-turned tail ending in filamentous claspers. Feeds mainly on beech.

▲ **Buff-tip** *Phalera bucephala*. Named for the buff wing-tips which, together with buff thoracic hairs, give the resting moth the appearance of a broken twig. 5-8, wherever there are trees and shrubs. Larvae, gregarious when young, feed on a wide range of deciduous trees and shrubs.

▲ **Chocolate-tip** *Clostera curtula*. Clear chocolate on wing-tip does not cross outer white line. 4-10 in 2 or 3 broods. Wooded areas. Larva is hairy: greyish blue with a broad yellow stripe on the back and orange spots on the sides. Feeds on poplar.

△ **Small Chocolate-tip** *C. pigra* is smaller and greyer, with indistinct chocolate tips. 4-10, with 2 broods in S. Fens and damp woodland. Larva is hairy: largely grey and yellow speckled with black. Feeds on sallows. N & C.

▲ **Iron Prominent** *Notodonta dromedarius*. Named for rust-coloured patches on forewing. 4-9 in lightly wooded areas. Larva is yellowish green to brown, with 5 slender humps on back. Feeds mainly on birch and alder. N & C.

▲ **Lesser Swallow Prominent** *Pheosia gnoma*. A distinct white wedge near rear edge of forewing. 5-9 in wooded areas. Larva is smooth and slender, purplish brown on top with yellow sides: a hump at the rear. Feeds on birch.

▲ **Swallow Prominent** *P. tremula* is larger and lacks conspicuous white wedge on forewing. Larva is green with a yellow stripe on each side. Feeds on poplar.

△s **Maple Prominent** *Ptilodontella cucullina*. 5-7, especially in hedgerows and woodland margins. Larva is glossy green with a pale line on each side and a purple hump at the rear. Feeds on field maple. C: mainly on chalk in B.

▲ **Great Prominent** *Peridea anceps*. Forewing brown to black: hindwing almost white. 4-7 in open woodland. Larva, pale green with pink and yellow diagonal stripes, feeds on oak.

▲ **Pebble Prominent** *Eligmodonta ziczac*. Named for the pebble-like blotch on wing-tip. 5-10, in 2 or 3 broods. Hedgerows and other wooded areas. Larva is greyish with a brown hind end: sometimes tinged pink or yellow: 2 humps near the middle and a third at the rear. Feeds on willows and poplars.

▲ **Coxcomb Prominent** *Ptilodon capucina*. Thorax normally has distinct crown of pale hair. Wings range from pale to very dark brown. 5-9 in 2 broods. Hedgerows and other wooded areas. Larva usually green with a yellow stripe on each side and a pair of red-tipped humps at the rear. Feeds on a wide range of deciduous trees.

▲ **Pale Prominent** *Pterostoma palpina*. Long palps project in front of head: very like a broken twig at rest. 5-8 in wooded areas. Larva is bluish green above and darker green below, with a yellow stripe on each side. Feeds on poplars and sallows.

▲ **Figure of Eight** *Diloba caeruleocephala*. Forewing bears clear figure 8. Hedgerows, woodland edges, and gardens. 9-10. Larva is bluish grey with black spots and yellow lines. Feeds on blackthorn, hawthorn, and other rosaceous trees.

Poplar Kitten

Sallow Kitten

Alder Kitten

Puss Moth

Buff-tip

Small Chocolate-tip

Chocolate-tip

Lobster Moth

Lesser Swallow Prominent

Swallow Prominent

Iron Prominent

Maple Prominent

Coxcomb Prominent

Pebble Prominent

Pale Prominent

Figure of Eight

Great Prominent

pinewood infested
by Pine Processionary larvae

Pine Processionary *Thaumetopoea pityocampa* Thaumetopoeidae. Hindwings white. Female much larger. In and around pinewoods 5-7. Larvae are dark, with tufts of brown hair, and they live communally in large silken tents on pine branches from autumn to spring. They march out to feed on the needles in single file – hence the common name. Feeding expeditions usually take place at night, but when the larvae are fully fed in late spring they march out by day to find suitable pupation sites. They may cluster on the ground for a while, as if deciding whether the conditions are right, and then they disperse to pupate singly in silken cocoons on or just under the ground. The larval hairs have very irritating properties and the caterpillars should not be handled. S & C (southern). A serious forest pest, sometimes so common that each tree bears several tents.

▲ **Oak Processionary** *T. processionea* has rather 'dirty' hindwings. Female is larger. 8-9, mainly in oakwoods, where the larvae live in silken tents on the trunks and larger branches in spring and early summer. They march in broader processions than the Pine Processionary when going out to feed on leaves at night and pupate communally in the tents. Their long hairs are extremely irritating. Although primarily associated with oaks, the species attacks several other broad-leaved trees. It has recently been spreading northwards from its original home in south and central Europe and is now established in southern England.

▲ **Pale Tussock** *Calliteara pudibunda* Lymantriidae. A very hairy moth flying 4-7 in wooded areas. Adults do not feed – a feature shared by the whole family. Striking larva, with dense white hair tufts like little shaving brushes, feeds on many deciduous trees. N & C. ▲ **Dark Tussock** *Dicallomera fascelina* is slightly smaller and darker, often with orange or yellow scales in the dark cross-lines. 7-8, mainly on heaths and moors.

▲ **Vapourer** *Orgyia antiqua*. Male flies by day. Female wingless, mating and laying eggs on or very near her cocoon. 6-10, with 2 or 3 broods, wherever there are trees and shrubs: often common in towns. Larva, easily identified by horn-like tufts of hair, feeds on a wide range of deciduous trees and shrubs.

▲ **Brown-tail** *Euproctis chrysorrhoea*. Wings usually pure white in both sexes. Abdomen largely brown above in male and greyish brown in female. Both sexes have tuft of brown hair at tip of abdomen: much larger in female, who uses hairs to cover eggs. It has been shown that, as well as concealing the eggs, the hairs provide active protection. The larvae in this family are clothed with irritating hairs, and these are incorporated in the silken cocoons when the insects pupate. On emerging from the cocoon, the new adult female collects some of the hairs with her abdominal brush and then uses them to protect her eggs. 7-8 in woods and hedgerows. Larvae live communally on blackthorn, hawthorn, and various other trees: sometimes an orchard pest. S & C.

▲ **Yellow-tail** *E. similis* has tuft of yellow or golden hair on abdomen. Male usually smaller and often with small black spot on hind edge of forewing. Wooded areas, especially hedgerows, 6-8. Larva feeds on hawthorn and many other deciduous trees and shrubs.

Gypsy Moth *Lymantria dispar* 7-9. Sexes markedly different: male flies by day but female is flightless. She covers eggs with blanket of yellow hairs from tuft at tip of abdomen. Larva feeds on many deciduous trees and is a serious forest and orchard pest. Most of Europe, but extinct in B, where it was reasonably common in the East Anglian fens until the mid-19th century. Occasional males cross the Channel and appear in southern counties. An asiatic race, whose females can fly, has recently become established in Germany and poses an even greater threat to forestry.

▲ **Black Arches** *L. monacha*. Female larger and rather sedentary. 7-9 in deciduous and coniferous woodland. Larva is grey and hairy with black spots and lines on the back. Feeds mainly on oak, but also on birch and various conifers.

♂ **Pine Processionary**   ♂ **Oak Processionary**

tent of Pine
Processionary larvae

♂   ♀

Vapourer

Pale Tussock

♂   ♀

Brown-tail

♂   ♀

♀

Yellow-tail

♂   ♀

Gypsy Moth

Black Arches   151

TIGER and ERMINE MOTHS Arctiidae. Stoutly-built, brightly coloured moths, usually hairy and often poisonous. The bold colours, especially on hindwings, warn birds of the unpalatability of these moths, although forewings often have cryptic patterns. The larvae are very hairy – many are known as woolly bears – and usually fed on docks, dandelions, and other low-growing plants. The family also contains the slender-bodied footmen (p. 154).

▲ **Garden Tiger** *Arctia caja*. Pattern very variable on all wings: forewing occasionally all brown and hindwing sometimes yellow instead of orange. 6-8 in almost any habitat.

▲ **Cream-spot Tiger** *A.villica* has cream or white spots on forewing, sometimes running together and occasionally much reduced. The black thorax with white sides is characteristic. 5-7 in scrubby and grassy places. Larva like that of *caja* but has chestnut head and shorter hair. S & C.

△s **Jersey Tiger** *Euplagia quadripunctaria*. 6-9 in open woodland and scrub, usually fairly dry. Flies in sunshine as well as by night. Roosts in vegetation in dull weather, sometimes in vast numbers as in the 'Valley of Butterflies' on the island of Rhodes. Larva is black with a broad yellow stripe on the back and pale spots on the sides. S & C: confined to Devon in B, but common in Channel Islands.

△ s **Scarlet Tiger** *Callimorpha dominula*. Markings vary: yellow occasionally replaces the red. Flies in sunshine 6-8. Fens, riverbanks, and damp woodland. Larva is dark grey with broken yellow lines and grey and black hair. Feeds on bramble, sallow, and other shrubs as well as on herbaceous plants.

▲ **Wood Tiger** *Parasemia plantaginis*. Pattern and colour vary: hindwing sometimes with red spots but may be completely brown, especially in mountains. Pale marks on forewing may also be reduced. Sides of abdomen yellow in male. Heaths, moors, woodland clearings, and other grassy places. 6-8, flying by day and night. Larva is black with short tufts of black and chestnut hair. N & C.

Pericallia matronula. Spots vary in size: those of hindwing separate or joined into a band. 5-7 in many habitats, often flying by day. Larva is dark brown or black with long brown hairs: polyphagous, taking 2 years to mature. Widely distributed in E. Europe, reaching eastern France.

Ammobiota festiva. Pattern very variable. Female usually has fewer and narrower pale bands and brighter hindwings. Less vivid and often just pink and grey in northern parts of range. 5-6, often flying by day, in dry grassy and scrubby habitats. Larva, very like that of Garden Tiger, is polyphagous on low-growing plants. S & C.

▲ **Ruby Tiger** *Phragmatobia fuliginosa*. Forewings reddish brown to dark brown, rather thinly scaled in centre. Hindwings largely grey in north: elsewhere largely pink. 5-9, with 2 broods in many areas. All kinds of habitats, but most common in damp grassland. Larva is dark brown and densely hairy.

P. maculosa has variable spot pattern, often much fainter than shown here. Hindwing darker red in female. 6-8 in rough, grassy places. Larva, velvety black with short brown hair, feeds on bedstraws. S & C.

Fall Webworm *Hyphantria cunea* Sometimes pure white, sometimes black-spotted. 7-8. Larva is yellowish green with black and orange warts and white hair. Lives communally in silken tent on various deciduous trees in autumn: a pest of fruit trees. An American species now established in Germany and some other parts of Europe.

Cymbalophora pudica. Forewing ground colour ranges from white to deep pink. 8-10 in scrubby and grassy places. Larva, greyish brown with short hair, feeds on various grasses. S: often abundant on Mediterranean coast.

▲ **White Ermine** *Spilosoma lubricipeda*. Black spots vary in size: occasionally absent. Abdomen yellow. 5-8 in gardens and many other habitats. Larva is dark brown and very hairy, with a thin red line along the back. It feeds on a wide range of low-growing plants.

▲ **Buff Ermine** *S. lutea* has variable pattern on cream to deep yellow wings. Habits like those of White Ermine but larva is paler brown, with no red line.

▲ **Muslin** *Diaphora mendica*. Sexes markedly different: female thinly scaled, with variable amount of black spotting and a white abdomen. 5-6 in hedgerows and open woodland. Male nocturnal, but female largely diurnal. Larva like that of Buff Ermine, feeding on low-growing vegetation. N & C.

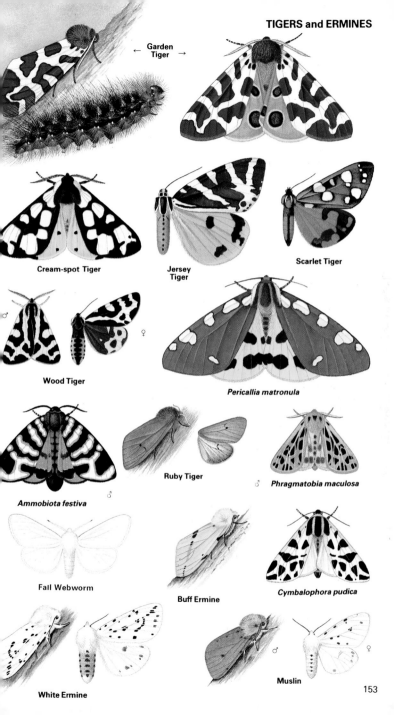

TIGERS and ERMINES

← Garden Tiger →

Cream-spot Tiger

Jersey Tiger

Scarlet Tiger

Wood Tiger   ♂   ♀

Pericallia matronula

Ammobiota festiva   ♂

Ruby Tiger

♂   *Phragmatobia maculosa*

Fall Webworm

Buff Ermine

Cymbalophora pudica

White Ermine

♂   **Muslin**   ♀

153

Rhyparia purpurata. Spots vary in size and may run together, especially on hindwing. 6-7 in well-drained areas, sometimes flying by day. Larva is dark grey with velvety black rings and grey and rust-coloured hairs. It feeds on a wide range of herbs and shrubs, especially *Genista* species. Most of Europe.

▲ **Clouded Buff** *Diacrisia sannio*. Sexes markedly different: amount of grey on male hindwing very variable. 4-8 on heaths, moors, and grassland. Male flies by night and day: female largely nocturnal. Larva is brown with a pale stripe along the back and clothed with brown hair. It feeds on a wide range of herbs and low-growing shrubs.

▲ **Cinnabar** *Tyria jacobaeae*. 5-8 in open habitats, mainly on sandy soils and other well-drained soils. Largely nocturnal, but often seen fluttering weakly by day. Larva feeds on ragwort. Widespread, but mainly coastal in north.

△ **Crimson Speckled** *Utetheisa pulchella*. Day-flying, 4-10, with 2 or 3 broods in south. Open and scrubby habitats. Hairy larva is greyish with white lines and black warts, and an orange band on each segment. It feeds mainly on forget-me-not and borage. Resident in S, migrating to C each spring: sporadic visitor to B.

Feathered Footman *Spiris striata*. Female lacks thick black veins on forewing and does not have feathered antennae. Day-flying 5-7, on heaths and grassland. Rests with wings wrapped round body. Larva is black with an orange stripe along the back and yellowish spots. It feeds on various low-growing plants. Widespread, but most common in S.

Setina aurita. Lines on forewing often replaced by rows of dots, especially at lower altitudes. Abdomen all black, all yellow, or a mixture. 6-9. Larva, dark brown with yellow spots, feeds on lichens. Alps and neighbouring mountains.

▲ **Common Footman** *Eilema lurideola*. Pale streak at front of forewing tapers strongly and does not reach apex. 6-8 in hedgerows, woods, and orchards. Rests with wings almost flat – only slightly rolled round body. Larva is hairy, grey with black lines on the back and an orange line on each side. Like most true footmen larvae, it eats lichens on trees and shrubs.

▲ **Scarce Footman** *E. complana* has pale streak of constant width from shoulder to wing-tip. Front edge of wing almost straight. 6-8 on heaths and moors and in damp woods. Rests with wings rolled tightly round body. Larva is greyish with a black line on the back and orange and white spots on the sides.

▲ **Dingy Footman** *E. griseola* has uniform pale streak but front edge of wing is strongly curved. Abdomen and hindwings dirty yellow. 6-8 in fens and damp woods. Rests with wings virtually flat. Larva is velvety black with a purplish stripe along the back and variable orange spots on each side.C.

△s **4-spotted Footman** *Lithosia quadra*. Sexes markedly different: female often much larger. 7-9, flying by day and night. Mainly in old woodlands. Larva is black with red and grey spots and a broad yellow stripe along the back. It eats lichens.

▲ **4-dotted Footman** *Cybosia mesomella*. Forewing sometimes much yellower. 6-7 on heaths and moors and in open woods. Larva is velvety black with tufts of black or dark brown hair. It feeds on lichens.

△ **Red-necked Footman** *Atolmis rubricollis*. 5-8, mainly in woodland. Larva is hairy: greyish with paler markings and red spots. It eats lichens.N & C.

▲ **Rosy Footman** *Miltochrista miniata*. Female is smaller. 6-8 in damp, wooded areas, including hedgerows. Larva is dark grey and very furry. It eats lichens. N & C.

△ **Dew Moth** *Setina irrorella*. Wings thinly scaled. Female smaller and darker. 6-8. Male often active by day. Mainly in coastal and montane habitats: also chalk and limestone hills with bare rock. The hairy larva is dark brown with yellow and white lines. It eats lichens on rocks.

▲ **Short-cloaked Moth** *Nola cucullata* Nolidae. Dark patch at base of forewings resembles a short cloak at rest. 6-7 in wooded and scrubby habitats. Larva is reddish brown with grey hair and white spots. It feeds on blackthorn, hawthorn, and other rosaceous trees and shrubs. Absent from far north.

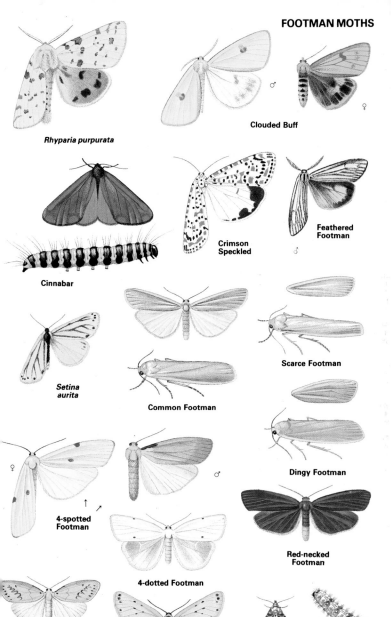

Rhyparia purpurata

Clouded Buff ♂ ♀

Cinnabar

Crimson Speckled ♂

Feathered Footman

Setina aurita

Common Footman

Scarce Footman

Dingy Footman

4-spotted Footman ♀ ♂

4-dotted Footman

Red-necked Footman

Rosy Footman

Dew Moth

Short-cloaked Moth

155

Noctuidae. A very large family with over 25,000 known species of stoutly-built moths. Forewings generally sombre and cryptically coloured, although hindwings may be brightly coloured. Sexes usually alike, but males often have tufts of hair at tip of abdomen. Vein M_2 of forewing is close to M_3 at base, thus distinguishing the family from the Notodontidae (p. 148). Forewing usually with three prominent spots or stigmata – the orbicular near the middle, the kidney-shaped reniform outside it, and the elongate claviform below it. At rest, the wings may be held roofwise or flat and overlapping. Larvae are usually plump and, with a few notable exceptions, they have little hair.

Forewing venation of a noctuid moth

M_2

M_3

▲ **Garden Dart** *Euxoa nigricans.* Forewing pale to very dark brown: claviform stigma usually indistinct. 6-8 on cultivated land and grassland: mainly in lowlands. Larva is pale brown or green with a double white stripe low on each side. It feeds on a wide variety of low-growing plants.

△ **Archer's Dart** *Agrotis vestigialis.* Ground colour grey to rich brown. Well marked claviform stigma (dart) and dark wedges near outer edge of forewing. 6-9, mainly on sandy coasts and heaths. Larva is grey and eats a wide range of low-growing plants.

▲ **Turnip Moth** *A. segetum* is distinguished from most other noctuids by its pearly hindwings – white in male, grey in female. Forewings pale grey to black. 5-10 in cultivated areas and waste land. Glossy larva, grey and tinged with purple, feeds mainly underground and damages crop roots.

▲ **Shuttle-shaped Dart** *A. puta* has dart-shaped orbicular stigma. Female darker, with pale border to orbicular stigma. Hindwing white in male, grey in female. 5-10 in most habitats. Mottled brown larva eats many kinds of herbaceous plants. S & C.

▲ **Heart and Dart** *A. exclamationis* is named for prominent reniform and solid black claviform stigmata. Forewings pale to dark brown. Black collar distinguishes it from several similar species. Open habitats, especially cultivated land. 5-9. Larva is brown above and grey below and feeds on numerous herbaceous plants.

▲ **Flame Shoulder** *Ochropleura plecta.* Readily identified by the pale streak on front edge of forewing. Hindwings shiny white. 5-9, almost everywhere. Larva, yellowish grey with a yellow stripe on each side, feeds on a wide range of herbaceous plants.

▲ **Flame** *Axylia putris.* Pale areas of forewing sometimes tinged with red. Wraps wings round body at rest and resembles broken twig. 5-7 in hedgerows, woodland margins, and cultivated land. Larva is mottled greyish brown with black markings and a hump at rear. It eats numerous herbaceous plants.

▲ **True Lover's Knot** *Lycophotia porphyrea.* Ground colour of forewing brick-red to purplish brown. Hindwings grey. 6-8, mainly on heaths and moors. Larva, reddish brown with paler lines, feeds on heathers.

▲ **Large Yellow Underwing** *Noctua pronuba.* Forewings pale grey to rich chestnut, the palest specimens being females and the darkest ones males. Always a jet-black spot or streak near wing-tip. Flight is fast and erratic, as in all yellow underwings, flashing the yellow hindwings and then dropping rapidly to ground to confuse predators (see p. 44). Rests with wings folded flat over body. 6-10, almost everywhere. Larva is brown or green with rows of tapering black dashes on back. It eats almost any herbaceous plant.
   △ **Lunar Yellow Underwing** *N.orbona* is like a small *pronuba* but has a black spot in hindwing. 6-9, mainly in open country. Larva feeds mainly on grasses.

▲ **Broad-bordered Yellow Underwing** *N. fimbriata.* Forewings greyish brown to chestnut: females lighter than males and often tinged with green. 6-9 in wooded areas. Larva, brown with black around spiracles, feeds on various deciduous trees.

▲ **Lesser Broad-bordered Yellow Underwing** *N. janthina* has no black spot in hindwing. 7-9 in hedgerows and other wooded areas. Larva, brownish with dark V-shaped marks, feeds on various herbs and shrubs. Absent from far north. ▲ **Least Yellow Underwing** *N. interjecta* has greyish brown to chestnut forewings with little marking. Hindwing has black spot underneath. 6-8 in open and scrubby country. Larva feeds mainly on grasses.
   ▲ **Lesser Yellow Underwing** *N. comes* has black spot in hindwing. Forewings range from grey to chestnut and very dark brown, without a black fleck near the tip. 7-9 nearly everywhere. Larva, like that of *pronuba*, feeds on various trees and shrubs.

▲ **Beautiful Yellow Underwing** *Anarta myrtilli.* Forewings greyish brown to purplish. Day-flying, 4-8, mainly on heaths and moors. Larva is green, marked with yellow and white, and is very difficult to see on its heather food-plant. △n **Small Dark Yellow Underwing** *A. cordigera* is similar but forewings are blacker and never tinged with red. Abdomen lacks pale bands. 5-6, mainly on moorland. Larvae, reddish brown with white lines, feeds on bearberry. N & C and southern mountains.

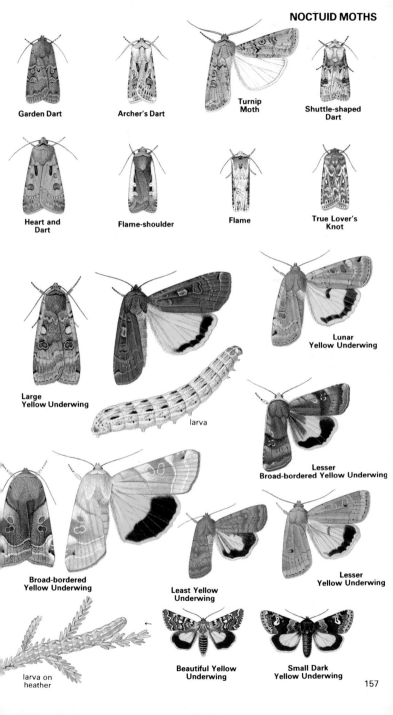

Garden Dart

Archer's Dart

Turnip Moth

Shuttle-shaped Dart

Heart and Dart

Flame-shoulder

Flame

True Lover's Knot

Large Yellow Underwing

Lunar Yellow Underwing

larva

Lesser Broad-bordered Yellow Underwing

Broad-bordered Yellow Underwing

Least Yellow Underwing

Lesser Yellow Underwing

larva on heather

Beautiful Yellow Underwing

Small Dark Yellow Underwing

157

▲ **Setaceous Hebrew Character** *Xestia c-nigrum*. Ground colour pale grey to purplish chestnut, with characteristic light and dark marking near front of forewing. Wings flat at rest. 5-10, but mainly autumnal: mainly lowland. Polyphagous larva is pale brown or green, heavily speckled with black.

▲ **Double Square-spot** *X. triangulum* has dark mark round orbicular stigma forming 2 almost square spots. Wings flat at rest. 5-7 in wooded areas. Larva is brown with black marks: polyphagous.

▲ **Ingrailed Clay** *Diarsia mendica*. Forewings vary from straw-coloured, through chestnut, to dark brown: usually dark in north. Wings flat at rest. 5-7 in woods and moors. Polyphagous larva is brown with black triangles on sides.

▲ **Green Arches** *Anaplectoides prasina* Black markings vary: green fades after death. Hindwings dark grey or brown with white fringe. 5-7 in deciduous woods. Larva, brown with darker markings, feeds on various herbs and shrubs.

△n **Great Brocade** *Eurois occulta*. Ground colour pale grey to black: pale orbicular and white-edged reniform stigmata always prominent. 6-8: moors and open woodland. Larva, purplish brown with yellow and white lines, feeds on bog myrtle. N & C.

▲ **Gothic** *Naenia typica*. Hindwings entirely grey. 5-8 in most lowland habitats. Larva is greyish brown with a dark line on each side and a few black dashes at the rear. Polyphagous. △s **Bordered Gothic** *Heliophobus reticulata* is similar but hindwings are white with darker edges.

▲ **Cabbage Moth** *Mamestra brassicae*. Forewings sometimes tinged reddish brown. Hindwings silvery grey with darker margins. All year, but mainly 5-8: very common on cultivated land. Polyphagous larva is green or dull brown with darker spots: often tunnels in cabbages.

▲ **Broom Moth** *Melanchra pisi*. Ground colour greyish brown to purplish. 5-7. Polyphagous larva is green to dark brown with bold yellow stripes.

▲ **Broad-barred White** *Hecatera bicolorata*. Ground colour white to bluish grey. 5-9. Larva is green or brown with dark diamonds on back. It feeds on flowers and buds of hawkweeds and other yellow-flowered composites.

▲ **Dot Moth** *Melanchra persicariae*. 5-9, usually in cultivated areas. Larva is green, brown, or purplish with a distinct hump at the rear. Polyphagous.

▲ **Bright-line Brown-eye** *Lacanobia oleracea*. 5-9, especially common in gardens and other cultivated areas. Larva, green or brown with a black and yellow stripe on each side, feeds on many woody and herbaceous plants and sometimes damages tomatoes, but prefers goosefoots and similar weeds.

▲ **Tawny Shears** *Hadena perplexa*. Ground colour off-white to dark brown. Claviform stigma broad and usually edged with black. 5-9. Larva is glossy pale brown, feeding on white campion.

▲ **Varied Coronet** *H. compta* flies 5-9 in gardens and open country. Larva is dull, yellowish brown and feeds in seed heads of pinks and campions. A recent arrival in B (mostly south-east).

▲ **Hedge Rustic** *Tholera cespitis*. Hindwing white (with grey margin in female). 7-9 in grassy places. Larva, green at first and then greyish brown, feeds on various tough grasses.

▲ **Feathered Gothic** *T. decimalis* has feathery antennae only in male. Wings more slender than Gothic: forewings strongly veined in white. Hindwings white with grey border in male: grey in female. 7-9 in grassy places.

▲ **Antler Moth** *Cerapteryx graminis*. Ground colour greyish brown to deep chestnut, with variable 'antler' pattern. Male smaller than female and normally darker. 6-9 in open country, especially in uplands: often flies by day. Larva is glossy greyish brown and feeds on grasses: often damages pastureland.

▲ **Pine Beauty** *Panolis flammea*. Forewing sometimes greyish brown. 2-5 in pinewoods. Larva feeds on pine needles and is a serious forest pest.

▲ **Clouded Drab** *Orthosia incerta*. Pale grey, through reddish brown, to purplish black: reniform and orbicular stigmata usually with pale outlines. 2-4 (sometimes earlier), mainly in wooded areas: common in gardens. Larva, bluish green with white dots and lines, feeds on shrubs.

▲ **Hebrew Character** *O. gothica* is easily identified by the heavy black mark around the orbicular stigma. Wings held roofwise at rest (unlike Setaceous Hebrew Character). 1-5. Larva is polyphagous, mainly on shrubs.

▲ **Common Quaker** *O. stabilis* is greyish brown to brick-red. 2-4 (sometimes earlier), mainly in wooded areas. Larva, bright green with yellow dots and lines, feeds on most deciduous trees.

NOCTUID MOTHS

Setaceous Hebrew Character

Double Square-spot

Ingrailed Clay

Green Arches

Great Brocade

Gothic

Cabbage Moth

Broad-barred White

Bright-line Brown-eye

↑

Dot Moth

Broom Moth

↑

Tawny Shears

Varied Coronet

Hedge Rustic

Feathered Gothic

Antler Moth ♀

Common Quaker

Pine Beauty

eggs

Clouded Drab

↑

Hebrew Character

159

▲ **Brown-line Bright-eye** *Mythimna conigera*. Pale yellowish brown to golden orange. 6-9 in hedges and woodland margins. Larva is pale brown with slender yellow lines and feeds on grasses, especially cocksfoot.

▲ **Clay** *M. ferrago*. Pale straw-coloured to brick-red. Male has triangular patch of black hair on underside. 5-8. Larva like previous species, feeding mainly on grasses.

▲ **Common Wainscot** *M. pallens* has straw-coloured to brick-red forewings: hindwings almost white (sometimes greyish in female). 6-10: especially common in damp grassland. Larva is pale brown with white lines on the back and a darker stripe on each side. It feeds on grasses.

▲ **Smoky Wainscot** *M. impura* has two or more conspicuous black dots on outer part of forewing: dark streak often less marked than shown here. Hindwing brownish grey. 5-8, mainly in grassy places. Larva like previous species.

▲ **Bulrush Wainscot** *Nonagria typhae*. Pale straw-coloured to brick-red. 7-9 in marshy areas, including ditches and river banks. Larva is pale brown and feeds and pupates inside bulrush stems (*Typha* spp).

▲ **Mullein** *Shargacucullia verbasci*. Ground colour pale straw to mid-brown. 4-6 in scrubby places and gardens: remarkably twig-like at rest. Larva is creamy white with black and yellow spots: feeds openly on leaves and flower spikes of mulleins and may completely destroy garden specimens. Absent from far north.

▲ **Shark** *Cucullia umbratica* has very narrow forewings, pale grey to rich brownish grey. Hindwings silvery in male, heavily clouded with grey in female. 5-7 in scrubby places, gardens, and waste land. Larva, greyish brown with black spots, feeds on sowthistle and lettuce.

Cucullia argentea. flies 6-8 in sandy areas.Larva, dull green with yellow lines along the back and a pink or red streak on each segment, feeds on the flowers and seeds of mugwort and related plants. Eastwards from Germany and Scandinavia.

▲ **Early Grey** *Xylocampa areola*. Sometimes darker and occasionally with a rosy tinge. 3-5 in hedges, gardens, and woods. Larva, yellowish brown with a dark line on each side and dark brown patches on the back, feeds on honeysuckle. Absent from far north.

▲ **Grey Chi** *Antitype chi*. Distinct black cross near middle of forewing: black marks may be heavier: ground colour often greenish, but this tends to fade after death. 8-10, mainly in open country: common in gardens. Larva is bluish green with green-edged white lines. It feeds on dandelions and other low-growing plants.

▲ **Beaded Chestnut** *Agrochola lychnidis*. Pale brown to brick-red, plain or mottled but always with 3 conspicuous spots on front edge of forewing. 9-11, often abundant at ivy blossom. Larva is yellowish green with white lines and spots. It feeds on a wide range of herbaceous plants and shrubs, especially sallows. Absent from far north.

▲ **Merveille-du-Jour** *Dichonia aprilina*. 8-10 around oak trees: hard to spot at rest on lichen-covered bark. Larva is greenish grey with zig-zag black lines on back. It feeds on oak buds and leaves and hides on trunks by day. Absent from far north.

▲ **Sprawler** *Brachionycha sphinx*. 10-12 in deciduous woodland: very well camouflaged at rest on trunks. Larva is pale green with yellow and white lines: rests with head and thorax raised. It feeds on oak and other deciduous trees. C.

▲ **Swordgrass** *Xylena exsoleta*. Variable amounts of black on forewings. 9-10 and again in spring after hibernation: all kinds of open habitats. Rests with wings wrapped round body . Larva is green with black spots and yellow and red stripes. It feeds on many low-growing plants and also on several trees and shrubs. Absent from far north.

▲ **Orange Sallow** *Xanthia citrago*. Forewings yellow to brick-red. 8-10.Larva is greenish grey with white lines and dots: feeds on lime. Not in far north.

▲ **Barred Sallow** *X. aurago* has pale yellow to orange ground colour. 8-10, mainly in and around beechwoods. Larva, reddish brown with pale dots and lines, feeds on beech and field maple.

▲ **Sallow** *X. icteritia* may have virtually no dark markings. 8-10 in hedgerows and scrubby places. Larva, reddish brown with darker spots and pale lines, feeds on sallow catkins in early spring and then various low-growing plants.

▲ **Green-brindled Crescent** *Allophyes oxyacanthae*. Forewings may lack green brindling, but always with prominent white fleck near hind edge. 9-10 in hedgerows and woodland: often on ivy blossom. Larva is purplish brown with twin pointed humps at rear. It feeds on hawthorn and related trees. Absent from far north.

NOCTUID MOTHS

Brown-line Bright-eye

Clay

♂ underside

Common Wainscot

Smoky Wainscot

llein

Shark

Bulrush Wainscot →

Cucullia argentea

pupa in *Typha* stem

arly rey

Grey Chi

Merveille-du-Jour

Sprawler

Swordgrass

Beaded Chestnut

Orange Sallow

Barred Sallow

Sallow

Green-brindled Crescent

161

▲ **Poplar Grey** *Acronicta megacephala*. Hindwings largely white. 5-8 in wooded areas, parks, and gardens. Larva is hairy: greyish with red and black markings and a square white patch near the rear. It feeds on poplars and willows.

▲ **Knotgrass** *A. rumicis* resembles previous species but has a clear white sub-marginal line: forewings sometimes almost black. Hindwings grey. 6-9. Larva is hairy, blackish brown with red and white spots. Feeds on knotgrass and many other herbs.

▲ **Sycamore Moth** *A. aceris* has very white hindwings. 5-7 in wooded areas, including town parks and tree-lined avenues. The very hairy and striking larva feeds on syca-more,maple, and other deciduous trees.

▲ **Grey Dagger** *A. psi* is named for black dagger-like marks on grey background. 6-7, mainly in lowlands. Larva feeds on hawthorn and many other trees.

▲ **Dark Dagger** *A. tridens* cannot be distinguished with certainty from *psi* without dissection, although it is often darker. Its larva, however, is very distinct.

△ **Alder Moth** *A. alni* flies 5-7 in deciduous woods. Young larva is grey with a white patch on the back and resembles a bird-dropping: later becomes black and yellow with long spatulate hairs on each side. It feeds on alder and various other deciduous trees.

△ **Miller Moth** *A. leporina* is very pale, with few black marks, often much smaller than shown here. 4-7 in woods and on damp heaths. Mature larva is pale green and almost completely covered with long, silky white hairs (often yellowish in north). It feeds on birch and various other deciduous trees. N & C.

Malachite Moth *Calotaenia celsia* 8-10 in coniferous woods. Larva is yellowish green with black 'warts' and a brown head. It eats grasses in summer. N & C (mainly eastern).

▲ **Marbled Beauty** *Cryphia domestica*. Grey may be replaced by green. 6-8 anywhere that lichens thrive: very hard to see at rest on lichens. Larva feeds on lichens.
▲ **Marbled Green** *C. muralis* is very similar but larger and the dark bar crossing the basal half of the wing does not reach the rear edge. S & C.

▲ **Nut-tree Tussock** *Colocasia coryli* 5-9 in hedgerows and open woodland. Larva is orange or brown with tufts of red or grey hair behind the head and a broken black stripe on the back. It feeds on hazel and various other trees. N & C.

△ **Copper Underwing** *Amphipyra pyramidea*. 6-8 in wooded areas. Rests with wings nearly flat. Larva is plump and green with white dots and stripes and a pointed hump at rear. It feeds on deciduous trees and shrubs.

△ **Svensson's Copper Underwing** *A. berbera* is almost identical to the previous species but underside of abdomen has no chequered fringe. Underside of hindwing also has more extensive reddish colour, not just a marginal band as in *pyramidea*, and a less distinct dark band.

▲ **Mouse Moth** *A. tragopoginis* gets its name for the mouse-like way in which it scuttles away when disturbed. Wings held almost flat at rest. 6-9 in woods, hedgerows, and gardens. Larva is green with narrow white lines and feeds on a wide range of herbs and shrubs.

▲ **Old Lady** *Mormo maura*. Named for its shawl-like pattern, this moth flies 6-8 in hedgerows, gardens (including town gardens), and light woodland. Larva is dull brown with white marks and orange spiracles. It feeds on herbs and shrubs. S & C.

Polyphaenis sericata. Forewings sometimes flecked with bluish white: stigmata often obscured but dark mark always present at wing-tips. 6-9 in scrubby places. Larva is yellowish grey and feeds on honeysuckle and other shrubs. S & C.

▲ **Straw Underwing** *Thalpophila matura*. 6-8 in grassy and scrubby places. Larva is pale to reddish brown with darker marks on the back. It eats grasses. S & C.

▲ **Angle Shades** *Phlogophora meticulosa*. Green areas may be replaced by brick-red: green usually fades to dull brown after death. Abundant everywhere and can be found at all times of year. Rests with wings wrinkled like a dead leaf. Larva is green or brown with darker chevrons on the back. Polyphagous and sometimes a garden pest.

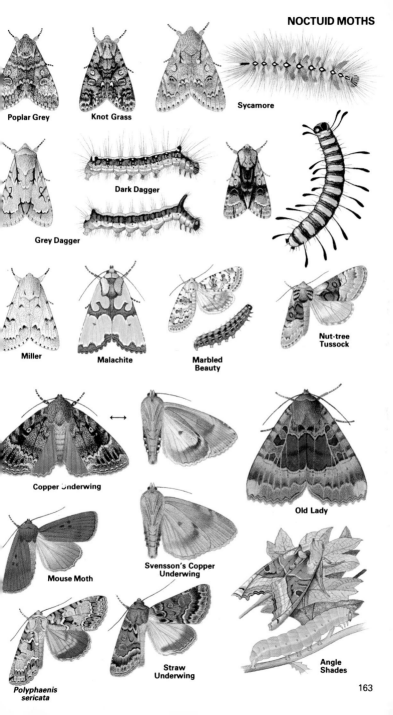

NOCTUID MOTHS

Poplar Grey

Knot Grass

Sycamore

Grey Dagger

Dark Dagger

Miller

Malachite

Marbled Beauty

Nut-tree Tussock

Copper Underwing

Old Lady

Mouse Moth

Svensson's Copper Underwing

Polyphaenis sericata

Straw Underwing

Angle Shades

163

▲ **Dunbar** *Cosmia trapezina.* Very variable: forewings ranging from greyish buff to deep brick. Cross-lines usually distinct and sometimes enclosing rust-coloured or even blackish central band. 6-8 in wooded areas, often on flowers. Larva is green with yellow lines and scattered black and white spots. It feeds on various deciduous trees and also eats other caterpillars, including its own species.

▲ **Olive** *Ipimorpha subtusa.* 6-8, mainly in wooded areas. Larva, green with black dots and white lines, feeds on aspen and other poplars.

▲ **Marbled Minor** *Oligia strigilis.* An extremely variable species, often difficult to separate from its relatives without examining genitalia. Abundant everywhere 6-8. Larva, purplish brown with yellow stripes, feeds on grasses. ▲ **Middle-barred Minor** *O. fasciuncula* often resembles *strigilis* but is usually redder and central band often more distinct. 5-7, mainly in damp habitats. Purplish brown larva feeds on grasses.

▲ **Small Clouded Brindle** *Apamea unanimis.* Reddish tinge may be absent, with more black mottling, especially in female. Reniform stigma usually clearly outlined in white. 6-8 in moist habitats. Larva is pale brown with dark-edged pale lines and feeds on moisture-loving grasses.

▲ **Common Rustic** *A. secalis* is another very variable species, with 3 common forms shown here. 6-8 in a wide variety of habitats. Larva is green with reddish lines on the back and feeds on grasses.

▲ **Dark Arches** *A. monoglypha* has forewings ranging from greyish brown to almost black: pale zig-zag lines always visible near outer margin. 6-10: abundant nearly everywhere and often coming in scores to light-traps. Larva is dirty white or flesh-coloured with black spots and a black head. It feeds on grasses, usually chewing through the bases of the stems.

▲ **Light Arches** *A. lithoxylea* flies 6-8 in most habitats. Larva is like that of *monoglypha* but has a brown head. Absent from far north.

▲ **Bird's Wing** *Dypterygia scabriuscula.* 5-10 in wooded areas: very well camouflaged at rest on tree trunks. Larva is reddish brown with black and white lines and yellow dots. It feeds on docks and related plants.

▲ **Rosy Rustic** *Hydraecia micacea.* Pink tinge varies in intensity. 9-10 in open country, especially coastal and cultivated areas. Larva is pinkish grey with black spots and feeds on docks and plantains: also on potatoes and other crops.

▲ **Frosted Orange** *Gortyna flavago.* Outer golden band often indistinct. 8-10 in open country, including both waste and cultivated land, especially in damp situations. Larva is pinkish with black spots and tunnels in stems of thistles and burdock: sometimes a pest of potatoes.

▲ **Ear Moth** *Amphipoea oculea.* Named for shape of reniform stigma. Coastal moths may be larger and paler. 8-9 in damp grassland: often abundant on flowers at night. Pinkish larva feeds on grasses.

△ **Burren Green** *Calamia tridens.* Reniform stigma often edged with rusty brown. Hindwing yellowish grey in male: whitish green in female. 8-9 in grassy and scrubby places. Larva, greenish brown with black spots, feeds on various low-growing plants. Only locality in British Isles is in western Ireland.

Synthymia fixa. Male has ash-grey forewing and pale yellow hindwing. 3-5 on dry hillsides. Larva, dark green with yellow and white lines, feeds on pitch trefoil. S: sporadic visitor to parts of C.

Spotted Sulphur *Emmelia trabealis.* Pale areas often deep cream in fresh specimens. Black markings also vary in number and intensity. 5-8 in rough, grassy places, especially on sandy soils. Flies late afternoon and at night. Larva, reddish brown with darker lines on back and yellow stripe on each side, feeds on bindweed. Absent from far north: in B recently extinct.

△ s **Four-spotted** *Tyta luctuosa.* Pale spot on forewing white or pink. Day-flying 5-9 in meadows and rough grassland. Greyish brown larva feeds on bindweed. S & C.

▲ **Cream-bordered Green Pea** *Earias chlorana.* Pale costal stripe and white hindwings distinguish this from Green Oak Tortrix (p.126). 5-8 in damp habitats. Larva, pale green with brown lines, feeds on osier and other willows.

▲ **Green Silver Lines** *Pseudoips fagana.* Female has white hindwings and paler red forewing fringes. 2nd-brood insects have only two white cross-lines. 5-8 in woods and hedgerows. Larva, pale green with a thin yellow line on each side, feeds on oak and other deciduous trees.

▲ **Scarce Silver Lines** *Bena prasina* has white fringes. 6-7 on oakwoods. Larva is green with oblique yellow bars on sides and a yellow-tipped hump near front. It feeds on oak. S & C.

△ s **Marbled Clover** *Heliothis viriplaca.* Pale patch on hindwing may be reduced. Day-flying 5-7 on flowery heaths and grassy places. Larva, green to purplish brown, feeds on a wide range of low-growing plants. Not in far north.

Dunbar

Olive

Marbled Minor

Middle-barred
Minor

Small Clouded
Brindle

Common
Rustic

Dark Arches

Light Arches

Bird's Wing

Rosy Rustic

Frosted Orange

Ear Moth

Burren
Green

♀ *Synthymia
fixa*

Spotted
Sulphur

Four Spotted

Cream-
bordered
Green Pea

Green
Silver Lines

Scarce Silver Lines

Marbled
Clover

▲ **Golden Plusia** *Polychrisia moneta*. 6-9 in hedgerows, gardens, and town parks: very fond of garden flowers. Larva white with black dots at first, becoming green with white spots and lines. Like the next 3 species, it has only 3 pairs of prolegs, including the claspers. It feeds on many herbaceous plants – especially garden delphiniums in B.

▲ **Burnished Brass** *Diachrysia chrysitis*. Metallic patches range from green to deep gold: inner and outer bands may join in middle. 6-9 in gardens, hedges, and rough ground. Larva, with just 3 pairs of prolegs, feeds on stinging nettles, deadnettles, and other weeds.

△s **Scarce Burnished Brass** *D. chryson* has one fairly small brassy patch. 7-8 in fens and other damp places. Larva feeds on hemp agrimony. S & C.

Slender Burnished Brass *D. orichalcea* flies 6-9 in rough and grassy places. Larva feeds on various composites. Resident in S, occasionally wandering to C & N.

▲ **Herald** *Scoliopteryx libatrix*. 8-10 and again in spring after hibernation, often in houses, as adult. Gardens, parks, and rough countryside. Larva feeds on willows and poplars.

△ **Gold Spot** *Plusia festucae*. Ground colour golden brown to chestnut. 6-9 in damp places. Larva feeds on grasses, sedges, and other waterside plants. Like those of the next 4 species, it is green with white spots and lines and has only 3 pairs of prolegs, including the claspers.

△n **Gold Spangle** *Autographa bractea*. Metallic spot sometimes deep yellow. 6-8, mainly in rough, upland country. Larva feeds on many low-growing plants and also on honeysuckle. N & C.

▲ **Beautiful Golden Y** *A. pulchrina*. Y-shaped mark, often broken in middle, sits on a rather confused and indistinct dark patch: reniform stigma clearly outlined in gold. 5-8 in gardens, hedges, and other scrubby places. Larva feeds on deadnettle and many other low-growing plants.

▲ **Plain Golden Y** *A. jota* has the Y-shaped mark, often broken, on a distinct and uniform brown rectangle: reniform stigma indistinct. Flies 5-8, usually at dusk, in same habitats as last species, and, like all members of the genus, is very fond of flowers. Larva feeds on a wide range of herbaceous plants and also on hawthorn.

▲ **Silver Y** *A. gamma* has grey to velvety black ground colour, occasionally tinged with purple. Upper part of Y sometimes indistinct. Abundant in gardens, town parks, and open country 5-11. Flies day and night and very common at garden flowers, continuing to beat its wings while feeding and appearing as a grey blur. Larva eats a wide range of herbaceous plants and may be a pest of peas and other crops in summer. Resident in S (where it flies all year), migrating to C & N in spring and producing a summer brood, some of which fly south in autumn: cannot survive winter in B.

▲ **Mother Shipton** *Callistege mi*. Named for forewing pattern, thought to resemble witch-like profile of the legendary Mother Shipton. Day-flying in grassy and scrubby places. 5-7. Larva is slender, pale brown with a creamy stripe on each side, and has only three pairs of prolegs. It feeds on clovers and other legumes.

▲ **Spectacle** *Abrostola triplasia*. Named for the pattern of hairs on front of thorax. 5-8 in gardens, hedgerows, and rough ground. Larva, pale green with white stripes and darker chevrons on back, has two humps near the front and a 3rd at the rear. It feeds on stinging nettle. ▲ **Dark Spectacle** *A. trigemina* is darker, with brown 'spectacles'.

Syngrapha ain. Resembles Silver Y but hindwings yellow instead of brown. 7-8 in montane larch forests. Larva is green with pale lines and 3 pairs of prolegs, including the claspers. It feeds on larch needles and has a long hibernation. C.

▲ **Blackneck** *Lygephila pastinum*. Amount of brown dusting on forewing varies, as does amount of black in reniform stigma. 6-7 in rough grassland and scrubby places, especially woodland clearings. Flies weakly. Larva, long and tapering, is greyish brown with 3 reddish brown stripes on the back. It feeds on tufted vetch. S & C. △s **Scarce Blackneck** *L. craccae* is very similar but has black dots on the front edge of the forewing. S & C.

▲ **Burnet Companion** *Euclidia glyphica*. Day-flying, 5-7 in rough grassy places. Larva has 3 functional pairs of prolegs, including claspers, and a vestigial pair in front of them. It feeds on clovers and other legumes.

Golden Plusia

Burnished Brass

**Scarce
Burnished Brass**

nder Burnished
Brass

Herald

Gold Spot

**Gold
Spangle**

Beautiful Golden Y

Plain Golden Y

Silver Y

Mother Shipton

Spectacle

Syngrapha ain

Blackneck

**Burnet
Companion**

△ **Clifden Nonpareil** *Catocala fraxini*. 7-8 in light woodland. Well camouflaged at rest on tree trunks. Larva, like those of the red underwings, is extremely hard to spot when stretched out on a twig. It feeds on poplars and ash. N & C (including Arctic): sporadic visitor to B.

▲ **Red Underwing** *C. nupta*. Flies 8-9 in light woodland, hedgerows, gardens, and town parks. Well camouflaged at rest but, like the yellow underwings (p. 156), it flies erratically when disturbed and flashes the red hindwings to mislead predators. Larva has several bud-like 'warts' on the back: fringes along the sides conceal shadows and allow the caterpillar to blend remarkably well with twigs when stretched out along them at rest. It feeds on willows and poplars. Absent from far north.

△ **Rosy Underwing** *C. electa* resembles the last species but hindwings are somewhat paler and forewings lighter grey with thin black lines. 7-9. Larva like that of the last species. S & C: sporadic visitor to B.

△s **Dark Crimson Underwing** *C. sponsa* usually has darker forewings than Red Underwing, with prominent white marks near centre: hindwings darker red, with strongly-angled W-shaped central black band. 7-8 in oakwoods. Larva, somewhat greener than that of Red Underwing, feeds on oak. S & C.

△s **Light Crimson Underwing** *C. promissa* is smaller than the last species, with greyer forewings and a much straighter central band on the hindwing. 7-8 in oakwoods. S & C.

Ephesia fulminea Forewings range from pale to dark grey, often with a violet tinge. 6-8 in scrubby places, including gardens. Larva is grey or brown with prominent 'warts' and a horn at the rear. It feeds on blackthorn and various other trees. S & C (southern).

Anua tirhaca 5-6 in dry, scrubby habitats. Some specimens have complete black border to hindwing, much broader in female than male. Larva is reddish or greyish brown, with thin dark lines on the back. It feeds on cistus and mastic shrubs (*Pistachia* spp.). S.

▲ **Beautiful Hooktip** *Laspeyria flexula*. Greyish brown to purplish brown, always dotted with black. 6-8 in hedgerows and woodland margins. Larva is bluish green with dark green points and black-tipped 'warts' on the back. Lower edges are fringed. It feeds on arboreal lichens. C. Unrelated to the true hooktips (p. 170).

▲ **Snout** *Hypena proboscidalis*. Much more slender than most noctuids, this moth is named for the long palps that project forward from the head. 6-9 in hedgerows and other rough habitats. Larva, slender and green with scattered black hairs arising from raised spots, feeds on stinging nettle.

▲ **Fanfoot** *Herminia tarsipennalis*. Another slender species, named because male has a large tuft of hair on the front leg. Male also has a swelling halfway along the antenna. Sub-marginal line starts before wing-tip. 6-7 in scrubby habitats, including gardens. Larva is greyish brown with black streaks and clothed with short hair. It feeds on bramble and various other shrubs. Most of Europe, but not far north or south.

▲ **Small Fanfoot** *H. nemoralis* has sub-marginal line starting at wing-tip. Male has no tuft on front leg and no antennal swelling. 6-7 in woods and hedgerows. Larva, similar to that of the last species, feeds on oak. Absent from far north.

The noctuid moths, sometimes known as owlet moths, form the largest of the moth families and their larvae include some serious crop pests. Many of these larvae live in the upper layers of the soil and are known as cutworms for their habit of coming out at night to chew right through the bases of young plants, leaving the stems and leaves lying on the surface. Even if they are not cut right through, the plants generally wilt and die, and slugs often get the blame. Freshly planted lettuces and brassicas are common targets for cutworms, but most species will attack and eat any plant of the right size. The worst offenders include the Large Yellow Underwing, the Turnip Moth, and the Heart and Dart, all described on p. 156. Many feed right through the winter, although they burrow deeply in very cold weather. They pupate in the soil when fully grown and most of the shiny brown, bullet-shaped pupae dug up in the garden belong to this group.

Clifden Nonpareil

Rosy Underwing

Red Underwing

Light Crimson Underwing

Ephesia fulminea

Dark Crimson Underwing

Beautiful Hooktip

Small Fanfoot

Anua tirhaca

Snout

Fanfoot

▲ **Pebble Hooktip** *Drepana falcataria* Drepanidae. Ground colour may be paler. 5-9 in woods and heathland. Wings held flat at rest. Larva, like all members of the family, tapers to a point at the rear and rests with both ends raised. It eats birch and alder.

▲ **Oak Hooktip** *Watsonsalla binaria*. 5-9 in woodlands. Larva, pale brown with yellowish marks on the back and a double-pointed hump behind the head, feeds on oak and birch. S & C.

▲ **Scalloped Hooktip** *Falcaria lacertinaria*. 5-9 in wooded areas and heathland. Rests with wings roofwise. Larva is light and dark brown with 2 humps behind the head and a 3rd at the rear. It feeds on birch and alder. Absent from far south.

▲ **Chinese Character** *Cilix glaucata*. 5-9 in gardens, hedgerows, and woods. Just like a bird dropping at rest. Larva has typical hooktip shape and is reddish brown, often purplish below, with 3 humps behind head. Mainly on hawthorn and blackthorn. S & C.

▲ **Peach Blossom** *Thyatira batis* Thyatiridae. 6-9, mainly in woodland. Larva is dark brown with oblique white lines and several humps along the back. It feeds on bramble and rests with both ends raised. N & C.

▲ **Buff Arches** *Habrosyne pyritoides*. 6-9 in woods and hedgerows. Larva is brick-coloured with a dark line on the back and a large white spot near the front on each side. It feeds mainly on bramble.

▲ **Figure of Eighty** *Tethea ocularis*. 80-mark usually distinct. 5-6 in wooded areas. Larva, dirty white with a grey line on the back, feeds on poplars.

▲ **Frosted Green** *Polyploca ridens*. 3-5 in wooded areas. Larva is yellowish green with black and white dots. It feeds on oak. S & C.

Family Geometridae.

A very large family, containing about 12,000 species of mainly flimsy moths with slender bodies and relatively large wings. The latter are generally spread horizontally at rest, often swept back into a triangular shape, although a few species hold their wings up like butterflies. Flight is generally weak. The larvae are hairless or only slightly hairy and have only 2 pairs of prolegs, including the claspers. They are known as loopers, from the way in which they arch their bodies into loops as they move along. Many are amazingly stick-like at rest.

△s **Purple-bordered Gold** *Idaea muricata*. Costal margin always purple, but wings otherwise completely yellow to completely purple. 6-7 in fens and other damp places, often flying at sunrise. Larva, pale brown with darker lines, feeds on marsh cinquefoil and other herbaceous plants.

▲ **Riband Wave** *I. aversata* may be greyish white or yellowish: bands may be indistinct. 6-9. The polyphagous larva is brown and wrinkled and tapers strongly towards the front.

Rhodostrophia calabra. Rosy areas may be darker red, especially in far south. 4-7. Larva, yellowish brown or grey with black bristles, feeds on broom and other legumes. S & C. **R. vibicaria** is normally paler than *calabra* and has sharply-angled hindwings. Pink bands strong or faint, but always with distinct edges. S & C.

△s **Lace Border** *Scopula ornata*. 5-9 in rough, grassy places, especially on chalk and limestone. Larva is pale brown above and greyish below, with several dark V-shaped marks on the back. It feeds on wild thyme and marjoram. ▲ **Cream Wave** *S. floslactata* commonly has only 2 prominent cross-lines and is sometimes almost unmarked. Ground colour sometimes yellowish white and may be smoky grey all over. 4-7 in wooded areas. Larva, greyish brown with darker markings and a notched head, feeds mainly on bedstraws. There are several similar species.
▲ **Small Bloodvein** *S. imitaria* has very angular wings. Ground colour often less orange than shown: stripe varies in thickness. 6-9 in hedgerows and other rough places. Larva is pale brown with 3 darker lines on the back. Polyphagous. S & C.

▲ **Bloodvein** *Timandra comae*. Ground colour ranges from cream to pale grey. 'Vein' is pink or purple and varies in thickness. 5-9 in hedgerows and other rough places, especially where damp. Larva is greyish brown with 4 dark spots on the back. It feeds on docks and other low-growing plants.

▲ **Clay Triple-lines** *Cyclophora linearia*. Ground colour ranges from yellow to pale brick: inner and outer cross-lines often missing. 4-9 in and around beechwoods. Larva, pale brown with yellow markings, feeds on beech leaves. S & C.

▲ **Mocha** *C. annularia*. Ground colour off-white to pale yellow: rings may be absent, especially on forewing. 5-9 in hedgerows and other wooded areas. Larva, dark green with yellow markings and a brown head, feeds on maple. S & C.

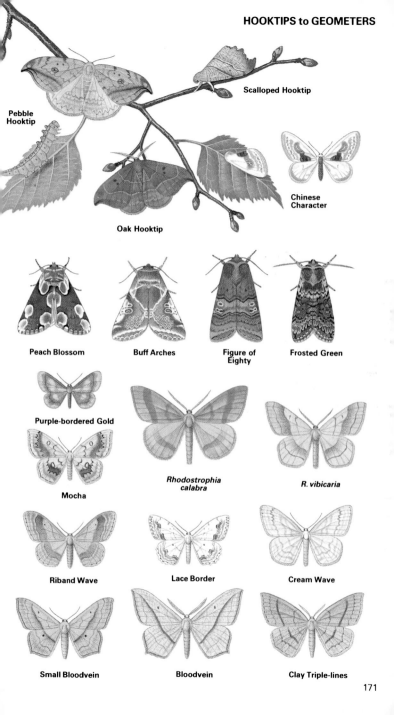

HOOKTIPS to GEOMETERS

Scalloped Hooktip

Pebble Hooktip

Chinese Character

Oak Hooktip

Peach Blossom

Buff Arches

Figure of Eighty

Frosted Green

Purple-bordered Gold

Mocha

Rhodostrophia calabra

R. vibicaria

Riband Wave

Lace Border

Cream Wave

Small Bloodvein

Bloodvein

Clay Triple-lines

▲ **Orange Underwing** *Archiearis parthenias*. 3-5 on heaths and in open woodland. Male flies around birches in sunshine: female flies little. Larva, green with white stripes and a black line along the back, feeds on leaves and catkins of birch. △ **Light Orange Underwing** *A. notha* is similar, but smaller and with plainer forewings.

▲ **Large Emerald** *Geometra papilionaria*. Bright green at first but, as in all emeralds, it fades after a few days: green may disappear altogether after death. 6-8 in woods, heaths and hedgerows. Twig-like larva is brown at first and then green.It feeds on birch, hazel, and beech.

▲ **Grass Emerald** *Pseudoterpna pruinata*. Bluish green at first, soon becoming grey. 6-8 on moors, heaths, and damp scrubby grassland. Larva is green with a dark line on the back and a pink line on each side. It feeds on broom and gorse. S & C.

▲ **Small Emerald** *Hemistola chrysoprasaria*. 5-8 in hedgerows and woodland margins, mainly on chalk and limestone. Larva is pale green with white dots and a brown head. It feeds on traveller's joy.

▲ **Blotched Emerald** *Comibaena bajularia*. 6-7 in and around oakwoods. Larva is reddish brown but camouflages itself with debris. It feeds on oak. C.

△s **Sussex Emerald** *Thalera fimbrialis*. Fringes chequered with red. Hindwing with 2 distinct points, separated by a crescent-shaped notch. 7-8 in scrubby and grassy places. Larva is yellowish green with red at front and rear and a red dorsal stripe. It feeds on a wide range of herbaceous plants. Absent from far north.

Euchrostes indigenata. 5-10 in rough and cultivated areas. Larva, bright green with red at each end, feeds on spurges. S.

▲ **Common Emerald** *Hemithea aestivaria*. Hindwing has a single point. 6-8 in hedgerows and wooded areas. Larva is green with reddish brown marks and black V-shaped marks on the back. It feeds on low-growing plants when young, and then on deciduous trees. S & C.

▲ **Little Emerald** *Jodis lactearia*. Pale green at first, soon fading to shiny white. 5-7 in hedges and woodland. Larva, thin and green with red spots, feeds on various deciduous trees and shrubs. S & C.

▲ **Light Emerald** *Campaea margaritata* 5-7, mainly in woodland. Larva is dark green to purplish brown and feeds on various deciduous trees 8-5, often chewing buds and young bark in winter. Not closely related to the other emeralds.

▲ **Mallow** *Larentia clavaria*. Forewings pale to deep brown: cross bands often indistinct. Chequered margins give wings a scalloped appearance. 9-11 in rough habitats. Larva is slender and green and feeds on mallows.

▲ **Shaded Broad-bar** *Scotopteryx chenopodiata*. Resembles Mallow but lacks chequered margins. 6-8 in grassy places. Larva, pinkish grey with black spots, eats grasses and assorted legumes.

△s **Chalk Carpet** *S. bipunctaria* flies 6-8 on chalk and limestone grassland. Larva, pale pinkish brown, feeds on clovers and trefoils. S & C.

△ **Chimney Sweeper** *Odezia atrata*. Jet black at first, becoming brown with age, but always with white streak at apex. Day-flying 5-7 in grassy places. Larva, green with dark lines on back, feeds on flowers of earthnut and other small umbellifers. N & C and southern mountains.

▲ **Treble Bar** *Aplocera plagiata*. 5-9 in rough grassy places: 2nd brood insects smaller and often with faint bars. Larva, dark green to reddish brown with darker and paler lines, feeds on St John's-worts.

▲ **Barred Yellow** *Cidaria fulvata*. 5-7 in gardens, hedges,and other scrubby places. Rests with abdomen raised. Larva, wrinkled green with yellow rings, feeds on roses.

▲ **Dark Spinach** *Pelurga comitata*. Central band varies in intensity. 6-8 in scrubby and grassy places, especially on coasts. Larva is brownish with V-shaped marks on back and feeds on seeds of goosefoot and related plants. N & C.

▲ **Phoenix** *Eulithis prunata*. 7-8 in gardens, hedges, and woodland margins. Larva, green to brown with pale triangular markings, feeds on currants and gooseberries.

▲ **Spinach** *E. mellinata*. Forewing ground colour pale yellow to brick: hindwing cream: chequered fringes on all wings. Rests with forewings at right angles to body and hindwings more or less hidden beneath them. 6-8, mainly in gardens. Larva, green with white lines, feeds on currant bushes. ▲ **Northern Spinach** *E. populata* is much darker and has no chequered fringes: forewing sometimes entirely brown. 6-8 in woods and on moors. Grey or brown larva feeds on bilberry and other shrubs. N & C: mainly northern in B. ▲ **Barred Straw** *E. pyraliata* resembles a pale Spinach but lacks chequered fringes and central cross-lines are closer together. 6-8 in hedges and woodland margins. Larva feeds on cleavers and bedstraws.

GEOMETER MOTHS

Orange Underwing

Large Emerald

Grass Emerald

Small Emerald

Blotched Emerald

Sussex Emerald

Common Emerald

Little Emerald

Light Emerald

Mallow

Shaded Broad-bar

Chalk Carpet

Chimney Sweeper

Treble-bar

Barred Yellow

Dark Spinach

Phoenix

Spinach

Barred Straw

Northern Spinach

▲ **Common Marbled Carpet** *Chloroclysta truncata*. Extremely variable. 5-6 and 8-10 in woods and hedgerows. Green larva is very slender, usually with reddish stripes on sides, and feeds on many trees and shrubs and also on wild strawberry. N & C.

▲ **Dark Marbled Carpet** *C. citrata* is equally variable and difficult to separate from the last species, but dark basal area of forewing generally has a sharper outline and hindwing is dirty white instead of mid-grey. 7-8 (more or less between the two broods of *truncata*) in woods and on heaths and moors. N & C.

▲ **Beautiful Carpet** *Mesoleuca albicillata*. 5-8, mainly in open woodland. Larva is green with reddish brown blotches on the back. It feeds mainly on bramble.

△ **Pretty Chalk Carpet** *Melanthia procellata*. 5-8 in old hedges and woodland edges, mainly on chalk and limestone. Larva, pale brown with darker lines, feeds on traveller's joy. S & C.

▲ **Red Twin-spot Carpet** *Xanthorhoe spadicearia*. Ground colour pale to dark grey: central band may be brick-coloured: twin spots may be obscure. Hindwing dirty white with grey clouding. 5-9. Larva is brownish grey with pale diamonds and black spots. It feeds on many low-growing plants. ▲ **Dark-barred Twin-spot Carpet** *X. ferrugata* has a darker central band, sometimes purplish, outlined in rich brown. Hindwing dark grey. 5-9. N & C. ▲ **Flame Carpet** *X. designata* flies 5-9 in damp woods and hedges. Larva, yellowish grey with black spots and assorted other markings, feeds on crucifers. N & C. ▲ **Silver-ground Carpet** *X. montanata* may have greyer ground colour and paler cross band. 5-8 in woods and hedges. Larva is purplish brown on the back and greyish on the sides. It feeds on bedstraws and other low-growing plants. N & C. ▲ **Garden Carpet** *X. fluctuata* has ground colour from white to dark grey: black marks also vary in extent. 4-10 almost everywhere. Larva, green to grey with pale diamonds on he back, feeds on brassicas and other crucifers.

▲ **Green Carpet** *Colostygia pectinataria*. Green usually fades to yellowish after a few days. 5-8 in hedges and other scrubby places, including heathland. Larva is greenish brown with red V-shaped marks and feeds mainly on bedstraws.

▲ **Common Carpet** *Epirrhoe alternata*. Dark markings black to greyish brown. Outer white band always contains a thin grey line (absent in the similar ▲ **Wood Carpet** *E. rivata*). 5-9 in woods and hedges. Larva, brown or green with various markings, feeds on bedstraws.

△ **Argent and Sable** *Rheumaptera hastata*. Northern specimens smaller and darker. Day-flying 5-7 on heaths and in open woods. Larva is shiny olive green with reddish marks on the sides and feeds on birch and bilberry. N & C.

▲ **Purple Bar** *Cosmorhoe ocellata*. 5-9 in most rough habitats. Larva is pale brown with a darker network and feeds on bedstraws.

▲ **Foxglove Pug** *Eupithecia pulchellata*. Flies 5-7. Larva, normally yellowish green and often marked with purple, feeds in foxglove flowers. ▲ **Currant Pug** *E. assimilata* is one of several similar species but can normally be distinguished by the prominent white mark at rear angle of forewing. 5-9 in gardens and hedges. Larva, yellowish green with darker green lines, feeds on currant and hop. N & C.

▲ **Narrow-winged Pug** *E. nanata*. Pattern varies, but relatively long and pointed forewings distinguish this from most other pugs. 5-9 on heaths and commons. Larva, very pale green with red spots, feeds on heather. N & C. ▲ **Lime-speck Pug** *E. centaureata* flies 5-10 in gardens and rough habitats. Like most pugs, it rests with its wings outstretched and front edge of forewing more or less at right angles to body. Larva is green or yellow, often with red spots, and feeds on flowers of yarrow, ragwort, and other composites.

▲ **Netted Pug** *E. venosata* may have darker forewings with less distinct network. 5-7 in hedges and other rough places. Larva, greyish brown with a greenish underside and 3 dark lines on the back, feeds in the seed capsules of campions.

▲ **Tawny Speckled Pug** *E. icterata* may lack brick-coloured patch on forewing. 5-8.Larva, reddish brown with a white line on each side, feeds on flowers of yarrow and other composites. ▲ **Bordered Pug** *E. succenturiata* may have dark clouding over much of forewing. 6-8 in rough grassy places. Larva is reddish brown with black marks on the back and feeds on leaves of mugwort, yarrow, and related composites. N & C.

▲ **Green Pug** *Pasiphila rectangulata*. Grey to black, often with little green. 5-8. Larva is relatively stout, pale green with a reddish stripe on the back, and feeds in buds and flowers of apple, hawthorn,and related trees. ▲ **V-Pug** *Chloroclystis v-ata* flies 4-9. Larva is green, normally with 3 reddish lines on the back. It feeds on the flowers of many plants, including hemp agrimony, traveller's joy, and bramble. S & C.

CARPET and PUG MOTHS

Common Marbled Carpet

Beautiful Carpet

Pretty Chalk Carpet

Dark Marbled Carpet

Red Twin-spot Carpet

Dark-barred Twin-spot Carpet

Green Carpet

Flame Carpet

Silver-ground Carpet

↑
Garden Carpet

Argent and Sable

Common Carpet

Purple Bar

Foxglove Pug

Currant Pug

Narrow-winged Pug

Lime-speck Pug

Netted Pug

Green Pug

Tawny-speckled Pug

Bordered Pug

V-Pug

Magpie
larva

Large
Thorn
larva

▲ **Magpie** *Abraxas grossulariata*. Pattern rather variable, but usually easily recognised. 6-8 in gardens, hedgerows, and other scrubby habitats. Larva (left) feeds on blackthorn, gooseberry, currants, and many others shrubs.

△ **Clouded Magpie** *A. sylvata* flies 5-7 in woodland, commonly resting on dog's mercury leaves and resembling bird droppings. Larva, cream with black and yellow lines, feeds mainly on wych elm.

▲ **Clouded Border** *Lomaspilis marginata*. Amount of dark spotting varies, females normally lacking black band across centre of each wing. 5-8, especially in damp woods and hedgerows. Larva is pale green with darker lines and feeds on sallows.

▲ **Scorched Carpet** *Ligdia adustata*. 4-9 in woods and hedgerows. At rest on bark, the dark patches break up the outline and render the moth very hard to detect. Larva is bright green with rust-coloured spots and is very like the stalks of the spindle leaves on which it feeds.

▲ **Large Thorn** *Ennomos autumnaria*. Pale yellow to almost brick-coloured, always with brown wing-tips. 8-10 in woods and hedgerows. Like most thorn moths, it often rests with wings raised at an angle. A regular visitor to light. Larva (left) feeds on hawthorn and other trees.

▲ **August Thorn** *E. quercinaria* ranges from pale yellow to almost brick-coloured: female usually paler than male. Cross-lines almost parallel, but inner line bends sharply inwards near front margin. 8-9 in wooded areas and also tree-lined suburban avenues. Larva is greyish brown and stick-like, with several 'warts' on the back. It feeds on oak and other trees.

▲ **Canary-shouldered Thorn** *E. alniaria* is named for its bright yellow thoracic hair. Wings range from pale to deep yellow, always tinged with brown. 8-10 in wooded areas, especially where damp. Twig-like larva feeds on alder, birch, and other trees.

▲ **Dusky Thorn** *E. fuscantaria* is like August Thorn, but cross-lines converge strongly towards rear edge of forewing. 8-9 in wooded areas. Larva is green and feeds on ash.

▲ **Early Thorn** *Selenia dentaria*. Ground colour yellowish grey to brown. Insects of spring brood (3-5) much larger than those of summer brood (7-9): females usually paler than males, especially on underside. Summer insects often more boldly marked. Rests with wings partly raised or else closed vertically above the body: underside resembles dead leaf. Woodland and hedgerows. Twig-like larva feeds on hawthorn and many other trees.

▲ **Purple Thorn** *S. tetralunaria* flies in woodland, with spring brood (4-5) darker and larger than summer insects (7-9). Basal part of wing ranges from chestnut to purplish black. Rests like Early Thorn: underside similar to upperside. Larva feeds on a wide variety of trees and shrubs. △ **Lunar Thorn** *S. lunularia* is distinguished by very ragged wing margins. 5-7 in woods and hedgerows. Brown, twig-like larva feeds on many trees and shrubs.

▲ **Lilac Beauty** *Apeira syringaria*. 6-9 in woods, gardens, and hedgerows. Rests with forewings strangely creased to resemble a dead leaf. Larva (below) has 2 hooked outgrowths on the back and is very hard to spot among the twigs. It feeds on lilac, privet, and honeysuckle.

▲ **Small Waved Umber** *Horisme vitalbata*. Dark stripe across wings and body breaks up outline and makes the moth very hard to spot at rest on tree trunks and fences. 5-9 in hedgerows and woodland margins. Larva is greyish brown with darker lines and feeds on traveller's joy.

Early
Thorn
larva

Lilac Beauty
larva

Lilac Beauty

Small Waved Umber

Magpie

Clouded Magpie

Clouded Border

Large Thorn

Scorched Carpet

August Thorn

Canary-shouldered Thorn

Dusky Thorn

♀ spring

spring

Early Thorn

♂ summer

Purple Thorn

spring

summer

Lunar Thorn

177

▲ **Scalloped Hazel** *Odontopera bidentata*. Ranges from dirty white to black, the latter mainly in the north. 4-7 in woods and hedgerows. Brown or green twig-like larva feeds on almost any deciduous tree or shrub.

▲ **Feathered Thorn** *Colotois pennaria*. Pale to dark brick-coloured. Male antennae strongly feathered. 8-11 in woods and hedgerows. Twig-like brown larva feeds on a wide range of deciduous trees and shrubs.

▲ **Scalloped Oak** *Crocallis elinguaria*. Ground colour ranges from pale cream to brick. 6-8 in woods and hedges. Twig-like greyish larva feeds on most deciduous trees.

▲ **Orange Moth** *Angerona prunaria*. Sexes differ markedly in colour: sometimes brown with orange (male) or yellow (female) band on each wing. 5-7 in woodland. Twig-like larva feeds on most deciduous trees and shrubs.

▲ **Scorched Wing** *Plagodis dolabraria*. 4-9 in woodlands. Twig-like larva, brown with darker markings and a large 'wart' at the rear, feeds on various trees.

▲ **Brimstone** *Opisthograptis luteolata*. 4-10 in hedgerows and other scrubby places, including gardens. Brown or green larva (below) feeds on hawthorn and other shrubs.

▲ **Speckled Yellow** *Pseudopanthera macularia*. Brown markings vary. Day-flying 5-6 in scrubby habitats. Bright green larva feeds on wood sage and other labiates.

▲ **Swallowtailed Moth** *Ourapteryx sambucaria*. 6-8 in gardens, hedges, and other scrubby places. Larva (below) feeds on ivy, hawthorn, and many other shrubs.

Brimstone larva

Swallowtailed larva

▲ **Winter Moth** *Operophtera brumata*. 10-2 in gardens, hedges, and wherever else there are trees. Male often comes to lighted windows: female virtually wingless. Larva, green with pale lines and a darker one on the back, feeds on almost any deciduous tree: a serious pest of apples.

▲ **Early Moth** *Theria primaria*. 1-3 in hedges and other scrubby places. Female wingless. Larva, generally pale green with darker blotches and pale lines, feeds on hawthorn, blackthorn, and other shrubs.

▲ **Spring Usher** *Agriopis leucophaearia*. Often much paler than shown, but forewings may be entirely black. Female wingless. 1-4 in wooded areas. Larva, green with yellowish lines, feeds on oak.

▲ **Scarce Umber** *A. aurantiaria* flies 10-12 in wooded areas. Female is wingless. Larva is brownish yellow with purplish marks on sides and feeds on many trees and shrubs.

▲ **Dotted Border** *A. marginaria* may have forewings darker than shown, but small dots usually visible on outer margins of all wings. Female wingless. 2-4 in hedges and other scrubby places. Larva, greenish brown with dark crosses on back, feeds on many trees and shrubs.

▲ **Mottled Umber** *Erannis defoliaria*. Very variable: forewings sometimes uniformly straw-coloured or dark brown. Female wingless. 10-3 in gardens, woods, and hedges. Larva ranges from straw-coloured to deep brown, usually with yellow patches along the sides. It feeds on almost any deciduous tree or shrub: often an orchard pest.

▲ **November Moth** *Epirrita dilutata*. 9-12 in wooded areas. Larva is green with deep red spots or lines and feeds on many trees and shrubs.

▲ **March Moth** *Alsophila aescularia*. 2-4 in gardens, hedges, and most wooded areas. Wings wrapped partly round body at rest. Female wingless. Larva, pale green with white lines, feeds on most deciduous trees and shrubs.

▲ **Small Yellow Wave** *Hydrelia flammeolaria*. 5-7 in woods and hedges: rests with wings widely spread. Larva, green with pale rings, feeds on maple and alder.

▲ **Rivulet** *Perizoma affinitata*. 5-7 in rough, grassy places. Larva is pinkish brown and feeds in seed capsules of campions.

▲ **Yellow Shell** *Camptogramma bilineata*. Ground colour yellow or brown: central band sometimes very dark. 6-8 in gardens and hedges. Larva is brown or green, paler below, and feeds on many low-growing plants. It bends into a ?-shape when resting.

▲ **Shoulder Stripe** *Anticlea badiata*. 3-5 in hedges and other scrubby places. Larva, generally green with paler rings, feeds on roses.

Small Yellow Wave   **Rivulet**   **Yellow Shell**   **Shoulder Stripe**

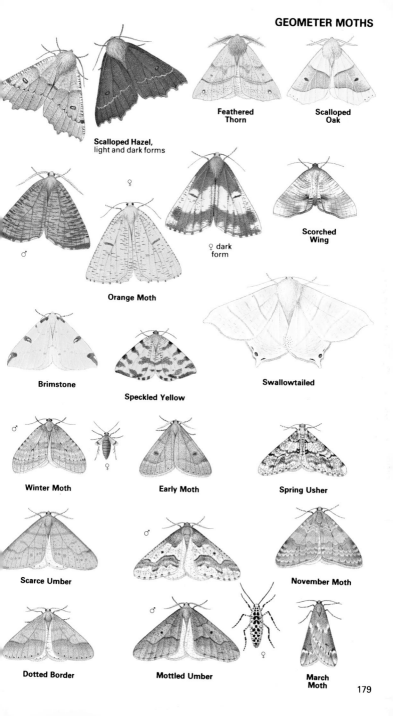

Scalloped Hazel,
light and dark forms

Feathered
Thorn

Scalloped
Oak

♀

♂

♀ dark
form

Scorched
Wing

Orange Moth

Brimstone

Speckled Yellow

Swallowtailed

♂

Winter Moth

Early Moth

Spring Usher

Scarce Umber

♂

Mottled Umber

♂

♀

November Moth

Dotted Border

March
Moth

179

Peppered Moth larva

Waved Umber

Oak Beauty larva

▲ **Peppered Moth** *Biston betularia*. Exists in two main forms – the speckled (normal) and the black (melanic). The latter was first noticed in the middle of the 19th century in industrial areas, where it clearly has an advantage on smoke-blackened trees and buildings, but it is now widespread in many other habitats and sometimes more common than the normal form. This industrial melanism has since been discovered in many other moths. The Peppered Moth flies 5-8 in woods and gardens. The larva (left) is greyish brown or bright green, with a deeply notched head. It feeds on many trees and shrubs.

△s **Oak Beauty** *B. strataria*. Flies 2-5, mainly in woodland. Larva (below left) feeds on oak and many other trees. S & C.

▲ **Pale Brindled Beauty** *Phigalia pilosaria*. 11-4 in hedgerows and woodland. Female is wingless and found mainly on tree trunks. Stick-like larva is greyish brown with darker bud-like 'warts' and feeds on most deciduous trees and shrubs. N & C.

▲ **Brindled Beauty** *Lycia hirtaria*. Ground colour grey or brown, usually heavily speckled with yellow. Female wings somewhat longer and narrower. 2-4, wherever there are trees, including town streets and parks. Larva is reddish brown or grey with yellow and red markings. It feeds on most kinds of deciduous trees and shrubs.

▲ **Waved Umber** *Menophra abruptaria*. Ground colour often much darker, especially in male. 3-6 in woods, hedgerows, and gardens. Remarkably well camouflaged at rest on trees and fences, where it always sits with its body horizontal and the wing pattern running vertically to match the furrows – which on tree trunks are almost always vertical. Larva is greyish, often marked with pink, and very twig-like. It feeds on privet, lilac, and other shrubs. Cocoon, spun on twigs and covered with fragments of bark and algae, is almost invisible. S & C.

▲ **Willow Beauty** *Peribatodes rhomboidaria*. Ground colour smoky grey or yellowish. One of several rather similar species, but distinguished from most of them by central cross-line on forewing having only one bulge (in front of middle). Male antennae strongly feathered. 6-9 in woods and gardens. Larva is reddish brown and feeds on ivy, hawthorn, and many other shrubs. S & C.

△ **Great Oak Beauty** *Hypomecis roboraria*. Black cross-lines vary in intensity and sometimes almost absent. 6-7 in oakwoods. The larva feeds on oak and closely resembles the twigs. S & C.

▲ **Engrailed** *Ectropis bistortata*. Markings vary in intensity, and ground colour often greyer. Male antennae not feathery. 3-9 in wooded areas. Larva is greyish and feeds on many deciduous trees and shrubs. N & C.

△ **Square Spot** *Paradarisa consonaria* has a clear square mark near outer margin of forewing. Male antennae not feathered. 4-6 in woodland. Larva feeds on numerous trees and shrubs, including pine. S & C.

▲ **Bordered White** *Bupalus piniaria*. Also called the Pine Looper. Male ground colour is white in northern Europe, including northern B, and yellowish in the south. Female is orange brown in north and yellowish elsewhere. All forms have brown wing-tips. 5-8 in coniferous woodland. Larva is green with pale stripes and feeds on the needles of many conifers, often causing severe damage in plantations.

▲ **Common Heath** *Ematurga atomaria*. Ground colour yellowish in male and white in female. Dark speckling often so dense as to make wings brown all over, but female usually less heavily speckled than male. Day-flying, 5-9 on heathland. Larva is grey to dark green, often with rows of white dashes on back. It feeds on heather, heaths, and various legumes.

Bordered White at rest

GEOMETER MOTHS

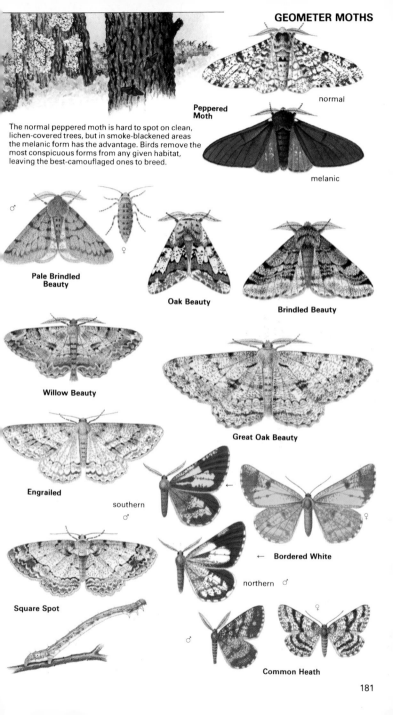

The normal peppered moth is hard to spot on clean, lichen-covered trees, but in smoke-blackened areas the melanic form has the advantage. Birds remove the most conspicuous forms from any given habitat, leaving the best-camouflaged ones to breed.

Peppered Moth

normal

melanic

Pale Brindled Beauty

Oak Beauty

Brindled Beauty

Willow Beauty

Great Oak Beauty

Engrailed

southern ♂

Bordered White

Square Spot

northern ♂

Common Heath

White Pinion-spotted

Common Wave

Clouded Silver

Common White Wave

▲ **Clouded Silver** *Lomographa temerata*. Silky white wings with a greater or lesser amount of dark grey shading readily distinguish this species, although clouding may be absent in some females. 5-6 in woods and hedgerows. Larva, green with reddish spots, feeds on blackthorn and several other trees and shrubs. C.

▲ **White Pinion-spotted** *L. bimaculata* has silky white wings like Clouded Silver, but black spots on front edge of forewing readily distinguish it. 4-6 in woods and scrubby places. Larva is dark green with purplish arrowhead marks on the back. It feeds on wild cherry, blackthorn, and other rosaceous trees and shrubs. C.

▲ **Common Wave** *Cabera exanthemata*. White, sprinkled with yellowish grey. Outer cross-line distinctly curved. 5-9 in wooded areas, especially where moist. Larva is green with yellow rings and black spots and usually has purplish marks on the sides. It feeds on sallows, alder, and various other trees.

▲ **Common White Wave** *C. pusaria* resembles Common Wave but is whiter (sometimes tinged with pink) and outer cross-line is virtually straight. 5-9, mainly in wooded country. Larva is normally purplish brown with white spots. It feeds on sallows, birches, and various other trees.

▲ **V-Moth** *Macaria wauaria*. Forewings may be darker: dark V near front margin usually distinct, although posterior arm may be faint. 6-8 in gardens and open woods. Larva is green or brown with white lines and black dots. It feeds on gooseberry and currant.

▲ **Latticed Heath** *Chiasma clathrata* has dirty white to yellowish brown ground colour. Lattice is dark brown or black, always more reticulate than in Common Heath (p. 180). 4-9 in grassy places, mainly day-flying. Larva, green with white lines, feeds on clovers and trefoils.

▲ **Brown Silver-line** *Petrophora chlorosata*. Forewings sometimes tinged with pink. 5-7 on heathland and other bracken-rich habitats. Larva, dark green with brown lines, feeds on bracken fronds.

△s **Straw Belle** *Aspitates gilvaria*. Forewings heavily speckled with brown in female. 6-8 in grassy places. Larva, pinkish grey with dark lines on the back, feeds mainly on low-growing plants. Local in S & C: mainly on chalk in B.

Psodos quadrifaria Yellow bands may be narrower. Day-flying 6-7. Larva is brown and feeds on a wide range of low-growing plants. Alps and other mountains of S & C.

CADDIS FLIES   Order Trichoptera

An order of nearly 6,000 species of holometabolous insects, almost all of which spend their larval life in water. About 400 species occur in Europe and 189 of them are found in the British Isles. The adults are mostly brownish, moth-like insects with relatively weak flight. Some fly by day, but most are active at night and often come to lighted windows and light traps, often quite a long way from water. There are normally four rather flimsy wings all covered with fine hairs, although the hindwings are generally less hairy and more transparent than the forewings. There are relatively few cross-veins, and the wings are held roofwise over the body at rest. The slender antennae, usually as long as the forewings and sometimes much longer, are held out in front of the head at rest. Ocelli are present or absent. Most adult caddis flies probably do not feed, although some species regularly lap nectar from waterside flowers. There is never a proboscis such as we find in most moths.

The head bears a pair of conspicuous maxillary palps, whose form is important in the classification and identification of the insects: some are very long, while others are short and swollen. Females always have 5-segmented palps, but the males of many species have fewer segments. The spurs on the tibiae are also valuable aids to identification, for their numbers vary from family to family. It is conventional to describe the spur pattern with a series of numbers: 2-2-4, for example, indicates that there are two spurs on the front tibia, 2 on the middle tibia, and 4 on the hind tibia. The spurs are usually very easy to see, but among the families Phryganeidae and Limnephilidae (p. 184) the legs also bear numerous spines, some of which may be at least half as long as the spurs. Take care that you really are looking at the spurs when counting them, and make sure that none has broken off in old or dried specimens.

The venation is another important factor in the identification of caddis fly families, although less easy to use. Classification revolves largely around the forking of the veins near the margin and also on the presence or absence of a discal cell near the centre of the forewing, but most of the caddis flies on the following pages can be recognised without looking at the veins. Separation of closely related species often necessitates examination of the genitalia.

Eggs are commonly laid in gelatinous masses in or on the water, although some are laid under stones on the beds of dried-up ponds and streams and hatch when the water returns in the autumn. A few species lay their eggs on overhanging vegetation and the larvae fall into the water when they hatch. The larvae are largely omnivorous, although some species show leanings towards either plant or animal food. The majority make portable homes or cases with small stones or plant fragments fitted on to a silken tube surrounding the body. The silk is produced by the larva's salivary glands. Each species builds to its own pattern, although closely related species have similar cases. The case is open at both ends, and more material is added to the front as the animal grows. The cases blend well with the surroundings and only the head and legs protrude when the larvae move about. A range of cases is shown on the following pages.

The larvae of some caddis flies are completely naked, while others shelter in silken nets. The latter are usually spun among water plants and they trap small animals and other food particles. Net-spinning species usually live in running water.

The insects pupate in their cases after cementing them to stones or other large objects. Species that make no larval cases construct simple pupation chambers of silk and sand. When the adult is ready to emerge, the pupa bites its way out of its case and swims to the surface or to the bank, where the adult bursts out and immediately flies away. The life cycle generally takes about a year.

▲ **Phryganea grandis** Phryganeidae. Spurs 2-4-4. Discal cell long and narrow. Male palps 4-segmented. Male is smaller and lacks black stripe in forewing. 5-8, with peak in early July: the largest British caddis fly. Breeds in still and slow-moving water, including large lowland rivers, with plenty of submerged vegetation. Case of spirally-arranged plant fragments. Absent from far south. ▲ **P. striata** is very similar but female has a more slender black stripe broken into 3 short dashes.

Oligostomis reticulata. Spurs 2-4-4. Mottled pattern combined with size readily distinguishes this species from most others. Hindwing has dark border and a dark stripe across the middle. Male palps 4-segmented. Larval case and habits like *Phryganea* . N & C. △n **Hagenella clathrata** is similar but has more dark clouding on hindwing. N & C.

Family Limnephilidae.
A large family in which the front leg never has more than one spur: formula 1-3-4 in most species. Forewings parchment-like with few hairs: discal cell fairly long and obvious. Hindwings rather broad and very transparent.

▲ **Glyphotaelius pellucidus**. Spurs 1-3-4. Readily identified by strongly notched or concave outer margin of forewing. Female less strongly marked: forewing often plain yellowish brown. Abdomen generally greenish. 4-10. Lakes and ponds: case of pieces of dead leaves, completely concealing larva from above. Absent from Iberia.

▲ **Limnephilus lunatus**. Spurs 1-3-4. Forewings, as in all members of this large genus, narrow with an almost straight front edge and sharply truncated at tip. Markings black or brown and variable, but always a pale crescent on outer margin. 5-11. Breeds in all kinds of water: sometimes abundant in watercress beds. Case of overlapping leaf fragments and other debris, sometimes with added shells and sand grains.
▲ **L. flavicornis** is similar but lacks pale crescent. Wings rather shiny: British specimens often much less marked, rarely with more than a dark line along rear edge of forewing. 5-11. Breeds mainly in small ponds. Case of various materials arranged in criss-cross fashion: occasionally made entirely of small shells. There are many other *Limnephilus* species, nearly all with clear patches on forewings, distinguished with certainty only by examining the genitalia.

▲ **Anabolia nervosa**. Spurs 1-3-4. Size very variable. Forewings often paler. 6-11. Breeds in still and running water but most common in streams. Case of sand grains, to which are attached a few of small sticks: the latter prevent trout and other fishes from swallowing the cases.

▲ **Grammotaulius nigropunctatus**. Spurs 1-3-4. Forewing rather pointed. Hindwing with an indented outer margin and a dark streak just in front of indentation: dark streak shows through delicate forewing at rest. 8-10. Breeds in marshy areas, including small ditches. Case of overlapping reed fragments. △ **G. nitidus** is larger and has a more pointed forewing, especially in the male. C.

▲ **Micropterna sequax**. Spurs 0-3-4 in male: 1-3-4 in female. 5-11. Very common at lights. Breeds in small, clear streams. Case of sand grains, but with a region of small stones, sharply demarcated, at the front. There are several similar species.

▲ **Halesus radiatus**. Spurs 1-3-3. Apex of forewing smoothly rounded, with a conspicuous pattern of finger-like, pale-edged grey streaks. Grey streaks and patches elsewhere in wing as well. 7-11. Breeds in running water. Case of assorted plant debris neatly fitted together: up to 3 slender twigs run the length of the case and project from both ends. ▲ **H. digitatus** is similar but larger: wing-tips slightly less rounded and pattern slightly less obvious. Case of debris and sand grains, but usually without sticks.

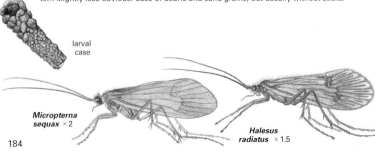

larval
case

**Micropterna
sequax** × 2

**Halesus
radiatus** × 1.5

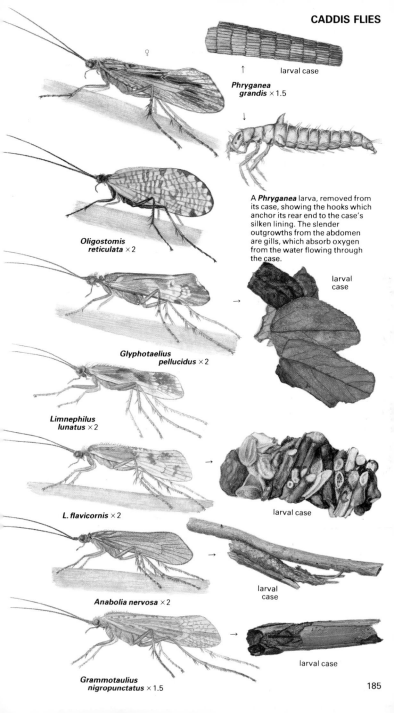

Phryganea grandis × 1.5

larval case

Oligostomis reticulata × 2

A *Phryganea* larva, removed from its case, showing the hooks which anchor its rear end to the case's silken lining. The slender outgrowths from the abdomen are gills, which absorb oxygen from the water flowing through the case.

Glyphotaelius pellucidus × 2

larval case

Limnephilus lunatus × 2

L. flavicornis × 2

larval case

Anabolia nervosa × 2

larval case

Grammotaulius nigropunctatus × 1.5

larval case

185

▲ **Brachycentrus subnubilus** Brachycentridae. Spurs 2-3-3, distinguishing this from near all other caddis flies: no other British species has this formula. Basal antennal segment stout and hairy. Male palps 3-segmented and very hairy. Female wings longer and more pointed. 3-7: very common around slow-moving rivers. Case of young larva made of plant debris and square in cross section: older cases of silk only and attached to vegetation. Larva strains food from water with comb-like middle legs.

▲ **Sericostoma personatum** Sericostomatidae. Spurs 2-2-4. Male palps 1-segmented and very broad and hairy: held in front of face like a muff. 6-9. Breeds in streams. Case of sand grains, very smooth and gently curved.

▲ **Goera pilosa** Goeridae. Spurs 2-4-4 and very conspicuous. Basal antennal segment very hairy. Male palps 3-segmented: 3rd segment long and bristly and held close to face. Body and wings yellow or greyish yellow. 5-9, around lakes and rivers. Case of sand grains with small pebbles at the sides.

▲ **Silo nigricornis**. Spurs 2-4-4. Basal antennal segment large and hairy. Male palps 3-segmented and very hairy: held in front of face. Male black when fresh: female brown. A hairy stripe runs through middle of male hindwing (see below). 5-8 near running water. Case like that of *Goera*. S & C. There are several similar species.

▲ **Lepidostoma hirtum** Lepidostomatidae. Spurs 2-4-4. Basal antennal segment longer than head and bearing long hairs. Male palps 2-3-segmented: short and club-like and very hairy. Male wings shorter and broader, with dark scales. 4-9. Breeds in still and running water. Case of vegetable debris and square in cross-section.

▲ **Hydropsyche pellucidula** Hydropsychidae. Spurs 2-4-4. Basal antennal segment slightly swollen. Last palpal segment much longer than the rest. No ocelli. Discal cell short and broad. Amount of mottling on forewing very variable. 5-9, flying in sunshine: very common. Breeds in still and slow-moving water. Larva spins net among gravel to trap food. There are many similar species, difficult to distinguish.

△ **Philopotamus montanus** Philopotamidae. Spurs 2-4-4. Last palpal segment longer than all the others together (see below). Ocelli present. Hindwings smoky grey. 4-8, mainly around upland streams. Larvae are net-spinners in swift-flowing streams. Wing pattern readily distinguishes this species in B, but there are several similar species on the continent.

▲ **Polycentropus flavomaculatus** Polycentropidae. Spurs 3-4-4 and very large. Last palpal segment about as long as all the others together. Antennae brown with *narrow* yellow bands. Wings very hairy. Female up to twice size of male. 5-9: one of the commonest caddis flies. Larva spins pouch-shaped net in slow-moving water. There are several similar species.

▲ **Tinodes waeneri** Psychomyiidae. Spurs 2-4-4. Last palpal segment long and slender. No ocelli. Veins very distinct: discal cell short and broad. Hindwing narrow, with front edge slightly cut away towards tip (see below). 5-8. Breeds in lakes and rivers, spinning galleries of silk, attached to stones and usually coated with mud. There are several similar, but generally smaller species.

▲ **Psychomyia pusilla**. Spurs 2-4-4. Hindwing sharply pointed and with a small spike on front edge (see below). 5-9: day-flying in warm weather, often in great swarms. Breeds like *Tinodes* in streams and rivers.

▲ **Hydroptila sparsa** Hydroptilidae. Wings very narrow, pointed, and extremely hairy. Spurs 0-2-4. Often scuttles over waterside rocks and plants: 5-9. Breeds in still or running water. Larva naked until final instar, when it makes a silken, sausage-shaped chamber coated with fine sand grains. There are many very similar species.

Silo: hindwing of ♂

Tinodes hindwing

Psychomyia hindwing

palp of *Philopotamus*   palp of female *Sericostoma*

palp of female
Lepidostoma

mature larval case

Brachycentrus subnubilus ×2.5

Goera pilosa ×2.5

lp →

head of ♂

Sericostoma personatum ×2

larval case of *Goera*

larval case of *Lepidostoma*

Lepidostoma hirtum ×3 ♀

Hydropsyche pellucidula ×2.5

Silo nigricornis ×2.5

Philopotamus montanus ×3

Polycentropus flavomaculatus ×3

Tinodes waeneri ×2
↓

larval galleries

Psychomyia pusilla ×4

Hydroptila sparsa ×8

▲ **Odontocerum albicorne** Odontoceridae. Spurs 2-4-4: large. Best distinguished by antennae, which appear distinctly toothed under a lens: basal antennal segment very thick. Wings silvery grey when fresh, becoming darker or yellowish with age. Hindwing of male with long tuft of hair along inner margin. Female larger than male. 6-10. Breeds in running water with stony bottom. Case of sand grains.

▲ **Molanna angustata** Molannidae. Spurs 2-4-4. No ocelli. Forewings dark grey to brown, with conspicuous venation, especially near tips. Legs rather long. Rests at an angle, with wings folded round body to resemble a piece of dead grass. 5-9. Breeds in slow and still-moving water with a sandy bottom. Case of sand grains: tubular, with a broad, flat shield on dorsal side. N & C.

▲ **Beraea pullata** Beraeidae. Spurs 2-2-4. No ocelli. Head projects forward between antennae. Palps long and stout: held upright in front of face in life. 5-7. Breeds in shallow water at edges of lakes and rivers, as well as in ponds and marshes. Case of sand grains: tubular and tapering and gently curved. There are several similar species.

▲ **Athripsodes cinereus** Leptoceridae. Spurs 2-2-2: all members of this large family have just 2 spurs on the hind tibia. Very long antennae, especially in males, are also a feature of the family. Palps very long and hairy. Colour and markings vary. Female smaller. 6-9: very common around lakes and large rivers. Case of sand grains: slender and tapering.

▲ **Ceraclea nigronervosa**. Spurs 2-2-2. Body entirely black. Forewing veins rather conspicuous. Hindwing very broad and triangular. Palps long and hairy. Female smaller. 5-7, around lakes and large rivers. Flight strong. Case of secretion, with irregular bands of sand grains. N & C.

▲ **Mystacides longicornis**. Spurs 0-2-2. Easily recognised as a rule by wing pattern, although this is occasionally obscured. Male eyes very large. Antennae very pale. Palps long and plumose and spread out to sides, almost like legs, at rest. 5-9: very common around lakes and ponds. Flight strong. Case of small stones or sand grains: almost straight and tapering very gently. Several closely related species have steely blue or black forewings.

▲ **Triaenodes bicolor**. Spurs 1-2-2. Readily identified by chestnut forewings when fresh. Antennae distinctly ringed. Palps very long. 6-9: often abundant around lakes and ponds. Case of very regular, spirally-arranged green leaf fragments: long and straight. Larva swims with aid of feathery middle legs: prefers weedy ponds.

△ **Rhyacophila obliterata** Rhyacophilidae. Spurs 3-4-4: large. First 2 palpal segments short and thick, the 2nd being almost spherical. Ocelli present. 6-9, mainly around upland streams. Larva makes no case and lives freely on stream bed. There are several closely related species, but *obliterata* is easily recognised by bright yellow wings when fresh, although colour fades after death.

▲ **Agapetus fuscipes** Glossosomatidae. Spurs 2-4-4. First 2 palpal segments short and thick. Wings narrow, black with golden hairs. Male has long yellow spine under abdomen. 5-12: one of the commonest caddis flies. Breeds in fast-flowing streams with stony bottoms. Case of small stones, domed above and flat below: often clothing submerged rocks in vast numbers.

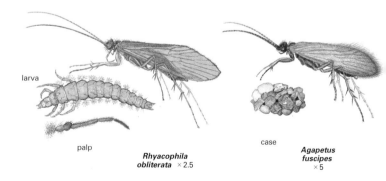

larva

palp

case

**Rhyacophila
obliterata** × 2.5

**Agapetus
fuscipes**
× 5

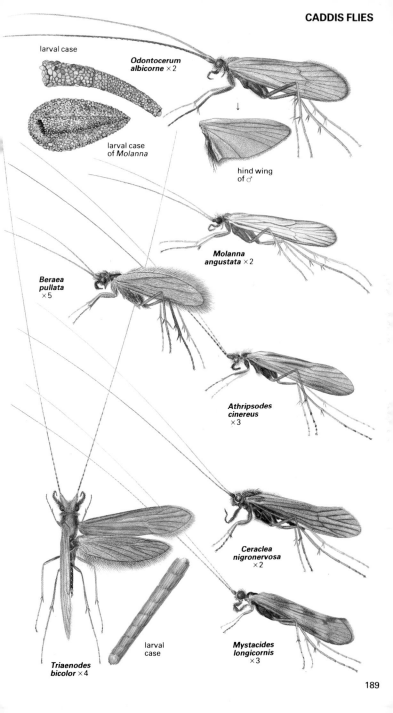

larval case

Odontocerum albicorne × 2

larval case of *Molanna*

hind wing of ♂

Molanna angustata × 2

Beraea pullata × 5

Athripsodes cinereus × 3

Triaenodes bicolor × 4

larval case

Ceraclea nigronervosa × 2

Mystacides longicornis × 3

TRUE FLIES   Order Diptera

An immense order of insects containing nearly 100,000 known species. The hindwings are reduced to minute pin-shaped structures known as halteres or balancers, which act as gyroscopes and help to maintain stability in flight. The single pair of membranous wings gives the order its name: 'two-winged'. A few species, mainly ectoparasites (p. 213), are entirely wingless.

Although a few hover-flies (pp 204-206) are able to crush pollen grains, flies feed essentially on liquids: mainly nectar, but many other liquids too. The females of mosquitoes, horse-flies, and several other groups feed mainly on blood, attacking both man and his domestic animals to get it. The blood-sucking in itself is serious only where the insects exist in huge numbers, but many carry dangerous diseases, such as malaria. The flies' mouth-parts vary with the diet. Female mosquitoes have needle-like jaws that fit neatly together to form a hypodermic syringe, complete with a protective sheath that is drawn back when the insect is about to pierce a victim. Female horse-flies have more blade-like jaws that cut the victim's skin: a fleshy pad then mops up the blood flowing from the wound. House-flies and blow-flies depend entirely on mopping up surface fluids with a pair of spongy pads at the tip of the mouth-parts, although they can deal with soluble solids like sugar by pouring digestive fluids on to them first. They spread disease by regurgitating over our food after sampling dung or carrion. Some flies do not feed at all as adults.

Compound **eyes** are always present, and often so large that they meet on the top of the head. This holoptic condition is most often found in males, but the females of some species also have it. The presence or absence of **ocelli**, which generally form a small triangle on the top of the head, often helps with identification, as do the form of the **antennae** and the arrangement of bristles on the head and **thorax**. The bulk of the thorax consists of the wing-bearing mesothorax, with the roughly triangular scutellum often prominent at the rear. In some flies, notably the parasitic tachinids (p. 212), there is also a post-scutellum bulging from underneath the scutellum itself. Each **foot** normally has two small pads, but some groups of flies have three on each foot.

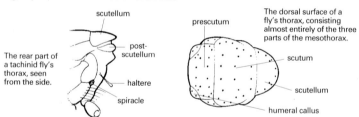

scutellum

post-scutellum

The rear part of a tachinid fly's thorax, seen from the side.

haltere

spiracle

prescutum

The dorsal surface of a fly's thorax, consisting almost entirely of the three parts of the mesothorax.

scutum

scutellum

humeral callus

Wing venation is extremely variable. Several schemes are in use for naming and numbering the veins: here we have used a simple numbering system for the major veins. Very close to the base of the front margin there is a small and often inconspicuous vein called the humeral vein. The sub-costa runs close to the front margin, often joining it about half way along although it reaches almost to the wing-tip in some species. The other main veins, sometimes termed long veins, can be numbered from the front. The first is commonly known as the radius, while the last two (6 & 7) are the anal veins. Venation is much reduced in many flies, especially towards the rear of the wing, and is often complicated by the branching of some or all of the veins. Some veins also fuse together, and it is not always possible to determine which vein is which simply by counting. But there are some useful clues: the anterior cross-vein always links veins 3 and 4, while the posterior cross-vein – usually near the centre of the wing – links 4 and 5. Many species have a discal cell near the centre: its shape varies a good deal, but the anterior cross-vein generally joins its anterior margin. Between the discal cell and the wing-base are generally two basal cells, whose relative shapes and lengths are important. The anal cell, if present, lies just behind the basal cells.

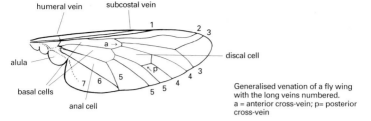

Generalised venation of a fly wing with the long veins numbered. a = anterior cross-vein; p= posterior cross-vein

The front or costal margin of the wing sometimes has one or two minute breaks in it, usually quite near the base and mainly in the smaller flies. The hind margin of the wing may have one or more distinct lobes near the base. The outer lobe, known as the alula, is generally the biggest and is quite obvious. The inner lobe, known as the calypter or thoracic squama, is generally minute, but in some flies – notably the house-flies and blow-flies – it forms a prominent flap over the haltere. These flies are known as calypterate flies.

Classification The flies are grouped into three sub-orders: Nematocera, Brachycera, and Cyclorrhapha. Members of the **Nematocera** (pp 192-197) have slender, many segmented antennae which are usually longer than the head and thorax together. Most of the segments are alike and there is no bristle or arista at the tip. The anal cell, if present, is open and gets wider towards the margin.

Antennae

Nematocera   Cyclorrhapha   Brachycera

The **Brachycera** (pp 198-205) are mostly much stouter flies whose antennae are always shorter than the thorax (Brachycera = short-horn). The antennae are quite stout and often horn-like. They are basically 3-segmented, although the 3rd segment is often strongly ringed and the antennae then appear to be many-segmented. Many have a terminal bristle. The discal cell is nearly always present and the anal cell is closed or strongly tapered towards the wing margin.

In the **Cyclorrhapha** (pp 204-216), the antennae are usually much less prominent. The three main segments are generally pendulous, and a slender bristle springs from the dorsal surface of the 3rd segment rather than from the tip. In most species, only the bristle is visible from above. It is the young stages, however, that reveal the main differences between the Brachycera and the Cyclorrhapha.

Larvae and Life Histories The larvae of flies are incredibly varied in form and habits, some living on land and some in the water, some inside plants, and others as parasites inside various other animals. They include many serious agricultural pests. The larvae have no true legs, although many have fleshy outgrowths that help them to wriggle about. The head is quite prominent in many nematocerans, and equipped with biting jaws. The brachyceran larva has a much-reduced head, which can be retracted into the thorax, although it still has biting jaws. The cyclorrhaphan larva has no real head and is the familiar, tapering maggot. Its jaws, at the narrow end, are represented by minute hooks whose main function is to scrape and tear at the food and release fluids that the maggot can imbibe.

There are normally four larval instars among the nematocerans, five to eight in the brachycerans, and only three in the cyclorrhaphans. The **pupa** is quite mobile in the first two groups, very much so in the mosquitoes and some other families. But the cyclorrhaphan pupa is quite immobile inside a hard, barrel-shaped puparium, formed from the hardened final larval skin. When ready to emerge, the pupa inflates a sac at the front of the head and the pressure forces up a round lid. The pale sac, known as the ptilinum, can often be seen in freshly-emerged flies, which therefore appear rather deformed, but it soon deflates and recedes into the head, leaving just a faint groove, shaped like an inverted U, around the bases of the antennae.

Tipula abdomen

CRANE-FLIES Tipulidae. Rather leggy flies commonly called **daddy-long-legs**. Legs readily break off when handled. Many are only mosquito-sized, but all can be recognised by the V-shaped thoracic suture and the lack of ocelli. A clear discal cell in outer half of wing, and two anal veins reaching wing margin. Larger species generally rest with wings extended: smaller species generally fold wings flat over body, and often bob up and down on their legs when at rest – hence an alternative name of bobbing gnats. Many of the smaller species form dense mating swarms. Female abdomen is pointed, for laying eggs in soil or other materials. Some females are wingless and can be seen on house walls in late autumn. Adults may lap nectar and other fluids, but do not feed much. Larvae live mainly as scavengers in soil or decaying matter, often in water.

▲ **Tipula maxima.** One of the largest crane-flies. Like most *Tipula* species, it rests with wings at about 90° to each other. 4-8, mainly in wooded areas. ▲ *T. vittata* is smaller and has a less extensive pattern. 4-6 in damp woods.

▲ *T. oleracea* is one of the commonest species. The wing is brown along the front, with a brown stigma, but otherwise plain. Antennae 13-segmented, with at least the first 3 segments brick-coloured. Female wings as long as abdomen. 4-10, but most abundant 5-6. ▲ *T. paludosa* is very like *oleracea* but antennae are 14-segmented (terminal one minute) and only first 2 segments are brick-coloured. Female wings shorter the abdomen, the latter often with rusty tinge. 4-10, but most abundant in autumn. Larvae of these two species are crop-damaging leatherjackets (p. 294).

▲ **Nephrotoma crocata.** Sides of thorax almost entirely black. Wings usually folded at rest. 5-8. Especially common in damp woods.

▲ **Spotted Crane-fly** *N. appendiculata* – illustrated here without its wings – has a very faint stigma: wing otherwise clear and shiny. 5-8, especially in cultivated areas. Larva, similar to that of *Tipula* is a common garden pest. ▲ *N. quadrifaria* is similar but has a dark stigma and dark streak below it. Both species hold wings flat over body at rest.

▲ **Limonia nubeculosa.** One of several species with spotted wings. Latter are folded flat at rest. Sub-costal vein runs into front margin, not into radius as in most other large crane-flies. No tibial spurs. Femur with 3 dark rings. All year, mainly in woodland.

▲ **Ctenophora atrata.** Antennae range from orange to black: strongly pectinate in male, toothed near tip in female. Male abdomen ranges from black to yellow, with spotted intermediate forms: female abdomen sometimes nearly all red. 4-7 in damp woods.

△ *C. ornata* has female antennae toothed throughout. 5-7 in woods. Both species breed in decaying timber; *atrata*, with its tougher ovipositor, preferring harder and less rotted wood.

▲ **Ptychoptera contaminata** Ptychopteridae. Resembles crane-flies but thoracic suture is U-shaped. No discal cell and only one anal vein. Legs with strong tibial spurs – much more prominent than in crane-flies. Abundant in damp places 5-10. Larva (p. 296) is aquatic. There are several similar species, all with spotted wings.

Liponeura cinerascens Blepharoceridae. A weak-flying insect with very long legs and a network of fine creases on wings. Ocelli present. Female predatory. Larva and pupa aquatic. Wings fully expanded, although folded, in pupa: latter 'explodes' at surface and adult flies away immediately, but wings never lose creases. One of several similar species living around upland streams in summer. S & C.

**Liponeura
cinerascens**
× 1.5

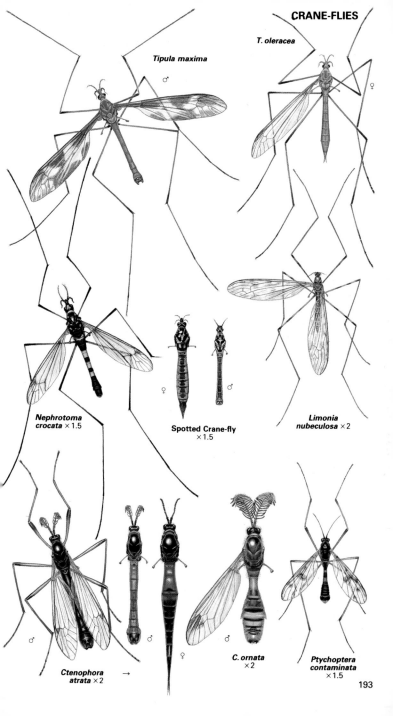

CRANE-FLIES

Tipula maxima ♂

T. oleracea ♀

Nephrotoma crocata ×1.5

Spotted Crane-fly ×1.5
♀ ♂

Limonia nubeculosa ×2

Ctenophora atrata ×2 →
♂ ♀

C. ornata ×2 ♂

Ptychoptera contaminata ×1.5

193

Culicine
at rest

Anopheline
at rest

▲ *Trichocera relegationis* Trichoceridae. Like a small crane-fly, but 2nd anal vein very short and sharply bent. Legs not decid-uous. Ocelli present. Abundant everywhere in winter, males forming dense mating swarms. Less common at other times of year. Larvae live in decaying matter. One of several similar species, mostly without a spot in middle of wing, known as winter gnats. ▲ *T. annulata* has a banded abdomen.

MOSQUITOES Culicidae. A large family of flies (over 1600 known species) with a long, forward-pointing proboscis that female uses to suck blood. Male, distinguished by bushy antennae, feeds on nectar. Male palps long and hairy: female palps always slender. Wing veins and margins clothed with scales. Mainly nocturnal, although some woodland species are active by day. Larvae (p. 296) are aquatic. Two groups are generally recognised – the culicines and the anophelines. Culicines rest with body slightly arched and abdomen almost parallel to surface: female palps very short. Anophelines, represented in Europe only by *Anopheles* species, are the malaria-carriers. They rest with body sharply inclined to surface and female palps are about as long as proboscis. Both groups fold wings flat over body at rest.

▲ *Culex pipiens*. Abdominal segments dark brown with white bands at front of each. Female abdomen blunt-ended. Male palps up-turned. Abundant everywhere, hibernating as adult in buildings. Rarely bites man in B. There are several similar species, but with less clearly banded abdomen.

▲ *Culiseta annulata*. One of the largest mosquitoes. Wings spotted. Legs and abdomen boldly banded. Common in many habitats, hibernating as adult in buildings. Bites man, often causing large blisters.

▲ *Aedes punctor*. Abdomen brown with yellowish bands, each notched in middle. Legs dark. Female abdomen pointed. Male palps swollen at tip. 3-10. Breeds in acidic pools, especially on heathland and in open woods. Regularly bites man. N & C.

Asian Tiger Mosquito *A. albopictus*, can be recog-nised by its conspicuous black and white stripes and the silvery white stripe running along the cen-tre of the head and thorax. The insect is a native of south-east Asia but has spread to many other areas, including southern Europe. Active mainly by day, it is particularly common around human habitation and can transmit several diseases, including den-gue fever and yellow fever.

Asian Tiger Mosquito

▲ *Anopheles plumbeus*. Female palps long: male palps clubbed, with hairy tip. Wings unspotted. Tuft of pure white scales on head (creamy white in *A. claviger*, which is generally rather browner). 3-10, mainly in woods: breeds mainly in wet tree holes. Bites man readily. Many *Anopheles* species have spotted wings.

▲ *Chaoborus crystallinus* Chaoboridae. One of a group known as phantom midges, closely related to mosquitoes but non-biting. Scales confined to wing margins. Female wings reach tip of abdomen. Male antennae plumose. Abdomen unbanded. Common all year except in the coldest weather. Usually near water: aquatic larva (p. 296) is almost transparent and called phantom larva.

▲ *Dixella aestivalis* Dixidae. Closely related to mosquitoes, but non-biting. No scales on wings. Sub-costal vein only about half length of wing. Antennae not plumose. Most of year, usually near water. Larva aquatic, usually bent into U-shape at surface (p. 297). There are several similar species.

▲ *Chironomus plumosus* Chironomidae. Posterior cross-vein absent: rear veins very weak. Wings shorter than abdomen and held roofwise over body at rest. Only male antennae plumose. Non-biting, feeding lit-tle if at all as adults. Common everywhere 4-9, males forming dense swarms. Aquatic larva (p. 297) is one of the blood-worms. One of many similar species known as non-biting midges. Some are green.

▲ *Sylvicola fenestralis* Anisopodidae. Resembles winter gnats (Trichoceridae) but has no V-shaped thoracic suture. Discal cell present. 2nd anal vein not sharply bent and not reaching wing margin. Common most of year, often in houses: one of several species known as window midges. Larvae live in decaying matter: very common in sewage beds.

Sylvicola fenestralis
× 3

Midge is a general term applied to small flies in several families and having no precise meaning

194

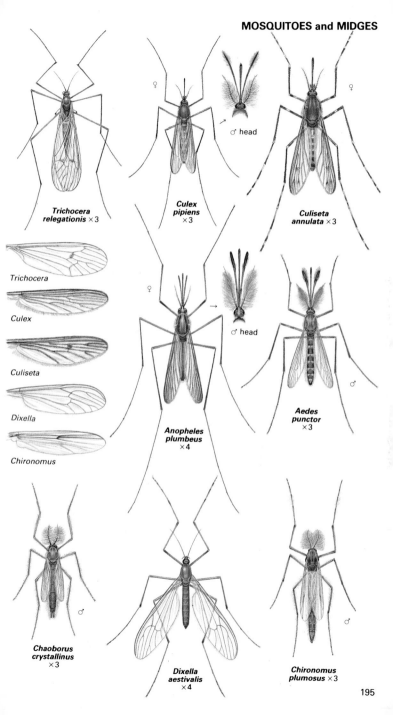

*Trichocera
relegationis* ×3

♀

*Culex
pipiens*
×3

♂ head

♀

*Culiseta
annulata* ×3

Trichocera

Culex

Culiseta

Dixella

Chironomus

♀

♂ head

♀

*Anopheles
plumbeus*
×4

♂

*Aedes
punctor*
×3

♂

*Chaoborus
crystallinus*
×3

*Dixella
aestivalis*
×4

♂

*Chironomus
plumosus* ×3

195

Simulium at rest

▲ **Simulium equinum** Simuliidae. One of many very similar species known as black-flies – not to be confused with the blackfly aphids (p. 94). Broad wings have characteristic venation, very faint in the rear. Strongly-humped thorax, best seen from the side. Female sucks blood and often flies in such numbers as to be a serious nuisance to horses and cattle: also attacks people. 3-10, especially common around hill streams. Larva (p. 297) is attached to stones in running water.

gall
of *Jaapiella*

▲ **Scatopse notata** Scatopsidae. Venation superficially like *Simulium* but wings narrower and thorax less humped. Ocelli present, unlike *Simulium*. Commonly enters houses and crawls over windows. Breeds in decaying matter. There are several similar species.

▲ **Jaapiella veronicae** Cecidomyiidae. Wings hairy, with very little venation. Antennae like minute strings of beads with whorls of hair. Swarms to lighted windows on summer nights. Larva causes hairy galls (left) on shoot tips of germander speedwell. Many very similar species, collectively known as gall midges, cause galls on a wide range of plants.

▲ **Sciara thomae** Mycetophilidae. Thorax strongly humped. Eyes meet above antennae. Tibiae spiny. Prominent fork in middle of wing. Common in houses, scuttling rapidly about or drifting slowly through the air. Breeds in all kinds of rotting matter. Abundant where mushrooms are grown, commonly damaging the crop. Larvae, like white worms with black heads, commonly feed in fungi and the insects in this family are known as fungus gnats.

▲ **Cerotelion lineatus**. First 2 long veins not linked by cross-vein. 6-10 in woods and other damp places. Larva carnivorous on other insects in fungi, especially those on tree trunks.

▲ **Platyura marginata**. First 2 long veins linked by cross-vein near wing-tip. Thorax with yellow hair: abdomen shining black. Femora yellow. 6-9, especially in wooded areas. Larvae inhabit silken web and are carnivorous on other fungus-eaters. C.

Culicoides

Pericoma

▲ **Culicoides obsoletus** Ceratopogonidae. One of the biting midges – very small flies with blood-sucking females. Thorax strongly humped. Forked vein in centre of wing: latter folded flat at rest. Male antennae plumose. Many species attack other insects, but *Culicoides* species take vertebrate blood: *obsoletus* and several similar species swarm in vast numbers in summer and often make life intolerable in northern and upland areas. They breed in waterlogged soil and peat.

▲ **Pericoma fuliginosa** Psychodidae. One of the owl midges or moth-flies, which are easily recognised by their hairy wings with many long veins. Some species rest with wings partly spread: others hold them roof-like over the body. Smaller species are mostly uniformly grey. Breed in decaying matter of all kinds. Abundant at sewage works. Often come to lighted windows at night.

▲ **St Mark's-fly** *Bibio marci* Bibionidae. Named because it often appears close to St Mark's Day (April 25th), this fly drifts slowly over vegetation with legs hanging. Like other members of the family, it has short, stout antennae inserted below the eyes. The latter well separated in female. A beak-like spine at tip of front tibia. Breeds in soil and rotting vegetation. Several similar species. ▲ *B. hortulanus*, with a brick-coloured upper surface in female, is not uncommon in gardens in spring, often pairing on sunny walls.

front leg of
St Mark's-fly

front leg of
Fever-fly

▲ **Fever-fly** *Dilophus febrilis*. Distinguished from *Bibio* species by circlet of small spines around tip of front tibia. Female has smoky wings: male wings clear with black spot like *Bibio*. On and around flowers, including apples and other fruit trees, 3-10: most common in spring. Flight is sluggish.

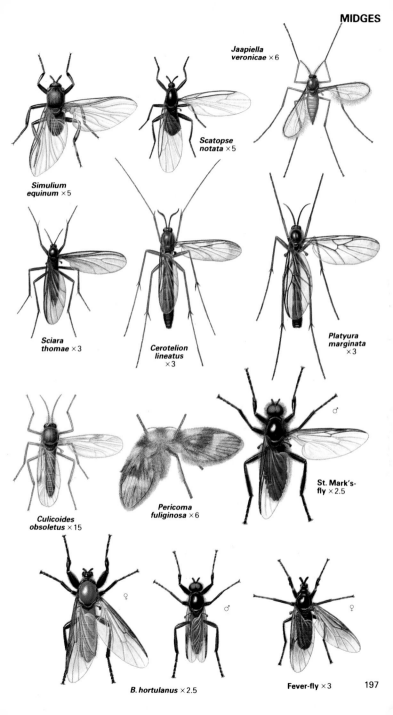

*Jaapiella
veronicae* ×6

*Scatopse
notata* ×5

*Simulium
equinum* ×5

*Sciara
thomae* ×3

*Cerotelion
lineatus*
×3

*Platyura
marginata*
×3

*Culicoides
obsoletus* ×15

*Pericoma
fuliginosa* ×6

St. Mark's-
fly ×2.5

♂

B. hortulanus ×2.5

♀

♂

Fever-fly ×3

♀

197

Stratiomys
potamida
♀ at rest

SOLDIER-FLIES Stratiomyidae. Flattened flies named for their usually bright and often metallic colours. Feet with 3 pads. Veins crowded in front part of wing, with small discal cell and relatively faint veins beyond it. Flight often weak, although some males hover and 'dance'. They visit flowers for nectar, but are most often seen sunbathing on ground or low vegetation. Wings folded flat at rest (left), often concealing the bright colours.

⬛ *Oxycera rara*. Scutellum with 2 spines. Legs largely yellow. 6-8 in damp woods and hedgerows. Breeds in moss and leaf litter. S & C. There are several similar species.

⬛ *Stratiomys chameleon*. Antennae long and pointed: distinctly elbowed, with 1st segment long. Scutellum with 2 spines. 5-9 in marshy areas: especially fond of umbellifers. Larva aquatic and carnivorous. ⬛ *S. potamida* has smaller yellow spots on 3rd abdominal segment in male and a narrow yellow band in female.

▲ *Chloromyia formosa*. Eyes very hairy. Scutellum not armed. Female abdomen less hairy than male, with blue-green and violet sheen showing through. 5-8 in woods, hedges, and gardens. Breeds in damp soil and leaf litter. *C. speciosa* has darker wings and yellowish hind tarsi. C.

▲ *Microchrysa polita*. Shiny green in both sexes. Antennae and legs black. Scutellum unarmed. 3-9 on shrubs and other lush vegetation: not uncommon in gardens. Breeds in dung and compost heaps.

⬛ *Beris clavipes*. Venation less crowded than in most soldier-flies. Scutellum with 4-6 black spines. 5-7 in damp areas with lush vegetation. ▲ *B. vallata* has no dark bands on abdomen. Wings are clearer, especially in female, and stigma more conspicuous.

▲ *Sargus bipunctatus*. Scutellum without spines. Veins more distinct in this genus than in most soldier-flies. Sexes differ markedly in abdomen. 8-10. Breeds in dung. S & C.

▲ *S. iridatus* has sexes alike, although female is broader at rear end. Wings uniformly smoky. 5-8. Breeds in cow dung.

△s *Odontomyia ornata*. Resembles *Stratiomys*, but smaller and with shorter, non-elbowed antennae. Scutellum with 2 small spines. Abdominal spots yellow or orange. 5-8, usually on flowers and leaves near water. Breeds in muddy water.

▲ *Oplodontha viridula*. Abdomen varies from white to orange or green, always with a central black stripe. Green becomes yellowish after death. 6-8 among reeds and other waterside vegetation. Breeds in water.

△s *Xylomya maculata* Xylomyidae. Related to soldier-flies, but venation is very different, with a closed cell behind discal cell. Mid and hind tibiae spurred. Feet with 3 pads. 5-6 in ancient woodland, usually around decaying stumps and logs in which the larvae feed.

△ *Xylophagus ater* Xylophagidae. Superficially like *Ctenophora* (p. 192), but venation and antennae quite different. Feet with 3 pads. Male thorax shiny all over: female thorax with 3 greyish stripes. 4-8, mainly in woodland. Breeds in dead deciduous trees. N & C. △n *X. cinctus*, in which female abdomen is reddish in middle, breeds in pine stumps. N & C.

▲ Snipe-fly *Rhagio scolopacea* Rhagionidae. Feet with 3 pads. 2nd long vein curves forward to enclose stigma. Anal cell open. Hind tibia with 2 spurs. 5-8, mainly in wooded areas. Rests head-down on tree trunks and other vertical surfaces. Larva (p. 294) lives in soil and is carnivorous. There are several related species, mostly with unspotted wings.

▲ *Chrysopilus cristatus*. Clothed with golden hairs and scales, although these easily rub off. Feet with 3 pads. Femora black. Hind tibia with 1 spur. 2nd long vein curves forward to enclose stigma. Anal cell closed and joined to wing margin by a stalk. 5-8 in woods and other damp or shady places. Breeds in rotting wood and leaf mould.

▲ *Atherix ibis*. Feet with 3 pads. Hind tibia with 2 spurs. 2nd long vein curves forward to enclose stigma. Anal cell closed and joined to wing margin by a stalk. Female greyer, with grey stripes on thorax. 5-7, rarely far from water. Larva is aquatic.

Snipe-fly at rest

SOLDIER-FLIES and SNIPE-FLIES

Oxycera rara ×3

Stratiomys chameleon ×2.5

Chloromyia formosa ×3

Microchrysa polita ×4

Beris clavipes ×3

Sargus bipunctatus ×2.5

S. iridatus ×2.5

Odontomyia ornata ×2.5

Oplodontha viridula ×3

Xylomya maculata ×2.5

Xylophagus ater ×2.5

Snipe-fly ×2.5

Chrysopilus cristatus ×2.5

Atherix ibis ×2.5

HORSE-FLIES Tabanidae. Stoutly-built, fast-flying flies with robust antennae. Eyes large and often brilliantly coloured and patterned in life. Veins form a broad Y-shaped fork across wing-tip. Feet with 3 pads. Most females are voracious blood-suckers, attacking large mammals, including man, with their blade-like mouth-parts. Males, often with slightly different patterns from females, are nectar-feeders. Almost always diurnal. Larvae (p. 294) live in damp soil and mud: some are carnivorous, other feed on decaying plant matter. About 160 of the 3,500 known species occur in Europe.

▲ *Tabanus bovinus*. Hind margin of head concave when seen from above (as in all *Tabanus* species). Eyes unbanded. Pale triangles on abdomen indistinct but usually reaching well into front half of each segment. Female palps very pale. 5-8 in pastures, especially near rivers. Breeds in muddy river banks.

▲ *T. bromius* ranges from yellowish grey to almost black. Eyes with one band. 5-9 on pastures: commonest of several similar species.

▲ *T. sudeticus* is very variable and often very like *bovinus*, but pale triangles shorter and generally more distinct. Female palps brownish. 6-8 in pastures and open woodland. Mainly upland in B.

△ *Hybomitra micans*. Eyes very hairy, especially in male, with 3 purplish bands. Palps, antennae, and legs all black. Sub-callus (swelling just above antennae) shiny black. 5-9 on moors and damp heaths. C and occasionally on mountains in S.

△s *H. muhfeldi* is distinguished from several similar species by the brownish (not black) swelling just in front of wing base. 5-8. Common in many places, but especially on damp grassland around lakes. (This genus distinguished from most other horse-flies, including all British species, by the very hairy eyes.)

Heptatoma pellucens. Distinguished by very long antennae and clear wings. Eyes with 4 bands. 5-9 in many habitats, wooded or open.

▲ **Cleg-fly** *Haematopota pluvialis*. Eyes fairly hairy. 1st antennal segment deeply notched near tip in female. Mottled wings, held roofwise at rest, characterise this genus. Colour and pattern of abdomen vary. 5-10. Especially common in damp, wooded habitats: one of the commonest horse-flies and a real nuisance to man, especially in thundery weather. Approaches silently. Partially replaced in uplands by the very similar ▲ *H. crassicornis*, which has a pale V or Y in the discal cell. There are many similar species.

△ *Chrysops relictus*. Middle tibia brownish yellow. Abdominal pattern varies, but always with black lobes on 2nd segment (less divergent in male than female). 5-9 on damp heaths and moors and in light woodland: rarely far from water. Breeds in muddy river banks and other wet places.

▲ *C. caecutiens* has black middle tibia. Male abdomen largely black: black marks on 2nd abdominal segment of female often much reduced. 5-9 in many habitats near water.

△ *C. viduatus* has brownish middle tibia. 2nd abdominal segment has a single dark spot, variable in shape and much larger in male. 6-9 in grassland and woodland clearings. The last two species are absent from Ireland. There are several other species, all with brilliant eyes. Wings generally have more extensive dark area in males. All *Chrysops* species have spurred hind tibia.

▲ **Dark-edged Bee-fly** *Bombylius major* Bombyliidae. The most familiar of numerous bee-flies, so called for the furry appearance of many of the species. Common at spring flowers, sucking nectar through long, rigid proboscis. Quite harmless. Hovers in sunny spots with high-pitched whine. Larvae attack grubs of solitary bees and wasps in their underground nests.

△s **Mottled Bee-fly** *Thyridanthrax fenestratus*. Has same hovering and darting flight as *Bombylius* and the rest of the family. Proboscis short and retracted into head when not in use. 6-8 in sandy habitats. Larvae parasitise caterpillars. N & C. Several similar species in S.

Anthrax anthrax. Dark body, more extensive dark areas of wing, and short proboscis distinguish this from *Bombylius*. 5-9, mainly in dry habitats. Larvae parasitise solitary bees.

△ *Villa modesta*. Like a clear-winged *Bombylius*, but proboscis is short and head more rounded. Male abdomen has no pale abdominal bands. 5-9 in sandy places, mainly coastal. Larvae parasitise caterpillars. There are several similar species.

Fallenia fasciata Nemestrinidae. Very agile, fast-flying and often hovering. Distinguished from bee-flies by very different venation and down-pointing proboscis. 5-8 in rather damp places, commonly feeding on thistles. Larvae feed on other insect grubs. S.

200

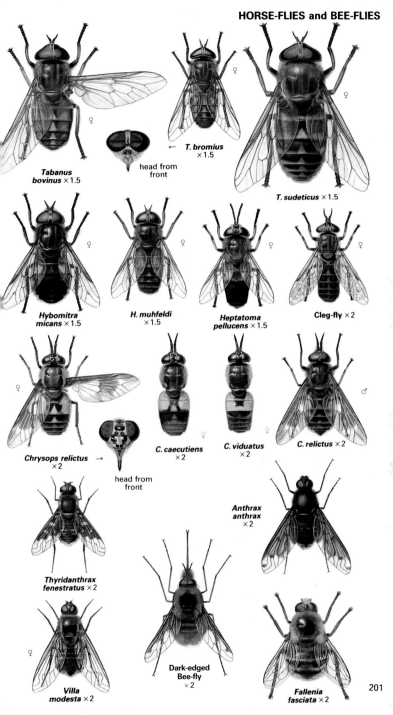

Tabanus bovinus × 1.5

← *T. bromius* × 1.5

head from front

T. sudeticus × 1.5

Hybomitra micans × 1.5

H. muhfeldi × 1.5

Heptatoma pellucens × 1.5

Cleg-fly × 2

Chrysops relictus → × 2

head from front

C. caecutiens × 2

C. viduatus × 2

C. relictus × 2

Thyridanthrax fenestratus × 2

Anthrax anthrax × 2

Villa modesta × 2

Dark-edged Bee-fly × 2

Fallenia fasciata × 2

201

Asilus
head from front

Asilus with prey

ROBBER-FLIES Asilidae. Very bristly predatory flies that generally chase and catch other insects in mid-air. Most species sit in wait and dart out when likely prey appears. The prey is then sucked dry with the stout proboscis, which projects horizontally or obliquely forward. There is a deep groove between the eyes in both sexes, the eyes never touching even in males. A 'beard' on the face protects eyes from struggling prey. Legs are sturdy and have 2 pads at most. Wings folded flat over body at rest. Larvae eat some dead vegetable matter, but most are at least partly predatory and some feed mainly on beetle and fly grubs in the soil.

△s **Asilus crabroniformis**. An unmistakable fly – one of the largest in B – inhabiting open country 7-10. A very strong flier. Breeds in cow pats and other dung.

Dasypogon diadema. First 2 long veins both reach wing margin: wing membrane ribbed. Front tibia has curved spine at tip. Male more uniformly black, with dark wings. 6-8 in scrubby places, especially coastal dunes. S.

▲ **Leptogaster cylindrica**. Feet without pads. Hind femur yellow. 3rd antennal segment ends in bristle. One of the slimmest robber-flies, it resembles a crane-fly in flight. It hunts in grassy places, flying slowly and plucking aphids from the grasses. 5-8. △ **L. guttiventris** is similar but has reddish hind femur.

△s **Dioctria atricapilla**. First 2 long veins reach margin. Beard rather sparse and, as in all *Dioctria* species, the antennae spring from a prominence high on the head. Female wings much lighter than male. 5-8 in grassy places.

△n **Laphria flava**. First 2 long veins join before reaching margin. 3rd antennal segment blunt, not with long bristle as in most other genera. 6-9 in pine woods. Breeds in pine logs and stumps. Confined to Scottish highlands in B. Several similar species, all furry and bee-like, live on the continent. △s **L. gilva** is much less furry than *flava*, with hairs lying flat. 6-8 in old woodland: breeds in tree stumps, especially pines.
△ s **L. marginata** is very similar but has yellow hairs on legs and thorax. 6-8 in oakwoods.

△s **Eutolmus rufibarbis**. First 2 long veins join before reaching wing margin. Legs black with yellow hair. 5-9. N & C. Several similar species live on the continent.

△ **Pamponerus germanicus**. First 2 long veins join before reaching wing margin. Bristles behind eyes bend sharply forward. Femora black: tibiae and tarsi orange or yellow with black tips. Wing base clear in female, not milky white. 5-7: mainly coastal.

△s **Acrocera orbicula** Acroceridae. Minute head appears to consist of nothing but the eyes. Antennae on top of head. Abdomen yellowish or brown, becoming darker after death. Thorax strongly rounded. 6-8 in grassy places: often on flowers, although adult does not feed. Larva parasitises spiders.

▲ **Thereva nobilitata** Therevidae. Resembles robber-flies, but no groove between eyes: male eyes touching. Face very hairy. First long vein much shorter than in robber-flies. Female abdomen largely golden, with last 2 segments shiny black. 5-8. Larva omnivorous in leaf litter. There are several similar species, difficult to separate. ▲ **T. annulata** male is silvery. Female is greyer and duller, with only last abdominal segment shiny black. 4-8 in sandy places, especially coastal dunes.

▲ **Window-fly** *Scenopinus fenestralis* Scenopinidae. Most often seen on windows, with wings tightly folded to give the fly a dark, bullet-like appearance. No bristles. Larva inhabits birds' nests and buildings, preying on grubs of other insects.

▲ **Empis tessellata** Empididae. Short triangular cell close to wing-tip is typical of this genus. Head almost spherical, with slender, down-pointing proboscis. Predatory on other flies, but also takes nectar. Often hunts on hawthorn and umbellifer flowers. 4-8. Larva lives in soil. ▲ **E. stercorea** is easily recognised by its yellow-brown colour with a black stripe along the back. 4-6 in lush, grassy places.

▲ **Hilara maura**. Venation like *Empis*, but triangular cell near wing-tip is longer and narrower. Swollen front tarsi of male produce silk, which the fly uses to wrap prey as a courtship gift for female. Swarms over water throughout the summer.

Acrocera orbicula × 2

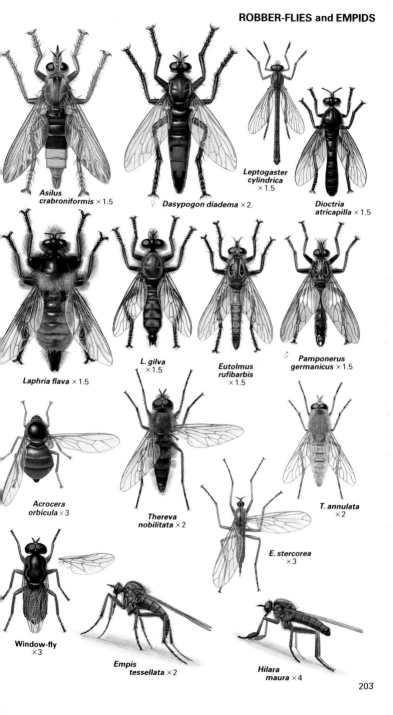

Asilus crabroniformis ×1.5

♀ *Dasypogon diadema* ×2.

Leptogaster cylindrica ×1.5

Dioctria atricapilla ×1.5

Laphria flava ×1.5

L. gilva ×1.5

Eutolmus rufibarbis ×1.5

♂ *Pamponerus germanicus* ×1.5

Acrocera orbicula ×3

Thereva nobilitata ×2

E. stercorea ×3

T. annulata ×2

Window-fly ×3

Empis tessellata ×2

Hilara maura ×4

203

Leptomydas corsicanus Mydaidae. Male much smaller and darker. Nectar-feeding with darting flight. 5-8 in rough, grassy places. Corsica only. Two similar species in Spain and another in Sardinia, all with clubbed antennae.

▲ **Lonchoptera lutea** Lonchopteridae. Pointed wings with no central cross-vein identify this small family. Last 2 veins join before reaching margin only in female. 4-10 in damp, shady places. Commonest of several similar species.

▲ **Phora atra** Phoridae. One of the scuttle-flies, so called for their active running. Front edge of wing spiny at base: most veins very weak. Abundant on shrubs in summer: males hover in shafts of sunlight. There are many related species.

Leptomydas corsicanus × 1.5

▲ **Sciapus platypterus** Dolichopodidae. Only one prominent cross-vein, as in all the family. 4th vein distinctly forked. Female lacks black and white markings on mid-tarsus. Hedgerows and tree trunks in summer. There are several similar species. All members of the family have a metallic sheen and prey on other small insects.

▲ **Dolichopus popularis**. Male genitalia very large, as in most members of the family. Female lacks plumes on mid-tarsus. Damp places throughout the summer, resting with front end raised. There are many similar species.

▲ **Poecilobothrus nobilitatus**. Male easily recognised by wing pattern: female like *Dolichopus*. Both sexes with 3rd and 4th veins wavy and convergent. 5-9 in damp places, resting on mud or on floating or waterside plants with front end raised.

HOVER-FLIES Syrphidae.

A family of about 5,000 species, with hovering and darting flight. Body shape very variable, but all species have a false margin formed by veins running more or less parallel to rear margin of wing. There is also a false vein near the centre – simply a thickening of the wing membrane and unconnected to any real vein. Vein pattern important in identification. Antennae usually short and drooping. Most are nectar-feeders, especially fond of umbellifers. Many mimic bees and wasps. The larvae live in a wide range of habitats and include predators, vegetarians, and scavengers.

▲ **Syrphus ribesii**. First 2 long veins both reach margin: anterior cross-vein is before middle of discal cell. Thorax greenish black with brown hair. Face has no black line. 4-11, often in swarms. Larva (p. 294) feeds on aphids.

▲ **Scaeva pyrastri**. Venation like *Syrphus*. Pale lunules on abdomen white or cream and of almost constant width. △**S. selenitica** has outer lunule arm much thinner than inner one. 6-10. Larva eats aphids.

▲ **Episyrphus balteatus**. Venation like *Syrphus*. Easily identified by additional narrow black bands on 3rd and 4th abdominal segments. 3-11 (may be all year in S). Often forms dense migratory swarms. Abundant in gardens. Larva eats aphids.

▲ **Xanthogramma pedissequum**. Venation like *Syrphus*. Distinctive body pattern and dark smudge on wing readily distinguish it from other yellow and black species. Abdomen very flat. 5-9. Larva feeds on aphids in ant nests.

▲ **Leucozona lucorum**. Resembles *Volucella pellucens* (p. 206), but distinguished by brown scutellum and *Syrphus*-like venation. 5-9. Larva eats aphids.

▲ **Rhingia campestris**. Venation like *Syrphus*, but easily identified by its snout. 4-11, mostly in hedgerows and light woods. Breeds in cowpats and other dung.
△s **R. rostrata** is very similar but has a slaty blue thorax.

▲ **Baccha elongata**. Venation like *Syrphus*. 4-10, hovering in and around damp vegetation but not easily seen because of slim build. Larva eats aphids.

△s **Doros conopseus**. Venation like *Syrphus*. Superficially like *Physocephala* (p. 208) but antennae quite different. Wasp-like in flight. 5-8, mainly in woodland. Larva believed to feed on aphids in soil.

▲ **Melanostoma scalare**. Venation like *Syrphus*. Male abdomen much slimmer than female: always parallel-sided. 4-11. Very common in gardens: especially fond of hawthorn blossom in spring. Larva eats aphids. There are several similar species.

▲ **Neoascia podagrica**. One of the smallest hover-flies. Venation like *Syrphus*, but outer cross-veins almost upright, destroying false margin. Abundant everywhere 3-10. Larva feeds in rotting vegetation. There are several similar species.

venation of *Neoascia*

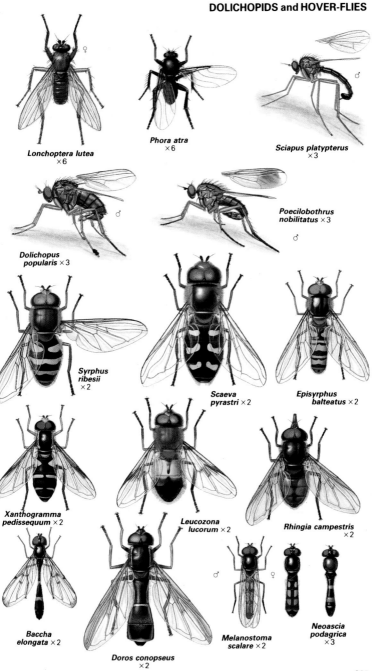

Lonchoptera lutea
×6

Phora atra
×6

Sciapus platypterus
×3

Dolichopus popularis ×3

Poecilobothrus nobilitatus ×3

Syrphus ribesii ×2

Scaeva pyrastri ×2

Episyrphus balteatus ×2

Xanthogramma pedissequum ×2

Leucozona lucorum ×2

Rhingia campestris ×2

Baccha elongata ×2

Doros conopseus ×2

Melanostoma scalare ×2

Neoascia podagrica ×3

▲ *Volucella bombylans*. As in all *Volucella* species, the first 2 long veins meet before reaching wing margin and the anterior cross-vein is before the middle of the discal cell. The false margin also bends sharply inwards at the front end. Antennae are feathery. Distinguished from its relatives by its dense hair, *bombylans* is a very variable species mimicking several kinds of bumble bees. 5-9. *Volucella* larvae (p. 294) all live as scavengers in the nests of wasps and bumble bees.

△s *V. zonaria*, easily recognised by its size and colour, is a good hornet mimic. It flies 5-9 in many habitats: not uncommon in suburban areas.

▲ *V. pellucens* resembles *Leucozona* (p. 204), but is bigger and has a black scutellum: venation also differs. 5-9, mainly in wooded areas: very fond of bramble blossom. Hovers at about head height (mainly the males).

▲ *V. inanis* is like *zonaria* but is smaller and has yellow at front of abdomen instead of brown. 6-9.

Milesia crabroniformis. First two long veins meet before reaching wing margin. Anterior cross-vein well beyond middle of discal cell. Anal vein bends sharply back to wing margin. 6-9, visiting various flowers and basking on the vegetation: a superb hornet mimic. Larva develops in rotting beech timber. S, mainly western.

▲ **Drone-fly** *Eristalis tenax*. Named for its remarkable resemblance to the drones of some races of honey bees. First 2 long veins meet before reaching wing margin: 3rd long vein with a deep U-shaped bend. Anterior cross-vein at about the middle of discal cell. Yellow or orange marks at base of abdomen often indistinct. Face has a wide black stripe down the centre. All year, hovering at about head height in sunshine: very common in gardens, often basking on walls in winter. Larva (p. 297) is the rat-tailed maggot, living in stagnant water. There are several similar species.
　　▲ *E. pertinax* has a narrow facial stripe and yellow tarsi on front and middle legs. 3-11 almost everywhere.

▲ *E. arbustorum* is smaller and has no facial stripe. Front and mid tarsi are dark. 4-10, mainly in open habitats.

▲ *Helophilus pendulus*. First 2 long veins both reach wing margin: 3rd long vein with a deep U-shaped bend. Anterior cross-vein at about middle of discal cell. Black line down centre of face. At least half of hind tibia yellowish. 4-10. Most frequent in damp places: fond of basking on waterside vegetation. Males hover just above water surface. Larva is like that of *Eristalis* and lives in muddy water. △ *H. hybridus* is similar but only basal third of hind tibia is yellowish.

▲ **Narcissus-fly** *Merodon equestris*. Venation like *Helophilus*. Hind femur with prominent bulge on underside of apex. Body essentially black with grey, tawny, or black hair. Mimics various worker bumble bees. 3-8. Larva lives in bulbs of narcissi and other plants, often causing severe damage. There are several similar species on the continent, mainly in S.

▲ *Myathropa florea*. Resembles a brightly marked Drone-fly, but readily distinguished by thoracic pattern and *Helophilus*-like venation. Pale markings vary in size, with western specimens tending to be darker. 5-10, mainly in wooded areas. Larva lives in stagnant water in hollow trees and similar places.

△s *Brachypalpoides lenta*. First 2 long veins reach wing margin. Anterior cross-vein beyond middle of discal cell and strongly oblique. Abdomen very flat. Black legs and red patch on abdomen distinguish this from several related species. 5-7. Breeds in rotting wood. Widespread but uncommon.

▲ *Chrysotoxum cautum*. Antennae long and forward-pointing, with 3rd segment about as long as other two together. First 2 long veins both reach margin. 5-8, mainly in woods and hedgerows: not uncommon in gardens and fond of basking on leaves. Breeds in ants' nests, where larvae eat aphids. S & C. There are several similar species, usually smaller. ▲ *C. festivum* is much blacker than *cautum*, with 3 pairs of narrow yellow bars on abdomen. The bars curve distinctly backwards in the outer region and do not reach the sides of the abdomen. The front half of the wing is yellowish brown, although this colour does not reach the wing-tip. 6-10 in grassy places. ▲ *C. bicinctum*, the commonest member of the genus in Ireland, has just 2 prominent yellow bands on the abdomen – on segments 2 and 4 – and an intense brown patch on the outer part of the wing. 5-9 in grassy places.

Chrysotoxum cautum
× 2

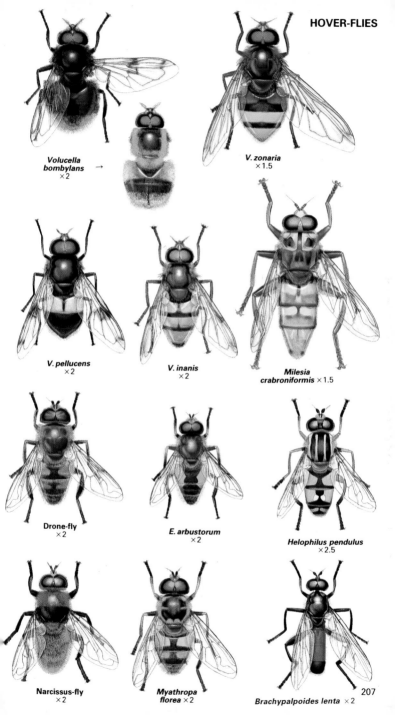

HOVER-FLIES

Volucella bombylans ×2 →

V. zonaria ×1.5

V. pellucens ×2

V. inanis ×2

Milesia crabroniformis ×1.5

Drone-fly ×2

E. arbustorum ×2

Helophilus pendulus ×2.5

Narcissus-fly ×2

Myathropa florea ×2

Brachypalpoides lenta ×2

207

Pipunculus campestris × 4

▲ **Pipunculus campestris** Pipunculidae. Female abdomen very shiny. Stigma often yellow at first, but may darken with age. 4-10 in woods and hedgerows: especially fond of bramble blossom. Larvae are internal parasites of leafhoppers. Large head, nearly all eyes, is typical of this large family. Venation, usually with a distinctly beaked sub-apical cell, is also characteristic. All are superb hoverers, often hovering low down in dense vegetation.

△ **Conops quadrifasciata** Conopidae. Long proboscis and antennae, and long, pointed anal cell near hind edge of wing. Hind femur yellowish brown. Female has small yellow pouch under 5th abdominal segment. 6-9 on umbellifers and composites, especially ragwort: mainly in dry habitats. Larva is internal parasite of bumble bees. There are several similar species. All members of the family have the pointed anal cell, but not all have the long proboscis and antennae.

△ **Physocephala nigra**. 5-7 on a wide range of flowers, especially in light woodland and scrubby places. ▲ *P. rufipes* is smaller, with a browner body and black antennae. Larvae of both species parasitise bumble bees.

△ **Myopa buccata**. Ocelli and short antennae clearly separate this from the last two species. Tip of 1st long vein very close to sub-costal vein. 4-8 on a variety of flowers: very fond of dandelions and hawthorn blossom. There are several similar species.

▲ **Platystoma seminationis** Platystomatidae. Prominent cream patch under end of abdomen. 5-10. Crawls rather slowly over rank vegetation in many habitats, especially in woods, hedgerows, and gardens. Rarely attracted to flowers, but has been seen sucking dead insects. Breeds in decaying matter. There are many similar species on the continent.

▲ **Melieria omissa** Otitidae. Face has deep grooves to accommodate antennae. Wing with 7 dark spots. Commonly waves wings slowly up and down as it rests on or walks slowly over vegetation. 5-8 on river banks and other damp places. Breeds in decaying matter. S & C. There are several similar species, differing slightly in pattern.

▲ **Seioptera vibrans**. Head red at front: face grooved. Body shiny blue or black. 3rd and 4th long veins converge slightly. Resembles sepsids (p. 210) in frantic wing-waving, but distinguished by larger size. 5-9 on trees and shrubs, especially lime. Feeds on aphids and other small insects. Breeds in decaying vegetation.

Family Tephritidae. A large family of rather small flies in which the wings are heavily mottled or pictured, as in the two previous families. Sub-costal vein sharply bent towards costa about half way along its length. Anal cell usually with a characteristically pointed extension. Female abdomen pointed, with rigid ovipositor. Larvae develop in fruits or elsewhere in plants, often causing galls.

▲ **Urophora cardui**. Anal cell blunt. Dark markings heavier in male. 5-8 in open country. Larvae induce very hard, egg-shaped many-chambered galls on stems of creeping thistle. Many similar species cause galls in composite flowerheads.

▲ **Cerajocera ceratocera**. Male has bristly horn on antenna. 6-8. One of several species causing galls in flowerheads of greater knapweed. The carpels become very hard and woody and can be felt by squeezing the dead flowerheads. N & C.

▲ **Celery-fly** *Euleia heraclei*. Eyes become reddish after death. Body and wing markings either blackish brown or pale reddish brown. 4-11. Larvae excavate mines in leaves of celery, parsnip, and other umbellifers.

△ **Mediterranean Fruit-fly** *Ceratitis capitata*. Wings with pink and yellow blotches. Thorax strongly humped. Female lacks the two spatulate, horn-like bristles on the head. Most of the year: continuously brooded in S. Larvae infest a wide range of fruits, including cherries, peaches, and oranges. S & C: not native in B but often imported in fruit. A serious pest in all the warmer parts of the world.

Rhagoletis cerasi. Head rather square in profile. Scutellum yellow: rest of thorax shiny black. 5-7. Larvae in wild and cultivated cherries. N & C: in B only through introduction in fruit. ▲ *R. alternata* has the whole thorax orange-yellow. Larvae in cherries and rose hips. N & C. Both species have very slow flight.

▲ **Anomoia purmunda**. Eyes green with 2 transverse red bands in life: becoming red when dead. Wing pattern very characteristic. 8-10. Larvae in hawthorn fruits. N & C.

Conops quadrifasciata ×2

Physocephala nigra ×2

Myopa buccata ×2

Platystoma seminationis ×3

Melieria omissa ×3

Seioptera vibrans ×3 ♀

Urophora cardui ×3 ♀

gall on thistle →

Cerajocera ceratocera ×3 ♀

Celery-fly ×3 ♀

→ leaf mine in celery

Mediterranean Fruit-fly ×3 ♂

Rhagoletis cerasi ×4

Anomoia purmunda ×3 ♀

grubs in cherry

209

▲ **Calobata petronella** Micropezidae. One of several long-legged species known as stilt-legged flies. 5-7, walking rather hesitatingly on foliage, mainly in damp places, and feeding on other small insects. Breeds in decaying matter. N & C.

▲ **Micropeza corrigiolata**. An even more slender stilt-legged fly, with a very flat, pointed head. Mid and hind coxae brownish. 5-9 on vegetation in damp and shady places. Not uncommon in shady gardens, where it probably breeds in compost heaps. △ **M. lateralis** has coxae all yellow and more yellow on abdomen. 8-10. S & C. **M. brevipennis** is all black with short wings. C.

Micropeza corrigiolata × 2.5

▲ **Coelopa frigida** Coelopidae. One of the kelp-flies, a small family distinguished from several similar groups by the very straight vein closing the anal cell, but best recognised by seashore habitat. *C. frigida* has a very flat body and waves over shore throughout the year: on coastal flowers in summer. Breeds in rotting sea-weed on beach. ▲ **C. pilipes** is similar but much hairier in male. The closely related ▲ **Malacomyia sciomyzina** flies with them but is not flattened. N & C.

▲ **Carrot-fly** *Psila rosae* Psilidae. One of many similar species, all with a pale streak running across basal part of wing although this is not always obvious. Front margin of wing with a distinct break about ¼ of the way along. Ocellar triangle very clear. 5-9. Larvae infest carrots, the leaves of infested plants often becoming rust-coloured.

▲ **Helcomyza ustulata** Helcomyzidae. Wings longer than abdomen and with prominent spines on front margin. 6th long vein reaches margin. Size varies a good deal. On sea-shore all year, with characteristic darting flight. Larvae live in sand or mud below high-tide level. N & C.

▲ **Coremacera marginata** Sciomyzidae. Dappled wings laid very flat over body at rest. Conspicuous, forward-pointing antennae. 6-10 in damp grassy and scrubby places. Larva preys on small molluscs. A few related species have all-yellow femora.

▲ **Lonchaea chorea** Lonchaeidae. One of several very similar shiny blue or greenish black flies with large, clear wings. Front margin distinctly broken at tip of sub-costal vein. Female with pointed ovipositor. 2-12 on bushes and herbage: movements rather sluggish. Breeds in decaying matter and under bark.

▲ **Sepsis fulgens** Sepsidae. One of several very similar species that wave their wings as they scuttle over the vegetation. Common on umbellifer flowers. Sometimes forms dense swarms in autumn, with hundreds of thousands of flies milling about on a small patch of plants. Hibernates as adult. Breeds in dung.

▲ **Psilopa nitidula** Ephydridae. One of many very small, shiny flies known as shore-flies, recognised by the presence of just one very long cell in hind region of wing: anal vein absent. Front margin with 2 small breaks. All year on margins of ponds and streams.

▲ **Suillia variegata** Heleomyzidae. Spines along front edge of wing. Distinguished from *Helcomyza* by smaller size, spotted wings, and much smaller anal cell. 3-12 in damp places. Breeds in fungi and decaying matter. Never on seashore.

▲ **Opomyza germinationis** Opomyzidae. One of several similar small flies with spotted wings, but distinguished from most by the long dark streak on front margin. 1st vein extremely short: 2nd and 3rd long veins converge strongly towards tip. Very common in leaf litter and grasses in moist habitats. Walks slowly: reluctant to fly. 6-10. Breeds in grass stems.

▲ **Frit-fly** *Oscinella frit* Chloropidae. A very small fly, often even smaller and paler after mid-summer. Ocellar triangle plate-like and very distinct, as in all members of the family. Anal cell absent. Abundant 3-11 in cereal fields, especially in oats and barley. Larvae tunnel in stems and ears and cause serious damage.

▲ **Lipara lucens**. One of the largest chloropids, but with relatively small eyes – well separated and with a very large ocellar plate between them. 2-11, mainly in marshy areas. Larva in a cigar-shaped gall (left) on common reed. There are several smaller but otherwise similar species.

▲ **Thaumatomyia notata**. Ocellar triangle very large in relation to head. This tiny fly is sometimes called the yellow swarming-fly because of its habit of entering buildings in vast numbers in autumn prior to hibernation. At other times it lives in rough vegetation. The larvae feed on root aphids in the soil.

gall of *Lipara*

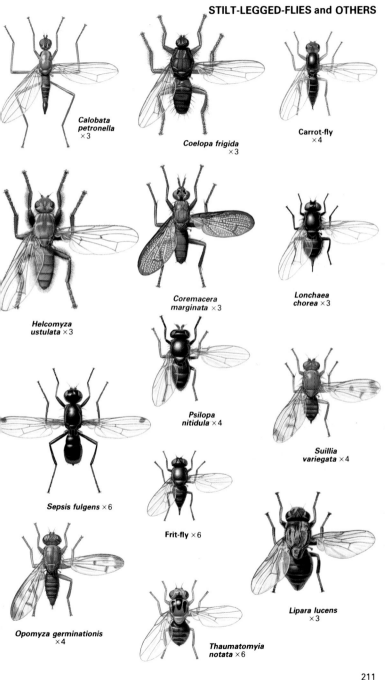

Calobata petronella ×3

Coelopa frigida ×3

Carrot-fly ×4

Helcomyza ustulata ×3

Coremacera marginata ×3

Lonchaea chorea ×3

Psilopa nitidula ×4

Suillia variegata ×4

Sepsis fulgens ×6

Frit-fly ×6

Opomyza germinationis ×4

Thaumatomyia notata ×6

Lipara lucens ×3

▲ ***Drosophila funebris*** Drosophilidae. One of many closely related species known as fruit-flies or vinegar-flies because of their liking for rotting fruit and other fermenting materials. Arista of antenna bears fine bristles and appears forked at tip (strong lens!). 2 clear breaks in front edge of wing. Long cell in hind region of wing, with short anal cell behind it, unlike Ephydridae and Chloropidae (p. 210). Most common in summer and autumn: all year in food and drink factories. Fond of wine, often settling on opened bottles and glasses. Breeds in decaying vegetable matter.

△ ***Leucophenga maculata***. Closely related to *Drosophila* but arrangement of head bristles differs. Easily identified by body pattern: thorax silver-haired in male and orange-brown in female. Breeds in fungi. S & C.

▲ ***Phytomyza ilicis*** Agromyzidae. 4-7 in woods, hedgerows, and gardens. Larva excavates distinctive mine in holly leaf. Mined leaves visible at all seasons, but grubs or pupae present only in spring and early summer. Easy to breed out adults. This large genus is distinguished from many similar groups by lack of posterior cross-vein, but specific identification of adults is difficult. All members of the family are leaf miners in their early stages.

LOUSE-FLIES Hippoboscidae.

Also known as flat-flies, these are flattened, blood-sucking parasites of birds and mammals. Head partly sunk into thorax. Long, toothed claws grip feathers or fur of hosts. Many have reduced wings, and even fully-winged species rarely fly. Instead of laying eggs, female periodically gives birth to a fully-grown larva, which pupates immediately. The related Nycteribiidae is a small family of completely wingless bat parasites in which the head folds back into a groove on the thorax.

▲ **Sheep Ked** *Melophagus ovinus*. Entirely wingless, never leaving hosts, although it can move from one sheep to another when they come into contact. It seems to do the sheep little real harm. *M. rupicaprinus* lives on the chamois.

▲ **Forest-fly** *Hippobosca equina*. Fully-winged in both sexes. On horses, cattle, and deer. Scuttles sideways with crab-like gait when disturbed. Mostly in wooded areas. 5-10, most noticeable when new adults are seeking hosts.

▲ **Deer-fly** *Lipoptena cervi*. On deer, especially red deer, mainly in wooded areas. Winged at first, but sheds wings on reaching host. New adults emerge in autumn and fly into trees, from where they drop on to passing animals.

▲ ***Ornithomyia avicularia***. Fully-winged. 6-10 on a wide range of woodland birds, including owls, pigeons, and thrushes: mainly on young birds, perhaps because older ones preen themselves better.

▲ ***Crataerina hirundinis***. Flightless, with much reduced wings. On martins and swallows. 5-10. Pupae overwinter in nests and new adults emerge when the birds return in spring. ▲ *C. pallida* has broader wings and infests swifts.

Family Tachinidae.

A large and rather variable family most of whose larvae are internal parasites of caterpillars and other young insects. Some attack adult bugs and grasshoppers. Adults are bristly and resemble Calliphoridae (p. 214), but distinguished from them by the prominent post-scutellum bulging beneath the scutellum. 4th long vein sharply bent. Thoracic squamae usually very large. Many species are common on flowers.

▲ ***Gymnochaeta viridis***. Resembles *Lucilia* (p. 214), but more bristly and with hairy eyes. Thorax may have golden stripes. On vegetation, especially tree trunks, 3-7. Eggs laid on plants and grubs bore into various moth caterpillars.

▲ ***Phasia hemiptera***. Size and colour vary a good deal, but male always has very broad wings and rather bug-like at rest. 4-8. Parasitises various heteropteran bugs, the female ovipositing directly into host.

▲ ***Dexia rustica***. Female much blacker. 6-8. Eggs laid on soil and larvae seek out grubs of cockchafer and related beetles.

▲ ***Gonia divisa***. Resembles *T. fera*, but wings lack yellow and head is more swollen in front. 3-6 in rough, grassy places. Eggs are scattered and grubs seek out caterpillars of noctuid moths.

▲ ***Tachina fera***. Jowls with yellow hair. 4-9 in woods and moist habitats: often abundant on waterside plants in late summer. Eggs are laid on plants and the grubs bore into the caterpillars of numerous butterfly and moth species.

▲ *T. grossa* resembles a bumble bee in flight. 2-9 in woods and heathland. A parasite of large caterpillars.

Gymnochaeta viridis × 2

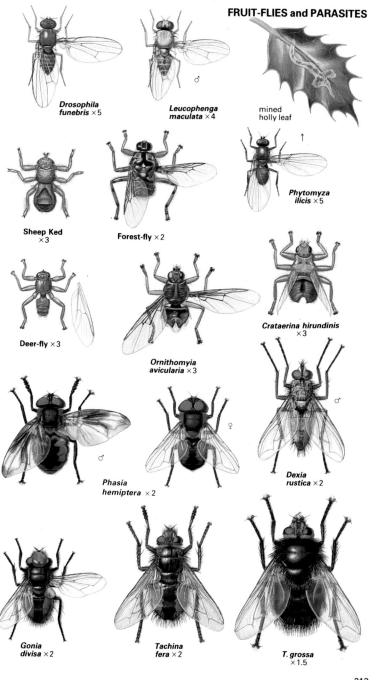

FRUIT-FLIES and PARASITES

Drosophila funebris ×5

Leucophenga maculata ×4 ♂

mined holly leaf

Phytomyza ilicis ×5 ↑

Sheep Ked ×3

Forest-fly ×2

Deer-fly ×3

Ornithomyia avicularia ×3

Crataerina hirundinis ×3

Phasia hemiptera ×2 ♂

♀

Dexia rustica ×2 ♂

Gonia divisa ×2

Tachina fera ×2

T. grossa ×1.5

BLOW-FLIES Calliphoridae. A large family of rather stout flies, resembling Tachinidae (p. 212) in having a fan of bristles close to haltere, but with little or no post-scutellum. 4th long vein usually bends *sharply* forward near tip. Adults soak up surface fluids with mop-like mouth-parts. Most common in summer, but many species are drawn out to bask by winter sunshine. Most breed in carrion and other decaying animal matter. A few larvae are parasites.

▲ **Bluebottle** *Calliphora vomitoria*. One of several similar flies common in and around houses: rests on sunny walls all year. Female attracted to meat and fish indoors for egg-laying. Larva (p. 294) is typical of whole family. ▲ *C. vicina* is almost identical but has reddish jowls (below eyes) instead of black.

▲ **Cluster-fly** *Pollenia rudis*. Golden hairs on thorax and chequered abdomen identify this fly, named for its habit of hibernating in dense clusters in attics and out-houses, usually with wings laid over each other on top of abdomen. Larvae parasitise earth-worms.

▲ *Cynomya mortuorum*. Brilliant blue or occasionally green, with yellowish jowls. On carrion but less common than bluebottle and greenbottle.

▲ **Greenbottle** *Lucilia caesar*. Bluish green to emerald, often becoming coppery with age. Eyes bare: jowls silvery. 4th long vein sharply bent. Size varies. On carrion, dung, and flowers everywhere: rarely indoors. Larvae sometimes live in wounds on sheep and other animals. Commonest of several very similar species in this genus.

▲ **Flesh-fly** *Sarcophaga carnaria* Sarcophagidae. One of several very similar species with large feet and red eyes. Size very variable. Common around houses, but not often inside. Breeds in carrion, female bringing forth young larvae instead of eggs.

HOUSE-FLIES and kin Muscidae. A large and rather variable family: often resemble blow-flies, but generally smaller and never with a fan of bristles near haltere. 4th long vein rarely bends sharply forward. Most species mop up fluids like blow-flies. Most breed in dung and other decaying matter, larvae being like those of bluebottle. Identification of many smaller species difficult, relying on bristle patterns and genitalia.

▲ *Eudasyphora cyanella*. Like *Lucilia* but 4th long vein bends gently forward. Eyes hairy. Green becomes coppery with age. Viviparous. Often overwinters in buildings with Cluster-fly. Several similar species.

▲ *Neomyia cornicina*. Like *Lucilia*, with 4th vein sharply bent, but jowls metallic green. On flowers, dung, and carrion. Larvae live in dung and are blue.

▲ *Mesembrina meridiana*. Enjoys basking on ground or vegetation: especially fond of umbellifer flowers. 3-10, mainly in woods and hedgerows. Breeds in dung.

M. mystacea is hairier, especially on middle tibia. Like *Volucella bombylans* (p. 206) in flight. 6-9, mainly on umbellifers and other flowers. Much of Europe, but only on mountains in S.

▲ *Helina reversio*. 4th long vein curves gently backwards. 4-10. Enjoys basking in all kinds of habitats from pinewoods to marshes. Many similar species.

▲ *Polietes lardaria*. Like a small Flesh-fly but with 4th long vein almost straight. 4-10 in open country and light woodland. Larva predatory in dung.

▲ *Phaonia valida*. 4th long vein almost straight, but differs from *Helina* and *Mydaea* in having a strong bristle on dorsal side of hind tibia (not easily detected). 4-11, basking on tree trunks and flowers. Many similar species.

▲ *Hydrotaea irritans*. Males of this genus have oddly-shaped front legs. Female plain grey, although abdomen may be reddish at base. 6-9, often swarming round human heads seeking sweat, especially in woodland. Larva partly predatory.

    ▲ *H. ignava*. Hind tibia of male curved and with tuft of soft hair. 4-10 on and around lush vegetation, especially among trees. Common in orchards. Hovers in shafts of sunlight. Breeds in decaying vegetation and manure, where larvae feed on other fly grubs. Abundant in poultry houses and on pig farms. The very similar ▲ *H. capensis* occurs in the same places.

    ▲ *Mydaea corni*. Scutellum yellow. A few bristles at base of 3rd long vein. 5-8, basking on flowers, foliage, and ripe fruit: especially fond of elder flowers.

    ▲ *Graphomya maculata*. 4th long vein bends quite sharply forward, thus distinguishing female from *Polietes*. Male wings have yellowish tinge, but female wings yellow only at base. 5-10, mainly on umbellifers. Larvae predatory in muddy pools and damp leaf litter.

Hydrotaea
ignava × 3

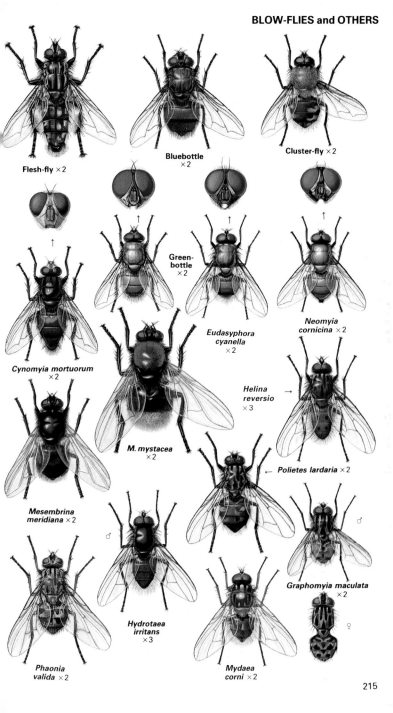

Flesh-fly ×2

Bluebottle ×2

Cluster-fly ×2

Green-bottle ×2

Eudasyphora cyanella ×2

Neomyia cornicina ×2

Cynomyia mortuorum ×2

Helina reversio ×3

M. mystacea ×2

← *Polietes lardaria* ×2

Mesembrina meridiana ×2

Graphomyia maculata ×2

♂

♀

Hydrotaea irritans ×3

Phaonia valida ×2

Mydaea corni ×2

215

▲ **Stable-fly** *Stomoxys calcitrans* Muscidae. One of the 'biting house-flies', both sexes being blood-suckers. Piercing proboscis points forward at all times, readily distinguishing this species from House-fly. 4th long vein gently curved. 4-10, mainly around farms and stables: often bites people. Breeds in dung and stable litter,

▲ **Common House-fly** *Musca domestica*. 4th vein sharply bent. Most common 6-9. Breeds in and around houses throughout the world. Especially numerous around farms and rubbish dumps where decaying matter abounds. ▲ **Face-fly** *M. autumnalis*, also called Autumn-fly, is very similar, especially female, but body more rounded and male has more orange on abdomen. Swarms over cattle: Sunbathes on walls and fences. Enters houses for hibernation in autumn – when House-fly population is declining.

▲ **Lesser House-fly** *Fannia canicularis* Fanniidae. Smaller and more slender than *Musca* and with 4th long vein almost straight. Female very dull, without clear patches at base of abdomen. Male flies incessantly round lights and other objects indoors. Larva (p. 294) feeds in various kinds of dung. There are many similar species.

▲ *Eustalomyia festiva* Anthomyiidae. Closely related to muscids but 6th long vein reaches wing margin. 4th vein almost straight. On flowers 5-8. Breeds in bodies of flies stored by solitary wasps.

▲ *Anthomyia pluvialis*. Abdomen much broader than *Eustalomyia* and very flat. 4-8 on umbellifers and other flowers, especially in damp places. Males 'dance' before rain. Breeds in decaying vegetation.

▲ **Cabbage Root-fly** *Delia radicum*. One of many very similar small flies. 3-11 on flowers and leaves. Susceptible to fungal attack, and corpses not uncommonly found clinging to vegetation in large masses. Larvae damage roots of brassicas.

▲ *Cordilura impudica* Scathophagidae. Outer half of costa hairy (lens!): wing clearly darker towards apex. Legs very spiky. 4-9, mainly in damp places. Frequents cow-pats and other dung, preying on small insects. Breeds in dung. There are many similar species.

▲ *Norellisoma spinimanum*. Identified by double row of bristles under front femur (lens!). Tibiae very bristly. Narrow brown (not black) bands on thorax. 6-9, mainly in damp places. Adults are predatory, but larvae feed in stems of docks.

▲ **Yellow Dung-fly** *Scathophaga stercoraria*. Golden-furred males swarm on fresh cow-pats and horse dung. Females are less furry and rather greyish: less common than males. Adults prey on other flies on the dung, while larvae develop in the dung. There are several similar species.

▲ **Warble-fly** *Hypoderma bovis* Oestridae. Hairy, bee-like fly, with 4th long vein bent sharply forward in line with posterior cross-vein. 6th vein reaches wing margin. 5-6. Adult does not feed. Eggs laid on cattle legs and larvae work their way through body to spend final 3 months in swellings (warbles) just under skin on the back. Fall out when mature and pupate on ground. Hides are ruined by the warbles and exit holes.

▲ *H. lineatum* is similar, although a little slimmer, with blacker veins and shorter hair.
▲ *H. diana* has a similar life history but attacks red deer.

Oedemagena tarandi. A parasite of reindeer, with a life history like Warble-fly. N.

▲ **Sheep Nostril-fly** *Oestrus ovis*. Wrinkled or warty surface characterises this fly. 3rd and 4th long veins join before reaching wing margin: 6th vein does not reach margin. 5-6, resting on rocks and walls in sheep country. Adult does not feed. Viviparous, with female depositing young larvae in sheep nostrils. The larvae feed on mucus and blood in the nasal cavity and sinuses for about 9 months and then pupate in the soil. The fly also attacks goats and various other mammals, including man on occasions.

Pharyngomyia picta. Life cycle like that of *Oestrus*, but living on deer. Widespread but rare.

▲ **Bot-fly** *Gasterophilus intestinalis* Gasterophilidae. 4th long vein almost straight. 7-9. Adult does not feed. Eggs are laid on legs of horses, donkeys, and mules: larvae enter mouth when legs are licked, and then pass into stomach to complete their growth attached to the lining. They pass out of the body to pupate in the soil. There are several similar species, mostly without brown on the wings.

Bot-fly × 2

Stable-fly
×2

Common House-fly
×2

Face-fly
×2

Lesser House-fly
×3

Eustalomyia festiva ×2.5

Anthomyia pluvialis ×3

← *Cordilura impudica* ×2.5

Norellisoma spinimanum ×2.5

Cabbage Root-fly
×3

Yellow Dung-fly
×2.5
♂

Hypoderma diana
×2
♀

Warble-fly
×2
♀

Oedemagena tarandi
×2
♀

Sheep Nostril-fly
×2
♀

Pharyngomyia picta
×2
♀

ANTS, WASPS, BEES, and their relatives

Order Hymenoptera

This immense order contains well over 100,000 known species. As well as the bees, wasps, and ants, it contains the sawflies and gall wasps and a bewildering assortment of ichneumons and other parasites. The range of size is enormous, from huge spider-hunting wasps down to the minute fairy flies (family Mymaridae) that pass their larval stages inside the eggs of other insects and are strong contenders for the title of the world's smallest insect.

The typical hymenopteran has two pairs of membranous wings, the front and hind ones being coupled by a row of minute hooks on the leading edge of each hindwing. The latter is usually very much smaller than the forewing and not always easy to detect, even when the insects are at rest. Wing venation is often much reduced, producing a network of large and often rather square cells not seen in any other group of insects. There is frequently a pigmented pterostigma towards the tip of the forewing, with a generally elongated cell, known as the marginal cell, beyond it. Just behind the pterostigma and marginal cell lies a row of two or three sub-marginal cells, which are of great value in identifying the insects, especially the bees and wasps. The pronotum is often no more than a narrow collar at the front of the thorax, but it sometimes extends back along the sides of the thorax to meet the tegulae. The latter are scales or swellings over the bases of the forewings. The form of the pronotum is another useful guide when identifying bees and wasps.

The head is usually rather hard and extremely mobile, being attached to the thorax by a slender neck. Three ocelli are usually present in addition to the compound eyes. The antennae are extremely variable in form, especially among the sawflies, and are often longer in males than in females. Mouth-parts are essentially of the biting type, equipped with toothed jaws for dealing with solid food, but many hymenopterans also lap up liquids and the bees feed largely on nectar. Most bees have developed long, tubular tongues in connection with their nectar-feeding habits, but they retain their biting jaws for nest-building and other chores.

The order is divided into two very distinct sub-orders – the Symphyta, containing the sawflies, and the Apocrita.

SAWFLIES   Sub-order Symphyta

The sawflies are readily distinguished from the other hymenopterans by the absence of any 'waist', the abdomen being joined to the thorax across its full width and showing little, if any narrowing at the front. The insects get their name for the female's ovipositor, which in most species is in the form of a minute saw. This saw is used to cut slits in plants, and the eggs are then laid in the slits. Each species has a distinct pattern of teeth on the saw, and it is often possible to identify a species just from the ovipositor. The horntails or wood-wasps (p. 222) are sawflies with drill-like ovipositors which are used to bore into timber.

 The saw-like ovipositor of a sawfly

Adult sawflies are mostly quite sturdy insects, although the stem sawflies in the family Cephidae (p. 222) are notable exceptions. The wings are folded flat over the body at rest. The antennae are mostly thread-like, but they are clubbed or feathery in some species. Most of the species are active by day and some, notably the pamphilids (p. 222), fly very rapidly in the sunshine. Others are rather sluggish and are more likely to scuttle away through the vegetation than to take to the air if disturbed. Some species are at least partly carnivorous, capturing other insects on the flowerheads of umbellifers and other plants, but most sawflies are vegetarians. They lap nectar and nibble pollen as they roam over the flowers.

Larval sawflies are almost all vegetarians. Most of them feed freely on the leaves and resemble the caterpillars of butterflies and moths, but they differ from these caterpillars in having at least six pairs of fleshy abdominal legs. The lepidopterous larvae have no more than five pairs of these prolegs (p. 111). Some sawfly larvae tunnel inside their food-plants and they have no abdominal legs. They look more like beetle larvae (p. 295) than caterpillars. These tunnelling larvae usually pupate inside the food-plant, but the other sawfly larvae generally pupate in cocoons in the soil or leaf litter or attached to the food-plant.

Sub-order Apocrita

By far the larger of the two sub-orders of the Hymenoptera, this group contains a very wide range of insects, including many parasitic and social species. The most obvious difference between this group and the sawflies lies in the possession of the typical 'wasp waist'. Although appearing to divide the thorax from the abdomen, the waist is, in fact, entirely in the abdomen if we stick strictly to anatomical criteria. The first segment of the abdomen, known as the propodeum, is firmly fused to the rear of the thorax and the waist comes just behind it. The whole of the abdomen behind the propodeum is known as the gaster, but for practical purposes we can consider the propodeum part of the thorax and equate gaster with abdomen. The narrow front part of the abdomen, which forms the waist, is known as the petiole (pedicel in ants) and may consist of one or two segments or just part of one segment. In a few families (p. 228) it is attached to the top of the propodeum, but it is generally attached near the bottom.

Entomologists split the Apocrita into two sections – the **Parasitica** and the **Aculeata**.

*The **Parasitica*** are almost all parasites, the females using their ovipositors to pierce the host tissues and to lay their eggs there. A wide range of other insects are used as hosts, and it is almost always the young stages that are attacked. Some of the parasites have extremely long ovipositors (p. 231) that can reach hosts tunnelling deep inside plants or even inside other animals. In this last instance, the parasite is known as a hyperparasite – parasitising an insect that is already living parasitically inside its host. Clearly, these parasites have extraordinary powers of detection – based on scent and vibration – to enable them to seek out their hidden hosts. Although most of the Parasitica attack other insects, some lay their eggs in the egg cocoons of spiders.

The young parasites grow up inside, or firmly attached to the outside of the host. Depending on the relative sizes of the parasite and its host, there may be anything from one to several hundred parasitic larvae in each host, which is gradually eaten alive. But the parasites are careful not to damage any vital organs until they themselves are almost mature. It would obviously not be in the parasite's interest to kill its host too early. The host usually dies at about the time that the parasites pupate – either inside or outside its shrivelled skin. Insects with this kind of life history, resulting in the eventual death of the host, are usually known as parasitoids. They are also known as protelean parasites, indicating that they are parasitic only in the larval state.

Best known of the parasitic hymenopterans are the ichneumons (p. 230), an immense and very varied group that can usually be recognised by having a prominent stigma in the forewing and more than 16 antennal segments. The front edge of the forewing is somewhat thickened, owing to the virtual fusion of the first long vein with the front margin and the consequent obliteration of the long narrow cell found in most other hymenopterans. Many ichneumons are quite large, but the rest of the Parasitica are mostly very small insects. They include the chalcids (p. 228), which often have beautiful metallic sheens, and the plant-feeding gall wasps (p. 226).

The bees, wasps, and ants belong to the **Aculeata**, in which the female's ovipositor is generally modified as a sting and use for paralysing prey or for defence. Wasps are essentially predatory insects: the adults often feed on nectar and fruit juices, but the larvae are almost always fed on animal matter. Bees are entirely vegetarian, feeding mainly on nectar and pollen, while the ants include predatory, vegetarian, and omnivorous species. Numerous social insects belong to this section, including all the ants and many bees and wasps. They live in colonies consisting of one or more fertile females (queens), a sprinkling of males (often only at certain times of the year), and numerous sterile females called workers. There are often marked differences between these castes – especially among the ants, where the workers are wingless. Ant and honeybee colonies are perennial, but the bumble bees and wasps produce annual colonies, with over-wintered queens starting new nests in the spring.

There is no hard and fast dividing line between the Parasitica and the Aculeata and there are several transitional families, such as the ruby-tailed wasps and velvet ants (p. 232). These families contain species with parasitic larvae, although the adults are anatomically closer to the Aculeata than to the Parasitica.

The larvae of the sub-order Apocrita – both Parasitica and Aculeata – are always surrounded by food and are poorly developed in comparison with the sawfly larvae. They are always legless and even the head is commonly reduced, especially in the parasitic species.

The following simplified pictorial key will enable you to identify the major groups of the Apocrita and to turn to the appropriate page, although only a very small proportion of species can be illustrated in this book.

1 Insects with abdomen attached near the top of the propodeum

Superfamily Evanioidea p. 228

1 Insects with abdomen attached near the bottom of the propodeum

  2 Antennae with more than 16 segments (lens!). Forewing with a distinct stigma: costal cell almost or quite obliterated

Ichneumons p. 230

  2 Antennae with less than 16 segments. With or without a stigma in forewing: costal cell may or may not be distinct

   3 Hindwing smoothly rounded, without any lobes or notches close to body on rear margin. Mostly very small insects

    4 Petiole of one or two segments, either scale-like or bearing distinct dorsal swellings. Antennae strongly elbowed. Often wingless.

Ants p. 234

4 Abdomen laterally compressed. Antennae not elbowed

Gall Wasps p. 226

4 Abdomen fatter. Antennae elbowed

Chalcids p. 228

3 Hindwing usually with one or two distinct lobes close to body on rear margin (sometimes only a small notch is discernible). Mostly medium-sized or large insects

5 Hindwing with no closed cells

lobes

Ruby-tailed Wasps and relatives p. 232

5 Hindwing with at least one closed cell

6 Pronotum reaches back to tegulae at bases of forewings

pronotum

tegula

7 Forewings folded longitudinally at rest. Eyes strongly emarginate

Potter, Mason, and **Social Wasps** pp 240-2

7 Forewings held flat at rest. Hind legs very long – much longer than abdomen. Body rarely very hairy

Spider-hunting Wasps p. 240

7 Forewings held flat at rest. Hind legs never much longer than abdomen. Body often very hairy. Often wingless

Velvet Ants and **Scoliids** p. 232

6 Pronotum does not reach back to tegulae, but forms a lobe on each side of thorax

tegula

8 Hind tarsi broad and often very hairy

Bees p. 244-252

8 Hind tarsi not broad and never very hairy

Digger Wasps pp 236-238

SAWFLIES   Sub-order Symphyta

Sawflies get their English name for the saw-like ovipositors of most females (see p. 218), although the horntails and a few others have drill-like ovipositors. The adults feed mainly on pollen, although some are partly carnivorous. Most fly weakly, usually by day. The larvae are almost all vegetarians, feeding openly on leaves or else tunnelling inside the plants. The free-living forms resemble the larvae of butterflies and moths, although they usually have more prolegs (see p. 218), but the tunnellers and some other larvae have greatly reduced legs. Some larvae induce gall-formation.

Megalodontes klugii Megalodontidae. Flat-bodied and fast-flying, mainly in sunshine. Antennae with flaps on the underside (see below). 5-8, usually on umbellifer heads. Larvae have no prolegs and live in communal webs on umbellifers. S & C.

▲ **Pamphilius sylvaticus** Pamphiliidae. One of several similar fast-flying, flattened insects. On flowers 5-7: usually active only in sunshine. Larva has no prolegs and lives in rolled leaves of hawthorn and other rosaceous trees.

△n **Acantholyda erythrocephala** Male head black behind antennae. Flies rapidly in pinewoods 4-6. Larvae have no prolegs and live communally in webs among pine needles. Sometimes a forest pest on the continent. N & C.

▲ **Xyela julii** Xyelidae. Varied shades of brown, with filamentous antennae. Female has long, slender ovipositor. Weak-flying 3-6, often visiting birch catkins. Larva has many legs and lives in male pine cones. Common on heathland. N & C.

△s **Xiphydria prolongata** Xiphydriidae. Long neck distinguishes this family. 6-8 in wooded habitats. Larva is almost legless and tunnels in sallows and poplars.
   △ **X. camelus** is similar but lacks red on abdomen. It breeds in birch and alder.

▲ **Horntail** Urocerus gigas. Siricidae. Named for prominent ovipositor: also called a wood-wasp, although it is harmless. 5-10, mainly in pinewoods but not uncommon on new housing estates, where adults emerge from building timbers. Flies in sunshine, with males usually around tree tops. Eggs are drilled into tree trunks and the almost legless larvae take 2 or 3 years to mature in the timber. The northern race (subspecies *taiganus*) has a black ovipositor sheath and male has more black on front of abdomen. There are several similar species in Europe.

▲ **Sirex juvencus** Male resembles Urocerus but has no pale patch behind eye. Antennae usually reddish at base, but may be all black in north. 5th tarsal segment always yellow. 5-10 in coniferous forests. Larvae tunnel in pine trunks. ▲ **S. noctilio** is similar but antennae are always black and 5th tarsal segment brown. Sirex species are often called wood-wasps. Several species occur in B, but most specimens come from imported timber. S. noctilio is the commonest.

ssp. taiganus

Orussus abietinus Orussidae. Antennae inserted below eyes (see below), not between them as in most sawflies: more slender in male. 5-8 in coniferous forests, but rare. Larva parasitises grubs of wood-boring beetles. No other sawfly has parasitic larvae. S & C.

Cephus pygmaeus Cephidae. One of several similar species, all with the slender bodies characteristic of the family. Yellow bands variable. Slow-flying 5-8. Common on flowers, especially yellow composites, in grassy places. The almost legless larvae tunnel in grass stems and are serious pests of cereals.

▲ **Arge ustulata** Argidae. Metallic blue or green: wings yellowish with yellow stigma. Antennae with only 3 segments, as in all this family, the 3rd segment being very long: less clubbed in male. 5-7. Slow-flying in scrubby places, mainly where damp. Larva is fully-legged and feeds on sallows, birches, and hawthorn.
   ▲ **A. cyanocrocea** has yellow costa in forewing, with dark smudge extending right across the wing behind the stigma. Hind legs yellow with black tips: sometimes all black in south. 5-7, usually on umbellifers. Larva feeds on bramble.

Orussus
head

Antenna of *Megalodontes*
with much enlarged
section to show the flaps.

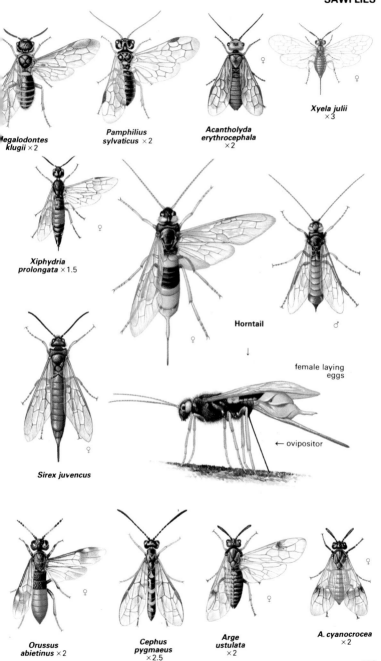

egalodontes klugii × 2

Pamphilius sylvaticus × 2

Acantholyda erythrocephala × 2
♀

Xyela julii × 3
♀

Xiphydria prolongata × 1.5
♀

Horntail
♀

♂

↓

female laying eggs

← ovipositor

Sirex juvencus
♀

Orussus abietinus × 2
♀

Cephus pygmaeus × 2.5

Arge ustulata × 2
♀

A. cyanocrocea × 2
♀

Hawthorn Sawfly emerging from
cocoon after cutting round one end
to form a lid

Blasticotoma filiceti Blasticotomidae. A rare insect (the only European member of its family), recognised by the distinctly pear-shaped cell in the middle of the forewing and the short antennae with only 3 obvious segments (4th segment forms a minute hook at tip). 5-7. Larva tunnels in fern stems. N & C.

⚠ **Abia sericea** Cimbicidae. Male thorax metallic green like abdomen. Antennae usually entirely reddish brown or orange, sometimes blackish. Fast-flying in grassy places 5-8: attracted to various flowers. Larva feeds openly on scabious leaves.
▲ **A. candens** is similar but female thorax green and antennae brownish at base and apex and yellow in middle.

▲ **Birch Sawfly** *Cimbex femoratus*. Dark band around all wing-tips. Fast-flying with buzzing sound in wooded areas 5-8. Larva is plump, greyish or bluish green, and feeds on birch. Spins a tough, sausage-like cocoon in an underground chamber.

⚠ **Hawthorn Sawfly** *Trichiosoma lucorum*. Hair may be very pale. 5-6 in hedgerows and other scrubby places. Larva (p. 297) feeds on hawthorn and spins a tough, sausage-like cocoon on the twigs. Adult cuts its way out with powerful jaws. The species seems to have declined markedly in recent years, possibly owing to widespread mechanical hedge-trimming. N & C. There are several similar species, not easy to distinguish.

▲ **Pine Sawfly** *Diprion pini*. Diprionidae. Abdomen dull, sometimes with pale bands in female. Antennae with more than 9 segments: strongly feathered in male. 5-8 in pinewoods: female rather sluggish and flying little. Larvae feed freely on pine needles, often in large groups: a serious forest pest. There are several similar species.

Family Tenthredinidae. The largest sawfly family, with nearly 1000 European species, many of which are garden pests. Antennae usually 9-segmented. Larvae usually free-living, with 6-8 pairs of prolegs: often gregarious. Many raise hind ends and wave them about when alarmed (see p. 295). Some are slug-like with reduced legs (see Pear Sawfly *Caliroa cerasi* on p. 295).

⚠ **Turnip Sawfly** *Athalia rosae*. One of several very similar species. Antennae with 10-12 segments. Costa black. Thorax yellow beneath. 5-10. Larva, greyish brown or black, feeds on various brassicas, especially turnips.

▲ **Allantus cinctus**. One of several similar carnivorous species with large, asymmetrical jaws. 5-8, often on umbellifers where it catches other small insects. Larvae feed on wild and cultivated roses and related plants.

▲ **Tenthredopsis litterata** Colour ranges from orange to black: female commonly with thorax and base of abdomen black and rest of abdomen red. 5-7. Larvae feed on grasses, especially cock's-foot grass.

▲ **Rhogogaster viridis** Amount of black varies, and green fades soon after death. Stigma uniformly green or straw-coloured. 5-7 in woods and scrubby places, usually on flowers where it catches other small insects. Larva is polyphagous on woody and herbaceous plants. There are several similar species.

▲ **Tenthredo atra** Antennae and stigma completely black. Female lacks red band on abdomen. 5-8. Larva feeds on a wide range of herbaceous plants, including potato and brassicas. One of several very similar species (65 *Tenthredo* species in N & C).

▲ **T. arcuata** is one of a number of very similar species with slightly clubbed antennae. Underside of male entirely yellow. Flagellum of antenna entirely black. 4-8 in grassy places. Larva feeds on red clover.

▲ **Cladius pectinicornis** Male antennae feathery, but much less so than in Pine Sawfly. 5-9 almost everywhere: one of the commonest sawflies. Larva is flat and green and rather hairy and feeds on undersides of rose leaves: also on strawberries and related plants. ▲ **C. difformis** is very similar.

▲ **Gooseberry Sawfly** *Nematus ribesii*. The amount of black on male abdomen varies a great deal. 4-9. Larva (p. 295) feeds on gooseberry and currant leaves, often stripping whole bushes. There are many similar species (about 40 in B).

▲ **Pontania proxima** 5-8 wherever white or crack willows grow. Larva causes the development of red bean galls on the leaves (paler on white willow than on crack willow). Less commonly attacks osier. Pupates in the soil. N & C. There are many similar species, whose larvae all live on willows and sallows, either in galls or in rolled-up leaves.

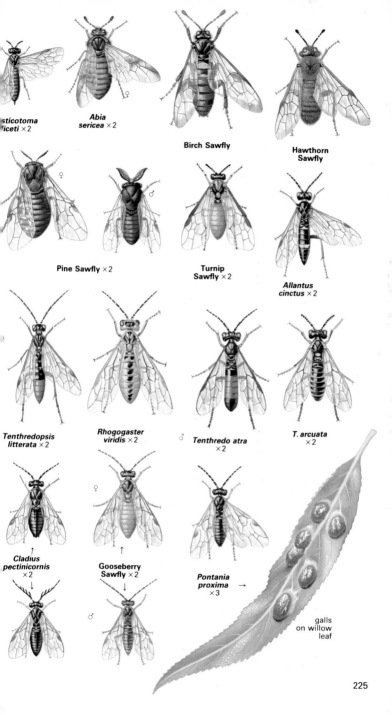

sticotoma liceti ×2

Abia sericea ×2 ♀

Birch Sawfly

Hawthorn Sawfly

Pine Sawfly ×2 ♀ ♂

Turnip Sawfly ×2

Allantus cinctus ×2

Tenthredopsis litterata ×2

Rhogogaster viridis ×2

♂ *Tenthredo atra* ×2

T. arcuata ×2

Cladius pectinicornis ×2 ↓

Gooseberry Sawfly ×2 ♀ ↓

♂

Pontania proxima → ×3

galls on willow leaf

225

WASPS, ANTS, and BEES   Sub-order Apocrita

GALL WASPS Cynipidae. Small, ant-like insects with laterally compressed abdomen and distinctive venation. Sometimes wingless. Nearly all species induce gall-formation in plants, especially oaks. Female lays eggs in the plants, and when the eggs hatch the tissues swell up around the grubs to form the galls. The larvae thrive on the nutritious tissues without appearing to harm the host plants. Unilocular galls contain just one chamber and usually a single larva, while plurilocular galls contain several chambers, each with its own larva. The insects always pupate in the galls, and many spend the winter in the pupal stage. Many species have complex life cycles, involving the alternation of bisexual and parthenogenetic generations. Each generation causes its own kind of gall. The parthenogenetic females differ slightly from females of the sexual generation. A few gall wasps do not induce gall-formation, but lay eggs in the galls of other species: their grubs may deprive the rightful occupants of food and cause them to die. Many parasites, including chalcids and ichneumons, also attack the gall wasp grubs. The insects emerging from a gall are thus not necessarily the gall causers.

△ **Phanacis hypochoeridis** causes plurilocular galls in cat's-ear stems. The galls are unusual in that they start to swell before the eggs hatch. Gall mature 8-9. Adult 5-7. Life cycle normal.

△ **Liposthenes glechomae** causes unilocular galls on ground ivy. Gall pea-sized, but several may coalesce. Gall mature 8-9. Adult 3-4. Life cycle normal.

△ **Diastrophus rubi** attacks young bramble stems, usually spindly stems low down on the plants, causing plurilocular, cigar-shaped galls up to 15cm long. Gall mature 10-11. Adult 4-6. Life cycle normal.

▲ **Diplolepis rosae** causes the bedeguar gall or robin's pincushion on wild roses: a plurilocular gall with a hard woody centre. Gall matures late autumn. Adults fly 4-6. Males very rare: females lay eggs without mating. No alternation of generations.

△ **D. eglanteriae** and ▲ **D. nervosa** resemble *rosae* but cause pea-like unilocular galls on the undersides of rose leaves. Those of *nervosa* are usually spiky and have been dubbed 'sputnik galls'. Both galls usually pink when mature in late summer. They fall to the ground in autumn and adults emerge in spring.

▲ **Neuroterus quercusbaccarum** causes common spangle galls on oak leaves in autumn. Galls fall to ground and parthenogenetic females emerge early in spring to lay eggs in oak buds. The new generation of grubs induces the formation of currant galls on young leaves and catkins 5-6. Male and female gall wasps emerge from these galls and, after mating, eggs are laid on the leaves, leading to a new generation of spangle galls. Silk button and smooth spangle galls also appear on oak leaves in autumn, caused by ▲ **N. numismalis** and ▲ **N. albipes** respectively. These insects resemble *quercusbaccarum* but galls of the sexual generation are inconspicuous swellings on young leaves.

▲ **Andricus kollari** induces unilocular marble galls on oak – green at first but brown and woody when mature 8-9. Parthenogenetic females emerge 9-10 and overwinter in sheltered spots before laying eggs in oak buds in spring. If eggs are laid on Turkey oak a bisexual generation is produced in little galls in the buds, but it is possible that the bisexual generation can be omitted and that the insect can produce a succession of parthenogenetic generations on pedunculate (common) oak or sessile oak. Artichoke galls are much-enlarged buds. They are caused by ▲ **A. foecundatrix**, which is similar to *kollari* but about half its size. The grub lives in a hard, egg-shaped inner gall that falls out when mature in the autumn. Parthenogenetic females emerge in spring and lay eggs in buds. The bisexual generation develops in tiny furry galls on male catkins 5-6.

marble galls
with adult
A. kollari

artichoke galls

GALL WASPS

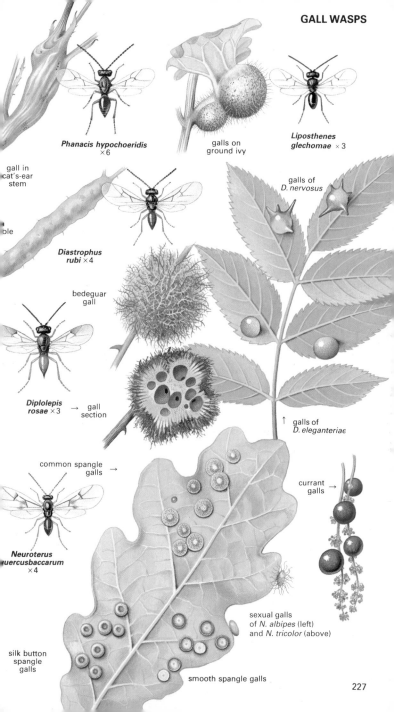

Phanacis hypochoeridis ×6

galls on ground ivy

Liposthenes glechomae ×3

gall in cat's-ear stem

ole

galls of D. nervosus

Diastrophus rubi ×4

bedeguar gall

Diplolepis rosae ×3 → gall section

↑ galls of D. eleganteriae

common spangle galls →

currant galls →

Neuroterus quercusbaccarum ×4

silk button spangle galls

sexual galls of N. albipes (left) and N. tricolor (above)

smooth spangle galls

asexual (knopper) gall of *A. quercuscalicis* on acorn ↓

asexual gall of *Andricus coriarius*

↑ sexual gall of *A. quercusramuli*

△ **Andricus quercusramuli** Cynipidae. Reddish brown with yellow legs. Males and females emerge 5-7 from cotton-wool-like galls that develop on male oak catkins. Parthenogenetic generation (rarely seen) develops in bud galls in early spring.

▲ **A. quercuscalicis** causes the knopper gall, a hard and irregular umbrella-like object on acorns. Larva is in a hard inner gall as in *A. fecundator* (p. 226). Parthenogenetic adults emerge 2-4. Bisexual generation induces galls on Turkey oak catkins.

A. coriarius induces spiky brown galls on downy oak and various other oaks in autumn. Only the parthenogenetic generation is known. S & C. ▲ **Cynips quercusfolii** causes the pale green to red cherry galls on the undersides of oak leaves in autumn. Parthenogenetic adults emerge 12-2 and lay eggs in buds, where bisexual generation induces purple or black galls in spring. ▲ **C. divisa** has a similar life history, but autumn galls are small yellow or red spheres with very hard walls. The much rarer **C. agama** has thin-walled galls.

▲ **Biorhiza pallida**. Males and females emerge from oak apples 6-7. The spongy, plurilocular galls contain many insects, but each gall contains only one sex. Females lay eggs on fine roots, where parthenogenetic generation develops in small brown galls. Parthenogenetic adults are wingless and emerge 2-4 of second year.

PARASITIC HYMENOPTERA

Hymenoptera, belonging to many different families, that spend their early lives inside or firmly attached to the young stages of other insects. The hosts remain alive until the parasites have grown up, but are eventually completely destroyed (see p. 219). Only a few of the families can be mentioned here.

△s **Evania appendigaster** Evaniidae. Gaster very small and attached to top of propodeum by very slender petiole: often waved flag-like, hence American name of ensign wasps. On flowers throughout summer. Larvae in oothecae of cockroaches.

△s **Gasteruption jaculator** Gasteruptiidae. Long, slender gaster attached to top of propodeum. Wings folded longitudinally at rest. On umbellifers in summer. Larvae in nests of solitary bees, feeding on grubs and stored food. N & C.

△s **Aulacus striatus** Aulacidae. Pear-shaped gaster attached to top of propodeum by short petiole. Long ovipositor. Around logs and tree trunks and on umbellifers and other flowers 6-9. Larva parasitises grubs of *Xiphydria camelus* (p. 222). N & C.

▲ **Torymus nitens** Torymidae. Hind coxa very large, as in whole family. Female uses long ovipositor to pierce young oak apples and other oak galls in summer. The grubs parasitise the gall wasp larvae. There are hundreds of similar metallic species in this and related families (collectively known as chalcids), all sharing the same simple wing venation and elbowed antennae. They are abundant in vegetation in summer.

▲ **Pteromalus puparum** Pteromalidae. Hind coxa not much larger than others. Larvae parasitise pupae of white butterflies, the female inserting her eggs before pupal case hardens. Adults emerge in large numbers from each infested chrysalis, with 2 or 3 generations per year.

Leucospis gigas Leucospidae. One of the largest of the chalcids. Hind coxa very large: hind femur much swollen and strongly toothed. Wings folded longitudinally at rest. Ovipositor curved over back. Flies in summer. Largely parthenogenetic: males found only in certain populations in SE. Larvae feed on grubs of solitary bees, especially *Chalicodoma parietina* (p. 246). S & C.

Pteromalus emerging from host pupa

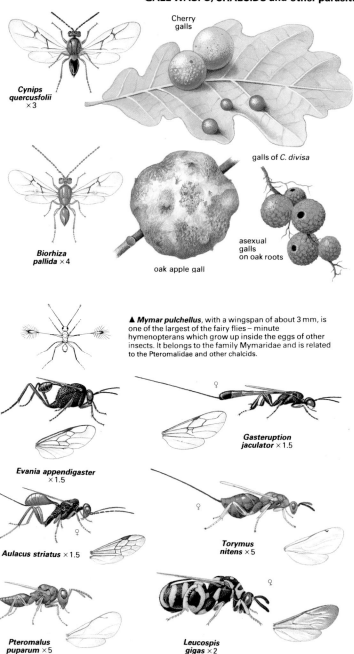

Cynips quercusfolii × 3

Cherry galls

Biorhiza pallida × 4

oak apple gall

galls of *C. divisa*

asexual galls on oak roots

▲ *Mymar pulchellus*, with a wingspan of about 3 mm, is one of the largest of the fairy flies – minute hymenopterans which grow up inside the eggs of other insects. It belongs to the family Mymaridae and is related to the Pteromalidae and other chalcids.

Evania appendigaster × 1.5

Gasteruption jaculator × 1.5

Aulacus striatus × 1.5

Torymus nitens × 5

Pteromalus puparum × 5

Leucospis gigas × 2

ICHNEUMONS Ichneumonidae. An immense group of parasitic insects whose larvae live in or on the young stages of other insects. Adults are rather slender, with long antennae of at least 16 segments. The front edge of the forewing appears rather thick, owing to obliteration of the costal cell, and there is a prominent stigma. A few species are wingless. Ichneumons are abundant in hedgerows and other dense vegetation, scuttling around and vibrating their antennae as they search for the scents of their hosts. Butterfly and moth caterpillars are the main hosts and generally just one egg is laid in or on each one. Endoparasitic species generally emerge after pupation of the host, much to the dismay of many people who collect caterpillars to breed out the adult butterflies or moths. Many other insects are used as hosts, and some ichneumons even use spiders. Female ichneumons often have a very long ovipositor to reach hosts deep inside plants or other animals. The family Braconidae is very similar in habits but readily distinguished by its venation: there is a long open cell towards the rear of the forewing (see below). Braconids tend to be smaller than ichneumons and often lay many eggs in each host.

△ *Agriotypus armatus.* Thorax has long, curved spine. Wings distinctly clouded. An ectoparasite of various case-bearing caddis flies. Female crawls into water and lays an egg in a case containing a fully grown larva or pupa. The grub consumes the pupa and then pupates in the case: adult remains in the case for the winter and emerges in spring or early summer. Cases containing pupae or resting adult *Agriotypus* can be recognised by a silken ribbon attached to one end and used in respiration.

▲ *Rhyssa persuasoria.* One of the largest ichneumons. Ectoparasitic on horntail larvae (p. 222): slender ovipositor drills deep into pine trunks to reach host. Not uncommon in pinewoods in summer. The brown and yellow *Megarhyssa superba* is even larger.

▲ *Pimpla hypochondriaca.* A very common endoparasite of various moth larvae and pupae, notably those of the Snout Moth (p. 168). All summer. There are several similar species, mostly a little smaller: one is an endoparasite of the pupa of the Large White Butterfly.

▲ *Lissonota setosa.* Resembles *Pimpla*, but larger and female has a very long ovipositor. Endoparasitic in larvae of the Goat Moth, the ovipositor being used to drill into tree trunks. The smaller, but otherwise similar ▲ *L. fundator* attacks clearwing larvae in stems. There are many similar species.

▲ *Diplazon laetatorius.* An abundant endoparasite of various hover-fly larvae. The egg may be laid in the host egg, and adult emerges from host pupa. There are several similar species.

▲ *Netelia testacea.* A very common ectoparasite of moth larvae. Abdomen flattened from side to side and arched upwards. Short ovipositor capable of piercing human skin if molested. Flies all summer: markedly nocturnal and abundant in light traps. There are several similar species but only *testacea* has dark tip to abdomen.

▲ *Ophion luteus.* Very like *Netelia*, but venation differs. Scutellum distinctly triangular. Late summer and autumn: very common. Endoparasite of various caterpillars. One of many similar species, with or without dark hind ends.

▲ *Protichneumon pisorius.* An endoparasite of hawkmoth larvae. Adult 5-9: not uncommon on umbels and other flowers.

▲ *Amblyteles armatorius.* Scutellum cream or yellow. Hind trochanter yellow. Very common on umbels in summer: hibernates as adult, often in caves. An endoparasite of many caterpillars, especially noctuids. One of several similar species.

▲ *Ichneumon suspiciosus.* One of many very similar species, difficult to separate with certainty. Very common on umbels in summer: hibernates as adult. An endoparasite of swift moth larvae and various noctuid caterpillars.

Cotesia glomerata × 5

▲ *Cotesia glomerata* Braconidae. Endoparasite in caterpillars of Large White and related butterflies. Up to 150 grubs in each caterpillar, emerging before it reaches pupal stage to leave just a shrivelled, empty skin. The grubs themselves pupate around the corpse in silken yellow cocoons. Adult spring and summer.

Cotesia cocoons surrounding dead host larva

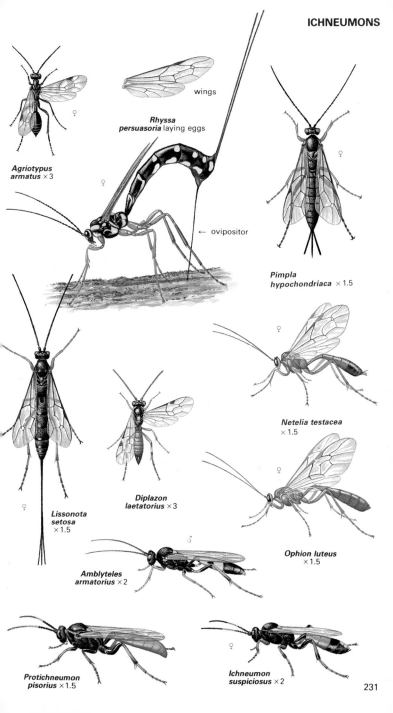

wings

Agriotypus armatus × 3

♀

Rhyssa persuasoria laying eggs

♀

← ovipositor

♀

Pimpla hypochondriaca × 1.5

♀

Netelia testacea × 1.5

♀

Lissonota setosa × 1.5

Diplazon laetatorius × 3

♀

Ophion luteus × 1.5

♂

Amblyteles armatorius × 2

Protichneumon pisorius × 1.5

♀

Ichneumon suspiciosus × 2

231

RUBY-TAILED WASPS Chrysididae. Metallic-coloured insects, often called jewel-wasps because of their bright colours. Also called cuckoo wasps because they lay their eggs in the nests of other insects – mainly solitary wasps and bees. The ruby-tail grubs eat the wasp or bee larvae and then feed on the stored food. A very hard cuticle protects adults from the stings of the host species, and most ruby-tails can also roll themselves up for extra protection – thanks to the flat or concave underside of the abdomen. Only three abdominal segments are usually visible from above. Female has ovipositor in a retractable tube. A sting is present, but not usually functional: most species lack venom.

Stilbum cyanurum. Tip of abdomen distinctly tapered, with 4 pointed teeth. Generally clear green with golden reflections, but head and thorax may be dull green or blue and abdomen reddish with a blue tip. Parasitises mason wasps and bees. 6-9. S & C (southern).

▲ *Chrysis ignita*. Commonest of several very similar species. Head and thorax green or blue, sometimes with golden sheen. 4 teeth at tip of abdomen sharply pointed and almost equidistant. Parasitises mason bees mainly, often seen running over walls and tree trunks in search of their nests. 4-9.

△ *C. fulgida* is readily distinguished from *ignita* by blue area at front of gaster. Parasitises digger and mason wasps. 5-9, in woods.

Parnopes grandior. Male has 4 abdominal segments visible from above: female has only 3, of which 3rd is much larger than the others. A thin, leaf-like projection from rear end of thorax. Abdomen not toothed at tip, but with several very tiny points. Tongue very long. Parasitises *Bembix* digger wasps. 6-8. S & C (southern).

▲ *Cleptes nitidulus*. Pronotum strongly narrowed at front and leading to a distinct neck. Thorax green or blue in male: black, red, and blue in female, usually tinged with green. Male has 5 abdominal segments visible from above: female only 4. Functional sting present. A parasite of sawfly larvae and pupae. 5-8. S & C. Sometimes placed in a separate family – the Cleptidae.

△s *Methocha ichneumonides* Tiphiidae. Male with 2 sub-marginals and a long, pointed marginal cell. Female wingless. Body very shiny in both sexes, but males very rare and reproduction is probably largely parthenogenetic. Female paralyses tiger beetle larvae with her sting and lays an egg on each one. 5-9 on heathland. S & C.

△s *Tiphia femorata*. 2 sub-marginals: marginal cell open in female but closed in male. Middle and hind legs red in female: black in male. Pronotum rather square in front. 7-8. Parasitises larvae of various chafer and dung beetles. S & C.

△ **Velvet Ant** *Mutilla europaea* Mutillidae. Male fully-winged: female wingless and ant-like, with a powerful sting. Both sexes with patches of silvery hair. 7-9 and again in spring after hibernation. A parasite of various bumble bees, feeding on the larvae in the nest. Most of Europe, but local. There are several similar species on the continent.

Myrmilla capitata. Wingless in both sexes. Head relatively large and square. Thorax parallel-sided. A parasite of various solitary bees. 4-8. S. There are several similar species, some with winged males.

Dasylabris maura. Male fully-winged, with dark wing-tips and 2 grey bands across abdomen. Female wingless, with strongly pear-shaped thorax. A parasite of *Ammophila* and other sand wasps. S & C (southern).

Scolia flavifrons Scoliidae. One of Europe's largest hymenopterans, with female up to 40mm long. Her head, larger than that of male, is chestnut-brown. Each yellow abdominal band may be split into 2 spots. Thorax and tip of abdomen may have reddish hairs in some areas. 6-8 in hot sunny places, visiting a wide range of flowers for nectar. Harmless to man despite its size. A parasite of the Rhinoceros Beetle (p. 264). S.

S. hirta is distinguished from several similar species by the 2 yellow bands and the strong violet tinge on wings. 7-10. A parasite of chafer grubs. S & C (southern).

△s *Sapyga quinquepunctatum* Sapygidae. 3 sub-marginals. Antennae distinctly thickened towards tip. Pronotum square in front. Male lacks red on abdomen but has yellow spots on 3rd and 4th segments. 5-8. A parasite of *Osmia* and other mason bees.

Sapyga quinquepunctatum × 2

Stilbum cyanurum ×2

Chrysis ignita ×2 ♀

C. fulgida ×2 ♀

at rest

Parnopes grandior ×2 ♀

Cleptes nitidulus ×3 ♀

Methocha ichneumonides ×2 ♂ ♀

Tiphia femorata ×2 ♀

Velvet Ant ×2 ♂ ♀

Myrmilla capitata ×2 ♀

Dasylabris maura ×2 ♀

Scolia flavifrons ♂

S. hirta ×1.25

ANTS Formicidae. A family of some 15,000 known species, all social. Workers are always wingless: sexual forms winged, but queens break off wings soon after mating. Antennae usually clearly elbowed. The narrow 'waist', known as the pedicel, has one or two segments. Sting not present in all species (usually absent in species with 1-segmented pedicel). There are carnivorous, herbivorous, and omnivorous species, with aphid honeydew prominent in many diets. European ants nest mainly in the ground. Some species have more than one queen in each colony. The dense swarms of flying ants that appear in summer and autumn are mating swarms. Unless otherwise stated, all ants illustrated here are workers.

Ants of the sub-family Myrmicinae have a 2-segmented pedicel. Other European ants have just one segment, usually scale-like.

non-Myrmicine

Myrmicine

▲ **Myrmica rubra**. Pedicel of 2 segments. Male blackish brown: queen and worker chestnut. Propodeum with 2 spines. Worker with sting. Omnivorous. Abundant in garden soils. Mating flights 7-10. One of several very similar species.

M. ruginodis is almost identical but the pedicel differs slightly in shape.

Pheidole megacephala. A very small ant with 2-segmented pedicel. Two kinds of worker, one with a very large head and jaws for cracking seeds, which are a major component of the omnivorous diet. Nests under stones in soil, often close to houses. S & C (southern): sometimes in buildings further north.

△ **Argentine Ant** *Iridomyrmex humilis*. A small and very slender ant with a 1-segmented pedicel bearing a well-developed scale. Head and thorax commonly dark brown like abdomen. Omnivorous. A native of S. America, now well established in and hard to eradicate from European buildings. Colonies increase and spread by fragmentation, without mating flights. Widespread in S & C: sporadic in B (heated buildings only).

▲ **Pharaoh's Ant** *Monomorium pharaoensis*. A very small ant with 2-segmented pedicel. Tip of abdomen usually darker than shown. Antennae 12-segmented, the last 3 broader than the others and forming a faint club. Omnivorous. A native of Africa, now a troublesome pest in heated buildings. Nests in tiny crevices. No mating swarms.

Camponotus vagus. One of the largest European ants, although size varies. Pedicel 1-segmented and much of body dotted with long pale hairs. Omnivorous, with a special liking for honeydew. Southern Europe, nesting in dead tree trunks and often causing losses to forestry by excavating galleries in felled trunks before they go to the sawmill. Several similar species live on continent, but none in B.
C. lateralis of southern Europe nests under stones and logs. Queen has brown head only: male is all black. Omnivorous. Workers forage on ground and tree trunks, often forming long columns and frequently associating with the superficially similar **Crematogaster scutellaris**, although latter is distinguished by 2-segmented pedicel and habit of carrying abdomen almost vertically when alarmed.

▲ **Black Garden Ant** *Lasius niger*. Pedicel 1-segmented. Dark brown to black. Omnivorous but regularly milking aphids for honeydew. Abundant everywhere, often under pavements and garden paths and sometimes nesting in or under house walls. ▲ **Yellow Meadow Ant** *L. flavus* is yellowish brown, but otherwise very like *niger*. Inhabits rough grassland, making the familiar ant-hills. Both species produce huge mating swarms, usually 7-8.

Messor barbara. Pedicel with 2 relatively long segments. Head red or black according to race: rest of body brown to shiny black. Two kinds of worker, one with much larger head than the other. Males have very small heads. Nests underground and feeds almost entirely on seeds, which are cracked open by the large-headed workers. Workers can be seen dragging seeds back to the nest from considerable distances. S.

△ s **Wood Ant** *Formica rufa*. Pedicel of one flattened, leaf-like segment. No sting, although the ant can fire formic acid from rear end when disturbed. Mainly in woods, making large mound nests with leaves and other debris. Several or many queens in each nest. Omnivorous, with a bias towards animal food. Protected by law in some countries because of its great value in destroying forest pests. Most of Europe, but mainly upland in S. Mating flight 5-6. There are several similar species.

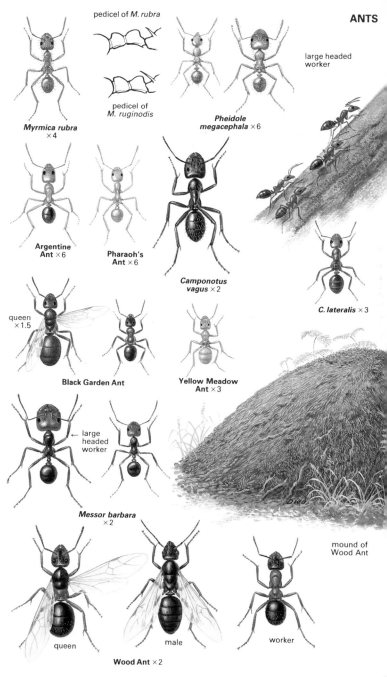

pedicel of *M. rubra*

pedicel of *M. ruginodis*

Myrmica rubra ×4

Pheidole megacephala ×6

large headed worker

Argentine Ant ×6

Pharaoh's Ant ×6

Camponotus vagus ×2

C. lateralis ×3

queen ×1.5

Black Garden Ant

Yellow Meadow Ant ×3

← large headed worker

Messor barbara ×2

mound of Wood Ant

queen

male

worker

Wood Ant ×2

DIGGER WASPS Sphecidae. Solitary wasps with a relatively broad head. Pronotum forms only a small collar, not reaching back to tegulae. Wings held flat over body at rest. Most species nest in ground: females often have a spiny comb on front leg for digging. Some species nest in decaying wood or hollow stems, and a few are masons and build with mud. The nests are stocked with various insects, paralysed by the female's sting. Several insects are usually put into each nest burrow, often in several separate chambers. Eggs are laid and the wasp grubs rely on the stored food until they pupate. There are some 9,000 known digger wasp species. The family is more closely related to the bees than to the other wasps.

▲ **Trypoxylon figulus.** One of several similar species with a slender, tapering abdomen. 1 sub-marginal cell. Inner margin of eye deeply notched. Nests in woodworm holes, hollow stems, and similar cavities: builds mud cells therein and stocks them with small spiders. 5-9.

▲ **Crabro cribrarius.** 1 sub-marginal. Male front tibia broad and plate-like. Male antennae appear deformed. Central yellow bands of abdomen divided. Continental specimens often with yellow on thorax. 5-9. Nests mainly in sandy soil: stocked with flies. There are many similar species.

▲ **Ectemnius cephalotes.** 1 sub-marginal. One of several similar species, distinguished from *Crabro* by normal front tibia in male and by grooved prolongation of abdomen in female. 6-9. Nests in rotten wood: stocked with flies.

△ **Crossocerus palmipes.** 1 sub-marginal. Face largely yellow. Front tibia and 1st tarsal segment of male expanded. 5-9 in sandy places: nest stocked with flies. One of several similar species.

Lestica clypeata. 1 sub-marginal. Body coarsely punctured. Male instantly recognisable by shape of head and front legs: female more normal, with yellow on thorax and a narrow grooved spike at tip of abdomen. 5-9. Nests in dead wood: stocked with small moths.

▲ **Oxybelus uniglumis.** Venation much reduced. Rear of thorax with 2 transparent flaps: propodeum with a small spine. Female with comb. 5-9. Nests in sand: stocked with flies carried back impaled on sting. There are several similar species.

Larra anathema. 3 sub-marginals. Abdomen sometimes entirely black: always shining. 6-9. Makes no nest. Follows mole crickets along their burrows and temporarily paralyses them with the sting. An egg is laid in each cricket, which soon wakes up and continues activity with the wasp larva inside it. S.

▲ **Pemphredon lugubris.** 2 sub-marginals, the first much larger than second. Abdomen distinctly stalked. Head and thorax hairy. 5-9. Nests in rotten wood: stocked with aphids. One of many similar species, most of which nest in bramble stems.

▲ **Mellinus arvensis.** 3 sub-marginals. Scutellum with large yellow spot. Abdomen with short petiole. 5-9. Nests in sand: stocked with large flies, especially hover-flies. △s **M. crabroneus** has paler markings and reddish antennae.

Palarus variegatus. 3 sub-marginals. Abdomen with distinct grooves between segments as in *Cerceris*, but more triangular and much yellower. 5-7. Nests in ground: stocked with assorted hymenopterans, including other digger wasps. S.

▲ **Astata boops.** 3 sub-marginals. Male eyes meet on top of head. Female antennae much shorter. Female with comb. 5-8. Nests in sandy soil: stocked with shield bug nymphs.

▲ **Mimesa lutarius.** 3 sub-marginals. Petiole shorter than 1st abdominal segment: keeled on top and straight when seen from side. Male usually has less red on abdomen. 5-8. Nests in sand: stocked with leafhoppers. There are several similar species.

▲ **Argogorytes mystaceus.** 3 sub-marginals. Male antennae extra long. Female with short comb. 1st abdominal tergite almost semi-circular. Yellow spot may be missing from 4th gastral segment. 5-9. Nests in soil: stocked with froghopper nymphs.

▲ **Nysson spinosus.** 3 sub-marginals, the 2nd being small and stalked in front. Rear edge of propodeum spiny. Front of abdomen often reddish. Cuticle very hard. 5-8. A cuckoo species, laying eggs in nests of *Argogorytes*. There are many similar species.

▲ **Cerceris arenaria.** 3 sub-marginals, the 2nd being stalked at front. Female with comb. 1st abdominal segment rounded, with 2 large yellow spots. Abdominal segments separated by distinct grooves. 5-9. Nests deep in sand: stocked with weevils. S & C. One of several similar species.

△s **Bee-killer** *Philanthus triangulum.* 3 sub-marginals. Head more rounded in front than in most digger wasps. Female with strong comb. Abdomen largely yellow, with or without black triangles. 7-9. Nests in sand: stocked with honey bees which are carried slung upside-down under body. Also known as the bee wolf, this wasp was extremely rare in B and confined to the south coast until recently but, perhaps as a result of warmer summers, it has expanded its range considerably and now occurs in many areas in the southern half of England. Much of Europe except far north.

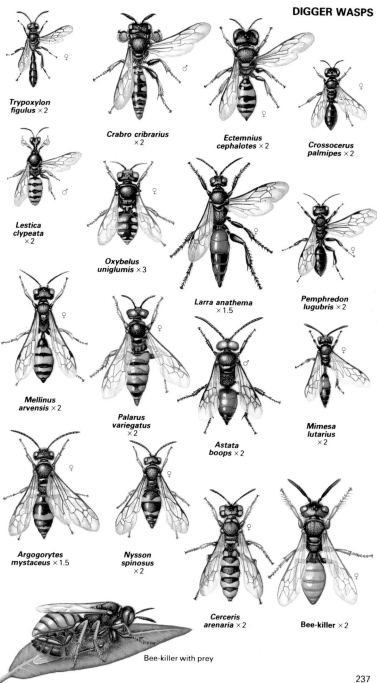

DIGGER WASPS

Trypoxylon figulus ×2 ♀

Crabro cribrarius ×2 ♂

Ectemnius cephalotes ×2 ♀

Crossocerus palmipes ×2 ♀

Lestica clypeata ×2 ♂

Oxybelus uniglumis ×3 ♀

Larra anathema ×1.5 ♀

Pemphredon lugubris ×2 ♀

Mellinus arvensis ×2 ♀

Palarus variegatus ×2 ♀

Astata boops ×2 ♂

Mimesa lutarius ×2 ♀

Argogorytes mystaceus ×1.5 ♀

Nysson spinosus ×2 ♀

Cerceris arenaria ×2 ♀

Bee-killer ×2 ♀

Bee-killer with prey

237

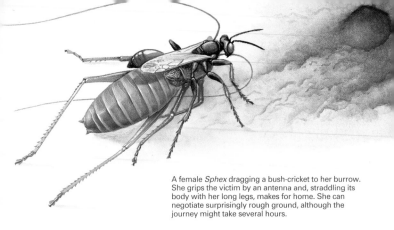

A female *Sphex* dragging a bush-cricket to her burrow. She grips the victim by an antenna and, straddling its body with her long legs, makes for home. She can negotiate surprisingly rough ground, although the journey might take several hours.

Sphex rufocinctus. 3 sub-marginals. Wing tinted yellow in female. Face clothed with silvery hair. Female with comb. Size very variable. 6-9. Nests in sandy soil: stocked with crickets and grasshoppers. S & C (southern): most common around Mediterranean. Commonest of several similar species.

Sceliphron destillatorium. 3 sub-marginals. Wings yellowish at base. Petiole yellow and almost as long as rest of abdomen. 5-8. Makes a nest of mud, attached to walls, rocks, tree trunks, etc: sometimes in buildings. Nests stocked with spiders. S & C (southern). **S. spirifex** is very similar but has no yellow on thorax: tegulae are black.

Liris praetermissa. 3 sub-marginals. Propodeum sub-rectangular and strongly grooved. 4-8. Nests in ground, often in pre-existing holes: stocked with crickets. S.

Dolichurus corniculus. 3 sub-marginals. Long pronotum with distinct neck. Almost square propodeum, strongly sculptured and keeled on top. Abdomen very shiny. Nests in hollow stems of bramble and other shrubs: stocked with cockroaches of genus *Ectobius*. 6-9. S & C (southern).

Ammophila sabulosa. 3 sub-marginals. Petiole 2-segmented, very long and slender and not sharply separated from rest of abdomen. Female with strong comb. 5-9. Nests in sandy places: stocked with non-hairy caterpillars. One of several similar species known as sand wasps, but distinguished from most others by entirely black legs.

Podalonia hirsuta. 3 sub-marginals. Thorax with bristly hairs, whitish in male and black in female. Petiole shorter than in *Ammophila* and more sharply separated from gaster. 3-8. Nests in sandy places: stocked with hairless or sparsely hairy caterpillars. Unlike most digger wasps, it catches prey before excavating nest.

Bembix rostrata. 3 sub-marginals. Resembles social wasps, but wings are held flat at rest. Mouth-parts with a beak-like extension. Comb on front leg in both sexes, but very large in female. Yellow abdominal bands sinuous and often broken in middle. 5-8. Nests in sandy places, often densely clustered: stocked with flies. Female brings more flies later to top up the larder, adjusting size of her captures to the increasing size of her larvae. There are several similar species.

Stizus fasciatus. 3 sub-marginals. Female has red or orange antennae. 5-8. Nests in sandy soil: stocked with crickets and grasshoppers. S. There are several similar species.

Ammophila tapping down the sand to close her burrow, using a small stone held in her jaws. Some species use their heads to tap down the sand.

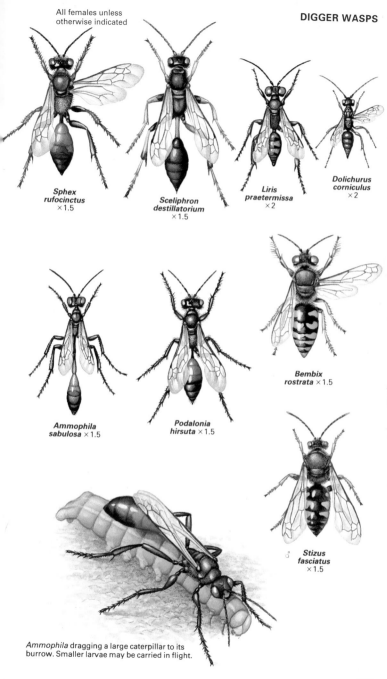

All females unless otherwise indicated

Sphex rufocinctus × 1.5

Sceliphron destillatorium × 1.5

Liris praetermissa × 2

Dolichurus corniculus × 2

Ammophila sabulosa × 1.5

Podalonia hirsuta × 1.5

Bembix rostrata × 1.5

♂ *Stizus fasciatus* × 1.5

Ammophila dragging a large caterpillar to its burrow. Smaller larvae may be carried in flight.

SPIDER-HUNTING WASPS Pompilidae. Solitary wasps using spiders as food for their young. Distinguished from digger wasps (p. 236) by pronotum extending back to tegulae at base of wings. Latter laid flat at rest: almost all with 3 sub-marginals. Males often much smaller than females: female antennae generally coil up after death. Legs long and slender: hind femur especially long. Generally nest in sandy ground, many females having strong combs on front legs for sweeping away the sand. Female makes several burrows, each one usually receiving a single spider and a single egg. Burrow is closed by tapping down sand with end of abdomen. Unlike most digger wasps, these insects catch prey before digging the burrow. A few species make nests.

> **Cryptocheilus comparatus.** One of the largest European pompilids. Collects wolf spiders, including the infamous tarantula, by following them into their tunnels or chasing them on the surface. Male often paler. 6-7. S.

△s **Caliadurgus fasciatellus.** Pronotum rather square in front. Male lacks red on abdomen and has no brown patch on wings. 6-9. Nest is a short vertical burrow in hard clay. Orb-web spiders are collected and stored vertically in the burrows.

△s **Ceropales maculata.** Female with visible sting sheath: male genitalia exposed. Female antennae do not coil after death. Legs not spiny. A cuckoo species, watching other pompilids excavating their burrows and then nipping in to lay an egg on the paralysed spider as it is being dragged into the nest. The *Ceropales* egg hatches quickly and its grub devours the rightful pompilid larvae as well as the spider. Adults often on umbellifer flowers 5-9.

> **Eoferreola rhombica.** Thorax (with propodeum) distinctly rectangular. Wings almost clear in male, which also has only 2nd abdominal tergite orange. Follows an eresid spider into its silken tunnel, paralyses it temporarily with the sting, and lays an egg on it. The spider recovers and the wasp grubs feed on it externally. 6-7. S & C (southern).

▲ **Anoplius viaticus.** Outer sub-marginal almost triangular. Tip of abdomen clothed with numerous stiff black hairs in female: broad and flat in male. 4-10, especially common on umbellifer flowers in spring. Chases wolf spiders. One of the commonest pompilids. S & C. Several similar species, but abdominal patterns differ.

▲ **Episyron rufipes.** Claws on all feet distinctly bifid. Female with strong comb. Thorax and propodeum with silvery scales (may be missing in worn specimens). White abdominal markings variable. Plucks orb-web spiders from webs. 6-9. *E. tripunctatus* of S & C is similar but has entirely black legs.

▲ **Pompilus cinereus.** Hairy bands on abdomen are blue-grey. Tip of female abdomen with scattered fine hairs. Female with strong comb. 5-9. Collects wolf spiders mainly, burying them temporarily while digging the main burrow. There are many similar species, often with orange bands on abdomen.

> **Celonites abbreviatus** Masaridae. 2 sub-marginals. Wings folded longitudinally at rest. Pronotum reaches back to tegulae. Abdomen very square in front. A solitary wasp making a small nest of clay cells on a stone. Unlike most wasps, it stocks its nest with pollen and nectar. 5-8. S & C (southern), especially near Mediterranean.
>
> **Ceramius lusitanicus.** 2 sub-marginals. Antennae spirally twisted at tip in male: normal in female. Abdomen rounded in front. Digs nest burrow in clay, forming several cells and stocking them with pollen and nectar. 5-7. SW.

POTTER and MASON WASPS Eumenidae. Solitary wasps, but closely related to social Vespidae (p. 242) and resembling them in folding wings longitudinally at rest. 3 sub-marginals. Pronotum reaches back to tegulae. Middle tibia with 1 spur. Almost all species black and yellow. Small nests built of clay or mud.

> **Delta unguiculata.** 1st abdominal segment bell-shaped and clearly separated from the rest. Nest is an irregular cluster of several cells, fixed to rocks or walls like a lump of hardened mortar: stocked with caterpillars. 6-8. S & C (southern).

△s **Eumenes coarctatus** is the common potter wasp of heathland. One of several similar species making vase-shaped nests on rocks and plants. Each vase is stocked with small hairless caterpillars and contains a single wasp grub. 6-9.

▲ **Odynerus spinipes.** Male antennae spirally rolled at tip, the rolled section entirely black. Male has paler hairs and 3 teeth on underside of mid femur. 5-9. One of several similar species nesting in sandy ground, especially on slopes: burrow entrance often with a curved chimney. Nest stocked with weevil larvae.

△ **Ancistrocerus antilope.** Male antennae not coiled: last segment bent back like a hook. Tegulae pointed at rear. 5-9. Nests in a wide range of cavities, divided by mud partitions and stocked with small caterpillars. Largest of several similar and very common species, not easily distinguished from each other.

SPIDER-HUNTERS, POTTERS and MASON WASPS

Caliadurgus fasciatellus ×2 ♀

Ceropales maculata ×2 ♀

Eoferreola rhombica ×2 ♀

Cryptocheilus comparatus ×1.5 ♀

Anoplius viaticus ×1.5 ♀

Episyron rufipes ×1.5 ♀

Pompilus cinereus ×1.5 ♀

Cryptocheilus stinging spider

Celonites abbreviatus ×2 ♀

Ceramius lusitanicus ×1.5 ♀

Delta unguiculata ♀

Eumenes coarctatus ×1.5 ♀

Odynerus spinipes ×1.5 ♀

Ancistrocerus antilope ×1.5 ♀

The vase-shaped nest of **Eumenes coarctatus**, made from sand and mud, is commony attached to heather. Several vases may be fixed together, though each remains a separate dwelling.

241

SOCIAL WASPS Vespidae. Eyes deeply notched or crescent-shaped. Wings folded longitudinally at rest, with most of abdomen exposed from above. Pronotum reaches back to tegulae. Middle tibia has 2 spurs. Insects live in annual colonies, each founded by a mated female (queen) in spring. Nests are built of paper, which wasps make from wood. A few hundred to several thousand female workers are reared in summer: always smaller than queens. Males appear in late summer: most often seen on flowers. They have longer antennae than females (13 segments compared with 12): base of antenna usually yellow beneath in males but yellow or black in females. Adults feed mainly on nectar and other sweet materials. Young reared mainly on other insects collected by workers. The colony disintegrates in autumn and only mated females survive the winter. Some species, known as cuckoo wasps, have no workers: they lay their eggs in the nests of other wasps. The following notes refer only to females: male patterns are more variable.

Common

German

Cuckoo

Red

Median Wasp

D. saxonica

Tree

Norwegian

D. adulterina

▲ **Common Wasp** *Vespula vulgaris*. Face usually with anchor mark: malar space (between bottom of eye and jaw) very short. Antennae black at base. Vertical yellow line behind eye broken by a black patch. Thoracic stripes parallel-sided. 4 yellow spots at rear of thorax. Nests in holes in ground or buildings: paper yellowish and formed into shell-like plates on outside.

▲ **German Wasp** *V. germanica*. Face with 3 dots: malar space very short. Antennae black at base. Vertical yellow line behind eye complete. Thoracic stripes usually bulge in middle. 4 yellow spots at rear of thorax. Nest like that of *vulgaris* but greyish.

△ **Cuckoo Wasp** *V. austriaca*. Face with 2 or 3 black spots: malar space very short. Antennae yellow at base. Only 2 yellow spots on thorax. Tibiae and 1st abdominal segment with long black hairs. Never any red on abdomen. A cuckoo in nests of Red Wasp. N & C.

▲ **Red Wasp** *V. rufa*. Face with thick vertical line, sometimes forming anchor-like mark: malar space very short. Antennae black at base. Only 2 yellow spots on rear of thorax. Tibiae without long hairs. 1st abdominal segment with long black hairs and often distinctly red. Subterranean nest covered with more or less smooth sheets. All Europe, but rare in S.

▲ **Median Wasp** *Dolichovespula media*. Face with slim black bar: malar space long (nearly as long as distance between antennal bases). Antennae yellow at base. Eye notch completely filled with yellow. Thorax often tinged red, especially on female and with 4 yellow or chestnut spots at rear. Generally the darkest of our social wasps, with large amounts of black on abdomen: often tinged with red. Nest hung in bushes and clothed with smooth sheets. After arriving in SE England in the 1980s, it spread rapidly and now occurs in most parts of B.

△s ***D. saxonica***. Like Norwegian Wasp but face bar often irregular. Thorax with pale hairs at sides. Abdomen never red.

▲ **Tree Wasp** *D. sylvestris*. Face clear yellow or with 1 black dot: malar space long. Antennae yellow at base. Thorax with pale hairs at sides and 2 yellow spots at rear. Nest a rather small ball, hung in bushes and covered with thin but tough sheets. Absent from far south.

▲ **Norwegian Wasp** *D. norwegica*. Face divided by vertical black bar: malar space long. Antennae yellow at base. Thorax with black hairs at sides and 2 yellow spots at rear. Abdomen often red in front. Nest like that of Tree Wasp but with looser covering. Widespread but most common in north.

D. adulterina. Black bar sometimes completely divides face: malar space long. Antennae yellow at base. A cuckoo species in nests of *saxonica*: not common.

△s **Hornet** *Vespa crabro*. The largest wasp, easily recognised by size and brown and gold colour. Nests in hollow trees, chimneys, and wall cavities, sometimes using the same site year after year (although a completely new colony). Populations fluctuate markedly from year to year in B.

Asian Hornet *V. velutina*. Smaller than *crabro*, with bright yellow tarsi and an orange-yellow band near the rear of the otherwise largely black or dark brown abdomen. Its nests hang from trees or buildings and are fiercely defended. A major enemy of honey bees, it also damages grape crops. Introduced from SE Asia in 2004, the insect has spread rapidly through the southern half of France and neighbouring parts of Europe and may well reach Britain in the near future.

Polistes gallicus. One of several very similar species known as paper wasps. Abdomen tapering in front and not hairy: pattern very variable. Nest is a small 'umbrella' without protective envelopes: often on buildings. S & C: most common in S. Occasional vagrants reach B.

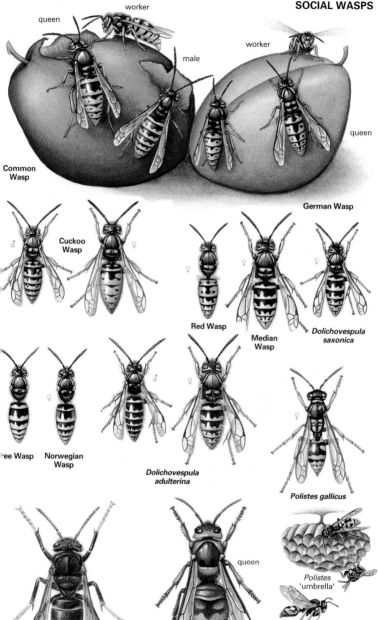

SOCIAL WASPS

queen

worker

worker

male

queen

Common Wasp

German Wasp

Cuckoo Wasp ♂ ♀

Red Wasp

Median Wasp

Dolichovespula saxonica

ee Wasp

Norwegian Wasp

Dolichovespula adulterina ♂ ♀

Polistes gallicus

queen

Polistes 'umbrella'

Asian Hornet

Hornet

All slightly enlarged

BEES A very large group of hymenopterans feeding on pollen and nectar. Although several families are mentioned on the following pages, the current trend is to put all the bees into a single family – the Apidae. The pronotum does not extend back to the tegulae (p. 218) and the body is generally rather hairy – an adaptation to pollen-gathering. Pollen is often carried back to the nest attached to the broad and hairy hind legs: among the honey bees and bumble bees, the hind tibiae are fringed with stiff hairs that form distinct 'baskets'. Some bees carry their pollen on the underside of the body. Only females are equipped for carrying pollen. Important features used in the classification and identification of bees include the sub-marginal cells (p. 218) and the form of the tongue. The latter is short and broad in *Colletes* and *Hylaeus*, but otherwise pointed and quite long.

Unless otherwise stated, all the bees described here are solitary species.

▲ *Colletes succinctus* Colletidae. 3 sub-marginals. Tongue short and broad. 7-9: ground-nesting in sandy areas. One of several similar species with bands of pale hairs on abdomen. Thoracic hairs paler in male.

△ s *Hylaeus signatus*. 2 sub-marginals. Tongue short and broad. Face almost entirely white in male: white spotted in female. Almost hairless: pollen carried in crop. Abdomen very parallel-sided, especially in male. 6-8 on bramble and umbellifers: nests mainly in sandy banks. S & C: one of several similar species.

Andrena Andrenidae. A large genus with many species superficially like honey bees. Abdomen often rather flat. 3 sub-marginals. Tongue short and pointed. Often known as mining bees, *Andrena* species generally nest in ground and appear mainly in spring. △ *A. hattorfiana* is the largest British species, largely dark brown with yellow near tip of abdomen. 6-9. △s *A. labiata* forages 5-6, almost entirely at speedwell flowers. Male has white hair on legs; female pale golden. S & C. △ *A. cineraria* male has less obvious black band on thorax and has white hairs on all femora: female has white hairs only on front femora. ▲ *A. haemorrhoa* is one of the earliest spring species – on blackthorn, dandelions, and sallows. Female has white face: male has pale brown face and yellower tip to abdomen. N & C. △s *A. pilipes* male has paler hair on thorax. Female has white pollen brush on hind legs. 3-5 and sometimes again 7-8: mainly on dandelions. △s *A. florea* male has paler head and thorax and very short antennae. Width of reddish abdominal bands varies, but first 2 segments usually largely red. Feeds mainly on white bryony. S & C. ▲ **Tawny Mining Bee** *A. fulva* feeds at currant and gooseberry flowers in spring, especially brightly coloured female. Often nests in lawns, with small mound around opening. C. △s *A. marginata* has yellowish or reddish brown abdomen in female: shiny black in male. 6-8 on scabious. S & C.

▲ *Panurgus banksianus*. 2 sub-marginals. Tongue short and pointed. Abdomen with black hair in male, brown in female. Latter with very prominent golden pollen brush on hind legs. Other legs with tawny hairs. 7-8 in sandy places.

Halictus Halictidae. Another large genus of ground-nesting bees. Abdomen more cylindrical than in *Andrena*: female with prominent bare patch at tip. Tongue short and pointed. 3 sub-marginals: basal vein (near centre of forewing) strongly curved, not ± straight as in *Andrena*. Mated females survive winter and fly again in spring: new generation of both sexes flies mid to late summer. ▲ *H. rubicundus* has clear yellow hind tibia. Abdominal bands of male entire. ▲ *H. tumulorum* is one of several greenish species. Female has paler legs. *H. scabiosae* is recognised by the very broad bands of pale hair on abdomen. S & C (southern). Many species show sub-social habits, with a few sterile females appearing late spring and doing a little food-gathering for the younger larvae in the nest.

▲ *Lasioglossum calceatum*. 3 sub-marginals. Tongue short and pointed. Male narrower, with more red on abdomen. Both sexes often with tufts of white hair. Usually nests in steep banks. △s *L. malachurus* resembles *calceatum* but has paler hair. S & C. ▲ *L. smeathmanellum* is metallic bronze or bluish green: male has less bright abdomen. This genus is ground-nesting, with flight times as in *Halictus*. Some species are sub-social, like some *Halictus* species.

△ s *Sphecodes spinulosus*. 3 sub-marginals. Tongue short and pointed. A cuckoo bee, laying eggs in nests of *Lasioglossum xanthopum*. Body ± hairless, for it collects no pollen. One of several similar species, some with dark wings and almost all with entirely black antennae. Flies late summer: mated females again in spring with host. S & C.

Sphecodes
spinulosus
× 1.5

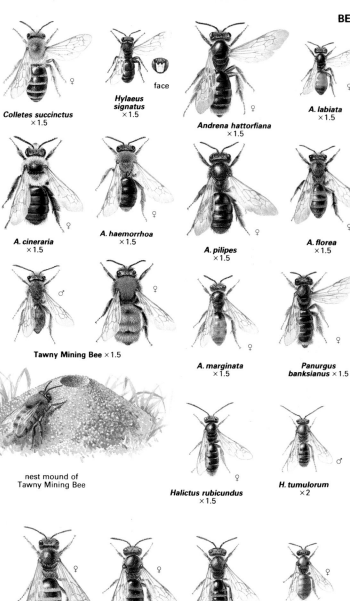

Colletes succinctus
×1.5

Hylaeus signatus
×1.5
face

Andrena hattorfiana
×1.5

A. labiata
×1.5

A. cineraria
×1.5

A. haemorrhoa
×1.5

A. pilipes
×1.5

A. florea
×1.5

Tawny Mining Bee ×1.5

A. marginata
×1.5

Panurgus banksianus ×1.5

nest mound of
Tawny Mining Bee

Halictus rubicundus
×1.5

H. tumulorum
×2

H. scabiosae
×1.5

Lasioglossum calceatum
×2

L. malachurus
×2

L. smeathmanellum
×2

245

Anthidium florentinum Megachilidae. 2 sub-marginals. Tongue long and slender. Distinguished from most of its relatives by yellow or brick-red thoracic borders. Flies all summer and nests in holes in ground, trees or walls. Nest lined with hairs plucked from plants. As in all members of this genus, males are noticeably larger than females. S & C (southern).

▲ ***A. manicatum*** has thorax almost entirely black. 6-8. Nests in pre-existing holes in timber or masonry: lined with plant hairs carried back in a ball under the body.

A. variegatum has thorax bordered with yellow and legs entirely yellow. Nests like *manicatum*. S & C (southern). There are about 30 similar species in Europe, some using plant hairs to line their nests and some using resin from conifers. Only *manicatum* occurs in B.

△s ***Stelis punctulatissima***. 2 sub-marginals. Tongue long and slender. A cuckoo species, with very little hair. Invades nests of *Osmia* and *Anthidium* species. Pale rear margins of abdominal segments distinguish it from the very similar △s **S. phaeoptera**.

▲ ***Chelostoma campanularum***. 2 sub-marginals. Tongue long and slender. A very slender, fly-like bee specialising in *Campanula* flowers. Female has dense orange pollen brush on underside of body. Nests in woodworm holes and other minute holes. Cannot turn round in burrows: backs in to off-load pollen but enters head-first to disgorge nectar. 6-8.

▲ ***C. florisomne*** is larger and female has creamy pollen brush. Male face with long pale hairs. Feeds mainly at buttercups. 6-9. Often nests in hollow stems, including straw and reeds of thatch. Males of both species often curl up in flowers at night.

▲ ***Osmia rufa***. 2 sub-marginals. Tongue long and slender. Male much smaller than female but with much longer antennae. Male face clothed with pale hairs: female face has black hair and a pair of short horns below antennae. Abdominal hairs denser in female. 4-7, nesting in holes in a variety of situations, often in walls. Cells made with mud. There are many similar species.

▲ ***Hoplitis spinulosa***. Resembles *Osmia* species, but thoracic punctures are elongate instead of round (not easy to see). Female has brick-red pollen brush under abdomen. Nests in empty snail shells, using dung for cell partitions. 4-7. S & C.

Chalicodoma parietina. 2 sub-marginals. Tongue long and slender. Male has browner body and lacks dark wing colour. 4-6, building small clay nests attached to stones, sometimes in large groups. S & C. There are several similar species, some building clay chambers in hollow stems.

△s ***Macropis europaea***. 2 sub-marginals. Tongue short and pointed. Thorax bordered by longer hairs in male, which also has swollen and curved hind legs: female hind tibia with pale yellow pollen brush. 7-8, feeding mainly on yellow loosestrife. Nests in ground and lines burrow with sticky sap of food-plant.

▲ ***Megachile maritima***. 2 sub-marginals. Tongue long and slender. Head relatively broad. Front of abdomen scooped out on dorsal surface: each segment with an entire pale terminal band. Female less brightly coloured and without dilated front legs: she has a dense pollen brush under abdomen – white at front and orange to black at rear. One of several species known as leaf-cutter bees because females cut oval and semi-circular pieces from leaves and use them to form sausage-shaped nest cells in plant stems and other crevices. 6-8. Mainly coastal.

▲ ***M. centuncularis*** female has a bright orange pollen brush under abdomen. Commonest of the leaf-cutters, it often attacks garden roses. 5-8. Usually nests in wood.

△s ***Dasypoda altercator*** Melittidae. 2 sub-marginals. Tongue pointed. Hinds legs with conspicuous golden tufts in female: male legs all clothed with dense yellow hair. Male also has thick yellow hair on face. Abdominal hair yellower than in female. 6-9, nesting in sandy soil. Mainly coastal in B.

△ ***Melitta haemorrhoidalis***. 3 sub-marginals. Tongue pointed. Male with longer and paler hairs on both thorax and abdomen. Resembles *Andrena* (p. 244) but tongue somewhat longer. 6-8, mainly on calcareous grassland. Often feeding at harebells. There are several similar species.

▲ ***Coelioxys inermis***. 2 sub-marginals. Tongue long and slender. One of several similar species with tip of abdomen pointed in female and spiny in male: no pale band on hind margin of 5th abdominal segment in this species. A cuckoo species laying eggs in nests of *Megachile* species. *Coelioxys* egg hatches first and grub destroys rightful egg. 6-8.

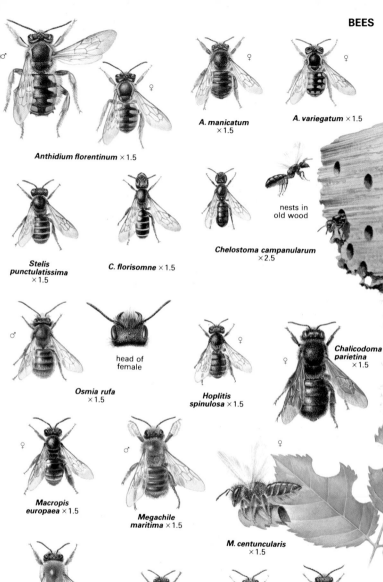

BEES

A. manicatum
×1.5

A. variegatum ×1.5

Anthidium florentinum ×1.5

nests in
old wood

**Stelis
punctulatissima**
×1.5

C. florisomne ×1.5

Chelostoma campanularum
×2.5

head of
female

Osmia rufa
×1.5

**Hoplitis
spinulosa** ×1.5

**Chalicodoma
parietina**
×1.5

**Macropis
europaea** ×1.5

**Megachile
maritima** ×1.5

M. centuncularis
×1.5

**Dasypoda
altercator** ×1.5

**Melitta
haemorrhoidalis** ×1.5

Coelioxys inermis ×1.5

△s **Nomada fulvicornis** Anthophoridae. 3 sub-marginals. Tongue ovate. A wasp-like bee, almost hairless and with variable amount of yellow on abdomen: 2nd and 3rd yellow bands always broken; 1st band often reduced to 2 small spots in female. 4-6, breeding as cuckoo in nests of *Andrena* species. There are many closely related species, some black and yellow and other red and black or brown and black.

▲ **Epeolus cruciger**. 3 sub-marginals. Tongue long and slender. Female legs entirely red. Almost hairless. 7-8, mostly in sandy areas. A cuckoo in nests of *Colletes* spp. N & C.

△ **Eucera longicornis**. 2 sub-marginals. Tongue long and slender. Male has extremely long antennae and a bright yellow face, but lacks the pale bands at tip of abdomen. His legs are also less hairy. 4-7, nesting in ground. There are several similar species.

head of *Anthophora*

head of bumble bee (p. 250)

▲ **Anthophora plumipes**. 3 sub-marginals. Tongue very long and slender. Extreme sexual dimorphism: female is jet black except for rust-coloured pollen brushes on hind leg, while male is brownish. Male has prominent fans of hairs on middle leg. Resembles bumble bees (p. 250), but eye reaches down to meet the jaw (left), with no cheek area such as occurs in bumble bees. Much quicker in flight than bumble bees, with much higher-pitched flight tone. Hovers well. 3-6. Very common in gardens, where fond of lungwort and other tubular spring flowers. Nests in ground and in soft mortar of walls. There are several similar species. △ **A. retusa** has only basal part of abdomen clothed with brown hair in male, and no fans of hair on middle leg. **A. hispanica** flies 1-3 in SW, nesting in sandy ground.

Melecta luctuosa. 3 sub-marginals. Tongue long and slender. 4-6, breeding as cuckoo in nest of *Anthophora retusa*. Absent from far north and many central areas: probably extinct in B. △s **M. albifrons** is very similar but has much smaller pale spots on abdomen and browner hairs on thorax. It is also a cuckoo in the nests of *Anthophora* species.

Tetralonia salicariae. 3 sub-marginals. Tongue long and slender. Male antennae very long, as in *Eucera*. 7-8, feeding mainly at flowers of purple loosestrife: occasionally at viper's bugloss and wild thyme. Local in S & C.

Xylocopa violacea Xylocopidae. Readily identified by its colour, this handsome bee flies in summer and autumn and again in spring after hibernation. Hind tarsus especially hairy in female: male has brush-like tuft on front tarsus. Fast flying, but not aggressive and rarely stings. It nests in dead wood, hence its common name of carpenter bee. The cell partitions are made of chewed wood fragments. S & C: vagrant to B and other more northerly areas. There are 3 other very similar species in western Europe.

△s **Ceratina cyanea**. 3 sub-marginals. Tongue long and slender. Metallic blue with white face in male; black face in female. Very little hair, even on legs of female. 4-6, nesting in hollow stems of bramble and other shrubs. Several similar species on continent.

▲ **Honey Bee** *Apis mellifera* Apidae. 3 sub-marginals. Apical cell slender and very long, reaching almost to wing-tip. Tongue long and slender. A social bee living in permanent colonies of perhaps 50,000 individuals. A native of southern Asia, but long established in Europe – in the wild as well as in domestic hives. The queen, who rules the colony, is rarely found outside the nest except when on her mating flight or when the bees are swarming, and in the latter instance she is completely surrounded by a mass of workers. The latter make up the bulk of the colony and forage from early spring to autumn. Drones (males) are plumper and appear mainly in early summer. There are several distinct strains or races of honey bees, some almost black and some with an extensive orange patch at the base of the abdomen. The Italian race, now common all over Europe, has a very marked orange patch. The strains hybridise very easily, however, and wild bees combine the features of many different strains.

Wild colonies usually build in hollow trees and similarly protected situations, but occasionally build in the open. The nest consists of several wax combs, suspended vertically – not horizontally like the wasps' combs – and without a protective envelope. Each comb consists of hundreds of 6-sided cells that are used for rearing the brood and for storing honey and pollen. New queens are reared when the old queen gets too old for the job and also when the colony becomes overcrowded. In the latter instance, the old queen flies off with a swarm of workers to start a new colony. The workers left behind enlarge selected cells on the comb and, by special feeding of the young grubs already in those cells, they produce new queens, one of which will eventually take control of the colony.

BEES

Nomada fulvicornis
×1.5

Epeolus cruciger
×2

Eucera longicornis ×1.5

head of male

Anthophora plumipes
×1.5

A. hispanica
×1.5

Ceratina cyanea
×1.5

Melecta luctuosa
×1.5

Xylocopa violacea
×1.5

♂

♀ (queen)

Tetralonia salicariae ×1.5

♀ (worker)

Honey Bee ×1.5

BUMBLE BEES Apidae. Relatively large and very hairy social bees of the genus *Bombus*, readily distinguished from *Anthophora* because the eyes do not reach down to the jaws (p. 248). The bees form annual colonies, with only mated queens surviving the winter to start new colonies in the spring. The nest may be under the ground – often in an old mouse hole – or among the bases of tall grasses, especially on sunny banks. The nest is essentially a ball of grass and moss with wax cells inside it. The young are reared on pollen and nectar, the pollen being carried home in large pollen baskets on the back legs. Some early spring workers are very small and it is hard to believe that they belong to the same species as the queens, but later workers are much larger as a result of better food supplies. Males, recognisable by their longer antennae, appear in summer. The bees illustrated here are all queens: workers and males are basically similar unless otherwise stated but the identification of all castes is complicated by marked regional colour variations. Some northern species produce very few workers – even none at all in the Arctic – because the short summer season in the far north simply does not allow time to build up a colony.

Bombus lapponicus. Very variable, with several sub-species. May have greyish yellow collar and scutellum. Abdomen almost entirely reddish, but yellow hairs often mingle with the red ones towards the rear. Nests on or just under the ground: few workers. Confined to northern Scandinavia, where often the dominant species, and high mountains.

△ *B. soroeensis*. Typical sub-species (*B.s. soroeensis*) has collar and 2nd abdominal segment yellowish and tail white. Male has 1st abdominal segment yellowish as well. Nests underground. The sub-species *B.s. proteus*, not found in B, is all black with an orange tail. Both sub-species are widely distributed on the continent, where they overlap and interbreed to produce numerous colour varieties.

▲ *B. jonellus* generally has yellow hairs on top of head. Collar, scutellum, and 1st abdominal segment yellow: tail white. Pollen basket reddish. Like a small *hortorum* but face is shorter and rounder. Mainly on coasts and heathland.

▲ *B. hortorum*. A relatively large bee with collar, scutellum, and 1st abdominal segment yellow: tail white. A rather 'scruffy' species with long hair. Pollen baskets black. Abundant everywhere: especially common in gardens. Usually nests on or just under the ground.

△s *B. ruderatus*. Often similar to *hortorum*, but yellow bands often narrower and darker and sometimes absent altogether. 1st abdominal band commonly broken. Hair generally shorter than in *hortorum*. Wings sometimes very dark. Nests underground. Much rarer than *hortorum* and absent from far north.

B. hypnorum. Identified by entirely rich brown thorax and white tail: front of abdomen may be black. Nests in hollow trees and other cavities above ground. In wooded areas in most parts of Europe.

B. subterraneus. A large, short-haired bee with a dull yellow collar and very narrow yellow band on scutellum: both bands may be much reduced. Tail off-white. Rear edges of abdominal segments often with brown fringes. Males largely greenish brown or brownish yellow with black bands. Nests below ground. Believed recently extinct in B.

▲ *B. lucorum*. Collar and 2nd abdominal segment lemon yellow: tail white. Male may have yellow scutellum as well, and other yellow bands may be extensive. A very early bee, abundant almost everywhere. Nests below ground.

▲ *B. terrestris*. Collar and 2nd abdominal segment orange or golden yellow (often reduced). Tail buff or tawny in B: white on continent. Worker and male always with whitish tail, sometimes tinged with ginger. Nests below ground. Very common, but absent from far north.

▲ *B. pratorum*. A relatively small bee with collar and 2nd abdominal segment yellow (sometimes interrupted): tail orange-red. Coat rather shaggy. Worker may lack yellow on abdomen. Male has wide yellow collar and more yellow on abdomen. An early bee: colonies often finished by end of July, although sometimes a 2nd brood. May nest well above ground – in birds' nests and nest-boxes, for example.

B. alpinus. Easily identified by black thorax and largely golden abdomen. Hind legs and pollen baskets very black: not brownish as in *lapponicus*. Nests above or below ground. Heaths and montane pastures in Alps and Scandinavia.

△ *B. monticola*. Collar and scutellum usually pale yellow, but scutellum may be black: whole thorax occasionally black. Abdomen largely red, becoming more orange towards the rear. Mountain and moorland: mainly northern.

B. confusus. Short-haired with swollen or humped thorax. Tail red and rather pointed. Male has very large eyes and greyish hairs on prothorax. S & C.

B. pomorum. Red tail has pinkish tinge. Male has yellowish grey collar and scutellum, with abdomen mainly red. Sandy areas.

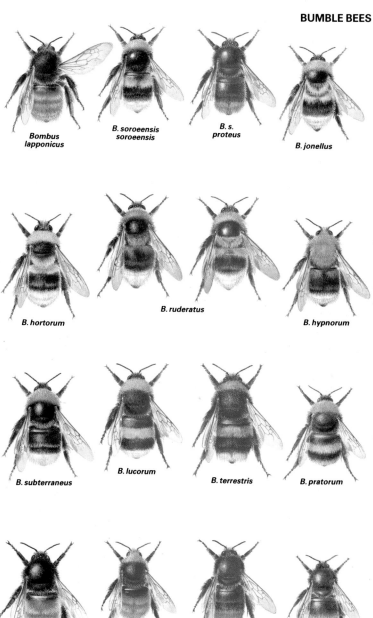

Bombus lapponicus

B. soroeensis soroeensis

B. s. proteus

B. jonellus

B. hortorum

B. ruderatus

B. hypnorum

B. subterraneus

B. lucorum

B. terrestris

B. pratorum

B. alpinus

B. monticola

B. confusus

B. pomorum

Bombus cullumanus. The insect illustrated is from Spain. The males show this general colour pattern everywhere, but in most parts of Europe the queens are black with a red tail and just a faint trace of yellow on collar and scutellum. They are thus superficially like *lapidarius*, but 1st segment of hind tarsus is shiny black, not downy yellow as in *lapidarius*. Widespread, but rare: extinct in B.

B. mendax. A variable species: pale bands may be missing from thorax and front of abdomen in Alps, but always present in Pyrenees. Tip of abdomen may be red, especially in male. Only in mountains.

B. mesomelas. The pale brown or fawn hair and prominent black band between wings easily identify this species. Front of abdomen sometimes golden: tip of tail black. Males greyish white and quite shaggy, with blacker band on thorax. Rear end more yellowish grey. Alps and Pyrenees.

△n **B. distinguendus**. A long-haired bee, predominantly brown with a black band between wings. Much brighter than *mesomelas*. Nests below ground. Not common. N & C (northern).

▲ **B. pascuorum**. Largely tawny, with variable amounts of black: very dark in N, but often foxy red in S. Coat thin and rather 'scruffy'. Nests on or above ground – often in old birds' nests. One of the last bumble bees to disappear in autumn.

| *B. hyperboreus* | *B. wurfleini pyrenaicus* | *B. lapidarius* |

B. gerstaeckeri. Thorax golden or orange yellow. Abdomen with scattered white hairs: sometimes entirely black. Face long and narrow. Alps and Pyrenees, usually feeding at *Aconitum* species.

△ s **B. sylvarum**. Thorax pale brown with black central area. Abdominal segments with pale fringes at rear. Tail orange to pinkish red. A relatively late species. Absent from far north.

B. hyperboreus. A large, brightly coloured, long-haired bee. Orange bands may be replaced by yellow. Black inter-alar band not wider than collar. Basal part of wing distinctly darker than outer edge. N.

B. wurfleini pyrenaicus. A colourful bee from the Pyrenees. Resembles Spanish form of *cullumanus*, but much larger and with less yellow hair on abdomen. Nests below ground. Further north, *B.w. mastrucatus* is just black with orange tail.

▲ **B. lapidarius**. Abdomen relatively long. Hair longer and thorax less humped than in *confusus* (p. 250). Male has broad yellow collar. Often nests under stones. Especially common in open country: often coastal in N. ▲ **B. ruderarius** is similar but has red pollen baskets instead of black.

CUCKOO BEES Social parasites once placed in the genus *Psithyrus* but now included in *Bombus*. No workers: females lay in nests of other *Bombus* species, often killing the reigning queen and leaving the host workers to rear the young cuckoos. Generally resemble the bees they parasitise, but coats are less dense and abdominal plates shine through. Females without pollen baskets. Wing membrane often dark. Females hibernate, but wake later than host species – waiting for the bumble bee nest to be established.

▲ **Bombus barbutellus**. Collar and scutellum yellow: front of abdomen may also be yellowish. Tail always white. Parasitises *B. hortorum*.

▲ **B. vestalis**. Mainly black, but with prominent golden collar and yellow and white patches near rear of abdomen. Parasitises *B. terrestris*: rare in N.

▲ **B. campestris**. Amount of yellow hair on scutellum varies. Abdomen sometimes all black, but usually with variable amounts of yellow hair, especially towards the rear. Male very variable: generally mainly yellow but may be all black. Parasitises *B. pascuorum* and is unusual in not resembling its host.

△ **B. rupestris**. Female very like *B. lapidarius*, which it parasitises. Male usually has some greyish yellow hairs on collar, scutellum, and front of abdomen. Widespread but not common.

hind leg of *Bombus* ♀

B. cullumanus

B. mendax

B. mesomelas

B. pascuorum

B. gerstaeckeri

B. sylvarum

B. distinguendus

♀

♂

Bombus barbutellus

♀

♂

B. vestalis

hind leg of ♀ cuckoo bee with no pollen basket

♀

♂

B. campestris

♀

♂

B. rupestris

BEETLES   Order Coleoptera

This is the largest order of insects, with well over 300,000 known species in the world and some 20,000 in Europe. About 4,000 live in the British Isles. The order contains the bulkiest of all insects – the fist-sized Goliath beetle, weighing about 100g – and also some of the smallest, many of them under 0.5mm long.

Beetles are easy to recognise as such, because the forewings, known as elytra, are tough and horny: and with the notable exception of the rove beetles (p. 260), they usually cover the whole abdomen. They normally meet neatly in the mid-line without overlap, giving the insects their characteristic armoured look. The only likely confusion is with some of the heteropteran bugs (p. 72), but these all have overlapping forewings whose tips are usually distinctly membranous. Also, the bugs have needle-like suctorial mouth-parts, whereas all beetles have biting jaws. Beetle hindwings are membranous, and folded beneath the elytra when not in use. They are sometimes absent, in which case the elytra may be fused together for extra protection. Rarely, as in the female glow-worm, the elytra are absent as well.

Compound eyes are usually well developed in the beetles, as are the antennae, whose shape is important in classification. Some antennae are distinctly 'elbowed', with the first segment (the scape) very long and the other segments forming an angle with it – as in the weevils (p. 284). Weevils usually bear their antennae on a prominent snout or rostrum, and the scapes can be retracted into grooves, called scrobes, on each side of it.

The prothorax is always large, and covered by a tough and often highly ornamented shield called the pronotum. In some beetles this shield almost covers the head as well. The rest of the thorax is generally covered by the elytra, except for a small triangle called the scutellum, which sits in the midline between the bases of the elytra. The legs vary a great deal with the beetles' habits. Dung beetles, for example, have broad front legs with strong teeth for excavating their burrows and manipulating the dung, while most water beetles have paddle-like hind legs for swimming. The number of tarsal segments on each leg (usually 4 or 5) and the shape of the coxa (the 1st segment of the leg) are also important, although not readily appreciated in the field.

Most beetles can fly, but most spend relatively little time in the air. They are essentially insects of the ground and the vegetation. Many live among stones and leaf litter, where the tough elytra provide valuable protection: the armoured and often tank-like look is no masquerade and it is surprisingly difficult to crush even a small specimen. With their biting jaws, both adults and larvae exist mainly on solid food, although some species lap nectar from flowers and some larvae have hollow mandibles through which they suck the juices of their prey. Different beetles exploit almost every kind of solid food: even the dried bones of animals, pepper, grain, or the dried wood of a chair leg. These dry foods present the insects with no problems because the elytra and the general thickness of the adult cuticle effectively prevent loss of body moisture. Nevertheless, the majority feed on living plant tissue, including roots and woody stems as well as leaves and fruits. The ability to exploit such a wide range of food – made possible by the biting jaws – has been one of the main factors in the success of the beetles throughout the world.

Life Histories All beetles undergo a complete metamorphosis, rarely with any form of parental care. The larvae (pp 295-7) are much more varied than the adults, although most use the same kind of food as their parents. Most have three pairs of legs, but weevil larvae, mostly living inside their food-plants and surrounded by provisions, are generally legless. Most European beetles have just one generation each year, normally passing the winter as larvae or adults – either active or in hibernation. Very few species pass the winter in the egg stage.

Water Beetles Beetles of several different families, notably the Dytiscidae and Hydrophilidae, have opted for life in the water, although most of them retain the power of flight and can move from pond to pond. The adults have generally evolved smooth outlines (pp 290-2), and many have broad, paddle-like hind legs. They remain essentially air-breathing insects and carry air supplies with them under the water. Among the dytiscids, the air is carried in the space between the elytra and the body, and the abdominal spiracles draw air directly from this reservoir. When the oxygen content has been exhausted, the beetle rises tail-first, breaks the surface with the tip of its abdomen, and draws fresh air into the reservoir. The hydrophilid beetles carry only part of their air supply under the elytra. The rest is held in a bubble 'strapped' to the underside of the body in a coat of fine, water-repellent hairs. This bubble gives the beetles a bright silvery appearance in the water. The hydrophilids come up head-first and break the surface with one of their club-shaped antennae. These are clothed with water-repellent hairs that form channels through which air is drawn into both reservoirs.

A few small water beetles have managed to dispense with surface visits altogether by developing a physical gill. A film of air is held around the body by a dense coat of extremely fine hairs. This film acts as a gill: it is in direct contact with the spiracles, and as oxygen is drawn from it more oxygen is drawn in from the surrounding water to redress the balance. This system is sometimes known as plastron breathing. The larvae of some water beetles have evolved true gills, which absorb oxygen directly from the water, but most are air-breathers like the adults and they come to the surface tail-first to draw air into their posterior spiracles. Although both larval and adult stages are spent in the water, nearly all water beetles pupate in the soil.

STYLOPIDS. These tiny insects, only 2-3mm long, grow up as internal parasites of bees, wasps, and homopteran bugs and are rarely seen, although they are quite common. Among the European species, only the short-lived adult males emerge from their hosts – through the inter-segmental membranes of the host abdomen. These males have relatively huge hindwings, but their forewings are club-shaped and act rather like the halteres of flies (p. 190). The adult females, which remain grub-like, do no more than protrude from their hosts' inter-segmental membranes. The males spend their few hours of freedom flying rapidly about in search of the females, which they smell out with their large antennae. Mated females give birth to small larvae which then search out new hosts. Unlike ichneumons and tachinid flies, the stylopids do not normally kill their hosts, although they commonly render them sterile. About 400 species are known, with about 30 in Europe.

Adult stylopids have no obvious relationship to other insects, but a study of larval structure and metamorphosis reveals a number of similarities with the oil beetles and others with parasitic larvae. For this reason, some entomologists regard the stylopids as a specialised group of beetles and place them in the Coleoptera. Other entomologists believe that the similarities with beetles are merely the result of similar lifestyles, and place the stylopids in a separate order – the Strepsiptera.

A stylopid male, showing the large hindwings and
club-shaped halteres derived from the forewings

TIGER BEETLES and GROUND BEETLES Carabidae.
Long-legged, fast-running predatory beetles with powerful jaws and very fine sensory bristles scattered over the body. The antennae are filamentous and usually 11-segmented. Tarsi are 5-segmented. Many species exhibit beautiful metallic or iridescent colours.

Cicindela
germanica
× 1.5

Tiger Beetles (*Cicindela* species) are sun-loving insects with huge eyes and jaws. The antennae are attached above the jaws and their bodies are somewhat flattened. Most fly well, with a loud buzzing sound. They hunt ants and other prey on the ground and usually live in open habitats. They are among the fastest runners in the insect world. The larvae (p. 295) construct burrows from which they ambush prey. About a dozen species live in Europe.

▲ **Green Tiger Beetle** *Cicindela campestris*. Legs and sides of thorax are coppery or purplish bronze and very shiny. Underside of abdomen metallic green. Elytral pattern varies and ground colour may be very dark. 5-7. Mainly on heathland, sand dunes, and other sandy places.

△ *Cicindela hybrida*. Elytra may have a greenish tinge, but margins always reddish, as are the edges of the thorax. Each elytron has 3 or 4 yellow marks. Underside of body metallic green. 8-9 and again 4-6 after hibernation. Heathland and dunes. Absent from far north.

△s **Wood Tiger Beetle** *C. sylvatica*. Similar to *hybrida*, but darker and with a distinct purplish tinge: yellow markings less heavy. Metallic blue below. Heathland and pinewoods. 5-9. N & C.

△s *C. germanica*. Smaller and more cylindrical than the other tiger beetles. Thorax distinctly bronze and elytra usually very dark green, often almost black. Elytral pattern usually confined to 3 small spots on outer margin of each side. Rarely flies. 5-9. Dry, grassy places in lowlands. S & C: south coast only in B.

Ground Beetles are generally less flattened than tiger beetles and largely nocturnal, although some of the more metallic species are active by day. The antennae are attached between the eyes and the jaws. Many are flightless, with vestigial hindwings and often with the elytra fused together. Front tarsi are strongly dilated in males. They eat a wide range of invertebrates and also take carrion: many eat plant matter as well. The larvae (p. 295) are active hunters like the adults. Most species are long-lived and adult throughout the year, although they hibernate in the coldest months. Several hundred species live in Europe.

Calosoma sycophanta. Elytra are golden green to brassy red and strongly striated. Flies well. Diurnal. Mainly in woodlands, adults and larvae living in trees and preying on moth larvae. They are important predators of gypsy and processionary moth caterpillars. Most of Europe but a sporadic visitor to B.

C. auropunctatum is recognised by the 3 rows of golden green dots on each elytron. Adults and larvae prey on moth larvae on the ground, although adults fly well. Diurnal. Most frequent in moist grassland. C.

△ *Carabus auratus*. Elytra and thorax green with a golden or brassy iridescence. Three broad ridges on each elytron. Flightless, with vestigial hindwings like most *Carabus* species. Gardens and other cultivated land, mainly in spring. Eats slugs, snails, and cockchafer grubs. S & C: occasionally introduced to B and establishing itself for short periods.

▲ **Violet Ground Beetle** *C. violaceus*. Elytra almost smooth, with a bright violet sheen around the edges and around the edges of the thorax. Common in many habitats, including gardens and hedgerows, hiding under stones and litter by day and emerging to hunt slugs and other prey at night. ▲ *C. nemoralis* has very convex elytra, especially in male, marked with fine ridges and rows of conspicuous pits. Bronzy to bright brassy green, becoming violet on the sides. Thorax is also purplish or bronze on the sides. Females are less shiny. Found in many habitats: especially common in gardens on the continent. Its habits are much like those of *violaceus* and most other *Carabus* species.

C. coriaceus. Resembles a large Violet Ground Beetle in shape, but thorax and elytra are dull black. Elytra patterned with coarse dots and wrinkles. Mainly in damp deciduous woodland.

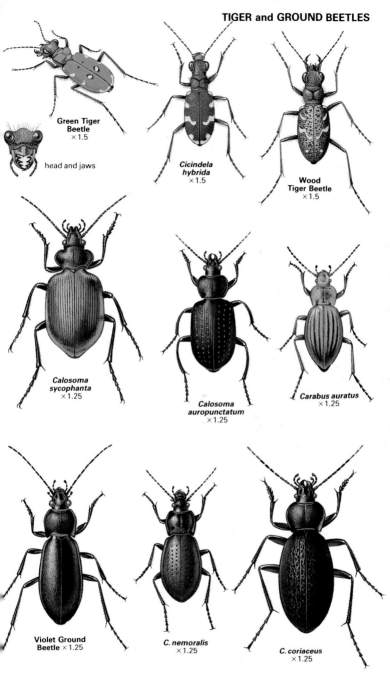

Green Tiger Beetle ×1.5

head and jaws

Cicindela hybrida ×1.5

Wood Tiger Beetle ×1.5

Calosoma sycophanta ×1.25

Calosoma auropunctatum ×1.25

Carabus auratus ×1.25

Violet Ground Beetle ×1.25

C. nemoralis ×1.25

C. coriaceus ×1.25

△ *Cychrus caraboides*. The narrow front end of this very convex beetle is associated with its diet of snails, the head being plunged deeply into the shells when feeding. Flightless, with elytra fused together. It squirts a jet of yellow liquid from the rear end when alarmed. Mainly in damp woodland.

▲ *Notiophilus biguttatus*. A sun-loving beetle with a bronze sheen that obliterates the elytral pattern from some angles. Flattened and very fast-running, feeding on mites and springtails and other small arthropods on the ground. Flightless. Abundant in gardens, grassland, and many other habitats. There are several similar species.

▲ *Elaphrus riparius*. Elytra sometimes metallic blue or bronze. Fully winged. Tarsi green. Sun-loving and fast-running. On bare sand and silt by ponds and streams.

↑
antenna-cleaning
notch on front
tibia of many
ground beetles

△s *Omophron limbatum*. The shape and colour immediately identify this ground beetle. Fast-running on bare ground around ponds and streams. Burrows in the sand.

△ *Broscus cephalotes*. Huge jaws and appetite to match. A prominent antenna- cleaning notch. Elytra dull black. Fully winged, but rarely flies. Lies in wait for prey in a burrow. Sandy places: mainly coastal.

△s *Callistus lunatus*. Dark areas of elytra with blue or green reflections. Antenna-cleaning notch. Fully winged. Diurnal, running rapidly over dry grassland, usually on chalk or sand: often coastal. S & C.

△ *Badister unipustulatus*. Several similar species with asymmetrical jaws. Antenna-cleaning notch. Fully winged. Among leaf litter and moss, usually near water.

▲ *Dyschirius globosus*. Smallest of many very similar species. Flightless. Usually lives near water, using spiny front legs to dig burrows in soft, sandy ground.

▲ *Dromius 4-maculatus*. Yellow spots may join on each elytron. Fully winged, with flattened body. Antenna-cleaning notch. Lives in trees and hibernates under bark.

▲ *Harpalus affinis*. Green to black, often strongly metallic: female less shiny. Antenna-cleaning notch. Fully winged. Open country, often on cultivated land. Largely vegetarian. A distinctive member of this very large family.

▲ *Pterostichus madidus*. Body and elytra black, like most members of this large genus, but legs usually chestnut, especially the femora. Antenna-cleaning notch present. Hind angles of pronotum blunt. Flightless. Common in gardens and other cultivated land, where it is fond of fruit and sometimes called Strawberry Beetle. ▲ *P. nigrita* is similar but legs are black and hind angles of pronotum sharp. Sides of pronotum strongly rounded. Fully winged. ▲ *P. cupreus* elytra range from brassy green to black: legs may be chestnut. Fully winged. Usually found near water.

△ *Agonum 6-punctatum*. Each elytron with a row of six small punctures. Fully winged. Antenna-cleaning notch. Usually found near water, often on bare soil and peat.

△ *Panagaeus bipustulatus*. Has antenna-cleaning notch. Lives in short, dry grassland. △ *P. cruxmajor* is slightly larger and lives in damp places.

△ *Lebia cruxminor*. Black elytral marks may link up with black scutellum to form a larger cross. Antenna-cleaning notch present. Climbs on grassland vegetation, feeding on other beetle larvae.

▲ *Amara aenea*. Elytra black with very fine striations and brassy green lustre. Fully winged. Antenna-cleaning notch. In short, dry vegetation in summer.

△s *Odacantha melanura* Thorax and elytral tips reflect blue or green. Fully winged. Antenna-cleaning notch. On reeds and other tall waterside plants.

▲ *Leistus ferrugineus*. Body and elytra yellow or brown. Jaws very broad and flat. Among grass tufts and debris, usually in open country.

△s **Bombardier Beetle**. *Brachinus crepitans*. When disturbed, it fires a burning, volatile liquid from its rear end like a puff of smoke, accompanied by a soft popping sound. Elytra reflect blue or green. Fully winged. Antenna-cleaning notch. Under stones in dry, open country, especially on chalk.

Odacantha
melanura
× 2.5

Leistus
ferrugineus
× 2.5

Bombardier Beetle
× 2.5

Cychrus caraboides
×1.5

Notiophilus biguttatus
×2.5

Elaphrus riparius
×2.5

Omophron limbatum
×2.5

Broscus cephalotes
×1.5

Callistus lunatus
×2.5

Badister unipustulatus
×2.5

Dyschirius globosus
×2.5

Dromius 4-maculatus
×2.5

Harpalus affinis
×1.5

Pterostichus madidus

P. nigrita
×1.5

P. cupreus
×1.5

Agonum 6-punctatum
×2.5

Panagaeus bipustulatus
×2.5

Lebia cruxminor
×2.5

Amara aenea
×2.5

259

▲ **Sphaeridium scarabaeoides** Hydrophilidae. A terrestrial member of a largely aquatic family (p. 292), with slender palps almost as long as antennae. Usually found tunnelling in fresh cow dung.

▲ **Hister 4-maculatus** Histeridae. Red spots may join up on each elytron. Feeds on fly maggots and other scavenging insects in horse and cow-dung. There are several similar species, all somewhat flattened with shiny, truncated elytra, elbowed antennae, and strongly toothed front tibiae (tooth pattern may help to separate species). Some live in carcases instead of dung. Many lack red spots. Apart from the short elytra, they resemble small scarabs (p. 264), but antennal club is solid and not composed of flaps.

BURYING BEETLES *Silphidae* Scavenging and carnivorous beetles with clubbed antennae and a very good sense of smell. The elytra are often strongly truncated, but most species fly well.

Nicrophorus species are the true burying beetles, burying small carcases (mice, birds, etc) by digging a shaft underneath them and hauling them down. They usually work in pairs and female lays eggs close to the buried corpse. Adults and larvae feed on the carrion and also on the other scavenging insects. They are also known as sexton beetles. Adults are seen mainly in spring and summer and are often attracted to lights at night. The antennae are very abruptly clubbed in this genus.

▲ **Nicrophorus humator** is one of few species with all-black elytra, but it can be recognised by the orange clubs on its antennae.

▲ **N. vespillo** is one of several species with orange-banded elytra. Both bands are almost complete in this species and the hind tibiae are strongly curved.

▲ **N. investigator** has the posterior orange band narrowly broken in the mid-line where the elytra join.

△ **N. interruptus** has both orange bands clearly interrupted.

▲ **N. vespilloides** has a broadly interrupted posterior orange band – often reduced to a small spot on each elytron – and entirely black antennae. ▲ **N. vestigator** is similar but has orange antennal clubs.

△ **Necrodes littoralis** resembles *Nicrophorus humator* but the antennae are not abruptly clubbed. Each elytron has 3 strong ridges and a large 'pimple' towards the back. Size is very variable. Usually on large carrion, which is not buried. Most often near the coast: frequently among stranded seaweeds on the shore. Summer.

▲ **Oiceoptoma thoracicum**. Elytra silky, each with 3 longitudinal ridges. A non-burying species found mainly in woodland – under dung and carcases and also in rotting fungi. Feeds on other insect larvae. Summer.

▲ **Dendroxena 4-maculata** lives mainly in oakwoods, feeding on moth larvae in the trees and on the ground. Most numerous in autumn and spring.

▲ **Silpha atrata**. Very glossy. A predator of snails, reaching deep into the shells to devour them. Woods and other damp, shady places.

ROVE BEETLES *Staphylinidae*. A very large family, with well over 1000 species in Europe. A wide range of sizes, with many very tiny species. The elytra are very short, leaving most of the abdomen exposed. Despite the short elytra, the hindwings are usually well developed and most species fly well. Many of the smaller ones fly by day, but the larger ones are mainly nocturnal. They are predators and omnivorous scavengers.

▲ **Creophilus maxillosus**. Elytral and abdominal pattern formed by grey and black hairs. Head and pronotum hairless. 5-10. Preys on other insects on dung and carrion and in rotting vegetation.

△s **Emus hirtus**. Very large and very hairy. 4-8. Feeds on other insects around fresh horse and cow dung. S & C.

▲ **Staphylinus caesareus**. Patches of golden hair on abdomen. 4-9. Usually on dung and carrion, where it feeds on other insects.

▲ **Devil's Coach-horse** *S. olens* is clothed with fine black hairs. Hides under stones and debris by day and hunts slugs and other invertebrates at night. Also called the cocktail because, when disturbed, it raises its rear end and opens its jaws wide in a threatening attitude. Common in woods, gardens, and hedgerows, and also in out-buildings.

Sphaeridium scarabaeoides ×2.5

Hister 4-maculatus ×2.5

Nicrophorus humator ×1.5

N. vespillo ×1.5

N. investigator ×1.5

N. interruptus ×1.5

N. vespilloides ×1.5

Necrodes littoralis ×1.5

Oiceoptoma thoracicum ×1.5

Dendroxena 4-maculata ×1.5

Silpha atrata ×1.5

Creophilus maxillosus ×1.5

Emus hirtus ×1.5

Staphylinus caesareus ×1.5

↑ **Devil's Coach-horse** ×1.5 ↓

261

▲ *Oxyporus rufus*. Smooth and shiny and distinctly arched in the middle. Adults and larvae live in various woodland toadstools. Most common in summer and autumn.

▲ *Paederus littoralis*. A flightless, predatory species with metallic blue elytra. Lives among debris on marshes, river banks, and other damp places. S & C.

▲ *Stenus bimaculatus*. Hairy, with black and yellow legs. Large bulging eyes are used for stalking springtails and other small prey. Lives around ponds and streams and in other damp places. Can skim over water surface by exuding an oily secretion from the rear end. Diurnal and sun-loving. One of many similar species.

▲ *Bledius furcatus*. Prominent horns on head and thorax of male: smaller in female. Gregarious, like other members of this large genus. Burrows in damp soil and feeds on algae. May emerge to fly in groups in the evening. S & C.

▲ *Philonthus marginatus*. Orange sides of thorax distinguish this species from other members of this large genus. It lives in dung and other decaying matter.

▲ *Tachyporus hypnorum*. One of several strongly tapering species. Lives among mosses and vegetable debris, including compost heaps. Most common in winter and spring.

△ s **Stag Beetle** *Lucanus cervus* Lucanidae. Named for the huge jaws (antlers) of the male, which are used to fight rival males in the breeding season. Female sometimes almost black. Antennae, as in all members of the family, are elbowed and have small flaps at the end, but the flaps cannot be brought together to form a club. Middle tibia has 3 small teeth. Size very variable. 5-8. Flies well, usually in the evening. Feeds on sap oozing from trees. Larva (p. 295) lives in decaying trees and posts, especially oak. S & C: becoming rare.

Stag beetles battling with their antlers. The stronger one wins, but neither is usually hurt.

▲ **Lesser Stag Beetle** *Dorcus parallelopipedus* resembles female stag beetle but middle tibia has only 1 tooth. Male never has antlers. 4-10, mainly in deciduous woods. Feeds on sap. Breeds in rotting stumps. S & C.

Platycerus caraboides. Rather flat, with a bluish iridescence in male and green in female. 4-9, flying mainly by day. Chews leaves and buds. Breeds in rotting wood. Widely distributed in deciduous woodland.

▲ *Sinodendron cylindricum*. Distinctly cylindrical. Male has rhinoceros-like horn on head: female just a small knob. 5-8, feeding on oozing sap. Breeds in rotting stumps, especially beech.

▲ *Trox scaber* Trogidae. Roughly sculptured elytra and pronotum, with bristly scales on the elytral ridges. Antennal flaps can be brought together to form a small club. Feeds mainly on small carcases, especially when dry, and often scavenges in owls' nests. Rarely flies. 4-8. Widely distributed but rare in N.

△ s *Odontaeus armiger* Geotrupidae. Strongly domed and very shiny. Male has slender, movable horn on head and smaller horn on thorax: female is hornless. As in the whole family, the antennal club is composed of movable flaps. 6-9, flying in the evening and also by day. Larva feeds on rabbit dung.

▲ **Dor Beetle** *Geotrupes stercorarius*. Superficially like some of the scarabs (p. 264), but easily distinguished because the jaws are clearly visible from above. Seven ridges on each elytron. Metallic green or blue below. Mainly on cow dung, digging shafts below it and burying the dung for breeding. Often flies in the evening. Also called the Lousy Watchman because it is commonly heavily infested with mites. 4-10. One of several similar species.

▲ **Minotaur Beetle** *Typhaeus typhoeus*. Very shiny, strongly-ribbed elytra. Male has 3 thoracic horns, but female has just 2 small points. Found mainly in sandy places, where it buries rabbit droppings and other dung on which adults and larvae feed. Flies in the evening.

Oxyporus rufus × 2

Paederus littoralis × 2

Stenus bimaculatus × 2

Bledius furcatus × 2

Philonthus marginatus × 2

Tachyporus hypnorum × 2

Lesser Stag Beetle

Stag Beetle

♂   ♀

Odontaeus armiger × 3

Trox scaber × 2

Sinodendron cylindricum × 1.5

Dor Beetle × 1.5

Platycerus caraboides × 1.5

♂

female head and thorax

Minotaur Beetle × 1.5

Scarabaeus pushing a
ball of dung along with
its hind legs

antenna of a chafer,
showing characteristic
fan-like flaps

SCARABS and CHAFERS Scarabaeidae. A very large family, with some 20,000 species in the world. The antennae are distinctly clubbed, the club consisting of several flaps that can be opened out to form a fan – especially noticeable in the chafers. The jaws are not visible from above. The elytra are normally truncated, markedly so in the chafers, leaving the tip of the abdomen exposed. Most species fly well. Many stridulate by rubbing the tips of the elytra against the abdomen. The scarabs are dung-feeders, while the chafers are vegetarians and often serious pests.

Scarabaeus semipunctatus. Numerous pits on pronotum: elytra almost smooth. Rolls balls of dung about with its hind legs, eventually burying them and eating them. Neighbouring beetles often wrestle over ownership of a ball. The rake-like front tibiae and the spiky head shield are used for raking up the dung and also for digging. Sandy shores around the Mediterranean. **S. laticollis** is similar but has ribbed elytra. S. **S. sacer** has smooth elytra and no pronotal pits: usually larger. S. There are several other species, differing slightly in the sculpturing of the pronotum and elytra.

▲ **Copris lunaris.** Female has shorter horn on the head. Usually associated with cow dung, digging shafts under it and burying large quantities in which the eggs are laid. Seen mainly in spring and autumn.

▲ **Aphodius fimetarius** and **A. rufipes** are two very common members of a large genus of dung beetles, all rather cylindrical. They are often attracted to lights at night. They feed on all kinds of herbivore dung, but do not burrow beneath it or bury it. A. rufipes is one of the largest European members of the genus.

Pine Chafer Polyphylla fullo. Female is slightly larger, but without the enormous scent-detecting flaps of the male antennae. Stridulates loudly. 6-8 in and around pinewoods, especially on sandy soils. Adults chew pine needles. Larvae feed on roots of sedges and grasses. S & C.

▲ **Cockchafer** Melolontha melolontha. Also called May-bug. Inhabits gardens, woods, and hedgerows. 5-6, often swarming round trees in the evening and crashing into lighted windows. Chews leaves of various deciduous trees. Larva (p. 295) feeds on roots of a wide range of plants, often causing severe damage to crops.

▲ **Summer Chafer** Amphimallon solstitialis. is like Cockchafer but pronotum is brown and much hairier. Only 3 segments to antennal club (4-7 in cockchafer). 6-7, swarming over rough grassland and round deciduous trees and shrubs day and night: mainly in dry places. Larvae feed on roots.

▲ **Garden Chafer** Phyllopertha horticola. Thorax sometimes almost black. Elytra often with green or blue iridescence. 6-7 in dry habitats, often swarming in sunshine. Adults feed on a wide range of woody and herbaceous plants and often damage fruit crops. Larvae feed on roots of cereals and other grasses.

Rhizotrogus aestivus resembles a Summer Chafer, but is less hairy, with long hairs only on thoracic margins. Usually a dark line in centre of pronotum. Grassy places. 4-6. Larvae feed on grass roots. S & C.

Rhinoceros Beetle Oryctes nasicornis. Up to 40mm long. Male has long, curved horn on head: female has just a small point. Flies on summer evenings. Breeds in rotting wood and leaves, and also in piles of sawdust at sawmills. Absent from far north.

Hoplia caerulea. Clothed with scales, which are brilliant blue in male and greyish brown in female. 6-8 in damp, grassy places, especially near streams. Larvae feed on roots. S & C (southern). **H. argentea** is greenish yellow, while several other species are reddish brown – like small summer chafers, but easily distinguished by their coatings of scales and also by the single large claw on the hind leg.

Anisoplia cyathigera. Found mainly in low-lying grassy places, often causing damage to cereals. 5-6. Larvae feed on roots and on decaying vegetation. S & C (southern).

Anisoplia cyathigera × 1.5

DUNG BEETLES and CHAFERS

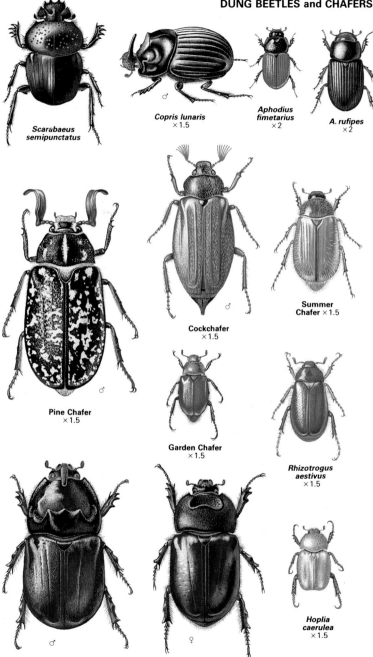

Scarabaeus semipunctatus

Copris lunaris
♂
×1.5

Aphodius fimetarius
×2

A. rufipes
×2

Pine Chafer
×1.5
♂

Cockchafer
×1.5
♂

Summer Chafer ×1.5

Garden Chafer
×1.5

Rhizotrogus aestivus
×1.5

Hoplia caerulea
×1.5

♂   ♀

Rhinoceros Beetle

265

▲ **Gnorimus nobilis**. Superficially like Rose Chafer, but elytra distinctly wrinkled and clearly separated from pronotum. 6-8, especially common on umbellifer flowers and flying strongly in sunshine. Breeds in rotting wood. Absent from far north.

△ **Bee Beetle** *Trichius fasciatus*. Very hairy. Elytra range from pale yellow to deep orange: black bars very variable. A tooth-like projection on middle tibia. 5-7, usually seen on flowers, especially thyme and roses. Breeds in rotting timber. *T. zonatus* and *T. abdominalis* are very similar but lack the tooth-like projection on middle tibia.

Oxythyrea funesta. Usually a coppery iridescence: white spots very irregular. Abundant in flowers of many kinds, often destroying flower buds of vines and fruit trees. 4-7. Larvae eat roots. S & C (southern).

▲ **Rose Chafer** *Cetonia aurata*. Elytra clearly flattened, usually green but may be bronze or even bluish black: always with some white marks. Slightly sinuate near apex (lens!). Coppery red beneath, with a rounded club-like process between middle coxae. 5-10, mainly in sunny places: nibbles many kinds of flowers, including roses. Larvae live in rotting timber and other vegetable refuse, including grass cuttings and piles of sawdust. S & C.

△ **C. cuprea** is green with a golden or bronze sheen, distinguished from Rose Chafer by the narrowing of the elytra towards the rear and a lack of any sinuous curve near the apex. White spots variable. Coppery violet beneath, with a rather square process between middle coxae. 5-9, visiting various flowers, especially in woods, and nibbling ripe fruit. Enjoys sunshine. Larvae live in ant nests.

C. aeruginosa is larger, with very smooth and shiny elytra and no white spots. 5-8 on flowers and also feeding at sap oozing from trees. Larvae feed in old oak trunks and stumps. S & C.

▲ **Serica brunnea**. Elytra dull yellowish brown and strongly ribbed. Like Summer Chafer (p. 264) but smaller and less hairy and with dark head. 6-8, mainly in sandy places. Often attracted to lights in evening. Larvae feed on roots.

△s **Omaloplia ruricola**. Similar to Garden Chafer (p. 264), but smaller and more rotund. 5-8, usually in warm and dry places. Flies day and night. Larvae feed on roots. C: on chalk soils in B.

BUPRESTID BEETLES Buprestidae. A family of some 15,000 rather metallic beetles living mainly in the tropics. Often bullet-shaped, with sharply pointed rear ends. They fly in the sunshine and are often seen on flowers. The larvae are flattened and tadpole-shaped, with a broad thorax, and live mainly under bark. The larvae are long-lived and are often carried far from home in timber. Only 12 species occur naturally in the British Isles.

Chalcophora mariana. Brown with a light bronze sheen. Pronotum and elytra with broad ridges and furrows. 5-10 in pinewoods.

Buprestis 8-guttata. Iridescent blue or green: pronotum with narrow yellow sides. Coniferous forests in summer. Larvae feed in young pines. Much of Europe, but rare.

B. rustica. Metallic green or blue, with a coppery or violet sheen. Summer, usually in pinewoods. The larvae live in rotting trunks and stumps.

Capnodis tenebrionis. Non-metallic, with grey pronotum and dull black elytra speckled with white. Summer, usually in sunny habitats and associated with blackthorn and other *Prunus* species. The larvae live in the older stems. S & C.

Lampra rutilans. Green, with a golden or bluish sheen. Elytra reddish on outer edges. 5-9, usually near old lime trees in which larvae feed.

△ **Anthaxia nitidula**. Male is green all over. Female head and pronotum purple or reddish: elytra blue or green. 4-7 on a variety of flowers. Larvae live in stems of rose, hawthorn, and related shrubs. S & C.

A. candens is easily identified by its striking coloration. 4-7, often on cherry blossom. Larvae feed in cherry trunks and branches. S & C.

A. hungarica. Male generally entirely green above, often with purplish sheen: female elytra green or blue. Both sexes are bright metallic purple beneath. 4-7 on various flowers, especially in and around oakwoods. Larvae live in decaying oak timber. S.

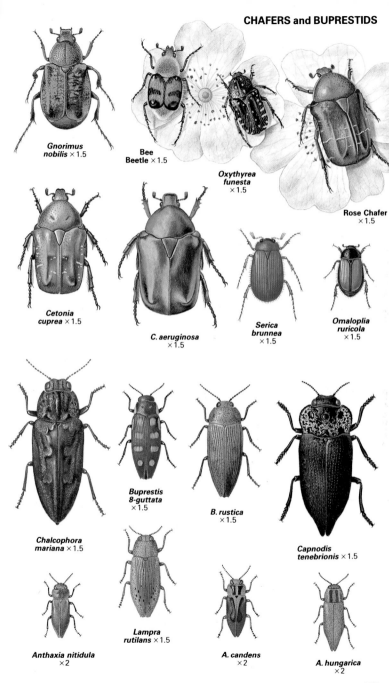

CHAFERS and BUPRESTIDS

Gnorimus nobilis ×1.5

Bee Beetle ×1.5

Oxythyrea funesta ×1.5

Rose Chafer ×1.5

Cetonia cuprea ×1.5

C. aeruginosa ×1.5

Serica brunnea ×1.5

Omaloplia ruricola ×1.5

Chalcophora mariana ×1.5

Buprestis 8-guttata ×1.5

B. rustica ×1.5

Capnodis tenebrionis ×1.5

Anthaxia nitidula ×2

Lampra rutilans ×1.5

A. candens ×2

A. hungarica ×2

Phaenops cyanea. Entirely blue but often tinged with green. Pine forests in warm regions. 6-8. Larvae develop in pine trunks.

Ptosima 11-maculata. Black with blue iridescence. Pale marks orange or yellow and very variable. 5-6. Larvae feed in *Prunus* species and are pests of cherry. S & C.

▲ **Agrilus pannonicus**. Dark green or blue with white spots. 5-7. Breeds in old oaks.

△ **A. viridis** is unmarked: often entirely green, sometimes entirely copper-coloured. 6-7 on sallows and other deciduous trees.

Isorhipis melasoides Eucnemidae. Like click beetles, but with some anatomical differences. 5-7. Adults and larvae (legless) in rotting beech and oak. S & C.

▲ **Melasis buprestoides**. Matt black, sometimes tinged with red. Thorax widest at the front. Female antennae only lightly toothed. 5-7. Breeds in various deciduous trees. Larvae legless. S & C.

CLICK BEETLES Elateridae. A large family (over 7,000 species) of elongate beetles named for the ability to leap into the air and right themselves when laid on their backs. The action is accompanied by a loud click. The larvae are slender and short-legged, vegetarian or carnivorous, and live in rotting wood or the soil.

△n **Ctenicera pectinicornis**. Green or coppery and very shiny. Female antennae only lightly toothed. 6-7 in grassy places. Larvae live in the soil. N & C. △n **C. cuprea** is sometimes entirely violet or copper-coloured. Female antennae only lightly toothed. Grassland. 5-7. N & C.

△ **Ampedus cinnabarinus**. Lightly clothed with rust-coloured hairs. Woodland, mainly in spring. Breeds in decaying deciduous trees, where larvae eat other grubs.

△ **A. sanguineus** is similar but has black pubescence. 5-8, mainly on woodland flowers. Breeds in rotting timber, especially conifers. △ **A. balteatus** frequents umbellifers and other flowers. 5-6. Breeds in dead evergreen and deciduous trees.

▲ **Common Click Beetle** *Agriotes lineatus*. Brown or yellowish with striped elytra and brick-red antennae. Much of the year, but seen mainly 5-7. Abundant on grassland and cultivated land. The larva (p. 295) is one of the infamous wireworms that cause much damage to crop roots.

▲ **Garden Click Beetle** *Athous haemorrhoidalis*. Clothed with grey or brown hair. Elytra strongly grooved. Abundant 5-8, especially in hedgerows and grassland. Larvae (wireworms) eat roots.

Selatosomus cruciatus. Black markings roughly in the form of a cross. 4-7, mainly in woodland and scrub. Larva lives in soil.

Cardiophorus gramineus. Deciduous woodland, especially on hawthorn flowers, 4- 5. Larva, very long and thin, feeds on other insects under bark. S & C.

▲ **Oedosthetus 4-pustulatus**. Rear yellow spots may be absent. River banks and other damp, grassy places, often under stones. 5-7. N & C.

Cebrio gigas Cebrionidae. Female, with short elytra and no hindwings, remains in her larval gallery all her life. Male flies in evening. 8-11. Larvae eat roots. S.

△ **Drilus flavescens** Drilidae. Male is winged but rarely flies. 6-7 among low-growing vegetation: female rarely seen. Larvae feed on snails.

▲ **Dascillus cervinus** Dascillidae. Covered with hair – greyish in male, yellowish brown in female. 5-7. Rough grassland, usually on flowers. Larvae eat roots.

▲ **Byrrhus pilula** Byrrhidae. Very convex. Brown or reddish. Among moss and short turf, especially in sandy areas. All year, but hibernates: most common in spring.

▲ **Microcara testacea** Helodidae. Thin-skinned and rather soft. Abundant in damp grassland and hedgerows in summer. Larvae are aquatic.

When disturbed, *Byrrhus* pulls in its legs and antennae and is easily mistaken for a seed

Dascillus cervinus × 1.5

Byrrhus pilula × 2

Microcara testacea × 4

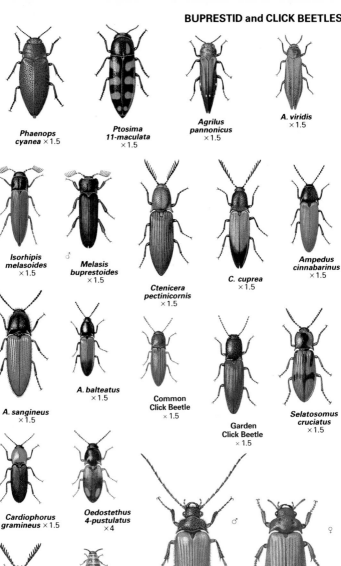

Phaenops cyanea ×1.5

Ptosima 11-maculata ×1.5

Agrilus pannonicus ×1.5

A. viridis ×1.5

Isorhipis melasoides ×1.5

Melasis buprestoides ♂ ×1.5

Ctenicera pectinicornis ×1.5

C. cuprea ×1.5

Ampedus cinnabarinus ×1.5

A. sangineus ×1.5

A. balteatus ×1.5

Common Click Beetle ×1.5

Garden Click Beetle ×1.5

Selatosomus cruciatus ×1.5

Cardiophorus gramineus ×1.5

Oedostethus 4-pustulatus ×4

Drilus flavescens ×2

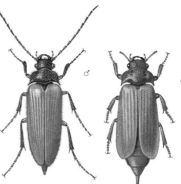

Cebrio gigas

SOLDIER and SAILOR BEETLES Cantharidae. So-called for the bright colours of some species, reminiscent of old military uniforms. Elytra are soft. The beetles are predators, often hunting on flowers of grassland, hedgerow, and woodland margin. They fly well in the sunshine. The larvae resemble those of ground beetles (p. 295) and hunt mainly on the ground.

▲ *Cantharis rustica.* Femora largely red. Abundant everywhere 5-8. ▲ *C. fusca* is similar but with black femora and the black spot near the front edge of the pronotum. ▲ *C. livida* has legs partly black and sometimes has black spot on pronotum. 4-8.

▲ *Rhagonycha fulva* is a very common species, often called the bloodsucker because of its colour, although it is harmless. Pronotum almost square and elytra always black-tipped. 5-8.

▲ *Malthinus flaveolus.* Elytra are ridged and short, leaving tip of abdomen exposed. Abundant on shrubs and among grasses, mainly near woodland margins. All summer.

△s **Glow-worm** *Lampyris noctiluca* Lampyridae. Males fly at night in search of wingless, larva-like females that sit in grass and emit greenish light from under rear end of abdomen. 6-7 on grassland, including roadside verges. Larva feeds on snails. Absent from far north and becoming rare in many other places. *Phausis splendidula*, common on continent, is a little smaller: female tawny brown with 3 spots of light.

Firefly *Luciola lusitanica.* Male flies after dark, emitting bright flashes about once every second from under rear end of abdomen. Female has smaller head and eyes and a very pointed abdomen. Although fully winged, she does not fly: she sits in vegetation and responds with flashes when she sees a male overhead. 5-7. Larva feeds on snails. S: not west of Rhône.

△s *Phosphaenus hemipterus.* Wingless female rarely seen: she sits among turf or stones and attracts wandering male with greenish light after dusk. 5-7. Larva is like that of Glow-worm and feeds on snails.

Family Cleridae. A family of brightly coloured and rather hairy beetles. Most are predatory as adults and larvae. The latter are often brightly coloured and feed on other grubs under bark and in timber. Most of the 3,000 or so species are tropical..

Denops albofasciata. Woods and woodland margins, 5-6. Larva feeds on grubs of various bark beetles. S & C.

▲ *Tillus elongatus.* Female has red thorax: male entirely black. On trunks of various deciduous trees, 6-7.

Opilo domesticus. In coniferous woodland and often in houses. 6-8. Breeds in dry softwoods, feeding on woodworm and other grubs. S & C. ▲ *O. mollis* is very similar.

▲ *Thanasimus formicarius.* Elytral pattern varies, but always with 2 pale cross bars. On tree trunks in spring. Feeds on bark beetle grubs in various trees. May enter houses in logs.

Clerus mutillarius. Spring and summer on old trees and logs, especially oaks. Feeds on other beetle grubs. S & C.

Trichodes alvearius. Dark bands blue or black, the front one forming a shallow U: elytra red at apex. Very common on umbellifers and other flowers 5-7. Larvae feed on grubs of solitary bees. *T. apiarius* is similar but front band is straighter and elytra are dark at apex. Both species widely distributed in S & C.

△ *Necrobia ruficollis.* Sometimes seen on flowers, but more often in tanneries and meat stores. Larvae eat skins and bones and dead insects. All year indoors: spring and summer out of doors. ▲ *N. rufipes*, with all-blue thorax and elytra, is more common in B.

▲ **Cardinal Beetle** *Pyrochroa coccinea* Pyrochroidae. Rather flat and found on flowers and old tree trunks and stumps 5-7. Larva (p. 295) lives under bark and feeds on other insects. N & C. ▲ *P. serraticornis* is similar but head is scarlet.

△n *Schizotus pectinicornis* resembles *P. coccinea* but has very feathery antennae and a black spot on pronotum. N & C.

Lygistopterus sanguineus Lycidae. Soft elytra, less flattened than cardinal beetles. Sun-loving and found on flowers, usually in woodland, 5-9. Larvae eat other grubs in rotting timber

△n *Dictyoptera aurora* resembles last species but pronotum is decorated with sunken pits. Elytra strongly ridged. Coniferous woods, 5-8. Larvae feed on other grubs under bark. N & C and mountains in S.

Dictyoptera aurora × 2

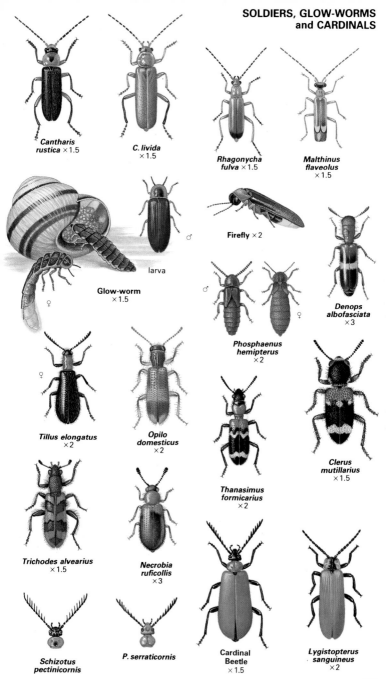

Cantharis rustica ×1.5

C. livida ×1.5

Rhagonycha fulva ×1.5

Malthinus flaveolus ×1.5

Glow-worm ×1.5

larva

♂

♀

Firefly ×2

Phosphaenus hemipterus ×2

♂ ♀

Denops albofasciata ×3

Tillus elongatus ×2

♀

Opilo domesticus ×2

Thanasimus formicarius ×2

Clerus mutillarius ×1.5

Trichodes alvearius ×1.5

Necrobia ruficollis ×3

Schizotus pectinicornis

P. serraticornis

Cardinal Beetle ×1.5

Lygistopterus sanguineus ×2

271

| **Malachius aeneus** ×2 | **M. bipustulatus** ×2 | **Anthocomus fasciatus** ×5 | **Endomychus coccineus** ×3 |

▲ **Malachius aeneus** Melyridae. A predatory beetle frequenting flowers in spring, especially in woods. Elytra rather soft. Male has outgrowths near base of antennae, used for holding female. S & C. ▲ **M. bipustulatus**, also with antennal swellings in male, hunts other insects among flowers and grasses. 5-8.

▲ **Anthocomus fasciatus**. Elytra soft, ground colour black or greenish black. Knees of front legs brownish. Summer. Predatory in grass and on various trees, and also in thatched roofs, from which red larvae often get into houses. S & C.

▲ **Endomychus coccineus** Endomychidae. Often mistaken for a ladybird, but much flatter and with longer antennae. A fungus-eater living under bark of dead or dying trees, especially beech. 4-6.

LADYBIRDS Coccinellidae. Small, domed, and usually hemispherical, although some species are oblong. Head sunk into pronotum. Legs short and retractable: tarsi 4-segmented but 3rd segment very small and concealed in bilobed 2nd segment. Usually brightly coloured and distasteful, but colour pattern is notoriously variable. Mostly carnivorous. Often hibernate in large masses. Larva (p. 295) also carnivorous: pupates openly on plants.

Epilachna chrysomelina. 6 black spots on each elytron, varying and often merging to form heavy black network. Vegetarian on gourd family: sometimes a pest of melons. All year in Mediterranean region. ▲ **Subcoccinella 24-punctata** eats all kinds of plants: a carnation pest in France. Very variable. Summer.

▲ **Coccidula scutellata** hunts aphids on various plants in marshy places. 7-8.
▲ **Scymnus frontalis** Elytra may lack red spots. Front of pronotum often reddish in male, always black in female. Dense vegetation in dry places. 5-7. S & C.

△ **Hippodamia 13-punctata**. More oval than many species. 4-9 in low marshy areas. Possibly extinct in B.

▲ **7-spot Ladybird** Coccinella 7-punctata. The ladybird, abundant everywhere 3-10.
△ **Eyed Ladybird** Anatis ocellata. Usually on or near conifers. 6-7. ▲ **Psyllobora 22-punctata** feeds largely on mildews. 4-8 in low vegetation and shrubs of all kinds.

▲ **2-Spot Ladybird** Adalia bipunctata Abundant everywhere 3-10. Black legs. Elytra very variable: black ground colour, especially common in north, helps heat absorption in smoky and cloudy regions. ▲ **10-Spot Ladybird** A. 10-punctata is similarly variable but has yellowish legs. 3-10.

▲ **Propylea 14-punctata**. Elytra range from almost all yellow to almost all black, with black spots merging together: always a black line along the junction of the elytra. Common on shrubs 4-9. ▲ **Cream-spot Ladybird** Calvia 14-guttata occurs mainly on shrubs and small trees. 4-9.

▲ **Harlequin Ladybird** Harmandia axyridis, a native of Japan, has recently been spreading through Europe at an alarming rate, competing with and even preying on native ladybirds. It is slightly larger than most European species and extremely variable, with up to 21 spots, but can be distinguished by the more or less triangular white mark on the head and the conspicuous red border around the underside of the abdomen.

LARDER BEETLES Dermestidae. Mostly sombre-coloured scavengers, clothed with scales or hairs. Clubbed antennae can be hidden under body. Many are cosmopolitan pests of stored foods and fabrics. Larvae are bristly and known as 'woolly bears'.

▲ **Larder** or **Bacon Beetle** Dermestes lardarius. Larvae and adults eat carrion in the wild and dried meats in store. All year, but hibernate in the wild. ▲ **Hide Beetle** D. maculatus has similar habits but damages hides and furs as well as stored foods.

▲ **Attagenus pellio**. Visits flowers 3-9: also common in houses. Larvae in birds' nests, furs, carpets, stored grain, etc. Sometimes called the fur beetle.

▲ **Varied Carpet Beetle** Anthrenus verbasci. Pattern varies. Adults eat pollen and nectar 3-9. Larvae (p. 295) eat dried material in birds' nests and buildings and also damage woollens and insect collections.

△ **Khapra Beetle** Trogoderma granarium. Adult does not feed, but larva is serious pest of stored grain and cereal products everywhere. All year in heated buildings.
T. angustum, much narrower than most other Trogoderma species, is a native of Chile now established in Germany and Sweden. A pest in insect collections.

*Epilachna
chrysomelina*
× 2

*Subcoccinella
24-punctata*
× 5

*Coccidula
scutellata*
× 5

**Scymnus
frontalis**
× 5

*Hyppodamia
13-punctata* × 3

**7-spot
Ladybird** × 3

**Eyed
Ladybird** × 2

*Psyllobora
22-punctata* × 3

  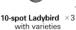

2-spot Ladybird × 3
with varieties

10-spot Ladybird × 3
with varieties

Harlequin Ladybird × 3   with varieties

*Propylea
14-punctata* × 3

**Cream-spot
Ladybird** × 3

Larder Beetle
× 2

Hide Beetle
× 2

Attagenus pellio
× 3

**Varied
Carpet Beetle**
× 5

Khapra Beetle
× 4

*Trogoderma
angustum* × 4

△ **Ptinus fur** Ptinidae. One of the 'spider beetles', so called for the rounded bodies of many of the females: sexes differ markedly in shape. Colour and pattern vary. Scavenges and breeds in dry organic matter indoors and out, often damaging museum specimens and other stored materials. *P. tectus* is more common in B, where it breeds in foodstuffs.

▲ **Furniture Beetle** *Anobium punctatum* Anobiidae. Dark brown to yellowish and very downy. Antenna with unusual and very characteristic 1-sided club. Abundant indoors and out, 5-7. Larva is the woodworm, tunnelling in dead coniferous and broad-leaved timber and causing serious damage. Escape holes of adults 1.5-2 mm across.

▲ **Death-watch Beetle** *Xestobium rufovillosum*. Hairy and, as in all the family, the head is more or less hidden from above. Breeds in old trees and building timbers – usually oak and other hardwoods, especially where damp. Tunnelling larvae cause immense damage to old buildings, but less common than furniture beetle. Adults appear in spring and make tapping noises to attract mates. Exit holes 3-4 mm across.

▲ **Ptilinus pectinicornis**. Antennae are simply toothed in female. 5-8, often indoors. Breeds in dry hardwoods.

▲ **Lesser Grain Borer** *Rhizopertha dominica* Bostrychidae. Pimply pronotum forms hood over head. Antenna with 3-segmented club. Adult and larvae feed on grain of various kinds, commonly infesting granaries and flour mills.

△ **Lyctus linearis** Lyctidae. One of the powder post beetles. Antennae with 2- segmented club. Breeds in old hardwoods, indoors and out, and reduces them to a very fine dust. 4-7.

▲ **Cadelle** *Tenebroides mauritanicus* Trogossitidae. Dark brown to black. Found mainly in food stores and bakeries, where adult and larva prey on other insects. Sometimes out of doors, under loose bark, in warmer areas.

▲ **Lymexylon navale** Lymexylidae. Soft, furry elytra. Female slightly larger and lacks feathery palps. 5-8, around dead and dying deciduous trees in which it breeds. Occasionally damages oak timbers. S & C.

△ **Hylecoetus dermestoides**. Only male has feathery palps. 5-6 around dead and dying trees, usually deciduous species. As like previous species, larva has horny plate at end.

▲ **Saw-toothed Grain Beetle** *Oryzaephilus surinamensis*. Silvanidae. 6 blunt teeth on each side of thorax. Usually in grain stores and warehouses, feeding on larvae of other insects, including grain weevils.

▲ **Glischrochilus 4-punctatus** Nitidulidae. Smooth and shiny: rear edge of thorax narrower than elytra. Clubbed antennae. 3-11 around conifers. Breeds under bark and in bark beetle galleries. ▲ **G. hortensis** is stouter, with sides of thorax more or less continuous with elytra. 5 tarsal segments. Feeds on oozing sap and over-ripe fruit 5-10.

▲ **Raspberry Beetle** *Byturus tomentosus* Byturidae. Clothed with fine hair. 5-7, gnawing raspberry buds and laying eggs in them. Larvae feed in the growing fruit.

▲ **Mycetophagus 4-pustulatus** Mycetophagidae. Superficially like *Glischrochilus*, but flatter and with 3-4 tarsal segments: pronotum semicircular. 4-9, usually on bracket fungi on deciduous trees: occasionally on dung.

▲ **Gnatocerus cornutus** Tenebrionidae. Female lacks horns, which are outgrowths from jaws. Feeds on flour in grain stores, flour mills, etc. Also under loose bark.

▲ **Confused Flour Beetle** *Tribolium confusum*. Confined to flour mills, granaries, and food stores. Feeds on flour and other cereal products.

▲ **Mealworm Beetle** *Tenebrio molitor*. Seen mainly in granaries, etc, where it damages grain and cereal products, but also breeds readily in old birds' nests in house roofs. Larva (p. 295) is the mealworm, widely sold in pet shops for feeding birds and other small animals. Occasionally out of doors, usually under bark, in summer.

△ **Diaperis boleti**. Shiny black with yellow or orange markings. Strongly domed. Feeds on fungi, mainly in woodland.

▲ **Churchyard Beetle** *Blaps mucronata*. A flightless, ground-living beetle of caves, cellars, stables, and other damp, dark places. Strongly nocturnal, like most members of the family. Scavenges on vegetable matter and emits a foul smell when alarmed.

Churchyard Beetle
× 1.5

WOOD-BORING BEETLES and others

Ptinus fur × 4

Furniture Beetle × 4

larval damage

Death-watch Beetle × 3

Ptilinus pectinicornis × 3

head from side

Lesser Grain Borer × 3

Lyctus linearis × 4

Cadelle × 2

Lymexylon navale × 2

Hylecoetus dermestoides × 2

Saw-toothed Grain Beetle × 5

Glischrochilus 4-punctatus × 4

G. hortensis × 4

Raspberry Beetle × 4

Mycetophagus 4-pustulatus × 4.

Gnatocerus cornutus × 4

Confused Flour Beetle × 4

Mealworm Beetle × 1.5

Diaperis boleti × 1.5

Lagria hirta
× 2

Cteniopus sulphureus
× 2

▲ **Lagria hirta** Tenebrionidae. Soft-bodied and rather sluggish. Head and thorax black or brown. 5-7, on flowers, usually in dry habitats. Larvae eat decaying matter in turf and leaf litter.

⚐ **Cteniopus sulphureus**. Soft-bodied. Head and thorax often almost black. 5-7 on flowers, usually on sand dunes and in other dry, sunny places. Larvae live at base of plants.

Oncomera femorata
× 1.5

Oedemera nobilis
× 2

Notoxus monoceros
× 4

Anthicus antherinus
× 4

A. floralis
× 4

▲ **Oncomera femorata** Oedemeridae. Elytra and body soft. Pollen-feeding on various shrubs, including ivy, 4-10. Larvae feed in decaying wood. S & C.

▲ **Oedemera nobilis**. Female is thinner and lacks swollen hind femora. Elytra pointed and gaping. Pollen feeding: common on a wide range of flowers 4-8.

Notoxus
head and thorax

△ **Notoxus monoceros** Anthicidae. An agile, ant-like beetle with a thoracic horn projecting over head. Elytra often black with just a pale triangle at tip. Among debris and turf on sandy ground: often on flowers.

⚐ **Anthicus antherinus**. Very agile. Usually on compost heaps and other vegetable debris or manure heaps. 5-10. ▲ **A. floralis** is very ant-like: whole body often dark. In manure and vegetable refuse. 5-10.

△s **Spanish Fly** *Lytta vesicatoria* Meloidae. One of the blister beetles, so called because they emit blistering fluids when alarmed. 5-8, chewing the leaves of various trees and giving out a strong mousy odour. Larvae in nests of solitary bees. S & C.

△ **Meloe variegatus**. One of the oil beetles, releasing a smelly, oily fluid when alarmed. Flightless, with short elytra overlapping at the front. 4-7 in grassy places, chewing leaves of various plants. Larva lives in nests of solitary bees. S & C. ▲ **M. proscarabaeus** is bluish black and, like all oil beetles, very variable in size. Male has kinked antennae. 4-7. △ **M. violaceus** is similar but more finely punctured on head and thorax. Habits are like those of *M. variegatus*. Male oil beetles are always smaller than females.

Mylabris polymorpha. Pale markings vary in shape and may be orange or yellow. On flowers in sunny places, feeding on pollen. 6-9. Larvae parasitise grasshopper eggs. S.

Spanish Fly
× 1.25

276

Meloe variegatus × 1.25

M. proscarabaeus
× 1.25

Mylabris polymorpha
× 1.25

LONGHORN BEETLES Cerambycidae. A family of more than 20,000 beetles, mostly with very long antennae arising from prominent tubercles. Antennae usually longer in males than in females. Body usually distinctly elongate and often rather flattened, but size is very variable and reflects the quality of the larval food. Elytra may be much broader than thorax. Tarsi appear to have only 4 segments, with 3rd segment bilobed and almost completely enclosing the tiny 4th segment. Tarsal segments much broader in males than in females.

Many species are very colourful, often with marked differences between the sexes, but there are also many sombre species. Most are fully winged and fly, by night or day, with a ghostly rising and falling motion. A few are fast and noisy. They feed on flowers, particularly the pollen, and leaves, although some species take little food in the adult state. Many can stridulate loudly by rubbing their thoracic plates together. They do this mainly when alarmed, and especially when handled.

A typical longhorn larva, showing the tapering body and very short legs.

The larvae are almost all wood-feeders, attacking both living and dead timber. Several species cause severe damage to forest and plantation trees. They are usually elongate, pale coloured, and flattened – especially those species that live just under the bark. The jaws are powerful, but legs are very short or absent. Wood is not a very nutritious food and larval life is consequently rather long – usually two or three years and sometimes much longer in dry, seasoned timber. Pupation takes place in an enlarged feeding tunnel or in a chamber hollowed out just under the bark. The larvae often go on growing after their trees have been felled and used for building, and with today's worldwide trade in timber the adults often emerge far from their native homes.

Several hundred longhorn species live in Europe, with about 70 species native to Britain. Most live in the woodlands. Their habits are all rather similar and only minimal descriptions are given on the following pages. The habitats given are essentially those of the larvae.

▲ **Tanner Beetle** *Prionus coriarius*. One of Europe's stoutest longhorns. Larvae live in tree roots. 6-9.

♀

Ergates faber. Up to 60mm long. Thorax spiny-edged: with 2 large spots in male. Larvae live in stumps in old pine woods. 7-9. S & C: mainly eastern.

Monochamus galloprovincialis. Antennae reddish brown. U-shaped hairy patch on scutellum. On pines. 6-9. Mainly S, but also plantations in C.

Morimus funereus. Flightless. Found on stumps and old trunks of deciduous trees, especially oak and beech. 5-6. S.

△ **Monochamus sartor.** Antennae black: banded with white in female. Scutellum entirely hairy. On dead and dying conifers: damages structural timbers. 6-8. C: mainly in upland regions.

× 1.5

▲ **Musk Beetle.** *Aromia moschata.* Sometimes coppery or blue. Emits musk-like secretion. Deciduous trees, especially willows. 6-8.

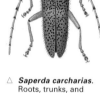

△ **Saperda carcharias.** Roots, trunks, and branches of young poplars: often a pest. 7-9.

△ **Lamia textor.** A lethargic species found around sallows and poplars: a pest of osier beds. 5-10.

△ **Oberea oculata.** Elytra strongly concave at apex. Larvae in young willow shoots. 5-8.

△ **House Longhorn.** *Hylotrupes bajulus.* Breeds in dry coniferous timber, often destroying telegraph poles and house timbers. 6-8.

▲ **Wasp Beetle** *Clytra arietis*. A superb wasp mimic, scuttling over tree trunks in sunshine with antennae waving. Pronotum very round. Common in gardens and hedgerows 5-7. Larvae in fence posts and other dead hardwood.

△ *Plagionotus arcuatus*. Sides of thorax strongly rounded. On dead oaks and beeches in sunshine. 5-7. Often breeds in structural timbers.

Chlorophorus varius. Sun-loving: often on flowers, especially umbellifers. Breeds in various hardwoods, including vines. 6-7. Mainly southern.

× 1.25

Cerambyx cerdo. One of Europe's largest beetles – up to 55 mm long. Flies around oaks, 6-8, mainly in evening. Larvae damage standing oak timber. S & C, occasionally imported into B in timber *C. scopoli* is smaller and blacker.

▲ *Strangalia maculata*. Elytra strongly tapered. Thorax almost bell-shaped. One of several similar species: pattern varies but base of each antennal segment always yellow. On flowers 6-8. Larvae in rotting deciduous trees stumps.

△ *Phymatodes testaceus*. Head may be black and elytra bluish. 6-8, often swarming at dusk. Breeds in dead and dying deciduous trees.

△ *Agapanthia villosoviridescens*. On flowers in hedges and damp places, 5-7. Breeds in stems of thistles and other herbaceous plants. N & C.

× 1.25

× 1.25

279

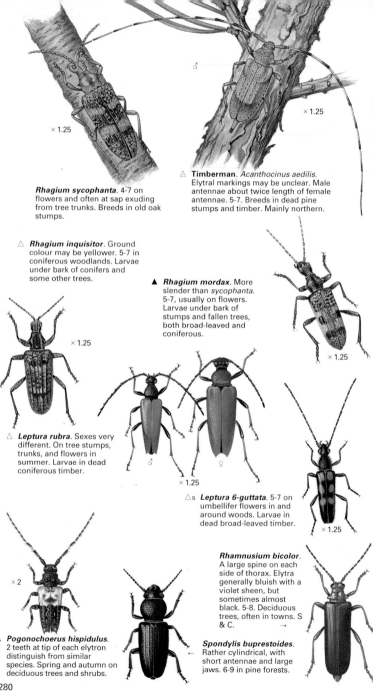

Rhagium sycophanta. 4-7 on flowers and often at sap exuding from tree trunks. Breeds in old oak stumps.

△ **Timberman.** *Acanthocinus aedilis.* Elytral markings may be unclear. Male antennae about twice length of female antennae. 5-7. Breeds in dead pine stumps and timber. Mainly northern.

△ **Rhagium inquisitor.** Ground colour may be yellower. 5-7 in coniferous woodlands. Larvae under bark of conifers and some other trees.

▲ **Rhagium mordax.** More slender than *sycophanta.* 5-7, usually on flowers. Larvae under bark of stumps and fallen trees, both broad-leaved and coniferous.

△ **Leptura rubra.** Sexes very different. On tree stumps, trunks, and flowers in summer. Larvae in dead coniferous timber.

△s **Leptura 6-guttata.** 5-7 on umbellifer flowers in and around woods. Larvae in dead broad-leaved timber.

▲ **Pogonochoerus hispidulus.** 2 teeth at tip of each elytron distinguish from similar species. Spring and autumn on deciduous trees and shrubs.

Spondylis buprestoides. Rather cylindrical, with short antennae and large jaws. 6-9 in pine forests.

Rhamnusium bicolor. A large spine on each side of thorax. Elytra generally bluish with a violet sheen, but sometimes almost black. 5-8. Deciduous trees, often in towns. S & C. →

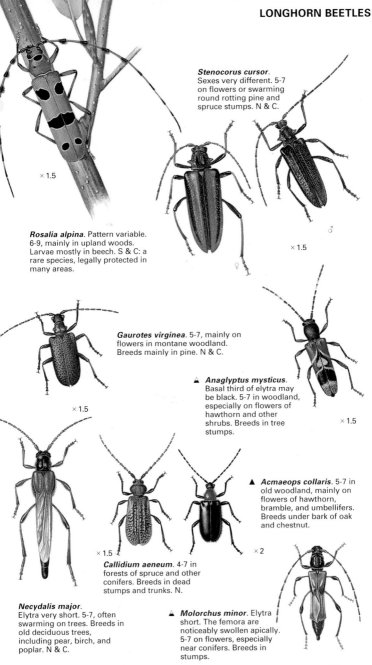

Stenocorus cursor. Sexes very different. 5-7 on flowers or swarming round rotting pine and spruce stumps. N & C.

× 1.5

Rosalia alpina. Pattern variable. 6-9, mainly in upland woods. Larvae mostly in beech. S & C: a rare species, legally protected in many areas.

× 1.5

♂

♀

Gaurotes virginea. 5-7, mainly on flowers in montane woodland. Breeds mainly in pine. N & C.

× 1.5

▲ **Anaglyptus mysticus**. Basal third of elytra may be black. 5-7 in woodland, especially on flowers of hawthorn and other shrubs. Breeds in tree stumps.

× 1.5

▲ **Acmaeops collaris**. 5-7 in old woodland, mainly on flowers of hawthorn, bramble, and umbellifers. Breeds under bark of oak and chestnut.

× 1.5

Callidium aeneum. 4-7 in forests of spruce and other conifers. Breeds in dead stumps and trunks. N.

× 2

Necydalis major. Elytra very short. 5-7, often swarming on trees. Breeds in old deciduous trees, including pear, birch, and poplar. N & C.

▲ **Molorchus minor**. Elytra short. The femora are noticeably swollen apically. 5-7 on flowers, especially near conifers. Breeds in stumps.

× 1.5

▲ **Pea Beetle** *Bruchus pisorum* Bruchidae. One of several similar beetles with truncated elytra, but distinguished by the two black spots at tip of abdomen. A serious pest of peas. Legless grubs develop in growing pods. Adults emerge in spring and commonly sunbathe on walls.

▲ **Bean Beetle** *Acanthoscelides obtectus*. Like *Bruchus* but pronotum distinctly triangular instead of semi-circular. Hind femur has 3 teeth. A pest of beans, breeding in stored seeds and growing crops.

Pea Beetle × 4   **Bean Beetle** × 4

LEAF BEETLES Chrysomelidae A family of over 25,000 known species, almost all leaf-eaters. Often brightly coloured and mostly with smooth, rounded outlines. Tarsi appear 4-segmented, but actually 5-segmented: 4th segment is minute and concealed in expanded 3rd segment. Some species might be confused with ladybirds (p. 270) but latter have only 3 visible tarsal segments. Larvae soft and slug-like although they have short legs.

▲ *Donacia vulgaris*. Elytra green or coppery with red or blue central area. On bur-reed 5-8. Larvae live in stems. One of several similar species on water plants.

▲ *Oulema melanopus*. Head and elytra blue or black. Abundant in grass and sometimes a minor cereal pest. 4-7, often sunning itself on walls.

▲ **Asparagus Beetle** *Crioceris asparagi*. A pest of asparagus, adults and larvae chewing the fine, needle-like branches. 5-8, hibernating as adult. S & C.

▲ **Lily Beetle** *Lilioceris lilii*. 4-8 on various members of lily family, including cultivated forms. Orange larvae are clothed with slimy black droppings. S & C: a major pest.

△ *Clytra 4-punctata*. 5-8 on vegetation near black ant nests. Scatters eggs on nest: larvae, protected by soil and excrement, eat scraps in the chambers and galleries.

▲ *Cryptocephalus hypochaeridis*. One of a large genus of very metallic beetles, commonly seen on flowers, especially hawkweeds and other yellow composites, in summer.

C. sericeus is golden green to bluish or purplish green. 4-7 in grassland, especially on yellow umbellifers. S & C.

C. bipunctatus occurs mainly on hazel, birch, and oak. 4-7.

▲ **Bloody-nosed Beetle** *Timarcha tenebricosa*. Strongly domed and flightless: smooth elytra fused together. Pronotum narrows strongly towards rear. One of the largest leaf beetles. Named for habit of exuding red blood from mouth when alarmed – this frightens birds. 4-8 in grassy places, walking slowly over turf and bare ground. Feeds on bedstraws. S & C. ▲ *T. goettingensis* is smaller, with pronotum almost parallel-sided.

▲ *Chrysolina polita*. Common all summer on herbage of river banks and other damp places, especially on mints. *C. grossa* of Mediterranean area is larger, with metallic blue thorax.

△ s *C. menthastri* is one of our most brilliant leaf beetles, found on mints and other labiates in damp places. 5-9. S & C.

△ s *C. cerealis* is usually metallic green with blue and red bands, but colours vary. Throughout summer in dry, sandy places, usually on wild thyme. S & C.

C. geminata is bronzy green or blue, sometimes all black. On St John's-worts (*Hypericum* species) throughout summer. N & C.

▲ *Gastrophysa viridula*. Usually golden green: sometimes bluish. Gravid female has enormously swollen abdomen. 5-8 on docks and related plants, normally on edges of ponds and streams.

△ **Colorado Beetle** *Leptinotarsa decemlineata*. A notorious potato pest, originally from N. America. Larvae (p. 295) and adults all destroy leaves, and also feed on tomato, nightshades, and related plants. Active 4-9, hibernating in soil as adult. Widely distributed in S & C: notify police if seen in B.

▲ *Chrysomela populi*. Pronotum dark green or bronze or almost black. Elytra orange to bright red, often with dark spots. On sallows and poplars 4-9.

C. 20-punctata has 10 irregular black marks on each elytron. 4-8, usually near water and normally on willows. C.

▲ *Phytodecta viminalis*. Shiny rusty brown: black marks variable and sometimes absent, but usually a black band or heart-shaped mark at rear of pronotum. 5-8, mainly on willows. N & C.

▲ *Lochmaea caprea*. Locally abundant on sallows in fens and other damp places: also on birch. 4-9. ▲ *L. crataegi* is redder and occurs on hawthorn.

leaf beetle tarsus showing the very small 4th segment almost enclosed in the 3rd segment

*Donacia
vulgaris*
×2

*Oulema
melanopus*
×3

Asparagus
Beetle ×3

Lily Beetle
×3

*Clytra
4-punctata* ×2

*Cryptocephalus
hypochaeridis*
×3

C. sericeus
×3

C. bipunctatus
×3

Bloody-nosed
Beetle ×1.5

Chrysolina polita
×2

C. menthastri
×2

C. cerealis ×2

C. geminata
×2

*Gastrophysa
viridula* ×2

Colorado
Beetle
×2

*Chrysomela
populi* ×2

C. 20-punctata
×2

*Phytodecta
viminalis* ×2

*Lochmaea
caprea* ×2

▲ ***Galerucella lineola***. A rather sombre, hairy beetle with pubescence lying parallel to suture. Often abundant on willows 3-9, feeding on flowers and leaves. Several similar species live on willows and other waterside plants.

▲ ***Galeruca tanaceti***. Shiny black. Elytra distinctly wider at rear end, especially in female, where abdomen may protrude beyond elytra. Roadsides and other grassy places, often quite dry, feeding on yarrow and other composites. 4-9.

▲ ***Luperus longicornis***. Male is more parallel-sided, with antennae much longer than body. On trees in damp places throughout the summer.

▲ ***Pyrrhalta viburni***. Very like *G. lineola*, but pubescence runs at right angles to suture. On wayfaring tree throughout summer, often reducing leaves to skeletons.

▲ ***Phyllodecta vitellinae***. Golden green, sometimes bluish or coppery. On poplars and willows, especially osiers, in spring and summer. Hibernates under bark.

△ ***Phyllobrotica 4-maculata***. 5-8, usually on skullcap in damp places.

▲ **Turnip Flea** *Phyllotreta nemorum*. One of the flea beetles – jumping species with enlarged hind femora. Like many other flea beetles, it is a pest of brassicas, including turnips. Adults feed mainly on seedlings, leaving them riddled with holes. Larvae tunnel in leaves and mature in autumn. Adults hibernate and reappear in spring to feed and lay eggs.

▲ ***Phyllotreta nigripes*** larvae feed on roots, but adult habits are like *nemorum*.

▲ ***Psylliodes chrysocephala***. Another troublesome flea beetle, with very large hind femora. Elytra sometimes yellowish brown. Larvae live in stems and mid-ribs of brassicas, especially cauliflowers and turnips. They also damage oil-seed rape. Adults nibble leaves and flowers. Winter is passed in the larval stage.

▲ **Potato Flea Beetle** *P. affinis* is common on nightshades and is sometimes a pest of potatoes (rarely a problem in B.) Adults nibble leaves while larvae tunnel in roots.

▲ **Green Tortoise Beetle** *Cassida viridis*. One of several similar species in which the pronotum and elytra extend well beyond the body. When pulled tightly down against a leaf they eliminate shadows and make the beetles very hard to see. Rear angles of pronotum rounded (more sharply angled in most other species). 6-9, usually in damp places on leaves of mint and other labiates. The larvae of all *Cassida* species (p. 295) camouflage themselves with excrement.

△ ***C. sanguinolenta*** is more convex and usually marked with red. It occurs on thistles and yarrow in grassland in summer.

WEEVILS A very large group, with over 40,000 known species arranged in several families. Most weevils have a prominent snout (the rostrum), with jaws at the end and elbowed antennae normally attached about half way along. Many are clothed with scales and many are flightless, often with elytra fused together. Almost all are vegetarians throughout their lives. Larvae are usually legless and usually live inside their food-plants: many live in seeds.

△ ***Anthribus nebulosus*** Anthribidae. Similar to *Bruchus* (p. 282), with short snout, although elytra cover abdomen. On various broad-leaved and coniferous trees and shrubs 5-7. Larvae have legs and feed on various scale insects.

▲ ***Rhynchites aequatus*** Attelabidae. On hawthorn and other rosaceous trees from spring to autumn. Female rostrum much longer than head and thorax together: male rostrum about as long as head and thorax together. There are several similar species, although their colours vary slightly.

 R. auratus ranges from brassy green to purple. 5-7 on blackthorn, the larvae living inside the kernel of the fruit. The largest member of its family, it is widely distributed but uncommon in Europe.

△ s ***Byctiscus populi***. Female lacks spines on front of thorax and has shorter rostrum. 6-9 on aspen and other poplars. Female rolls leaf around eggs. △s ***B. betulae***, found on birch, hazel, and various other trees, is similar but has very shiny, metallic legs. Both species often blue or violet.

▲ ***Apoderus coryli***. Head narrows at rear, forming a distinct neck. 5-7, mainly on hazel. Larva feeds in rolled-up leaf.

▲ ***Attelabus nitens***. Like *Apoderus* but head not narrowed at rear. 5-7 on young oaks and sweet chestnuts. Larva feeds in rolled-up leaf.

▲ ***Apion frumentarium*** Apionidae. One of several similar species in this large genus. All are small, with characteristically pointed fronts. On docks, especially in damp habitats. 5-8.

▲ ***A. pomonae*** Rather downy: elytra sometimes greenish blue. Legs black. 5-8 on peas and vetches: larvae feed in the pods.

tortoise beetle
camouflaged
on leaf

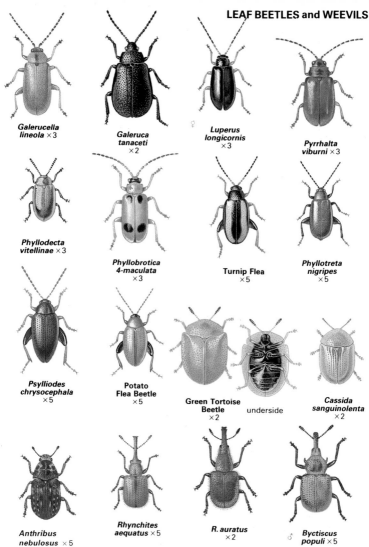

LEAF BEETLES and WEEVILS

Galerucella lineola ×3

Galeruca tanaceti ×2

Luperus longicornis ×3 ♀

Pyrrhalta viburni ×3

Phyllodecta vitellinae ×3

Phyllobrotica 4-maculata ×3

Turnip Flea ×5

Phyllotreta nigripes ×5

Psylliodes chrysocephala ×5

Potato Flea Beetle ×5

Green Tortoise Beetle ×2   underside

Cassida sanguinolenta ×2

Anthribus nebulosus ×5

Rhynchites aequatus ×5

R. auratus ×2

Byctiscus populi ×5 ♂

Apoderus coryli ×3

Attelabus nitens ×3

Apion frumentarium ×5

A. pomonae ×5

▲ **Otiorhynchus clavipes** Curculionidae. One of our largest weevils, with very long antennae. Distinguished from *Liparus* and some other similar weevils by short rostrum with antennae attached to the upper surface instead of the sides. Pale markings due to clusters of hairs, which often rub off with age. On hawthorn and other rosaceous trees and in dense grass tufts in summer. ▲ **Vine Weevil** *O. sulcatus*, slightly smaller and with a tooth on the front femur, attacks a wide range of garden and greenhouse plants and is particularly troublesome on pot plants. The larvae chew roots. There are several similar species. Adults are mostly nocturnal.

▲ **Phyllobius pomaceus**. One of several similar species clothed with golden green or bluish green scales: scales easily rub off and older specimens may be bald and black. Front femur toothed. Abundant on nettles 4-9.

▲ **Polydrusus tereticollis**. 4-6 in oak, aspen, and alder coppice. Elytra with alternating bands of bronze and paler brassy scales. This genus can usually be distinguished from *Phyllobius* because front femur is usually untoothed.

P. picus inhabits birch, oak, and beech in summer. Patches of pale scales often missing in older specimens. S & C.

▲ *P. formosus* is very shiny. 4-7 on deciduous trees, especially birch.

▲ **Pea Weevil** *Sitona lineatus*. Prominent eyes and striped elytra. Abundant on peas, clovers, and other legumes in autumn and spring: hibernates as adult. Nibbles leaf margins, leaving them with frilly edges. Larva feeds in root nodules. A serious pest of peas in some years. There are several similar species.

△s **Lixus paraplecticus**. Elytra dark, clothed with yellow scales. On stems of various umbellifers in damp places in autumn and spring: hibernates as adult. S & C: possibly extinct in B.

▲ **Cionus hortulanus**. Grey or greenish grey, with shiny rostrum and two more-or-less equal black spots on the back. 6-9 on dark mullein. Larva feeds externally, surrounded by gelatinous secretion. S & C. There are several similar species, but the black spots are unequal.

▲ **Pine Weevil** *Hylobius abietis*. Pubescent patches usually pale but may be deep chestnut: legs black or deep red: femora toothed. A serious pest of pine and spruce, damaging young shoots by chewing bark and stopping growth. Adult all year, but hibernates and seen mainly 4-10. Larvae develop in old stumps.

H. piceus, usually a little larger, is associated mainly with larch. N & C.

Liparus glabrirostris. Superficially like *Hylobius*, but plumper and elytra clearly rounded at front without angled 'shoulders'. Rather shiny. On umbellifers, butterbur, and other waterside plants in upland regions in spring and summer. C. △s **L. germanus** has yellow scales on pronotum as well.

▲ **L. coronatus** is smaller, often without yellow scales on elytra. In turf and other low-growing vegetation in spring and early summer. Larvae feed in roots, including cultivated carrots.

▲ **Pissodes pini**. Resembles *Hylobius* but more slender, with antennae inserted further back on rostrum. Femora not toothed. On pine and spruce, mostly in upland forests but lower down in N. Hibernates as adult. Larva under bark of living or dead conifers.

▲ **Cryptorhynchus lapathi**. Pale scales are white or yellowish. On willows, poplars, birches, and alders in spring and summer. Larvae develop in timber and may kill branches and small trees: a serious pest in osier beds.

△ **Apple Blossom Weevil** *Anthonomus pomorum*. Eggs are laid in flower buds of apple and pear. The flowers do not open properly and the larvae develop inside them. The buds eventually fall and adults emerge later to hibernate under loose bark.

▲ **Grain Weevil** *Sitophilus granarius*. Chestnut brown or black: elytra shiny. All year in granaries and similar places, breeding in stored grain of all kinds.

▲ **Notaris bimaculatus**. Striped pubescence often less obvious in older specimens. On waterside vegetation, including sallows and sedges, in spring. There are several similar species.

△ **Dorytomus longimanus**. Male has extremely long front legs. Both sexes with very long shiny black rostrum. 4-9 on poplars. Larvae in catkins and young shoots.

▲ **Nut Weevil** *Curculio nucum*. Female uses long rostrum to gnaw into young hazel nuts. She then lays an egg there and larva feeds on developing kernel. The grub remains in the nut until it falls in autumn, and then chews its way out and pupates in the soil. Rostrum is shorter in males and antennae are attached nearer the tip. 4-7, often visiting hawthorn flowers for pollen and nectar. ▲ **C. villosus** is black with scanty grey scales and a red antennal scape. Grubs develop as inquilines on oak apple galls of *Biorhiza pallida* (p. 228). ▲ **C. salicivorus**, only 2.5mm long, is black with a scaly white covering. Abundant on willows in summer, its larvae living in galls of *Pontania* sawflies (p. 224). *C. elephas*, with longer and straighter rostrum, breeds in acorns and sweet chestnuts. 6-9. S & C (mainly south).

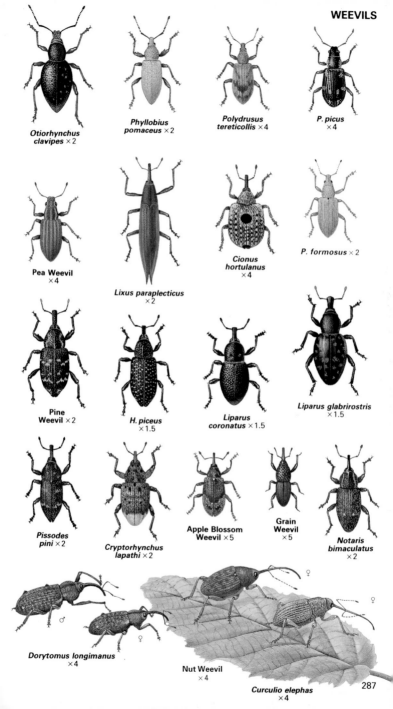

Otiorhynchus clavipes × 2

Phyllobius pomaceus × 2

Polydrusus tereticollis × 4

P. picus × 4

Pea Weevil × 4

Lixus paraplecticus × 2

Cionus hortulanus × 4

P. formosus × 2

Pine Weevil × 2

H. piceus × 1.5

Liparus coronatus × 1.5

Liparus glabrirostris × 1.5

Pissodes pini × 2

Cryptorhynchus lapathi × 2

Apple Blossom Weevil × 5

Grain Weevil × 5

Notaris bimaculatus × 2

Dorytomus longimanus × 4

Nut Weevil × 4

Curculio elephas × 4

287

BARK BEETLES Scolytidae. Cylindrical beetles, related to weevils but with almost no rostrum. Head almost hidden from above. Antennae distinctly elbowed. Elytra usually concave at rear and used as shovels when excavating. Adults normally mate in a chamber under the bark of the host tree, and female then excavates one or more galleries in which she lays her eggs. The larvae then make their own tunnels just under the bark and produce characteristic patterns (right) as they leave the main galleries and chew their way through the nutritious tissues. After pupation, adults emerge through small holes in the bark. A few species live deeper in the timber.

△ *Xyleborus dryographus*. Dark orange to chestnut. Male has a pit at front of pronotum and is more pointed in front. Adults and larvae bore deeply into timber – mainly oak and chestnut – and feed on fungi growing on the tunnel walls. S & C.

△ **Pityogenes chalcographus**. Deep brown to black, with 3 teeth on each side of elytral hollow. Mainly on spruce, often swarming round trees 5-6. Sometimes a 2nd brood in late summer. Female makes radiating galleries from nuptial chamber and larvae tunnel at right angles from them. △ *P. bidentatus*. Only the male has the 2 downward-pointing teeth on each side of elytral hollow. On pine and spruce.

♀

Xyleborus dryographus
× 6

Pityogenes chalcographus
× 6

P. bidentatus
× 6

Ips typographus
× 5

△ **Ips typographus**. Very hairy and much larger than *Pityogenes*. Elytral pit has 3 teeth on each side. 5-7. Breeds in spruce, with 2 vertical egg galleries made by two females mated to one male.

△ **Pine-shoot Beetle** *Tomicus piniperda*. Chestnut to black. Mainly in stumps of pine. Main gallery vertical with pairing chamber at base. Adults hibernate and are active mainly in spring, when they nibble the shoots. △n *T. minor* is similar, but galleries are like those of Ash Bark Beetle. N & C.

Pine-shoot Beetle
× 4

Ash Bark Beetle
× 4

Elm Bark Beetle
× 4

Pinhole Borer
× 4

▲ **Ash Bark Beetle** *Leperisinus varius*. Black, with irregular pattern of scales. 4-10 in 2 broods. Usually breed in diseased or fallen trunks and branches of ash. Main galleries horizontal, with 2 more or less equal arms. Adults often emerge in large numbers from logs brought indoors for the fire.

▲ **Elm Bark Beetle** *Scolytus scolytus*. Notorious carrier of Dutch elm disease, the adults carrying spores from tunnels and infecting new trees as they chew the young shoots. 5-9. Egg gallery vertical and quite short: larval galleries irregular.

△ **Pinhole Borer** *Platypus cylindrus*. Platypodidae. Very cylindrical. 6-7, producing characteristically splintery debris when tunnelling before egg-laying. Usually in oak, larvae tunnelling deeply into standing trunks or unseasoned logs. S & C.

Pityogenes chalcographus

Ips typographus

Ash Bark Beetle

Elm Bark Beetle

Pine-shoot Beetle

Dytiscus renewing air supply, which is carried between the body and the elytra

Family Dytiscidae A large family, related to the ground beetles (p. 256) although much modified for life in the water. The head is sunk partly back into the thorax and the whole body outline is smoothly rounded, while the hind legs are usually broad and flat and fringed with hairs for efficient swimming. Males of many species have swollen front tarsi, with which they grip the females while mating. The beetles renew their air supplies by coming to the surface tail-first. They nearly all fly well. Most can be found throughout the year, although they may hibernate in the coldest months. Adults and larvae are all fiercely carnivorous.

▲ **Great Diving Beetle** *Dytiscus marginalis*. Reddish brown with a deep green sheen, although latter fades after death. Pronotum has yellow border all round. Male elytra very smooth: female elytra usually dull and ribbed. Weedy ponds and other still waters: often very common. Larva (p. 297) and adult both attack frogs and newts as well as fishes, tadpoles, and various invertebrates. *D. latissimus* is larger and blacker, with elytra expanded sideways. Prefers large lakes. N & C. There are several similar species, mostly without yellow all round the pronotum.

 Cybister laterimarginalis resembles *D. marginalis* but pronotum has yellow only at the sides. 3-7 in still and running water in lowlands. Not in far north.

▲ *Acilius sulcatus*. Elytra shiny in male: ribbed in female, with dense hair between ridges. Black pattern on elytra often indistinct. Ponds and other still or slow-moving water.

▲ *Platambus maculatus*. Readily identified by its pattern, although this does vary slightly. 5-10. Occurs in some well-aerated lakes, but mainly in running water – from fast-flowing mountain streams to weedy rivers and even brackish stretches: prefers stony or sandy bottoms. Absent from far south.

△ s *Noterus clavicornis*. Yellowish brown to brick-coloured. Very convex and tapering markedly towards the rear. Antennae dilated, especially in male. 3-10 in densely vegetated ponds and lakes. Widely distributed, but local. Often placed in a separate family – the Noteridae.

▲ *Nebrioporus depressus*. Clothed with short hair. Elytra toothed near apex. Amounts of black and yellow on elytra vary, some beetles being largely black and others mainly yellow. Yellow deepens with age. Essentially a bottom-dwelling species with legs less modified for swimming than in most other dytiscids. Lakes and rivers with gravelly beds.

▲ *Laccophilus minutus*. Rather flat, with distinctly lobed hind tarsi. Elytra sometimes quite green and frequently decorated with pale spots. Ponds and ditches.

▲ *Hygrotus versicolor*. Relatively large eyes, together with the characteristic elytral pattern, distinguish this from several closely related species. Very common in lakes, canals, and slow-moving rivers.

▲ *Hydroporus palustris*. One of several closely related species, but usually distinguished quite easily by the orange or yellow borders of the elytra. The rest of the elytral pattern varies and may be absent. Very common in all kinds of still water, including mountain tarns.

▲ *Ilybius fenestratus*. One of several very similar species with unequal claws on hind feet. Most are black or bronze, but *fenestratus* has a reddish tinge above and a red underside. 4-10 in ponds and lakes: less often in slow-moving streams. Larva (p. 297) is typical of many dytiscids in shape. N & C.

▲ *Colymbetes fuscus*. Distinguished by its narrow shape (relative to *Dytiscus*) and by the yellow margins of elytra and thorax. Often with a green iridescence. Abundant in weedy and muddy ponds and ditches.

▲ *Agabus bipustulatus*. Antennae and front legs reddish brown: rest of body black, with a faint shine in male but dull in female. Claws on hind feet equal. In standing water of all kinds: often abundant. Flies very readily and not uncommon at lights at night. There are several similar species, but most are smaller.

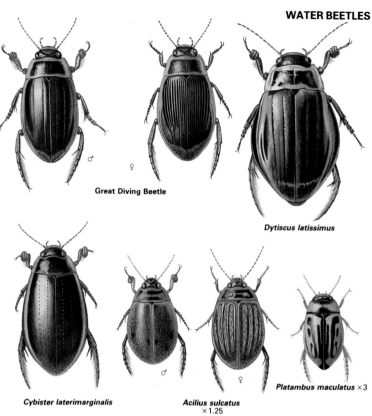

Great Diving Beetle

♂ ♀

Dytiscus latissimus

Cybister laterimarginalis

♂ ♀

Acilius sulcatus
×1.25

Platambus maculatus ×3

Noterus clavicornis ×3

Nebrioporus depressus ×3

Laccophilus minutus ×3

Hygrotus versicolor ×3

Hydroporus palustris ×3

Ilybius fenestratus ×1.5

Colymbetes fuscus ×1.5

Agabus bipustulatus ×1.5

▲ **Haliplus fulvus** Haliplidae. Very convex, with rows of elongate punctures on elytra. Hind coxae very large. A poor swimmer, with hind tarsi not broad. Crawls on plants and stones in weedy pools and streams, browsing on algae. Larva (p. 297) has long 'tail'.

▲ **Screech Beetle** *Hygrobia herrmanni* Hygrobiidae. Very convex, with large eyes. Legs hairy, but not broad. Squeaks when alarmed by rubbing tip of abdomen against elytra. Adult and larva (p. 297) feed on invertebrates in muddy ponds. S & C.

▲ **Whirligig Beetle** *Gyrinus natator* Gyrinidae. One of several very similar species whirling round and round on surface of still and slow-moving water, often in large groups: dive when disturbed. Middle and hind legs very short and paddle-like. Each eye in 2 parts, one looking down into water and one looking across surface. Larva (p. 297) and adult both predatory, feeding largely on mosquito larvae. Adults hibernate.

Great Silver Beetle
renewing air supply

▲ **Hairy Whirligig** *Orectochilus villosus*. Antennae, legs, and underside of body orange. Upper surface hairy. Nocturnal, but otherwise like *Gyrinus*.

Family Hydrophilidae. This family contains both aquatic and terrestrial species (see p. 260). Palps are long and act as antennae: true antennae are short and clubbed. Aquatic species are usually omnivorous scavengers in still and slow-moving water. They are poor swimmers, with legs little modified, and they crawl over submerged vegetation. There is an air reservoir under the elytra and another enclosed by hairs on underside of abdomen: underside of body thus looks silvery in water. Air supply is replenished by coming up head-first and breaking the surface with one of the antennae. Larvae nearly all carnivorous. Most species are adult all year, although they may hibernate.

▲ **Great Silver Beetle** *Hydrophilus piceus*. One of Europe's largest beetles. Shiny above, with greenish sheen in life: very silvery below when seen in water. A sharp spine under thorax. A better swimmer than most hydrophilids. Scavenges on plant debris and also eats water snails. Still water with much weed and mud. Widespread, but becoming rare through loss of habitat. Larva on p. 297.

▲ **Laccobius sinuatus**. Readily identified by convex shape and thoracic pattern, although elytra often very pale. Long hairs on middle and hind tarsi. Mainly small, slow-flowing streams: sometimes ponds and brackish pools: several similar species.

△ **Spercheus emarginatus**. Brick-coloured or yellowish brown: strongly domed. Carnivorous, hunting among roots and debris in muddy water.

▲ **Helophorus aquaticus**. Easily recognised by 5 ridges on thorax. Very hairy beneath. Mainly in still water, including ditches and brackish pools: often in debris at water's edge. Several related species are similar, but all are smaller.

▲ **Enochrus testaceus**. Pronotum and elytra yellow to brick-red: head black, although it may be yellow in front of eyes. 2nd segment of palp dark. Still and slow-moving water: often in debris at water's edge. Larvae are caterpillar-like.

▲ **Hydrochus elongatus**. Protruding eyes and large pronotal pits distinguish this genus, of which *elongatus* is the largest species. Head and pronotum black or green: elytra usually very dark, occasionally green. Weedy still water, mainly in spring.

△ **Hydrochara caraboides**. Like Great Silver Beetle in shape and habits, but no more than half its size and less pointed at the rear. Still water.

▲ **Hydrobius fuscipes**. Shiny black elytra, often with blue or green iridescence in life. Legs long and rust-coloured. Hind femur hairy. Abundant in still water and debris. Larva on p. 297.

▲ **Dryops auriculatus** Dryopidae. Densely hairy. Antennae very short and stout. In and around ponds and streams, gripping plants and debris with strong claws.

▲ **Heterocerus flexuosus** Heteroceridae. Very hairy. Heavily spined front legs used to tunnel in mud or sand in and around ponds and streams. Flies readily at night. There are several similar species, all scavengers.

▲ **Elmis aenea** Elmidae. Cannot swim, and lives among stones, moss, and algae – usually in fast-flowing water. Grips with strong claws. Vegetarian. The beetle uses plastron respiration (p. 255) and does not have to surface for air.

Haliplus fulvus
×3

Whirligig Beetle
×3

Hairy Whirligig
×3

Screech Beetle
×3

*Laccobius
sinuatus* ×3

*Spercheus
emarginatus* ×3

**Great Silver
Beetle**

*Helophorus
aquaticus* ×3

*Enochrus
testaceus*
×3

*Hydrochus
elongatus* ×3

*Hydrochara
caraboides* ×2

*Hydrobius
fuscipes*
×3

*Dryops
auriculatus*
×3

*Heterocerus
flexuosus* ×3

Elmis aenea
×7

TERRESTRIAL LARVAE

Insects with a complete metamorphosis (p. 8) are markedly different in the young and adult stages. The young are always wingless and often feed on totally different foods from the adults. They are called larvae and a selection is illustrated here to show the wide variation in form. Page numbers refer to the descriptions of the adult insects. Fly larvae are always legless, but nevertheless display an immense range of form (see also p. 191). Most Hymenoptera larvae are legless, because they are generally completely surrounded by food and do not need to move. Larvae (caterpillars) of butterflies and moths are illustrated on pages 112-181. Sawfly larvae often resemble them but have more than five pairs of prolegs on the hind part of the body. Some aquatic larvae are illustrated on the next two pages.

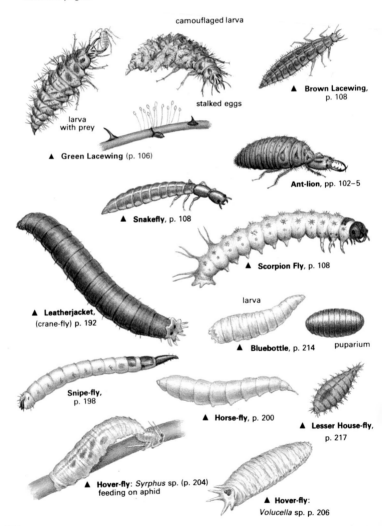

camouflaged larva

stalked eggs

▲ **Brown Lacewing,** p. 108

larva with prey

▲ **Green Lacewing** (p. 106)

Ant-lion, pp. 102–5

▲ **Snakefly,** p. 108

▲ **Scorpion Fly,** p. 108

▲ **Leatherjacket,** (crane-fly) p. 192

larva

▲ **Bluebottle,** p. 214   puparium

Snipe-fly, p. 198

▲ **Horse-fly,** p. 200

▲ **Lesser House-fly,** p. 217

▲ **Hover-fly:** *Syrphus* sp. (p. 204) feeding on aphid

▲ **Hover-fly:** *Volucella* sp. p. 206

TERRESTRIAL LARVAE

▲ **Gooseberry Sawfly**, p. 224

▲ **Hawthorn Sawfly**, p. 224

▲ **Pear Sawfly** (Pear Slug), p. 224

▲ **Sawfly** *Croesus septentrionalis* in alarm position

▲ **Ground Beetle**, p. 256

▲ **7-spot Ladybird**, p. 272

pupa →

← **Tiger Beetle**, p. 256

▲ **Click Beetle** (Wireworm), p. 268

△ **Glow-worm**, p. 270

△ **Cardinal Beetle**, p. 270

▲ **Mealworm**, p. 274

Colorado Beetle p. 282

larva

pupa

▲ **Cockchafer** (most segments divided dorsally into three regions). p. 264

△s **Stag Beetle**, p. 262

▲ **Carpet Beetle** (Woolly Bear), p. 272

▲ **Tortoise Beetle**, p. 284

mostly somewhat enlarged

AQUATIC NYMPHS and LARVAE

Many insects spend their early lives in fresh water and their adult lives in the air. Mayflies, dragonflies, and stoneflies are familiar examples. These all exhibit partial metamorphosis and their young stages, known as nymphs, show some similarity with the adult form despite living in water. A range of their forms is shown below. Mosquitoes and many other flies also grow up in water, but these insects have a complete metamorphosis and their young, known as larvae, are totally unlike the adults. Some of their larval forms are shown on these pages. Caddis flies have a similar life history and their larvae are illustrated on pages 184-189. Water beetles live in the water throughout their lives but, having a complete metamorphosis, their larvae are still very different from the adults. A selection of water beetle larvae is shown on the opposite page.

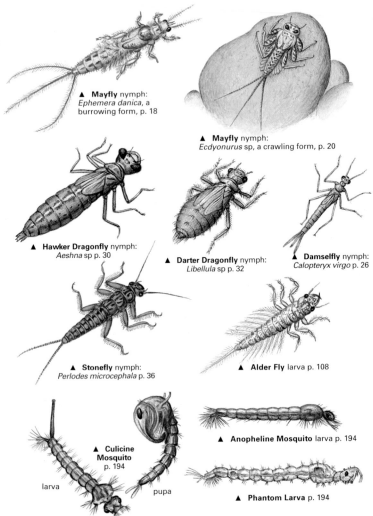

▲ **Mayfly** nymph: *Ephemera danica*, a burrowing form, p. 18

▲ **Mayfly** nymph: *Ecdyonurus* sp, a crawling form, p. 20

▲ **Hawker Dragonfly** nymph: *Aeshna* sp p. 30

▲ **Darter Dragonfly** nymph: *Libellula* sp p. 32

▲ **Damselfly** nymph: *Calopteryx virgo* p. 26

▲ **Stonefly** nymph: *Perlodes microcephala* p. 36

▲ **Alder Fly** larva p. 108

▲ **Culicine Mosquito** p. 194

larva

pupa

▲ **Anopheline Mosquito** larva p. 194

▲ **Phantom Larva** p. 194

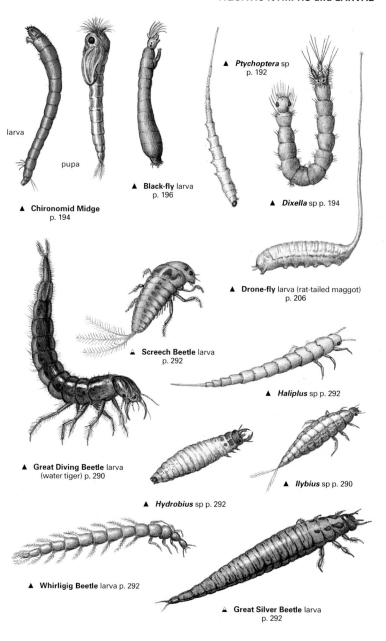

larva

pupa

▲ **Chironomid Midge**
p. 194

▲ **Black-fly** larva
p. 196

▲ *Ptychoptera* sp
p. 192

▲ *Dixella* sp p. 194

▲ **Drone-fly** larva (rat-tailed maggot)
p. 206

▲ **Screech Beetle** larva
p. 292

▲ *Haliplus* sp p. 292

▲ **Great Diving Beetle** larva
(water tiger) p. 290

▲ *Hydrobius* sp p. 292

▲ *Ilybius* sp p. 290

▲ **Whirligig Beetle** larva p. 292

▲ **Great Silver Beetle** larva
p. 292

mostly somewhat enlarged

The Other Arthropods

The insects form just one class, albeit a very large one, of the immense animal group known as the arthropods, all of which have jointed limbs. Examples of some of the other classes are illustrated on this and the following pages to show how they differ from insects, with which they are commonly confused.

CENTIPEDES Class Chilopoda Elongate, predatory arthropods with just one pair of legs to each body segment: hind pair of legs long and sensory. A pair of poison claws surround the head, but no British species is dangerous to man. *Stigmatogaster* lives in soil and leaf litter, and *Necrophloeophagus* lives in the soil. *Cryptops hortensis* usually lives under bark or stones, as do the many very similar species of *Lithobius* – all with 15 pairs of legs when mature. The long-legged and very fast *Scutigera coleoptrata* lives mainly on rocks and walls, often indoors. *Scutigerella immaculata* is like a very small centipede, but it is a vegetarian and belongs to a group known as symphylans. It lives in soil and can be a pest in greenhouses.

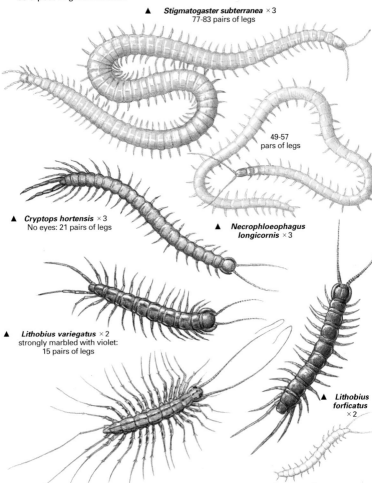

▲ *Stigmatogaster subterranea* × 3
77-83 pairs of legs

49-57
pars of legs

▲ *Cryptops hortensis* × 3
No eyes: 21 pairs of legs

▲ *Necrophloeophagus longicornis* × 3

▲ *Lithobius variegatus* × 2
strongly marbled with violet:
15 pairs of legs

▲ *Lithobius forficatus* × 2

△s *Scutigera coleoptrata* 15 pairs of legs

▲ *Scutigerella immaculata* × 4

Centipedes and millipedes are sometimes collectively known as myriapods (= many feet), although they are not closely related. They are all basically nocturnal.

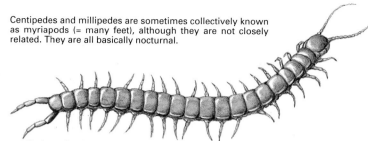

Scolopendra cingulatus, the largest European centipede, is yellowish brown to olive green. It occurs in scrubby habitats around the Mediterranean. Its bite is painful and potentially dangerous.

MILLIPEDES Class Diplopoda Generally elongate arthropods with two pairs of legs on each body segment. Relatively slow-moving and feeding on living and dead plant matter. Body segments essentially circular in cross section, but flat-backed millipedes, such as ***Polydesmus***, appear flat because segments have flat extensions on upper surface. ***Polymicrodon polydesmoides*** and ***Oxidus gracilis*** have similar extensions, but upper surface remains domed. Millipedes are most common in leaf litter and other decaying vegetation, but ***Tachypodoiulus niger***, one of several species that coil up when disturbed, often climbs tree to browse on mosses and algae. It is often found under loose bark. The **Spotted Snake Millipede**, *Blaniulus guttulatus*, lives mainly in cultivated soil and is a pest of potatoes. (See also p. 300.)

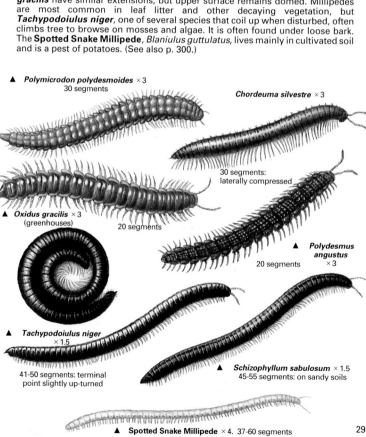

▲ *Polymicrodon polydesmoides* × 3
30 segments

Chordeuma silvestre × 3

30 segments: laterally compressed

▲ *Oxidus gracilis* × 3
(greenhouses)

20 segments

▲ *Polydesmus angustus* × 3

20 segments

▲ *Tachypodoiulus niger* × 1.5

41-50 segments: terminal point slightly up-turned

▲ *Schizophyllum sabulosum* × 1.5
45-55 segments: on sandy soils

▲ **Spotted Snake Millipede** × 4. 37-60 segments

rolled up
×2

Glomeris marginata ×1.5

G. connexa ×1.5

▲ **Glomeris marginata**. One of the pill millipedes – short, stout species that can roll into balls. In leaf litter and debris. Glossier than Pill Woodlouse (below) and with many more legs.

G. connexa is one of several red-spotted species found under stones on the continent.

WOODLICE Order Isopoda Land-living crustaceans with 7 pairs of walking legs. Although terrestrial, most still require damp habitats. Most live as scavengers in decaying vegetation. About 30 species are native to B. **Oniscus asellus, Porcellio scaber**, and **Philoscia muscorum** are all common in gardens. **Ligia oceanica** lives on the sea shore. The **Pill Woodlouse**, Armadillidium vulgare, lives in slightly drier places. When rolled up it is distinguished from the Pill Millipede by the numerous small plates of the rear end.

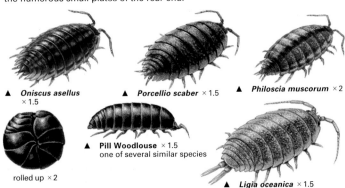

▲ **Oniscus asellus** ×1.5

▲ **Porcellio scaber** ×1.5

▲ **Philoscia muscorum** ×2

▲ **Pill Woodlouse** ×1.5 one of several similar species

rolled up ×2

▲ **Ligia oceanica** ×1.5

The Arachnids This class of arthropods, which includes the spiders and scorpions and their relatives, are the most frequently confused with insects, but they are readily distinguished by having 4 pairs of legs. They never have wings and their bodies are never clearly divided into 3 regions.

FALSE SCORPIONS Order Pseudoscorpiones Mostly minute predatory arachnids with poison claws, harmless to people. Garypus beauvoisi is one of the largest and lives on the seashore in S. Others, generally very much smaller (perhaps only 2mm long), live in leaf litter and even in buildings – often among books where they feed on booklice (p. 98). About 25 species occur in B.

Garypus beauvoisi ×3

TICKS and MITES Order Acarina A very heterogeneous group of arachnids, mostly very small and globular and with relatively short legs. **Sheep Tick**, Ixodes ricinus, lives in grassy places and feeds on many mammals: young will attach themselves to and take blood from people. Mites are vegetarian, carnivorous, parasitic, or scavenging. The carnivorous **Velvet Mite**, Eutrombidium rostratus, is often common on garden paths in spring. **Red Spider Mite**, Panonychus ulmi, is a serious pest of fruit trees. **Hydrachna globosus** is one of many very similar water mites feeding on other tiny aquatic animals.

larva

▲ **Sheep Tick** ×3

▲ **Velvet Mite** ×3

▲ **Red Spider Mite** ×6

▲ **Water Mite** ×3

Other Arthropods: ARACHNIDS

SCORPIONS Order Scorpiones Arachnids with large claws (pedipalps) and a slender tail tipped with a sting. Nocturnal predators, mostly tropical but with a few species in southern Europe. *Euscorpius flavicaudis* lives in cracks in walls and buildings, protruding its claws at night to catch passing insects. Harmless to man. S & C: established in some dockland areas of B. *Buthus occitanicus* lives under stones in S. Its sting is painful and can be dangerous to infants.

Euscorpius flavicaudis × 1.5

Buthus occitanicus × 1.5

HARVESTMEN Order Opiliones Arachnids resembling spiders, but body undivided and 2nd pair of legs the longest. No venom and no silk. Generally mature in late summer – hence the name. Mainly nocturnal, feeding on a wide range of other small animals, both living and dead. About 24 species live in B. *Leiobunum rotundum* is abundant everywhere, often resting on walls and tree trunks by day. *Phalangium opilio*, found in dense vegetation, has a pure white underside and male has horned chelicerae. *Nemastoma bimaculatum*, like other short-legged species, lives on the ground in turf and leaf litter.

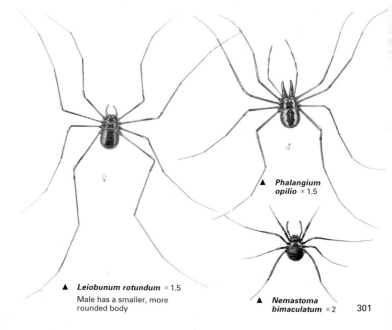

♀

♂

▲ *Phalangium opilio* × 1.5

▲ *Leiobunum rotundum* × 1.5
Male has a smaller, more rounded body

▲ *Nemastoma bimaculatum* × 2

301

SPIDERS

The spiders (Order Araneae) are the most familiar of the arachnids (see p. 300) and, with the possible exception of the mites, they are also the largest group. The spider body is in two parts – the relatively hard cephalothorax at the front and the softer abdomen behind – and this distinguishes them from the harvestmen (p. 301). The dorsal surface of the cephalothorax is called the carapace. The 1st pair of legs are the longest, and there are no antennae, although a pair of palps at the front of the cephalothorax act like antennae and could be mistaken for them. Male spiders have clubbed palps that they use in courtship and mating. There are usually eight simple eyes, not necessarily all the same size, arranged in various patterns on the front of the cephalothorax. Some spiders have only six eyes and some have even fewer.

Spiders are all predatory creatures and many spin elaborate silken snares to trap insects. The most familiar of these snares are the orb-webs (see below), but there are many other designs. Several different kinds of silk are produced in glands that fill most of the spider's body. The threads are extruded from the rear end through three pairs of spinnerets. These are usually very small, but in some spiders they protrude well beyond the tip of the abdomen. The silk is used for wrapping eggs, making shelters and life-lines, and for wrapping prey, as well as for making webs. But not all spiders actually make snares: many actually go hunting, while others merely lie in wait and leap on passing prey. The spider's weaponry consists of a pair of poison fangs called chelicerae, which are hinged just under the front of the carapace. The prey is usually stabbed just behind the head, where the nerves are concentrated, and its is quickly paralysed by the venom. It may then be wrapped in silk before being drained of its body fluids. Digestive juices are pumped into the victim to liquefy the tissues, for the spider can ingest only liquid food. Several spiders in southern Europe can give painful and potentially dangerous bites, but very few of the British species can pierce human skin and even then the effects of their venom are usually very minor.

ORB-WEB SPIDERS Araneidae The spiders in this large family spin more or less circular webs. The orb is built in a framework, whose shape depends on the available supports. Most of the webs are slung in bushes, but walls and fences are equally acceptable. The orb consists of a number of radii on which are laid sticky spiral threads. The droplets of gum that provide the stickiness show up well on misty or frosty mornings. Waxy hairs on its feet prevent the spider from becoming trapped itself, but insects are quickly snared. While waiting for prey to arrive, most orb-web spiders retreat to a shelter a short way from the web, although they remain in contact with it via a signal thread. Some spider species spin a non-sticky central platform on which they rest, and some of these species also produce a stabilimentum – an area of broad zig-zag bands of silk spun between certain radii (below). Males are usually much smaller than females and have to approach very carefully during courtship to avoid being eaten. Most species pass the winter in the egg stage and mature in late summer. This is when the webs are at their largest and most obvious.

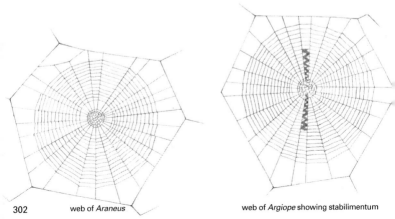

web of *Araneus*   web of *Argiope* showing stabilimentum

WEB-SPINNING SPIDERS

▲ **Garden Spider** *Araneus diadematus* Easily recognised by the white abdominal cross that gives it the alternative name of cross spider. Abundant in gardens, on fences and in hedgerows. Generally rests under a nearby leaf.

▲ *A. quadratus* has a very rounded abdomen, ranging from deep green to brick-red but always with 4 prominent pale spots. Especially common on heathland.

▲ *Araniella cucurbitina* is one of the smallest orb-web spiders, often spinning its web across a single leaf. Has a red spot under tip of abdomen. Abundant in a wide range of trees and bushes.

△s *Argiope bruennichi.* Yellow or cream with wavy black lines: carapace distinctly silvery. Female body up to 25mm long, but male only about 4mm long. Web (opposite) has a vertical stabilimentum. Common in bushes and long grass in S & C. *A. lobata*, an unmistakable spider of southern Europe, spins its web, like that of *bruennichi*, in shrubs and dense herbage.

▲ *Zygiella x-notata.* Abdomen with dark leaf-like pattern edged with pink. Web has 2 empty sectors near top. Very common around window frames and on garden sheds. Some closely related species live on bushes.

Garden Spider × 1.5

Araneus quadratus × 1.5

Araniella cucurbitina × 1.5

Argiope bruennichi

Argiope lobata × 1.5

Zygiella x-notata × 2

▲ *Metellina segmentata* Tetragnathidae. Colour varies, but pattern ± constant: carapace with dark V or tuning-fork mark. Sexes almost equal in size. Web has no central platform and is generally slung at an angle in vegetation of all kinds. Abundant in gardens in spring as well as autumn.

Metellina segmentata × 2

web of *Zygiella*

303

▲ *Amaurobius similis* Amaurobiidae. Makes lace-like webs on old walls and fences, wherever there are small crevices into which it can retreat. Webs bluish when fresh, but usually greyish and rather scruffy: not remade regularly like orb-webs and new silk is added somewhat haphazardly. ▲ *A. fenestralis* is similar but slightly smaller and more boldly marked. It likes slightly damper habitats than *similis* and is common on tree trunks. ▲ *A. ferox* is slightly larger than *similis* and almost black, although a faint skull and cross-bones pattern can usually be seen on the abdomen. It likes much damper places than its two relatives and can usually be found lurking under logs and stones and in damp buildings.

▲ *Pholcus phalangioides* Pholcidae. Commonly known as the daddy-long-legs spider: easily identified by very long legs and cylindrical body. Hangs from flimsy web in buildings. Insects flying into web are secured by more silk thrown over them by the long legs. Also eats other spiders. Vibrates web rapidly when alarmed. S & C. *P. opilionoides* of continental Europe is similar but smaller. △ *Psilochorus simoni* is much smaller, with a globular abdomen.

▲ *Linyphia triangularis* Linyphiidae. Male abdomen slender, without the triangular patterns. Dome-shaped sheet-web abundant in hedgerows and bushes in autumn: spider hangs upside-down from lower surface. Irregular scaffolding threads above sheet impede insects, which fall on to sheet and are caught before they can escape. Sheet not sticky. There are several similar species. ▲ *L. montana*, with plainer and darker abdomen, is equally common. Its web sags to form a hammock. The money spiders that make small sheet webs in the grass also belong to this family.

△s *Eresus cinnaberinus* Eresidae. Sometimes called ladybird spider, although female, with a very square carapace, is velvety black all over. The spider makes a burrow with a silk awning over it and a flimsy web on the surrounding ground, and feeds mainly on beetles and grasshoppers. Females never leave their burrows, but males wander freely in search of females in spring. Sunny slopes, especially on heathland, in S & C: extremely rare and legally protected in B, where until recently it was believed extinct.

▲ *Segestria senoculata* Segestriidae. 6 eyes. Hides in crevices in walls and bark, with a dozen or so silken trip-wires radiating from its silk-lined retreat. Male has relatively longer legs. One of several similar species.

Steatodea paykulliana Theridiidae. Carapace dark brown to black. Male much more slender, with white stripe at front of abdomen and pale chevrons down the middle: legs banded brown and black. Lurks under stones in summer. Female bite said to be poisonous to humans. S & C (southern). ▲ *S. bipunctata* is chocolate brown, with a white band around the front of the abdomen: male also has a white central stripe. Usually in and around houses, often spinning its flimsy web under window-sills.

▲ *Enoplognatha ovata*. Red stripes often absent, but top of abdomen may also be entirely red. Abundant on nettles and other dense vegetation in summer. Female rolls leaves and deposits bluish-green egg sac among them. Web is a flimsy, 3-dimensional trellis, sticky on the outside.

▲ *Theridion sisyphium*. Readily identified by its attractive pattern. Spins 3-dimensional web in hedges and bushes: particularly fond of gorse. The web is like flimsy scaffolding, with interlocking horizontal and vertical threads. Central area is sticky and traps small flying insects. The spider makes a thimble-like shelter in upper part of web, using silk and plant fragments. Female rears her brood here and feeds them when they are very young – puncturing prey so that they can suck up the fluids, or actually regurgitating fluids for them. 5-9.

▲ *Tegenaria gigantea* Agelenidae. One of the house spiders, of which several similar species can be found in houses and other buildings, especially in autumn when males run about in search of mates. Females adult all year and much plumper than males. Triangular sheet-web spun in neglected corners, with tubular retreat at apex. Abundant in sheds and other out-buildings and also common out of doors. Females can survive for several years, and can exist for several months in houses without either food or drink.

▲ *Agelena labyrinthica* makes a conspicuous sheet-web close to the ground among grasses and other low vegetation. Sheet leads into tubular retreat from which spider rushes when food arrives. Web is not sticky, but surface is covered with a network of trip-wires, like *Tegenaria* web, and small insects find escape difficult. 7-8 in rough vegetation of all kinds. *A. gracilens* of S & C is very similar but makes web higher up in bushes.

△ **Water Spider** *Argyroneta aquatica* The world's only truly aquatic spider. Constructs a bell-shaped web under water and fills it with air bubbles. Lives in this air-filled web by day and hunts in the water at night: will also dart out to catch passing insects by day. Air supply renewed periodically by bringing fresh bubbles from surface. Male often larger than female. Still and slow-moving water.

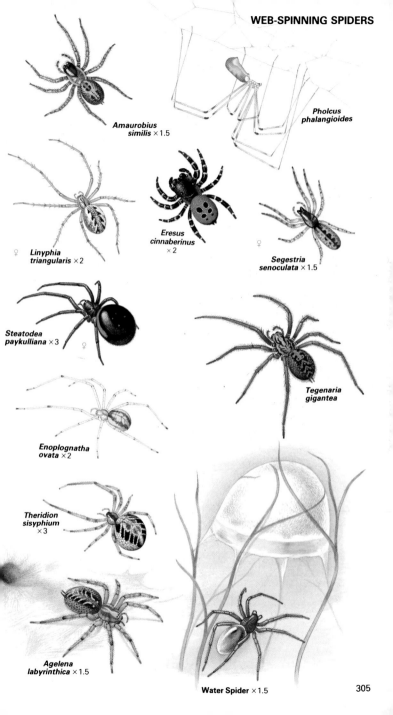

Amaurobius similis × 1.5

Pholcus phalangioides

♀ *Linyphia triangularis* × 2

Eresus cinnaberinus × 2

Segestria senoculata × 1.5 ♀

Steatodea paykulliana × 3 ♀

Tegenaria gigantea

Enoplognatha ovata × 2

Theridion sisyphium × 3

Agelena labyrinthica × 1.5

Water Spider × 1.5

▲ **Pisaura mirabilis** Pisauridae. Grey to rich brown: male markings stronger. Hunts in nettle-beds and other dense vegetation. Sunbathes on leaves with front 2 legs on each side extending forward and very close together. Female carries egg sac in fangs. When eggs are about to hatch she attaches sac to vegetation, spins a silken tent over it, and stands guard until youngsters disperse – hence common name of nursery-web spider. 5-7.

△ **Dolomedes fimbriatus**. 5-8 in swamps and margins of still water. Often sits on floating leaf with front legs resting on water surface to pick up vibrations, and then darts over surface to capture insects or even tadpoles and small fish. Submerges when alarmed. △s *D. plantarius* is very similar, although often a little paler.

▲ **Drassodes lapidosus** Gnaphosidae. Spinnerets prominent. A nocturnal hunter, spending daytime in a silken chamber under stones etc. Prey includes other spiders and is rapidly bound with broad bands of silk. There are several similar species.

▲ **Pardosa amentata** Lycosidae. One of several very similar species of wolf spiders that hunt prey on the ground and on low vegetation. Males use clubbed palps to signal to females with a kind of semaphore. Female carries her wide-seamed egg sac attached to spinnerets. Young ride on her back for a few days after hatching. Sunny places with some moisture and shelter: enjoys basking on stones. 4-9. Often common in gardens.

Lycosa narbonensis. This large wolf spider is one of the true tarantulas. It lives in a burrow and races out to catch passing insects. Its bite is painful to humans, but not usually dangerous. Mediterranean.

▲ **Dysdera crocota** Dysderidae. 6 eyes. Carapace without the usual central depression. Abdomen grey, cream, or flesh-coloured. A nocturnal hunter with huge fangs for capturing woodlice. Spends daytime under stones and debris: fond of compost heaps, where it finds both warmth and woodlice. 5-9. ▲ *D. erythrina* is slightly smaller. Both species can pierce human skin.

CRAB SPIDERS Thomisidae. These are spiders that lie in wait in flowers and elsewhere and pounce when prey arrives. The first two pairs of legs are longer than the others and the spiders have a crab-like sideways walk. Most deceive prey with superb camouflage.

▲ **Xysticus cristatus**. Commonest of several similar species. 4-9 in low herbage.

▲ **Misumena vatia**. Female pale green, white, or yellow and able to change from one colour to another. Sometimes with thin red lines on abdomen. Male very much smaller than female. 5-7, usually on flowers.

▲ **Diaea dorsata**. Female carapace bright green in life, but fades after death. Male has reddish brown carapace and yellowish legs with brown rings or spots. 5-7 in trees and bushes, including conifers.

Heriaeus hirtus. Unusual among crab spiders in being hairy. Male abdomen pale yellow. Both sexes may have red streak along top of abdomen. Lurks among hairy plants 5-7. S & C (southern).

▲ **Zebra Spider** *Salticus scenicus* Salticidae. One of the jumping spiders, which stalk prey and leap on to it from a distance of 2-3cm. Very large central eyes. 5-8, usually on sunny rocks and walls.

△s **Evarcha arcuata**. A jumping spider living mainly on heather. Male abdomen plain black. 5-9.

△s **Atypus affinis** Atypidae. Fangs directed downwards. Burrows in sunny banks and makes a closed tubular web that spills out from burrow to lie on ground. When prey walks on the web the spider rushes up, stabs it, and pulls it into the tube through a slit cut with the fangs. Males roam freely in search of mates in autumn. *A. piceus* is darker.

△s **Scytodes thoracica** Scytodidae. 6 eyes. Stalks prey very slowly and spits sticky, venomous threads to trap it. Nocturnal: rarely seen outside buildings. S & C.

♀

Atypus affinis
× 1.5

'finger' web of Atypus

fly trapped by
sticky threads

Scytodes thoracica × 2

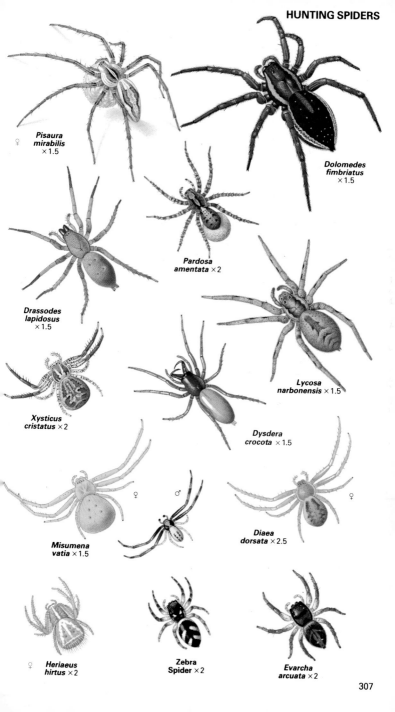

Pisaura mirabilis ×1.5

Dolomedes fimbriatus ×1.5

Pardosa amentata ×2

Drassodes lapidosus ×1.5

Lycosa narbonensis ×1.5

Xysticus cristatus ×2

Dysdera crocota ×1.5

Misumena vatia ×1.5

Diaea dorsata ×2.5

Heriaeus hirtus ×2

Zebra Spider ×2

Evarcha arcuata ×2

Glossary

The numbers given after most of the entries refer to the pages on which the terms are illustrated or described in greater detail.

Abdomen Hindmost of the 3 main divisions of the insect body. p. 6

Alula Conspicuous lobe of the wing membrane in certain flies. p. 190

Anal (1) Concerning the anus or hind end of the abdomen. (2) Concerning the hindmost region of the wing.

Antennae The 'feelers' - the pair of sensory organs on the head p. 5

Antenodal Veins Small cross-veins at the front of dragonfly wings. p. 22

Apical At or concerning the apex of any organ.

Appendage Any limb or other organ attached to the body by a joint.

Apterous Wingless.

Apterygote Any primitive wingless insect. p. 16

Arista A bristle-like branch of the antenna in certain flies. p. 191

Basitarsus 1st and usually the largest segment of the tarsus (foot).

Brachypterous Short-winged.

Calypter A flap-like outgrowth from the thorax of certain flies. p. 190

Campodeiform (larva) Flattened and elongated, with well-developed legs and antennae. Typified by lacewing larva. p. 294

Caste Any of the three or more distinct forms in a colony of social insects. p. 218

Caudal Concerning the tail or rear end.

Cell An area of wing bounded by veins. p. 7

Cerci The paired appendages, often thread-like, at the tip of the abdomen in many insects. p. 16

Cheek (= gena)

Chelicerae The jaws or fangs of an arachnid. p. 302

Claspers (1) The last pair of legs of a caterpillar. (2) Modified cerci (q.v.), used by males of some insects to grasp females during mating. p. 48, p. 102

Clavus Part of the forewing in heteropteran bugs. p. 70

Clypeus Lower part of the insect face, just above the mouth-parts. p. 5

Corbicula Pollen basket on the hind leg of many bees. p. 248

Corium Main part of the forewing in heteropteran bugs. p. 70

Cornicle One of the paired tubular outgrowths from the aphid abdomen. p. 94

Costa A long vein, usually forming the front edge of the wing.

Coxa Basal segment of the insect leg. p. 6

Cross-vein Any short vein linking two neighbouring longitudinal veins. p. 7

Cubitus One of the major longitudinal wing veins. p. 7

Cuneus Part of the forewing of certain heteropteran bugs. p. 70

Discal Cell A large or near central cell near the middle of the wing. p. 7

Distal Concerning that part of an appendage furthest from the body.

Ecdysis The skin-changing or moulting process. p. 8

Ectoparasite A parasite (q.v.) living on the outside of its host.

Elbowed (antenna) With 1st segment (scape) longer than the rest and with a distinct angle between 1st and 2nd segments. p. 235

Elytron Tough forewing of a beetle or earwig.

Emarginate Distinctly notched or indented.

Embolium A narrow strip along the front edge of the forewing in certain heteropteran bugs. p. 70

Endoparasite A parasite (q.v.) living inside its host's body.

Endopterygote Any insect with a complete metamorphosis. p. 8

Epiproct Central 'tail' of bristletails and mayflies. p. 16, p. 18

Eruciform (larva) Caterpillar-like.

Exopterygote Any insect with partial metamorphosis, with the wings developing gradually on the outside of the body. p. 8

Femur 3rd and often largest segment of the insect leg. p. 6

Filiform (antenna) Thread-like.

Flagellum That part of the antenna beyond the second segment. p. 5

Frenulum Bristle or group of bristles linking fore and hind wings in many moths. p. 110

Frons Upper part of the insect face, between and below the antennae. p. 5

Gall Abnormal growth of a plant caused or induced by insects or other organisms in the tissues. p. 226

Gaster Main part of the hymenopteran abdomen. p. 220

Gena (= cheek) That area of the insect head below and behind the eye. p. 5

Geniculate (= elbowed)

Genitalia Copulatory organs.

Genus A group of closely related species, all sharing the same first name. Plural: genera.

Glabrous Hairless.

Haltere Modified hindwing in true flies. p. 190

Hemelytron Forewing of heteropteran bugs. p. 70

Hemimetabolous Having an incomplete metamorphosis. p. 8

Holometabolous Having a complete metamorphosis. p. 8

Humeral Vein A small cross-vein near the base of the wing. p. 7

Imago The adult.

Inquiline An insect or other animal living in the nest or home of another species without causing it any direct injury, although it may compete with its host for food. Inquilines living in plant galls, for example, eat the gall tissues and may indirectly cause the death of the rightful occupant.

Instar The stage of development between any two moults. p. 8

Intercalary Vein A longitudinal vein running in from the wing margin but not directly connected to any major vein. p. 20

Larva Young stage of an insect with complete metamorphosis. p. 8

Macropterous Fully winged.

Mandible The jaw.

Marginal Cell Any cell bordering the front margin of the wing.

Media A major longitudinal vein near the middle of the wing in most insects.

Mesothorax 2nd of the 3 thoracic segments.

Metamorphosis Change from young to adult form. p. 8

Metatarsus (= basitarsus)

Metathorax 3rd of the 3 thoracic segments.

Micropterous With very short wings.

Moniliform (antenna) Composed of bead-like segments.

Moulting (= ecdysis)

Mouth-parts Collective name for the jaws and other feeding appendages around the mouth. p. 5

Nodus The small notch or kink in the front edge of a dragonfly wing, and also the short cross-vein just behind it. Also called the node. p. 22

Nymph Young stage of an insect with incomplete metamorphosis. p. 8

Ocellus A simple kind of eye. p. 5

Ootheca Egg case of mantids and cockroaches. p. 60, p. 62

Ovipositor Egg-laying tool.

Palp A small, sensory leg-like extension of the mouth-parts. p. 5

Parasite An organism spending part or all of its life on or in another species (the host), taking food from it but giving nothing in return, although it does not usually kill its host.

Parasitoid An insect that lives as a parasite only during its early stages, using just a single host individual – usually another insect – which invariably dies when the parasitoid matures and has no further use for it.

Parthenogenesis Virgin birth.

Pectinate (antenna) Comb-like. p. 271

Pedicel (1) 2nd segment of the antenna. (2) The waist of an ant. p. 5, p. 234

Petiole The narrow part (waist) of the hymenopteran abdomen. p. 219, p. 220

Plumose (antenna) Feathery.

Proboscis Any feeding apparatus used for sucking up fluids.

Proleg Any of the stumpy or fleshy legs on the hind part of a caterpillar. p. 111

Pronotum Upper surface of 1st thoracic segment. p. 6

Propodeum 1st abdominal segment of bees, wasps, and other hymenopterans in the suborder Apocrita. p. 219

Prothorax 1st of the 3 thoracic segments.

Proximal Concerning the basal part of an appendage, nearest to the body.

Pterostigma (1) A small coloured area near the wing-tip of many insects. (2) a prominent cell in the wings of psocids. p. 23, p. 98

Puparium Barrel-like pupal case of many flies. p. 190

Quadrilateral An important cell in the damselfly wing. p. 22

Radial Sector Posterior of the 2 main branches of the radius: often abbreviated to Rs. p. 7

Radius A major longitudinal vein in the front half of the wing. p. 7

Rostrum A beak or snout, especially in bugs and weevils. p. 70, p. 284-6

Scape 1st segment of the antenna. p. 5

Scutellum Large, often triangular plate extending back from the top of the mesothorax. p. 70, p. 190

Spur A large and often movable spine on the legs of many insects. p. 183

Stigma (= pterostigma)

Subcosta The longitudinal vein just behind the front edge of the wing. p. 7

Tarsus The insect foot. p. 6

Tegmen Leathery forewing of grasshoppers, cockroaches, and related insects, although the term is not often used today. Plural: tegmina.

Tegula A small lobe or scale overlying the base of the forewing. p. 218

Thoracic squama (= calypter)

Thorax Middle of the 3 main body sections, carrying the legs and wings.

Tibia One of the segments of the insect leg: often the longest. p. 6

Triangle An important region near the base of the dragonfly wing.

Trochanter One of the segments of the insect leg, between the coxa and the femur and usually very small. p. 6

Tympanum The ear drum of various insects. p. 48

Vertex The top of the head, between and behind the eyes. p. 5

Vestigial Poorly developed or degenerate.

Index of English Names

Index of Genera and Species

Acknowledgments

The author is extremely grateful to all the numerous friends and colleagues who have generously helped with their answers to questions and expert criticism – particularly to the following: Dr P.C. Barnard, Mr S.J. Brooks, Mr P.S. Broomfield, Mr D.J. Carter, Mr B.H. Cogan, Mr M.C. Day, Mr G.R. Else, Mr P.D. Hillyard, Mrs J.A. Marshall, Mr R.D. Pope, Mr J. Quinlan, Dr D.R. Ragge, Mr W.J. Reynolds, Mr C.R. Vardy and the late Dr I.H.H. Yarrow.

He also thanks the Trustees and staff of the British Museum (Natural History) for making specimens available for study and painting, and is also very grateful in this respect to Mr B.R. Baker and Mr C. Sizer of Reading Museum and Art Gallery and to Mr M. Scoble of the Hope Department of Entomology at Oxford.

Most of all, we are grateful to our artists. Principally, **Denys Ovenden** contributed the whole initial design, all the line-drawings, his imaginative advice throughout, and painted the Odonata, Orthoptera, Hemiptera, the bees and many of the minor groups; **Richard Lewington** the Lepidoptera, Coleoptera and much of the Hymenoptera; and **Stephen Falk** (while still a student at London University) the Diptera. **René Préchac** painted the Trichoptera, **Anthony Hopkins** the wasps, and **John Wilkinson** the plates of stoneflies, larvae and myriapods. **David More** has in 2012 contributed the painting on p.130. **Hermann Heinzel**, throughout the book, made many invaluable contributions to conception and design.